# LAW & ECONOMICS: TOWARD SOCIAL JUSTICE

# RESEARCH IN LAW AND ECONOMICS: A JOURNAL OF POLICY

Series Editors: John B. Kirkwood and
Richard O. Zerbe

Recent Volumes:

Volume 20: An Introduction to the Law and Economics of Environmental Policy: Issues in Institutional Design – Edited by T. Swanson

Volume 21: Antitrust Law and Policy – Edited by J. B. Kirkwood

Volume 22: General Issue – Edited by R. O. Zerbe and J. B. Kirkwood

Volume 23: Introduction to Benefit-Cost – Edited by R. O. Zerbe

RESEARCH IN LAW AND ECONOMICS: A JOURNAL OF POLICY VOLUME 24

# LAW & ECONOMICS: TOWARD SOCIAL JUSTICE

EDITED BY

**DANA L. GOLD**

*Seattle University School of Law, USA*

Emerald

JAI

United Kingdom – North America – Japan
India – Malaysia – China

JAI Press is an imprint of Emerald Group Publishing Limited
Howard House, Wagon Lane, Bingley BD16 1WA, UK

First edition 2009



**Reprints and permission service**
Contact: booksandseries@emeraldinsight.com



**British Library Cataloguing in Publication Data**
A catalogue record for this book is available from the British Library

ISBN: 978-1-84855-334-7
ISSN: 0193-5895 (Series)

# CONTENTS

## SECTION B: SEEKING SOCIAL JUSTICE THROUGH LAW AND ECONOMICS

# LIST OF CONTRIBUTORS


| | |
|---|---|
| *William W. Bratton* | Georgetown University Law Center, USA |
| *Naomi Cahn* | George Washington University Law School, USA |
| *Devon W. Carbado* | University of California Los Angeles School of Law, USA |
| *June Carbone* | University of Missouri-Kansas City School of Law, USA |
| *Claire Moore Dickerson* | Tulane University Law School, USA |
| *Kent Greenfield* | Boston College Law School, USA |
| *Daniel J. H. Greenwood* | Hofstra University School of Law, USA |
| *Mitu Gulati* | Duke University School of Law, USA |
| *Thomas W. Joo* | University of California, Davis, School of Law, USA |
| *Robin Paul Malloy* | Syracuse University College of Law, USA |
| *David Millon* | Washington & Lee University School of Law, USA |
| *Cheryl L. Wade* | St. John's University School of Law, USA |

# PREFACE

We are delighted to publish the papers from the symposium on social justice sponsored by the Center on Corporations, Law & Society of the Seattle University Law School. These papers address an impressive array of business and social issues and provide a penetrating assessment of whether existing legal doctrines and approaches promote social justice. True to the theme of this series, the authors frequently utilize economic analysis, but they also point out where they think it does not apply or needs to incorporate new developments. The exceptional quality of this volume reflects the distinguished credentials of the authors, the extraordinary efforts of the Special Editor, Dana Gold, the former director of the Center, and the support of the Dean of Seattle University Law School, Kellye Testy.

John B. Kirkwood
Richard O. Zerbe
*Series Editors*

# INTRODUCTION

In the Fall of 2006, the Center on Corporations, Law & Society (CCLS) at Seattle University School of Law, in collaboration with Professor Jack Kirkwood, co-editor of this *Research in Law and Economics* book series, hosted a symposium to explore the relationship between law and economics principles and the promotion of social justice. CCLS has a robust history facilitating scholarship about the role corporations and corporate law plays in promoting, as well as undermining, social, economic, and environmental justice, having organized numerous conferences with published proceedings on topics connecting corporate law and governance to health care,[1] first amendment protections,[2] business ethics,[3] and diverse progressive social movements, including environmental activism, worker rights, racial justice, and electoral democracy.[4] Given that corporations play such a dominant role in almost every aspect of society, and given that much of governing corporate law doctrine and theory derives from neoclassical law and economics, the theme of the symposium, *Law and Economics: Toward Social Justice*, was both natural and fundamental to CCLS's work. This book-volume is a collection of the papers accepted for presentation at the symposium and revised for publication.

We defined the term social justice broadly, reflecting a vision of society that embraces more than traditional economic efficiency and that includes, for example, a reduction of subordination and discrimination based on race, religion, gender, sexual orientation, age, disability or class; increased wealth dispersion throughout all sectors of society; a safe and healthy environment; worker rights; and a flourishing political democracy.[5] The nationally recognized scholars who enthusiastically participated in this project contributed relevant and valuable papers that approach from different perspectives the question of the role economic analysis plays in law as it relates to this vision of social justice.

The papers in this volume fall into two general categories, though each can be read (and was written) independent of an organizing framework within the general topic. The papers in the first category, *Economics and Business Law: Challenges to Social Justice*, tease apart some of the presumptions undergirding legal theory and doctrine in the business arena.

The chapter by Robin Paul Malloy, *Economics as a Map in Law and Market Economy*, opens the volume with a call for awareness of both the usefulness and limits of any disciplinary framework for making decisions, particularly those, like in law as well as economics, which affect societal interests. He reminds us that economics provides a useful map for understanding market transactions, but that we must not confuse the map, which as a system of interpretation is informed by culture, values, language and norms, with the exchange process itself. And to the extent that the law, itself a map and process of interpretation, relies on economics to navigate the interests of parties involved in exchanges, Malloy argues that it is a mistake to believe that applying economic analysis to law renders law or policy neutral, objective, or scientific. While economic and legal concepts can be useful in solving problems, they cannot substitute for applying normative judgments about a course of action that advances particular values, such as social justice. They are tools, but not ends in themselves.

This reminder that theories contain embedded values and assumptions and, while useful, should not be taken as truisms, is echoed in William Bratton's deconstruction of US corporate law's theoretical debates. In *An Anatomy of Corporate Legal Theory*, Bratton categorizes the primary debates in US corporate law and concludes that despite significant theoretical disagreements in four principle areas, there is at root basic consensus about the objectives of the firm, namely to facilitate productivity through management's freedom of action and to minimize the cost of capital. He artfully shows that these objectives of corporate law neither flow from nor embrace a specific theory – indeed, they limit the range of theoretical debates to those that accept the premises of delegated decision making and low-cost production. That corporate law pursues these objectives without consistent reference to one theoretical framework creates little space for, but significant protest from, those calling for a different set of objectives for the firm at the outset – such as social responsibility or power granted to constituents other than management, such as workers. Bratton argues that the objectives of corporate law are so firmly established that the doctrine will continue to navigate but not resolve theoretical disputes, and that social justice objectives that seek to limit externalities and protect the public interest will necessarily have to be satisfied, as they are now, outside of the boundaries of corporate law through regulation.

Bratton's description of an objective-driven corporate law regime makes one wonder if, in this particular area of law at least, critiques of corporate law and theory, let alone new ideas for law reform to promote social justice, are futile exercises. This cynical view did not hinder the remaining scholars in this volume from critiquing and offering alternatives to the theoretical "map," to reference Robin Paul Malloy's chapter, used by law and economics business scholars that frequently leads to outcomes that cause social and economic injustice. In *The Single Constituency Argument in the Economic Analysis of Business Law*, David Millon describes how in corporate law, bankruptcy law, and antitrust law, law and economics scholarship tends to advocate for the interest of a single constituency in each area (shareholders, creditors, and consumers, respectively) to promote efficiency in the market – and generally, the theory is largely implemented in the legal doctrine in each of these areas of business law. Millon argues that the single-constituency argument is not only a veiled objection to using the law towards progressive, redistributive ends that would value the interests of workers, small business owners, and other constituencies affected by business conduct, but it is in fact a regressive position that favors and seeks to maintain the existing distribution of wealth and power.

In a similar critique of how corporate law theory is geared to maintaining existing power structures, Kent Greenfield takes aim at one of the most powerful concepts in economics, law, and politics – the notion of "choice." In *Corporate Law and the Rhetoric of Choice*, Greenfield argues that the rhetoric of choice, rooted in an economic theory of the voluntary, rational actor, since belied by significant advances in behavioral economics research, when applied in corporate law has the effect of maintaining the existing power structure of the corporation that excludes stakeholders such as employees or communities. By invoking the choice rhetoric that maintains that people have "chosen" to accept their relationship to the corporation and thus also the effects of corporate conduct, social justice interests are effectively excluded. Greenfield argues that replacing the concept of "choice" with that of "consent," which may account for factors such as access to and quality of information or available alternatives, might be an important shift that could facilitate socially just outcomes.

Daniel Greenwood's chapter, *The Dividend Puzzle: Are Shares Entitled to the Residual?*, continues the theme of revealing the underlying values in corporate law theory (and practice) that result in maintaining the status quo and marginalizing non-manager corporate stakeholders. Greenwood argues that the idea that shareholders are entitled to the corporate surplus is not grounded in law or economics, but rather is a function of the political value of share-centered metaphors: shareholders' rhetorical claims of firm "ownership" bestow a greater amount of entitlement and power than they in fact have as a matter of law, and managers benefit from share-centered rhetoric as a justification for excessive CEO compensation as well as a distraction from evaluating their true effectiveness by focusing on stock performance rather than the long-term values of job creation and wealth distribution. By exposing the weaknesses of the arguments promoting sharecentric ideology and practice, Greenwood seeks to foster a more honest discussion about the political choices related to wealth distribution and power that flow from corporate governance theory and practice.

Finally, Claire Moore Dickerson in *Corporate Social Responsibility: Lessons from the South on Law and Business Norms* presents a study in comparative corporate law to argue that in areas of divergence between positive law and societal norms lie opportunities to promote corporate social responsibility. By comparing how social norms in the African country of Cameroon both track and, more significantly, diverge from the applicable business laws, Dickerson offers a model to look at the extent to which corporate governance law in the US does, and does not, reflect political beliefs about the role of corporations in society. She argues that business law standards will be only marginally effective at influencing corporate behavior because cultural norms are so powerful, but in those areas where social norms diverge from the law – for instance, when corporations and business owners engage in conduct that respects the community or values employees rather than just focusing on shareholder interests – that is precisely where law reform efforts to promote social justice should be concentrated.

In the second category of papers, *Seeking Social Justice Through Law and Economics*, the contributing scholars take specific issues of social justice – racial, gender, and marriage equality – and look at how traditional law and economics principles influence achieving justice in each context. Thomas Joo in *The Discourse of "Contract" and the Law of Marriage* critiques how the rhetoric of "contract," used to imply obligations derived from consent, is used to analogize marriage as something that should be based solely on consent of the parties. In a critique on the power and problems of rhetoric similar to that invoked by Kent Greenfield and Dan Greenwood, Joo argues that when the contract *analogy* is invoked for an approach to marriage, the rhetoric associated with contract – presumptions of efficiency, liberty, enforceability, and neutrality – obscures not only actual contract law doctrine, which depends on the contract's relationship to public welfare in addition to the parties' consent, but also the existence, let alone complexity, of rich debate in contract law and theory. Joo seeks to ensure that just as the discourse around marriage is recognized as normative and political, the contractarian arguments in favor of, or against, marriage should be recognized as normative and political as well.

Naomi Cahn and June Carbone offer a new critique of the rational actor model, arguing that developments in both behavioral economics and behavioral biology dictate a reexamination of the role gender plays in understanding market transactions. In *Behavioral Biology, the Rational Actor Model, and the New Feminist Agenda*, Carbone and Cahn revisit Carol Gilligan's work on moral development by documenting important new research in economics and biology that establishes distinct gender differences in how men and women experience motivation and relationships. The outdated and inaccurate rational actor model needs to be replaced, they argue, with a new methodology that incorporates the insights of behavioral economics and biology to advance a legal and economic agenda focused not on efficiency and markets but rather one that supports a functioning society built on qualities such as trust, cooperation, and care. A more realistic understanding of the role of gender will inform feminism as well as law and economics, with the goal of advancing a more progressive paradigm that considers societal interests and not just those of the individual transactions between non-existent rational actors.

The final two chapters in the volume both focus on racial justice in the corporate workplace. In *Race to the Top of the Corporation: What Minorities Do When They Get There*, Devon Carbado and Mitu Gulati seek to debunk two primary myths about achieving success and equality in the workplace. The first is that climbing the workplace ladder is not merely a function of being more productive or qualified than one's competitors – being able to navigate corporate culture and politics is essential to reaching the top echelons of the institution. The second, and the primary focus of their chapter, is that racial minorities who succeed at navigating the institutional landscape to reach the top may not, contrary to assumptions, be either committed or empowered to help racial minorities on the rungs below. If corporate leaders, racial justice advocates, and scholars believe that minorities at the top of the corporation will help ameliorate discrimination, when in fact those minorities have incentives to preserve their places at the top and maintain the status quo, it may be critical to consider new approaches in law and business to promoting nondiscrimination. The authors' insight that the same behaviors that lead to minorities' success may also maintain discrimination in the corporate workplace is important for any efforts geared towards promoting racial justice throughout the corporate hierarchy.

In their chapter, Carbado and Gulati compellingly describe how racial minorities have incentives to defy stereotypes to succeed in the workplace; this also demonstrates the existence and power of those racial stereotypes.

Their work informs Cheryl Wade's chapter, *Workplace Racial Discrimination and the Professionals at the Center of Corporate Hierarchies*, as she focuses on those African Americans who are not at the "top of the corporation" but rather remain, for the most part, in the bottom and middle of the corporate workplace. She argues that law and economics analysis of the problem of employment discrimination, which tends to focus on individual choices, presumed efficiency found in homogenous groups, and the costs of implementing antidiscrimination policies, ignores both the force of negative assumptions and stereotypes against African Americans as well as the context – the true costs and harm – of workplace racial discrimination. Wade maintains that a more accurate accounting of the costs of discrimination – economic, socioeconomic, and psychological, which she describes in detail – creates a powerful opportunity to reduce discrimination in the workplace. If corporate cultures openly acknowledged the existence and effects of racism instead of promoting hollow diversity efforts (this would be a very different corporation than the typical one described by Carbado and Gulati), the behavior of hundreds of individuals working within that corporate culture could be transformed. The prospect of promoting racial justice within the workplace through an honest accounting of the existence and effects of prejudice is a hopeful, and perhaps even achievable, goal.

A theme that runs through all of the chapters in this volume is how unexamined assumptions and rhetoric can undermine social justice. By exposing the flaws in many of the assumptions that underlie law, policy, and scholarship – and indeed by exposing the existence of some of the assumptions and rhetoric that are used with such frequency that they are taken as truisms – this collection begs us to question governing legal and economic doctrines and theory as we consider reforms needed to promote a more just society.

Societal interests are generally protected only through reactive mechanisms that are in place to mitigate harm caused by corporate conduct and prejudice: regulations that offer patchwork protections for the environment, workers, women, and minorities, or litigation that seeks a remedy for an injustice that has already occurred. The authors here ask us to question the assumptions and rhetoric that may be the source of social injustices in the first place: Does the accepted legal purpose of corporate law dictate marginalization of stakeholder interests? Does the rational actor theory perpetuate gender inequity and erosion of societal trust? Does the rhetoric of choice and consent threaten equality? Do diversity efforts obscure an honest accounting and real reduction of discrimination? The questions themselves are a necessary first step on the path of identifying the threats to social justice and possible solutions. This volume paves the way.

# NOTES

1. See Corporate Ethics & Governance in the Health Care Marketplace (2004). *Seattle Journal for Social Justice* (Fall/Winter), *3*(1), 205–428.
2. See Corporations and the First Amendment: Examining the Health of Democracy (2007). *Seattle University Law Review* (Summer), *30*(4), 847–1030.
3. See Business Ethics in the Corporate Governance Era: Domestic & International Trends in Transparency, Regulation and Corporate Governance, co-hosted with the Albers Business Ethics Initiative (2007). *Business and Society Review* (Summer), *112*(2), 163–313.
4. See New Strategies for Justice: Linking Corporate Law with Progressive Social Movements, co-hosted with the Equal Justice Society and the UCLA Critical Race Studies Concentration (2005). *Seattle Journal for Social Justice* (Fall/Winter ), *4*(1), 225–382.
5. This definition was taken from Dean Kellye Testy's (2002, p. 1244) law review article, Linking Progressive Corporate Law with Progressive Social Movements. Dean Testy is the co-founder of the Center on Corporations, Law & Society at Seattle University School of Law.

# ACKNOWLEDGMENTS

Jack Kirkwood invited me and the Center on Corporations, Law & Society to organize the symposium that would generate this unique and compelling volume. His and Richard Zerbe's trust in me to guest edit this volume of their *Research in Law and Economics* book series set a high bar for me as well as the contributors, and I am grateful for their support and patience as two residential moves and the birth of my daughter, Aziza Gold Morrison, delayed completion of this project. Equally important to this project was my husband, Robert Morrison, who offered constant support (and childcare) during our tremendous life changes that coincided with the completion of this book. In addition to Jack Kirkwood, Margaret Chon and Kellye Testy offered wise counsel and support in shaping the symposium and ultimately this volume. Christopher Rideout graciously offered guidance on editing to me and my Student Fellows (and fellow editors), Amy Worrell-Kneller, Meghan Eagan, Hillary Mohr, and Ian Adams. I am particularly grateful for their invaluable and thoughtful work on these chapters. My research assistant, Kevin Jussell, performed the herculean task, with enthusiasm and tenacity, of conforming the citation style used by law scholars to the Harvard referencing system used by Emerald Publishing.

Finally, I am grateful to all of the contributors to this volume. I am personally thankful to each of them for being so responsive and committed to me and this project and for their understanding and patience while the project was on unanticipated "hold" during the aforementioned life transitions. Additionally, although each paper is compelling and provocative in its own right, taken as a whole, the volume is all the more rich for containing such outstanding scholars committed to rigorous inquiry and social justice in one place.

## REFERENCES

Testy, K. (2002). Linking progressive corporate law with progressive social movements. *Tulane Law Review*, *76*, p. 1227.

Dana L. Gold
*Editor*

# SECTION A
# ECONOMICS AND BUSINESS LAW: CHALLENGES TO SOCIAL JUSTICE

# ECONOMICS AS A MAP IN LAW AND MARKET ECONOMY*

Robin Paul Malloy

## ABSTRACT

*S.I. Hayakawa said, "The map is not the territory." Taking this as my theme, I explore the idea of economics as a cultural-interpretive map that can be usefully employed to navigate the legal landscape. As a map, economics facilitates our understanding of law in a market context. At the same time, the map is not the metaphorical territory that it represents, just as economics is not the market exchange process to which it refers. Therefore, we must be careful not to conflate our conception of the economic map with our understanding of the legal territory.*

*© Robin Paul Malloy, all rights reserved (2008). This paper is an original essay that includes intermittent text and notes from two of my books with Cambridge University Press, *Law in a Market Context: An Introduction to Market Concepts in Legal Reasoning* (Malloy, 2004), and *Law and Market Economy: Reinterpreting the Values of Law and Economics* (Malloy, 2000) (quoted text in this paper is not an indicator of what in this paper does or does not come from these two books). Further discussion and details related to the ideas discussed herein can be explored in these earlier books.

**Law & Economics: Toward Social Justice**
**Research in Law and Economics: A Journal of Policy, Volume 24, 3–20**

**ISSN: 0193-5895/doi:10.1108/S0193-5895(2009)0000024005**

## INTRODUCTION

For the past 20 years, I have extensively written and lectured on two primary areas of the law, the first area being on real estate transactions, finance, and development, and the second area being on the relationship between law and market theory. Both of these areas converge in the sense that transactional law is about the ability to use the law to capture and create wealth. It is natural therefore, for someone with my interest, to turn to economics and market theory for ideas and tools that can be helpful in the development of a useful and pragmatic theory of transactional lawyering.

Early on in my work, I became conscious of the fact that both law and economics were systems that involved the lawyer in the process of interpretation. The lawyer's stock and trade is the use, development, and manipulation of meaning. The successful lawyer communicates effectively using a variety of mechanisms (metaphor, narrative, grammar, analogy, etc.) to capture the essence of a deal and move a transaction toward the successful completion of its objective. At the same time, economics also involves a process of interpretation. Most fundamentally to economics, the exercise of choice involves a process of interpretation. Choice is not simply about a calculus of costs and benefits; it is about the interpretation of costs and benefits, and about determining what costs and benefits to include as relevant to a decision. As an interpretive process, choice is an exercise of conscience, and an expression of one's humanity.

This realization triggered an interest in a third area of study over these past 20 years, and that is legal semiotics: the study of law as a system of signs, and more specifically how signs function to generate meanings and values in law. Signs are ideas that have meaning, and we can explore the way in which ideas and meanings change over time. In particular, we can examine the changes in the meanings, and hence values, of law that result from the introduction of economic concepts into legal reasoning.

In this chapter, therefore, I explore how these three interests (law, markets, and semiotics) come together. I make two points. First, I discuss the way in which economics functions as a map for navigating our legal landscapes. Second, I elaborate on this theme in presenting an argument for using these "maps" to reduce the indeterminacy and subjectivity of legal reasoning.

## THE MAP IS NOT THE TERRITORY

As a starting point for better understanding the position I give to economics in addressing law in a market context, let me offer a deceivingly simple quote from S.I. Hayakawa. He said, "the map is not the territory" (Hayakawa & Hayakawa, 1990, pp. 13–21).

A map, like any semiotic sign, is a partial and incomplete representation of that to which it refers (Malloy, 2004, pp. 68–69; Malloy, 2000, pp. 41–43). A roadmap, for example, is useful in the task of navigating around town but it tells us little about the quality of schools, home prices, crime rates, climate, or other important characteristics that collectively give meaning and value to a particular property located along a particular street in a given community. Likewise, a deed to property represents an interest in a specifically described piece of land but it is not itself the land to which it makes reference. The deed is a semiotic representation of the property and creates opportunities for wealth-enhancing moves that make land transfers easier, and which give rise to the ability of the owner to mortgage the land, and to put the value it represents into various streams of commerce.

In a similar manner we can appreciate the idea of economics as a map. When we look at the relationship between law and economics we can understand that economics and various economic concepts and metaphors such as the prisoner's dilemma, the tragedy of the commons, the Coase theorem, Arrow's impossibility theorem, and the theory of efficient breach, to name a few, are all maps (Malloy, 2004, pp. 124–211). They are all maps and models attempting to represent, in some partial and incomplete way, the process of human exchange to which they make reference. Economics is not, however, the exchange process itself, but is merely one of a number of cultural-interpretive (semiotic) "maps" that can be referenced in the process of interpreting and influencing the meanings and values of social organization.

The error made by many engaged in the enterprise of an economic analysis of law consists of collapsing the map with the territory; that is, of believing that what they do with the economic model is in fact done to the underlying market-exchange process. This mistake leads to an inability to appreciate the function of economics as an interpretive device, and this in turn leads to the mistaken belief that economics brings neutrality, objectivity, and science to law.

Economics does not bring science to law; it brings a cultural-interpretive code to law that facilitates the framing and comprehension of certain relational experiences in law. As with any such code, it operates within a social context and is given authoritative meaning through normative adherence to its conventionalized value structure.

I am interested in the encoding and decoding of the models and maps of the human practice of exchange; of the networks and patterns of exchange within and between communities and the individuals who comprise these communities. Who initiates exchange? What is permitted as the subject/object of exchange? How do the networks and patterns of exchange vary with reference to a variety of characteristics such as race, gender, age, education, and geographic location? Putting exchange into historical context might allow us to better understand the constraints and path dependencies of law reform across time and place.

We must be careful when confronted with competing and conflicting maps emerging from people situated in alternative cultural-interpretive communities. We must consciously explore the ways in which law functions to conventionalize certain maps at the expense of others. This is because legally favored cartographers exercise authoritative influence over the codes of social organization by virtue of their position in establishing a cultural-interpretive hierarchy that conventionalizes decision-making authority in favor of a particular interpretive group (Malloy, 2004, pp. 64–69, 74–76). This influences the allocation of scarce resources and constrains the people, groups, and institutions having responsibility for generating, responding to, or otherwise participating in future decisions and exchanges.

In the language of semiotics, these cultural-interpretive hierarchies (these maps of authoritative and conventionalized interpretive norms) operate as *indexical referents* that mediate and inform the process of interpretive choice (*ibid.*, pp. 70–84). In this context, the pursuit of self-interested behavior is directed at two primary objectives. First, it is directed at the pursuit of strategic opportunities for interpretive influence within the given hierarchy (within a particular worldview or market frame), and second, it is directed at the pursuit of either reinforcing or replacing the given interpretive hierarchy (*ibid.*). This means that we either try to act strategically within the rules that we are confronted with, or we try to change the rules. Thus, contested understandings of the market reflect struggles over the conventionalized decision-making process, with the understanding that authoritative influence in this process can result in a greater share of the distribution of wealth (*ibid.*, p. 67).

This idea of a *cultural-interpretive hierarchy* can be understood by comparison to an operating system in a computer (Malloy, 2000, pp. 170–171; Malloy, 2004, p. 67). The operating system conventionalizes the computing environment and only compatible software will work in the system. Any software that is incompatible with the conventionalized operating system is rendered inoperative. This control over the meanings and values that are expressed within the system is very valuable as is evidenced by the market position of the Microsoft Corporation. Microsoft dominates the market with its operating system and this makes it very difficult for software companies that do not use compatible software. By dominating the market for operating systems, Microsoft controls the interpretive hierarchy of computer software and this enhances both its market power and its economic position. In a similar way, control over the cultural-interpretive environment of law and market economy gives primacy and power to discourses, meanings and values which are compatible with the dominant interpretive hierarchy. In other words, if I have the power of a high court judge and I require all legal cases to be approached from an economic point of view, I make legal argument difficult for those people who want to discuss problems in terms that are not readily priced for easy cost and benefit analysis, and for those who want to address a conflicted relationship through feminist or critical race theory.

Economic concepts are important in all of this analysis because economics provides a formal representational sign system, or "language," for "mapping" certain parts of the underlying process of exchange that is the subject of my investigation (Kevelson, 1988; Kevelson, 1993; see also Malloy, 2004; Malloy, 2000). It is also important that we be familiar with basic economic tools so that we can examine the way in which the introduction of economic concepts into law changes the underlying meanings and values of the law itself.

In furtherance of this discussion, a simple diagram (Fig. 1) represents the relationships among law, markets, and culture, with a particular focus on the way in which people experience the intersections of these three spheres of interest (Malloy, 2004, p. 62). Understanding that each of these spheres (law, markets, and culture) is itself a semiotic system, I consequently have attempted to develop a meta-semiotic or layered semiotic approach that bridges or maps the relationships between these three spheres.

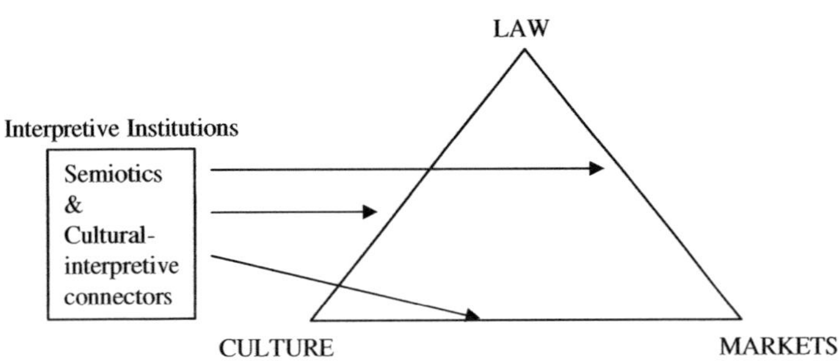


*Fig. 1.* The Relationship among Law, Markets, and Culture.

The way in which people experience the intersections among law, markets and culture are understood by means of interpretive institutions (semiotic and cultural-interpretive connectors), and they vary by such characteristics as race, gender, age, religion, income, education level, and geographical location, among others. In Figure 1, law mediates the tension between the market and culture, where the market expresses the motivations of rational and self-interested actors directed by what Adam Smith referred to as an *invisible hand*, and culture expresses the interests of the community, which in some sense operates as might Adam Smith's notion of the *impartial spectator*. Although we know that no spectator is truly impartial, we can appreciate the constraint that community norms and standards place upon interpretation in both the areas of the market and of law. In my approach, law functions ideally when it mediates the tension between self-interest and the public interest so that collectively we might identify and promote our *common* interests.

In my work I use economic concepts and ideas to organize and make more comprehensible many of the market elements of a transactional legal problem; at the same time, I am cautious about the usefulness of an economic calculus. Caution is advised for many reasons.

First, economics is used to map a complex system, which is the underlying practice of human exchange to which it refers. However, complex systems under chaos theory are unable to be evaluated for optimal outcomes (Kauffman, 1995). Complex systems theory informs us that systems with multiple degrees of freedom (multiple actors and multiple courses of action and inaction) generate multiple sets of plausibly good outcome choices. There is, in other words, often more than one way to achieve a reasonably good outcome without being able to say that one outcome choice is absolutely superior to any other. Some choices can be shown to be suboptimal and these can be eliminated from the set of plausibly good options under consideration. In most cases, however, we are left with multiple courses of action where no one course of action is mathematically superior to any other. Liability may fall in different places, different legal rules and policy choices may come into conflict, but economics will not be able to endogenously resolve the choice-making process. Thus, it is a misconception to believe that economics can help us identify the most efficient legal rule or the optimal-rule choice in a given set of circumstances. Economics can only present us with ways of identifying and justifying plausibly good sets of outcome options. The ultimate choice between the resulting set of plausibly good options involves a normative one grounded in experience, ethics, and aesthetics (Malloy, 2000; Malloy, 2004).

Second, any distribution of wealth within a system can be determined to be efficient, so efficiency tells us little about legal and cultural concerns with respect to distribution. Distribution questions raise the need for normative evaluation (Malloy, 2000, pp. 126–129).

Third, a foundational idea in economics is that individuals pursuing their own self-interest end up promoting the public interest even though it was no part of their original design. This is the position of equivalence between self-interest and the public interest, a position that even economics casts into doubt with its many models showing the failure of this convergence between self-interest and the public interest because of such things as transaction cost, the commons problem, and the prisoner's dilemma (Malloy, 2004, pp. 114–211). Consequently, normative judgment must be exercised in framing the questions to be asked and in determining the nature of the exchange relationship to be investigated. For example, one might look at the question of legalizing prostitution and see it as a simple two-party transaction which meets the test of both Pareto and Kaldor–Hicks efficiency. On the other hand, one might decide to frame the matter of prostitution more broadly and see this as an exchange with numerous spillover effects and externalities (i.e., public health concerns, and the effects of the commodification of women, for example) such that the two individual transactors are incapable of capturing and considering all of the costs of their transaction on their own. The 'best' market outcome, therefore, depends in part on how one sets the frame of the transaction, and how one draws the line with respect to the relevant costs and benefits to be considered.

Fourth, because it is easy to manipulate the way in which legal problems are framed, one can totally recast the economic analysis by shifting the legal landscape, as in recasting a conflict from contract law to tort law (moving from a contract action based on privity of contract requirements to a tort action for breach of a duty to a person who could be reasonably expected to rely, or recasting an installment contract for deed into a constructive mortgage) (*ibid.*, pp. 10–11, 82–84). Such moves easily recharacterize the legal problem, trigger different rule choices, and require different economic tools for analysis. The characterization of the legal problem is also, therefore, a normative one.

And fifth, economics applied to law leads to ambiguous results because many important cultural values that shape the choice-making process are influenced by cultural factors that are not easily expressed in quantitative terms. Thus, such values are left out of the economic and market equation, and there is no normative justification for law to proceed as if such exclusion is either natural or desirable.

Having set the initial stage, what follows is a further elaboration on the way in which economics can be useful in assisting us in reducing the indeterminacy of legal reasoning, even as we recognize its limitations.

## THE MAP CONSTRAINS THE PURELY SUBJECTIVE

As explained above, the art of lawyering involves a process of interpretation. This process is a semiotic process involving the continuous encoding and decoding of meanings and values through exchange, where exchange is not limited to commercial activity, but understood broadly to encompass all forms of interaction, substitution, and value and meaning transformation – including that which occurs in language. It is a process grounded in the idea of humans as sign-making and sign-interpreting beings. Prototypical sign systems include: law, economics, language, music, fashion, architecture, and a full range of ways in which people communicate ideas among and between each other (Malloy, 2004, pp. 1–9). I have referred to this semiotic process applied to law as a *cultural-interpretive* approach "because this term expresses the semiotic ideas that the individual interpretive actor is situated within a cultural context and that a culture, in essence, is an implicit interpretive system" (*ibid.*).[1]

This perspective informed my work as I first started exploring the connections between semiotic interpretation theory and law and economics.[2] At first only a few people expressed an interest in the way in which the market might be understood as a 'place' of meaning and value formation, nor was there a good understanding of economics as a method of interpreting certain market-exchange relationships. Initially there was resistance to seeing economics as a cultural-interpretive device for organizing legal inquiry and reasoning. I offered a humanities-based rationale for the reference to economics as a useful mapping device and explained how it could be understood without accepting it as a 'science'. My work demonstrated the way in which the importing into law of economic models, paradigms, metaphors, and concepts was transforming the underlying meanings and values of law. The economic analysis of law was not simply about making law more efficient; it was about shifting the cultural-interpretive framework of law in a way that gave primacy to a particular political and socio-legal hierarchy. Over the years interest has grown with respect to understanding economics as a cultural-interpretive device capable of drawing attention to useful information and of influencing the underlying meanings and values of the law.

Using legal semiotics and the cultural-interpretive approach permits one to examine new questions that are not being explored by people doing more traditional work in law and economics. Legal semiotics focuses on the process of exchange itself: the idea being that market theory is really about our understanding of the human practice of exchange, and so we need to think about law in terms of the networks and patterns of exchange. This analysis considers who initiates exchange, what is permitted as an object/subject of exchange, and how exchange varies with reference to a variety of characteristics such as race, gender, age, education, and geographic location, among others.

In understanding economics as a map applied to organize our understanding of market exchange, it is possible to imagine alternative market arrangements. Rather than assuming that markets are driven only by a concern for the calculus of wealth maximization, one can assume that other values come into play in the process of exchange. People may act to improve their position in life but they need not do so in order to maximize individual gain at the expense of others. In exploring alternative market arrangements and exchange values, one comes to appreciate the dynamic malleability of economics. And, even as one comes to understand the fluidity of economic analysis, one also comes to appreciate the ability of market tools to focus and constrain our understanding of wealth trade-offs in dealing with law in a market context (Malloy, 2004; Malloy, 2000).

One way in which law seeks to project constraint with reference to economics is by employing economic analysis as a cultural-interpretive *sign* for asserting a sense of science, neutrality, and objectivity *in* law. This is important because objectivity is central to conceptions of justice as being neutral. Objectivity is assumed to further the goals of equality and fairness through law by rendering justice blind to such characteristics as income, class, race, gender, religion, ethnicity, and geographic origin. And, to the extent, that economics can direct legal inquiry to measurable and identifiable trade-offs between conflicting claims, it can create a framework for a constrained evaluation of the innumerable choice options that confront us as public-policy makers.

Using economics as a way of projecting a sense of objectivity in law sheds light on the role of "objectivity" as a *sign* in semiotics. In semiotics, a sign does not stand for something in all respects; it is partial and incomplete. A sign is an idea that has meaning. A sign is not invariant or absolute.

> A sign ... is something which stands to somebody for something in some respect or capacity. It addresses somebody, that is, creates in the mind of that person an equivalent sign, or perhaps a more developed sign. (Peirce, 1955, pp. 99–100; Malloy, 2000, p. 70)

"Objectivity" is a sign that can be understood in a market context as being a representation or an interpretation of "bounded objectivity;" that is, as being constrained and not entirely subjective and indeterminate. In legal economic reasoning, bounded objectivity means that a legal argument or conclusion is capable of being interpreted by other legal actors as reasonably independent of personal feelings, opinions, and prejudice because of the logic of the inferences to be drawn from stated economic assumptions. It means that we can say that something is an "objective" statement of the law or a "true" conclusion in the application of the law to a given set of facts, not because it is the "absolute truth" but because it functions as an argument or conclusion that fits within the cultural-interpretive networks and patterns of exchange of the given market assumptions. It is, in other words, constrained by its "fit" within the authoritative maps of economics applied to legal reasoning. In this sense it is not fully indeterminate. At the same time, however, the conclusions are not absolutely objective because the constraining assumptions are capable of manipulation and adjustment. We could, for instance, attain a different set of plausibly good outcomes by shifting from one form of economic efficiency (Pareto) to another (Kaldor–Hicks). There are many tools and framing devices in our economic tool kit and by carefully selecting we can drive different outcomes. In each case, however, we are constrained by the logical relationship between and among the tools we use, and by the ability of the selected tools to produce outcome choices capable of matching the reasonable experiences and expectations of the people affected thereby.

Economics provides a cultural-interpretive framework capable of enhancing the bounded objectivity of legal reasoning. It is useful as a "map" that helps us to understand and communicate about observable and experienced exchange relationships. For example, we do experience scarcity and a need for choice making, and there are things that are usefully described in terms of transaction costs. Some situations are also made comprehensible by reference to the Coase theorem, the prisoner's dilemma, public choice, the efficient breach, and the tragedy of the commons, among other market concepts. And, even while there are a number of "maps" to chose from, using market concepts and economic tools to frame inquiry and to inform discussion is not arbitrary because many market concepts are helpful and connect us to the experienced world in which we engage in the human practice of exchange. Thus, while economics cannot provide us with a calculus for identifying the *optimal* course of action in law, it can help us identify *useful* framing devices that support logical inferences capable of being understood as reasonably independent of personal and subjective belief.

Assuming that an exogenous normative argument justifies the use of a particular map in a given circumstance, the map itself constrains the set of plausibly good legal arguments and outcomes. The map establishes critical "sign posts" and criteria by which to evaluate the soundness of a given choice option. In this sense the map draws attention to important considerations that might have otherwise been overlooked, while simultaneously constraining the reasonably inferable set of plausibly good outcomes.

Expanding on the aforementioned, we can usefully employ economic terms and concepts in law even as we understand that they offer a partial and incomplete picture for legal reasoning. Economic concepts and models are used to represent the exchange process, but they are not the exchange process itself. This can be better understood if one thinks in terms of the way in which a legal description "represents" a particular piece of property even though it is not itself the property to which it refers.[3] The legal description simplifies the process of identifying and transferring the property, but it is not the property and it does not represent all of the characteristics of the property. It is a partial and incomplete representation. In a similar sense, economic concepts function as signs that define, simplify, and facilitate exchange, but like the legal description mentioned earlier, these concepts are merely partial and incomplete representations of underlying exchange processes which are complex and dynamic.

Thus, economic concepts function as partial and incomplete representations even though they may be useful for understanding the constraints and the dynamics of a particular situation. In this way, economics is like a map. A road map, for example, is useful for assisting in the task of driving around town but it tells one little or nothing about the quality of schools or home prices, and gives no indication of crime rates, climate or other important characteristics that collectively give meaning to a particular property located along a particular street in a given community. In this respect, the map is not the territory, and the market model is not the market-exchange process. Nonetheless, economics, as a cultural-interpretive device, facilitates the mapping process and can help us identify a finite set of plausibly useful courses of socio-legal action.

We can better appreciate this function when we consider the form of legal argument. From an interpretive point of view, the market is understandable as a complex and dynamic web of representational networks and patterns of exchange wherein the nature, scope, and content of these exchange relationships inform social meaning and value.[4] Borrowing from Peirce, I identify a three-step process (Malloy, 2004, pp. 72–85).

Fig. 2 depicts a cultural-interpretive form of legal argument for law and market economy using Peirce's triadic theory of signs (firstness, secondness,

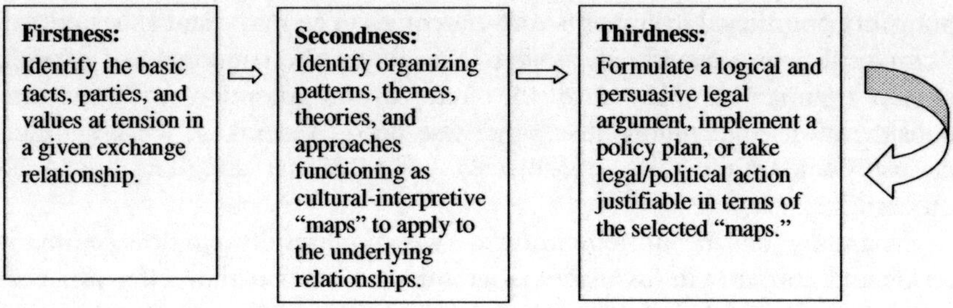


*Fig. 2.* The Structure of Legal Argument.

and thirdness) (Malloy, 2000, pp. 23–50). In this diagram the firstness is the exchange itself; it arises in an experiential context of social or interpretive conflict or tension. Secondness frames, filters, and influences the encoding and decoding of socio-legal meanings and values. It "maps" the relationship between a particular exchange and other such exchanges or qualities; it is comparative in nature. In practice this involves organizing the facts in relation to particular patterns of legal and economic argument, and connecting the facts to legal themes and approaches that serve as potentially good frames, references, and representations for resolving the matter in a favorable manner. Thirdness involves the development of a logical and persuasive argument (normative justification) in support of the frames, references, and representations selected and used in reaching a given conclusion. To be influential as a legal argument, thirdness must flow logically and plausibly from the maps applied in secondness. Thirdness, as a contingent conclusion, also supports the refined identification of "significant" facts relative to facts that are argued to be of less or no significance to the given exchange. Thirdness is what gets constituted as law, or what gets justified and represented as a legal rule, holding, or conclusion.

After drawing an initial conclusion, the process is repeated and refined by taking the tentative conclusion and using it to go back and revisit the initial fact pattern related to the exchange relationship. This may give rise to a need to focus on slightly different facts than were considered on the first pass through of the analysis. Theoretically, this process of moving from firstness, secondness, thirdness and back again can go on indefinitely, but the demands of everyday life will cut it short. This process is referred to as *semiosis* (*ibid.*, pp. 21, 33–35, 87; Malloy, 2004, p. 74), and as we move through this process we construct alternative mappings of the exchange relationship in question.

In simple terms, this three-step model provides an organized way of thinking about legal-economic reasoning and legal argument. It represents thought in motion. In firstness it indicates the need to identify the basic nature of the exchange and dispute. In secondness it instructs us to look for ways of understanding the exchange or dispute in comparative relationship to patterns of legal argument, given particular economic assumptions and constraints. Thus, we think in terms of classifying and categorizing the basic facts with reference to particular areas of law and various approaches to contemporary market theory. We draw on maps such as those provided by the Coase theorem, the prisoner's dilemma, and various approaches to cost and benefit analysis using alternative discount rates and pricing factors. It is understood that we can influence the conclusions and arguments to be presented in thirdness by the way in which we select and apply the maps of secondness. At the same time, the selected maps impose constraints and limitations as to the logical inferences and conclusions that can be drawn. Thus, constraints of the chosen economic "map" reduce personal subjectivity even as the map selection process leaves room for creativity and normative judgment in structuring the sets of plausibly good legal arguments.

There are interpretive limitations to using economic "science" to solve complex socio-legal problems (Malloy, 2004, pp. 93–104; Eco, 1990). This is because the market exchange process cannot be fully captured by an economic calculus – there are values and experiences that are difficult or impossible to capture on an economic "map." Selecting the appropriate cultural-interpretive maps involves normative analysis outside the scope of traditional neoclassical economics.[5]

### *An Example*

This balancing between the constraining elements and the ambiguity of using economics in law is best understood with an example. Let us assume that we work in a large hotel. Imagine that we have been instructed by the hotel manager to prepare a large ballroom for a meeting that will be taking place later in the day.[6] We are instructed to go to the room, examine the various pieces of furniture in the room, and to arrange the room in the most efficient manner. When we get to the room, we are confronted with a space of a given size and shape, with particular lighting fixtures, and other characteristics. We also take note of a variety of furniture including chairs and tables of various styles and shapes. The physical characteristics of the room cannot be changed (size, shape, etc.) and we are instructed that none of the furniture can be taken from the room.

In this situation, the nature and characteristics of the room and the furniture operate as constraints to the ways in which the room can be arranged. In other words, there are real world constraints to the way we can "socially construct" the relationships within this particular room. At the same time, however, there are also numerous ways in which we might exercise some influence over relationships in the room by virtue of our authority to rearrange the furniture. The arrangement of the furniture by itself may signal important meanings, as in identifying important people with a head table, or it might shape conversation or influence physical movement based on the spacing we use around and between tables. An important problem from the outset, however, involves our ability to determine the most efficient arrangement of the furniture in the absence of a predetermined use for the room. If the room is to be used for a lecture we may want to arrange a head table or podium with all the other tables and chairs facing the "front." If, on the other hand, the room is to be used for a round table discussion, or for a job fair, we might arrange the room differently. Likewise, if the room will be used for dancing we will need to push tables and chairs to the side so that ample space can be left open for the activity. In short, the idea of efficiency can be ambiguous in the absence of a predetermined goal or objective.

Once we are clear about the use of the room, we can begin to make progress at identifying plausibly good alternatives for arranging the room in a useful way, or in other words, once a normative decision is made with respect to our given objective we can then seek to achieve that goal in a more cost-effective manner.

The physical constraints of the room are real world constraints; just as are concerns for externalities, transaction costs, and Coasian bargaining problems. Even with these physical constraints, however, there is still an opportunity to influence the organization of the room. Within these constraints there are probably several good ways of setting up the room for any particular purpose. While some of the arrangements might be awkward or inappropriate, it is quite possible that several different arrangements could be equally suitable (likewise with framing a legal conflict). Experience and experimentation will help in the decision-making process – they may also trigger ideas for the future construction of different types of rooms (the development of new legal rules and doctrines, for example).

The problem of arranging furniture in our hypothetical room is, of course, a metaphor for law. In the real world of human interaction and exchange there are always numerous "rooms" to arrange. In seeking to arrange these rooms we are constrained by convention and by physical limitations, yet we must not be misled into thinking that we have no power to influence the understanding of these rooms and their contents. We can influence these understandings and facilitate favorable arrangements (outcomes) by carefully manipulating the use of market concepts in legal reasoning. To do this, we need to understand economic terms and concepts while appreciating their primary semiotic function as elements of secondness in the structure of legal argument – we need to understand them as tools for advancing particular ends and not as ends in themselves. Economic tools are useful maps but as maps they are always partial and incomplete.

Therefore, the point of this example is that it illustrates the need to exercise normative judgment when integrating economic terms and concepts into law. Without a normative decision on how to use the room, in the first instance, one cannot make sense of a request to arrange the room in the most efficient way. Similarly, in the real world, economics does not provide law with an objective calculus capable of freeing us from the challenge and opportunity of exercising normative judgment. Economics can help illuminate the constraints that we confront, and it can help us develop useful maps of potentially good courses of action. Economics cannot, however, help us identify the optimal course of action, even as it helps us understand problems in new ways and provides us with a useful "language" for analysis (Malloy, 2000, pp. 137–148; Kauffman, 1995, pp. 248–262, 268–269).[7]

Moreover, economics does not make law fully objective, and it does not substitute for more traditional jurisprudential reasoning. Consequently, while there are limitations to our ability to shape specific outcomes (there are problems of scarcity, for example), there is still plenty of room to "arrange" law and legal institutions to advance particular normative values – even when economic analysis is incorporated into legal reasoning.

We can observe this advantage in using cost and benefit analysis to aid in legal reasoning. In *U.S. v. Carroll Towing Co.* (1947), for instance, we substitute a basic cost and benefit analysis for an ambiguous standard of *reasonable care* in the effort that should be expended to prevent accidental injury to another. Likewise, in *Vande Zande v. Wisconsin Dept. of Admin.* (1995), the ambiguous requirement for making a *reasonable accommodation* in the workplace for people with disabilities is replaced with the need to do a cost and benefit analysis such that a reasonable accommodation is given meaning by defining reasonableness in terms of the benefits outweighing the costs.[8] In each of these two cases we can appreciate the subjectivity of selecting certain economic tools to assist in our legal analysis. At the same time, economic tools and references (maps) help us focus on relevant information and establish a testable (or contestable) framework for making logical inferences and conclusions – inferences and conclusions that can be persuasive because they are not fully the subjective and indeterminate beliefs of the author. They can be validated or refuted by others making reference to the same (or different) maps. The use of such economic tools does not lead us to one optimal conclusion but it does reduce the ambiguity of legal reasoning by reference to a particular set of tools for analysis. Rather than leaving the legal decision maker free to apply *any* normative understanding of "reasonable care" or "reasonable accommodation," reasonableness can be given a wealth-implicating context and texture through economics. Selecting and quantifying the economic maps to be applied involves a normative judgment, and the selection of any given map, with its inherent wealth and value implications, should be publicly contested and debated.

## CONCLUSION

In the end I believe we must seek to strike a fair balance between the use of economic tools that provide us with useful and meaningful insight into the market sphere, and tools that provide us with the ability to understand the human condition at a cultural and aesthetic level. This means that we need to strike a fair balance in our cultural-interpretive approach between the use of maps provided by economics, and such other insightful codes as those provided by feminist theory, critical theory, sociology, anthropology, and other disciplines. While none of these maps is in itself complete, all of these maps work to more fully inform us about the underlying practice of human exchange.

## NOTES

1. For two definitions of culture that I incorporate into my work, see also Hall (1997):

> Culture ... is not so much a set of things – novels and paintings or T.V. programs and comics – as a process, a set of practices. Primarily, culture is concerned with the production and exchange of meanings – the "giving and taking of meaning" – between members of a society or group. To say that two people belong to the same culture is to say that they interpret the world in roughly the same ways and can express themselves, their thoughts and their feelings about the world, in ways which will be understood by each other. (Malloy, 2004, pp. 1–2)

See also Throsby (2001):

> "Culture" is ... a set of attitudes, beliefs, mores, customs, values and practices which are common to or shared by any group. The groups may be defined in terms of politics, geography, religion, ethnicity or some other characteristic .... The characteristics which define the group may be substantiated in the form of signs, symbols, texts, language, artifacts, oral and written tradition and by other means. (Malloy, 2004, pp. 3–4)

2. See generally, Kevelson (1993, pp. 199–218). Kevelson explains with reference to some of my early work:

> ... the triadic linking of law, economics, and semiotics makes its most recent debut in the work of Robin Paul Malloy ...
>
> Malloy shows how signification of cultural values evolve and are transformed through use and exchange in living community. He suggests that it is by using the instrument of semiotic inquiry, in the sense that all theories have instrumental purpose, that we can begin to perceive and explain previously undisclosed processes of value development, i.e., aspects of emerging value which appear only as a result of a certain way of being observed.
>
> Every use and mention of a term and every attempt to redefine and sharpen the meaning of a term creates an asymmetrical relationship between the known and the new, just as every marketplace transaction changes the value of the objects exchanged and increases the meaning of each, so that the value of each becomes off-balanced from its previous marketplace value and acquires, as if repricing were redefinition, an increase in meaning. (Kevelson, pp. 205–206)

3. For example, the formal metes and bounds, government survey, or plat based description that appears in the deed and mortgage only represents the property at issue (see Malloy & Smith, 2007, pp. 205–230). Note that representation occurs in a variety of areas and not just with respect to real estate. For example, the corporate form of organization operates as a representation that extends the authority and action of an individual or group. It permits action and exchange with a different and legally distinct identity, and permits the legal entity to act beyond the identity of the real people whose interests it represents. This extended representation can itself be limited, however, with such concepts as acting *ultra vires* (beyond the authority of the entity), or by the process of "piercing the corporate veil."

4. Law and market economy examines exchange systems, and the scientific method of inquiry used in semiotics to understand exchange systems reveals that they are like a "web" with indefinite boundaries (Peirce & Buchler, 1955, p. xii). This is also a point raised in general chaos or complex systems theory (Kauffman, 1995, pp. 270–287 (discussing co-evolving webs in complex systems)). In studying these webs of exchange it is important to investigate and understand discourse across a number of conventionalized boundaries (see Kevelson, 1996, pp. 11, 63, 78, 109, 131; Kevelson, 1993, pp. 27–28, 62–64).

5. It involves a reference to Peirce's ideas on the normative sciences. For a good discussion of Peirce's views on the normative sciences, see Potter (1997) (discussing the normative sciences as including esthetics, ethics, and logic).

6. See Malloy (2004), pp. 101–103; see also Malloy (2000), p. 147 and Deely (1990), p. 42 (using a home furnishings example to discuss semiotic relationships signaling different meanings even as the contents of the room remain constant).

7. It is impossible to optimize a course of action in a complex system – one can only hope to make a reasonable compromise within a wide range of constraints (Kauffman, 1995, pp. 268–269).

8. Many more examples and cases can be found in Malloy (2004).

## REFERENCES


Deely, J. (1990). *Basics of semiotics* (p. 42). Bloomington, IN: Indiana University Press.

Eco, U. (1990). *The limits of interpretation.* Bloomington, IN: Indiana University Press.

Hall, S. (1997). *Representation: Cultural representations and signifying practices.* London: Sage Publications.

Hayakawa, S. I., & Hayakawa, A. (1990). *Language in thought and action* (5th ed., pp. 13–21). New York, NY: Harcourt, Inc.

Kauffman, S. (1995). *At home in the universe: The search for the laws of self-organization and complexity* (pp. 248–262, 268–269, 270–287). New York, NY: Oxford University Press.

Kevelson, R. (1988). *Law as a system of signs* (pp. 167–201). New York, NY: Plenum.

Kevelson, R. (1993). *Peirce's esthetics of freedom: Possibility, complexity, and emergent value* (pp. 199–218). New York, NY: Peter Lang.

Kevelson, R. (1996). *Peirce, science, signs (semiotics and the human sciences)* (pp. 11, 63, 78, 109, 131). New York, NY: Peter Lang.

Malloy, R. P. (2000). *Law and market economy: Reinterpreting the values of law and economics.* Cambridge: Cambridge University Press.

Malloy, R. P. (2004). *Law in a market context: An introduction to market concepts in legal reasoning.* Cambridge: Cambridge University Press.

Malloy, R. P., & Smith, J. C. (2007). *Real estate transactions: Problems, cases and materials* (3rd ed., pp. 205–230). New York, NY: Aspen Publishers.

Peirce, C. S., & Buchler, J. (Eds). (1955). *Philosophical writings of pierce* (pp. 99–100). New York, NY: Dover.

Potter, V. G. (1997). *Charles S. Peirce on norms & ideals.* Bronx, NY: Fordham University Press.

Throsby, D. (2001). *Economics and culture.* Cambridge: Cambridge University Press.


### Cases


*United States v. Carroll Towing Co.*, 159 F. 2d 169 (2d Cir. 1947).

*Vande Zande v. State of Wisconsin Department of Administration*, 44 F. 3d 538 (7th Cir. 1995).

# AN ANATOMY OF CORPORATE LEGAL THEORY

William W. Bratton

## ABSTRACT

*This chapter collects and categorizes the principal theoretical debates respecting corporate law in the United States. What emerges is not a synthetic whole but a dialectic framework. Corporate law's theoretical debates do not resolve; their arguments and conclusions are determined by metapolitical preferences and unverified notions about aligning productivity incentives. But despite the debates, the acknowledged premise that corporations exist to create wealth by producing goods and services at a profit directs all theories of corporate law to two objectives. First, corporate law encourages long-term investment and risk-taking by facilitating a delegation of decision-making authority from the providers of capital to the expert managers who deploy it. Second, corporate law facilitates investment in producing assets at the lowest possible cost of capital, securing the presence of liquid trading markets in corporate securities.*

## 1. INTRODUCTION

In *The Anatomy of Corporate Law*, seven corporate law academics offered a concise and successful synthesis of the corporate law of the world's largest

**Law & Economics: Toward Social Justice**
**Research in Law and Economics: A Journal of Policy, Volume 24, 21–41**

**ISSN: 0193-5895/doi:10.1108/S0193-5895(2009)0000024006**

national economies (Kraakman et al., 2004). Impressed by that effort, this chapter undertakes a contrasting exercise in synthesis. It collects and categorizes the principal theoretical debates in corporate law, offering a concise outline of corporate legal theory in the United States. No synthetic whole integrates the theoretical disagreements, and corporate legal theory reveals itself as more a forum for ongoing and unresolved debates than a unitary system of assertions.

At the highest level of generality, however, the corporate law debates do proceed within implicit parameters that follow from the law itself. Because corporate law addresses a limited set of matters concerning business organizations, it necessarily stays focused on two core economic objectives. First, it carves out a zone of freedom of action for productive enterprise, and second, it seeks to facilitate enterprises' capitalization at the lowest possible cost. No assertion about corporate law or policy that fails to recognize and work with these objective functions registers in debates in the field. Questions and initiatives respecting the corporation's relations with outside society and corporate law's appropriate role in integrating firms within society are not thereby foreclosed, so long as the proponent takes care to recognize and interrogate the firm's economic objectives. Thus does corporate legal theory make all discussants welfare consequentialists who keep their eyes on productivity, whatever their economic, political, or ethical predispositions.[1]

The chapter's five sections proceed as follows. Section 2 identifies the core objectives of corporate law in the United States – freedom of action for management and the minimization of the cost of capital. Section 3 describes corporate legal theory's conceptual framework in four subject categories relating to various aspects of the firm, setting out the principal components of its unresolved debates. Section 4 places this conceptual framework in historical context, evaluating the two theoretical paradigms that dominated corporate law during the 20th century: the trust paradigm of Berle and Means and the contractarian paradigm of law and economics. This discussion shows that both paradigms lost salience because their proponents failed to accord sufficient recognition to corporate law's core objectives. Section 5 turns to contemporary disputes about the terms of the shareholder–manager–agency relationship, highlighting the interplay between leading debating points and the law's allowance of competing and inconsistent means to the end of achieving its dual objectives of freedom of action and cheap capital. What emerges from this analysis is that even as the competing theories offer means to resolve the tensions in the law's structure, the law declines the offers. Rather than endorsing a given theory, corporate law mediates its own internal tensions with open-ended terms and piecemeal resolutions. Section 6 takes up the problem of setting the firm's legal boundaries. Here, corporate law and its core objectives send a clear set of instructions, defining a narrow boundary that results in persistent and legitimate theoretical protests from those calling for social responsibility and constituent empowerment.

## 2. IMPLICIT PARAMETERS: THE PURPOSES OF CORPORATE LAW

Corporations exist to create wealth by producing goods and services at a profit. There would be no reason to put up with them if they did not succeed as economic producers. Indeed, real-world firms that fail to do so disappear in the long run. Corporate law's objective function follows from these home truths. Under the usual formulation, corporate law seeks to maximize the wealth generated by firms. But that usual formulation is problematic – no one really knows when wealth is being maximized, and, even if someone derived a plausible maximizing template, corporate law would make no attempt to impose it. The usual formulation should be relaxed and restated accordingly: corporate law facilitates the attempt to maximize the value produced by the firm.

A narrower formulation favored by many – that the firm and hence corporate law should maximize shareholder value – is not in fact legal doctrine. The shareholder value maximization norm follows from a particular conception of the optimal incentive alignment within the firm, a conception contestable in theory.[2] Although the shareholder value norm figures prominently in corporate law debates, it does not set the debates' parameters. Nor has the norm ever dictated the law's terms, even as it has had its moments of influence.

The objective function of corporate law, then, is more capacious than it may first appear, which fuels rather than resolves theoretical debate. Meanwhile, corporate law historically has pursued the stated objective of maximizing wealth created by firms, which influences regulatory results and bequeaths a conceptual context. That context provides a base for fleshing out the objective function's terms – an exercise that should be undertaken with care. A body of law's statement of its own purposes carries more positive than normative weight. A regulatory framework cannot by virtue of its own existence establish its own legitimacy; it takes a theory to do that. Nor does competitive evolution in history guarantee a single, first-best contextual outcome. Comparative corporate governance teaches that there are many possible legal frameworks within which actors can competitively producc a widgct or construct and operate a communications network.[3] Nor, finally, can it be asserted that an inherited regulatory context controls, for at a theoretical level everything remains contestable even if the doctrinal context tends toward stasis. We bear these caveats in mind as we seek more particular instructions from the doctrine.

US corporate law emerged in its present form in the state of New Jersey between 1888 and 1896, taking shape as an enabling regime that accorded management a wide zone of freedom of action respecting management and financial policy. Mandates provided the means to the ends. Management was to have absolute control over investment and financial decisions, as well as control of the corporate agenda, including both the terms of the corporate contract and end-period decisions like mergers. Beyond these mandates lay a largely enabling regime. The framework changed little during the 20th century. Subsequent innovation occurred primarily at the level of national lawmaking, centered on the capital markets and the federal securities laws. There the purpose was the assurance of liquidity, an essential means to the end of the lowest possible cost of capital in a system characterized by widespread holding of securities.

The doctrinal template suggests a more particular statement of the general purpose of wealth creation. It can be broken down into two primary components, each of which implies a corollary, one set situated on the left side of the balance sheet and the other on the right side.

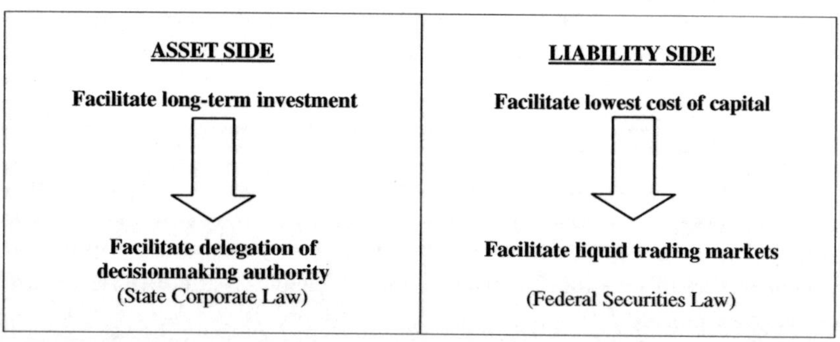


On the left side, it is corporate law's job to encourage long-term investment and the risk-taking implied therein. That purpose implies a corollary: facilitation of a delegation of decision-making authority from the providers of capital to the expert managers who deploy it. (The corollary extends over to the right side of the balance sheet to include substantial management discretion over financing.) On the right side, it is corporate law's job to facilitate investment in producing assets at the lowest possible cost of capital. A corollary again is implied: the law should secure the presence of liquid trading markets in corporate securities.

## 3. CATEGORIES OF DEBATE

The foregoing description of corporate law's objectives should garner general assent. Corporate law also articulates means to these accepted ends. Theoretical disagreements break out at this stage. The debates proceed within four subject matter categories, with persistent points of debate within each category that can be described as binary opposite positions, as follows:

1. Debates about the *appropriate scope of regulation* and the *degree of reliance accorded private ordering in solving problems*:
   - Public vs. private
   - Mandatory vs. enabling
   - Federal vs. state
2. Debates about the *objectives of regulation* and *normative priorities*:
   - Trust vs. contract
   - Fairness vs. efficiency
   - Substance vs. process
   - Protection of expectations vs. dynamism
   - Government enforcement vs. reputational enforcement
3. Debates about the *terms of the corporate agency relationship* and the *allocation of authority* within the firm:
   - Entity vs. agency
   - Management discretion vs. shareholder choice
   - Managerialism vs. shareholder value
4. Debates about the *boundaries of the firm* and the *firm's responsibility to outsiders*:
   - Outsiders (other constituents) vs. insiders (shareholders and managers).

There are conceptual ties among the various points of debate within given categories and across the four categories. And, as with all binary opposing positions, one by definition falls on the left side and the other on the right, inviting ordering along political lines. In the ordering here, the right-side binaries in all four categories yield a larger theoretical and political perspective in combination – the point of view of mainstream law and economics. The left-side binaries in Categories 1, 2, and 4 may variously be described as regulatory, progressive, or antimanagerial. The left side in Category 3, in contrast, resists these appellations. More generally, even as conceptual ties bind various positions mooted across the debates, the connections do not necessarily imply hard theoretical boundaries. Political, methodological, and doctrinal affinities can vary from debate to debate – a given discussant can gravitate to a right-side position in one debate and a left-side position in another without being accused of inconsistency.

A more particular description of the categories and positions follows.

*Category 1: Debates about the appropriate scope of regulation and the degree of reliance accorded private ordering in solving problems.* Problems respecting the governance of firms can be characterized in different ways depending on the political, economic, and social perspectives the particular observer brings to bear. Different observers likewise bring different regulatory strategies to bear in addressing the same problem. Further, in a federal system like that of the United States, a given regulatory strategy may be deployed at different levels of government, with different observers having different views about the choice. Three binary conceptual frameworks describe positions taken in these debates:

- Public vs. private
- Mandatory vs. enabling
- Federal vs. state.

The public/private contrast goes to the definition of the scope of a corporate law problem. A public characterization signals recognition of a wide range of affected interests and the view that appropriate regulation addresses them all. A private characterization of the same subject matter restricts regulatory recognition to a narrow range of inside interests and, stressing the voluntary nature of the insiders' participation, resists regulation. The mandatory/enabling contrast goes to the mode of regulatory response. Mandates direct results, constraining the choices of actors in firms in order to advance a normative objective. Enabling responses, in contrast, are default rules that leave affected actors the option of framing their own regulations. State corporate law in the United States is largely enabling, while the federal law governing the capital markets is largely mandatory. The federal/state binary references this mandatory/enabling divide and also a historical pattern of regulatory allocation. The federal/state binary also has a public/private aspect; under an informal federalism norm, federal law addresses trading markets, adding disclosure, antifraud, and insider-trading mandates in pursuit of a stated public interest, whereas all other corporate subject matters concern internal affairs and presumptively are left to the states. The United States states, constrained by the pattern of charter competition that began in New Jersey in 1888, privilege private ordering and enabling solutions. But, because the federal/state regulatory allocation is not set constitutionally, the presumption favoring state control yields to new federal regulation as political demands arise – regulations that sometimes break the historical pattern of federal/state allocation.

*Category 2: Debates about the objectives of regulation and normative priorities* This category sets out particulars that both support and reflect the more general perspectives in the preceding category. More particularly, the public characterization and willingness to mandate in Category 1 follow from the concerns expressed in the positions on the left side as shown in the diagram; the private characterization and preference for private ordering solutions in Category 1 follow from the concerns listed on the right. Five binaries describe debates in this category:

- Trust vs. contract
- Fairness vs. efficiency
- Substance vs. process
- Protection of expectations vs. dynamism
- Government enforcement vs. reputational enforcement.

Claims favoring regulation in corporate law tend to begin with the observations that the law empowers the managers of large firms and that the power's exercise impacts the interests of a range of other actors, sometimes negatively. Normative objections follow from observers who find these injuries troubling. For them the concept of trust pulls together both the positive observation and the normative objection: one actor's empowerment implies the trust of the subordinated actor and entrustment invites the imposition of legal responsibility on the empowered actor. The four succeeding left-side positions in this category set out more particular implications of a trust relationship. Entrustment triggers expectations of fair dealing in disempowered actors. Protection of those expectations necessitates substantive review of the entrusted actor's behavior. Government intervention and enforcement follow as a corollary – given disempowered actors, private ordering is an intrinsically inadequate source of protection. Significantly, none of these assertions necessarily conflict with corporate law's fundamental objectives. In the case of trust relationships between managers and providers of capital, for example, substantive review of the empowered managers, though it narrows their freedom of action, only does so for the purpose of minimizing the cost of capital. Restrictions that actually succeed in making capital cheaper are, in the case of equity capital, highly unlikely to detract from net productivity. The likelihood of adverse effects increases when debt capital becomes the beneficiary, but even here constraints on opportunism need not necessarily be undue.

Opponents of regulation start with a contrasting observation. They stress the voluntary nature of actors' engagements with firms. Cases of injury accordingly are normatively unproblematic because the injured actor consented in advance and had a chance to arrange for compensation. The concept of contract pulls together both the positive observation and the normative response: those who apply it stress its consonance with the freedom of action objective and go on to assert a normative presumption against mandatory regulation. These regulatory opponents simultaneously put contract to positive use, using it to describe the legal firm as well as the economic firm. The efficiency objective stated on the right side of the second binary restates the overall objective of productivity, bringing it to bear against outside substantive review of management actions in the name of fairness on the theory that outside review inhibits freedom of action and thus enhancement of the value of the firm's assets. The next binary restates this point; to protect expectations is to look backward, whereas productivity looks forward toward a dynamic economic environment.

Finally, because all government intervention implies costs, not just out-of-pocket costs, but opportunity costs in the form of chilled incentives, freely contracting actors in need of protection will prefer reputational enforcement. Some proponents combine this point with the contractual characterization of the legal firm to claim that all fiduciary law should be subject to reversal by contract. Where the government does intervene under the fiduciary rubric to protect an investor for the purpose of minimizing the cost of capital, process solutions that remit decisions to actors within the firm are preferred to substantive, outside review of management actions, which can inhibit productive initiative.

*Category 3: Debates about the terms of the corporate agency relationship and the allocation of authority within the firm.* This category focuses on a narrower range of subject matter – the governance structures that set the balance of power between managers and shareholders. Three binaries suggest themselves:

- Entity vs. agency
- Management discretion vs. shareholder choice
- Managerialism vs. shareholder value

Recall that the dual purposes of productive investment and low capital cost do not by themselves yield a determinative organizational template. There may be multiple means to the end. US corporate doctrine admits this multiplicity at a very basic level, giving us the first binary. In the classical doctrinal conception, the corporation is an entity and the powers of the board of directors are original and undelegated. Even as the shareholders elect the board, they are not accorded the rights of principals in an agency relationship. However, and unfortunately for the goal of doctrinal coherence, corporate law also frequently lapses into an agency characterization, the lapses being much encouraged by the economic theory of agency. Entity and agency coexist in tension in the doctrinal structure.

The ambiguity in the structure of the legal firm invites this category's debates over the line dividing management and shareholder authority. The entity conception goes with a preference for management discretion and a stress on the need for freedom of action. The agency conception goes together with the shareholder value objective, a stress on the cost of capital objective, and suggestions for enhanced shareholder choice in governance matters. Particular contests center on topics like shareholder access, proxy regulation, and takeover defense.

*Category 4: Debates about the boundaries of the firm and the firm's responsibility to outsiders*. Here, a single binary captures the matters at stake:

- Outsiders (other constituents) vs. insiders (shareholders and managers).

The outsiders appear on a standard list of corporate constituents excluded from fiduciary protection and remitted to self-protection through contract – employees, creditors, suppliers, customers, and communities. Debates over this hard result touch on a range of subjects, including limited liability, takeover defense, employee rights in firm governance, and financial contract interpretation. Discussants draw on the concepts described in Categories 1 and 2, pitting public values, fairness, and protection of expectations against private ordering, contract, and dynamism. The Category 4 debates, then, ultimately return us to Category 1, only to start the debates over.

## 4. THE SCOPE AND NORMATIVE CONTENT OF REGULATION

The debates described in Categories 1 and 2, while ongoing, have undergone a notable historical evolution. This part traces that evolution, highlighting the limiting effect of the corporate law purposes described in Part I.

Two theoretical paradigms dominated corporate law in the mid- to late 20th century, succeeding one another in time. First came a trust paradigm, most famously articulated in 1932 by Adolf Berle and Gardiner Means in *The Modern Corporation and Private Property*. It was eclipsed around 1980 by a contract paradigm that originated in economics during the 1960s and 1970s. By now, both have lost salience. In both cases the loss results from failure to hew to corporate law's bottom-line objectives.

Let us look first at Berle and Means. They highlighted the public aspects of what theretofore had been seen as a private subject matter. Enabling corporate law, they said, had facilitated the appearance and success of the large, mass-producing, management-controlled corporation. This had been a reactive rather than a purposive development – a change that followed from underlying economic facts. But the law thereby had become implicated in the creation and perpetuation of an unsatisfactory governance arrangement – the separation of ownership and control.

According to Berle and Means (1991), the big corporations of the 20th century had split the classical entrepreneurial function between salaried executives, who sat atop hierarchical organizations, and anonymous equity participants, who held small stakes and prized market liquidity over participation. This presented problems of competence and responsibility absent in an ideal, classical capitalist world inhabited by self-employed individual producers. In the classical model, market competition effectively controlled the producers, constraining both the incompetent and the greedy and legitimating private economic power. Corporate mass production on a large capital base broke those parameters, with firms taking on significant social attributes as well as economic power. Industrial oligarchs exercised unified control over the wealth under their charge, and the law played a role in investing the power. Therefore, said Berle and Means (p. 219), corporate property should no longer be deemed private property. That assertion supported a presumption favoring new regulation.

Berle and Means, however, recommended no pervasive system of government oversight. Instead, they focused on the problem of management self-dealing in an enabling context. Corporate insiders were writing their own contracts, with immunity clauses and waivers of shareholder rights allowing much diversion of corporate profit to managers' pockets (pp. 128, 220, 312). The law, said Berle and Means, would do a better job if it were rewritten to follow basic principles of trust law. More particularly, there should be a pervasive equitable limitation on powers granted to corporate management (or any other group within the corporation) by the enabling system: power should be exercisable only for the pro-rata benefit of all the shareholders (p. 220).

Berle and Means (p. 242) had in mind an overarching standard to be applied by common-law judges as an ex-post constraint of the enabling system: no language in a corporate charter could deny or defeat the fundamental equitable control of the court. Meanwhile, enforcement of the equitable limitation safely could be remitted to the state judiciary. In Berle and Means' view, charter competition impacted only statutes, leaving the common law of fiduciary duties as the one area of corporate law remaining robust: "Flexible and realistic" judges, "if untrammeled by statute," could be expected to find solutions to problems that demanded a remedy (pp. 197, 295).

While Berle and Means limited their trust paradigm's class of beneficiaries to the corporation's shareholders, many of the paradigm's subsequent proponents expanded the zone of beneficiary to debate Category 4, including other corporate constituents and the public interest. The "public" characterization in *The Modern Corporation and Private Property* invited the extension. So did the theory's emphasis on managerial power: to mid-20th century observers, power implied responsibility and, given the separation of ownership and control, responsibility needed to be imposed in law (Nader, Seligman, & Green, 1976, pp. 1, 7).

Events, however, did not unfold in accordance with the Berle and Means description. The "public" characterization never made the theory-to-practice transition, and the courts stubbornly refused to assume the management-oversight role. Things probably would not have changed very much had the judiciary accepted the invitation. Fiduciary duty was too narrow a framework to support a progressive revision of corporate law that better integrated management power within the wider social and political context. Eventually, economic and political developments overtook the trust paradigm. By the 1970s, new views emerged about the best means to the generally accepted end of creating wealth. A sense of national competitive failure combined with a loss of faith in regulatory problem-solving trumped the paradigm's motivating concerns.

Contract displaced trust. A new contractarian paradigm appeared, rebutting both the trust paradigm's description of separated ownership and control and its call for regulation. The new theory recast the operative description, so that the firm became a series of contracts joining inputs and outputs among rational economic actors – a "nexus of contracts." This view made corporate law a part of a governing contract and equity capital just another contractual input (Jensen & Meckling, 1976, p. 310). The imperfections identified under the trust paradigm reemerged under the denomination "agency costs," costs that firms must minimize due to the free market's competitive force. Managers were no longer seen as empowered actors and responsibility was no longer seen as a problem. When managers failed, they got removed, one way or another. Either a hostile offeror took over the company and threw them out,[4] a high agency-cost base caused the firm to fail to survive in the product market, or the management labor market held the poor managers accountable. These market constraints caused management incentives to be focused on long-run productive success for the firm. In this market-driven picture, corporate property again became private, the regulatory agenda went blank, and a powerful presumption arose against new intervention (Bratton, 1992, pp. 186–190).

The contract paradigm amounted to an ideological mirror image of the trust paradigm. It accordingly suited deregulatory policy agendas. That fit alone should have carried it to unquestioned and continued ascendancy in corporate law discussions. But it instead ran into an unanticipated public choice problem when the enabling system transformed itself in the process of dealing with hostile takeovers. Historically, corporate control always had been contestable in the trading market. But, prior to the 1980s, such contests when they occurred did not fundamentally challenge management empowerment. Low stock-market valuations changed that in the 1980s. Corporate lawmakers responded by interposing frictions that diminished the takeover threat and preserved freedom of action for management. This undermined the contract paradigm's positive story, which relied on market contracting to import incentive compatibility to the agency relationship.

The contract paradigm also failed to synchronize with corporate law at a normative level. Corporate law seeks to create wealth and looks at freedom of contract only as a means to the end. The contract paradigm's proponents stressed individual freedom and contract as ends in themselves. But corporate law is not a place where a commitment to individual freedom causes a zone of right to be identified and protected for its own sake. Nor does corporate law's facilitation of exchange imply anything approaching the economic ideal of property rights in a zone of free contract. Corporate law routinely suppresses alternative contractual arrangements in order to secure its objective of protecting management's freedom of action. The states' "enabling" codes in fact build on mandates. The delegation of power to management is mandatory,[5] as is management agenda control respecting the terms of the corporate contract. Ultimate, albeit indirect shareholder control also is mandated: one class of shares must retain full voting rights.

Apart from these mandates, much of corporate law does work as a contract, but not all. Significant parts of the whole evolve in an ongoing process of identifying and correcting perceived contract failures, again toward the end of clearing the field for management freedom of action and market liquidity. State antitakeover law performs the former function. The federal corporate law regime performs the latter function, protecting liquidity by requiring management truth-telling via disclosure.

If there was an era in which free contract came close to describing corporate law, it was the 1920s, after New Jersey stripped most of the mandates from its corporate code in the late 19th century and before Congress enacted the federal securities laws. But the meaning of free contract in corporate contexts was evolving even in the 1920s, moving away from the Victorian preference for individual choice and unanimous consent toward a more facilitative, majoritarian regime. Simply, deal making by insiders trumped freedom of contract.[6] With the exception of a brief period around 20 years ago, when contractarianism was hotly debated in corporate legal theory, no one has ever thought that the shareholder–manager relationship could satisfactorily be dealt with in the legal framework of arm's length contract, least of all the Victorians themselves.

The "nexus of contracts" corporation, then, never worked as description. Its positive claims served more as talking points in a wider normative campaign against regulatory innovation, particularly in fiduciary law. The anti-regulatory campaign retains vitality, pursuing the dual goals of management freedom of action as against regulators and shareholder choice as against management. Interestingly, the campaign now proceeds on both fronts as a rearguard action. The contractarians' theoretical reinforcement of the primacy of state law made no difference when a Congress frightened by voter disgust with corporate scandals enacted the Sarbanes–Oxley Act. The contractarians lost their battle for shareholder choice over corporate control much earlier, when antitakeover regulation appeared in the 1980s to chill the market for corporate control. Here too, state law has never fit the contractarian description. Although management freedom of action never absolutely trumps shareholder choice as a state law proposition, the underlay of charter competition weights the state law mediation between the two groups in management's favor. The law accordingly remains relatively impervious to the stronger normative claims of the contractarians and their economic theory of agency.

No overarching metatheory has succeeded the trust and contract paradigms to dominate thinking in the field. Welfare consequentialism still prevails, but no master set of instructions drives theoretical discussions about the means to the end. Today's theorists tend to think in terms of incentive compatibility and to confront incentive problems piecemeal, and, as ever, financial results in history have a way of shaping discussions.

Management self-dealing reemerges as a serious problem in the wake of the failure of the contractarians' market-control story. As a result, the trust paradigm's stress on fiduciary instructions remains a theme in contemporary debates. The separation of ownership and control also retains a place in the operative description of the large firm, no longer absolutely determinative, but still salient. The market paradigm's deregulatory presumption retains force, even as the nexus of contracts framework slowly recedes and fewer and fewer observers look to spontaneous order to solve agency problems, and hierarchy returns to the theoretical description of the firm. But the contractual description will never disappear because contract remains what it always has been – a significant component of corporate arrangements. Economics remains the dominant interdisciplinary referent, but the methodological menu is expanding.

## 5. AGENCY

Today's focal point debates occur in Category 3, where the line between management and shareholder authority has become more hotly contested than ever. As we have seen, the doctrine itself triggers the debate by simultaneously dispensing the two organizational models – entity, which privileges management empowerment, and agency, which suggests shareholder-centered controls on management discretion.

To isolate the points of tension, return to Section 2's balance-sheet picture of corporate law's objectives. On the left side of the balance sheet, corporate law mandates delegation and invests management with discretion, letting success or failure emerge in practice. It then makes a second mandate, remitting the vote for the board of directors to the shareholders, expecting the vote's aggressive exercise in case of failure. But the shareholder collective-action problem makes the dual dispensation problematic. Two points of conflict arise: one concerns shareholder access and the proxy solicitation process; the other concerns the hostile takeover. Characterizing the firm as an entity with the goal of encouraging risk-taking and long-term investment suggests that existing barriers to shareholder intervention serve the end of wealth creation. The agency characterization, however, with its corollaries of principal control and shareholder choice, suggest that a stronger threat of removal and shareholder legislative intervention would improve operating results.

Turning to the right side of the balance sheet, corporate law protects liquidity, facilitating exit as the primary shareholder defense against adverse selection problems. Management proponents focus on this, suggesting that the old Wall Street Rule of exit over voice still suffices to protect shareholder interest (and, with a degree of inconsistency, simultaneously questioning the intensity of federal regulations designed to keep the exit door open). But corporate law also seeks to reduce the cost of capital on the right side, even as it accords management discretion over financing decisions. This objective again raises the takeover question, with shareholder-choice advocates pointing to the cost of equity capital to counter the left-side claim made by management's defenders of perverse effects on investment incentives. Right-side questions also come up about other terms of the agency relationship. Opportunistic managers can self-deal at the expense of the marginal interest holder, causing the cost of equity capital to rise. To the extent that the law can intervene to control such conduct cost-effectively, it arguably should do so, even though the intervention entails a review of management decisions and constrains freedom of action. Here we enter the territory of the duty of loyalty and the ongoing and always-contested job of drawing the territorial line between business judgment and transactional scrutiny.

Corporate law makes no attempt to resolve these disputes in favor of either side. It instead intervenes to mediate on a piecemeal basis. We have mediation rather than solutions because both sides tell plausible stories about the impacts on wealth. Apparent, but unverified, welfare gains and plausible, but unverified, stories about perverse incentives crop up everywhere in this vicinity – the negative effects of management entrenchment vie with those of the short-term focus of institutional shareholders; the deadweight costs of management pocket-lining vie with those implicated by systems of enforcement; and the beneficial financial effects of equal returns for equally situated shareholders vie with the negative effects of constraints on transactional freedom. We have no empirical means to determine correct, across-the-board outcomes for disputes such as these. But, under the deregulatory presumption bequeathed by the contractarians, the theoretical burden of persuasion lies with those arguing for regulatory innovation.

Contemporary trends in the practice follow suit. Under the deregulatory presumption, the focus devolves on governance processes, with heavy reliance placed on the institution of the board of directors. Self-regulatory strategies prevail, their plausibility bolstered by the appearance of activist institutional investors. We also see this in the proliferation of voluntary codes of good practice and accompanying hortatory discussions among governance experts. Delaware fiduciary law falls into this pattern too, with its ever-increasing reliance on internal processes to solve conflicts of interest problems. At the same time, high-profile compliance failures by unsuccessful managers have prompted politicians to embed self-regulatory governance agenda items in the federal mandatory disclosure system. The overall result is anything but deregulatory, thus feeding the ongoing debates.

## 6. THE BOUNDARIES OF THE FIRM AND LEGITIMACY

Corporate doctrine in the US does not attempt to confer legitimacy on those it empowers, even as it does bestow limited liability. The incorporating states and their regime of general incorporation long ago surrendered substantive review of business projects in order to clear the field for action. Legitimacy is left to management to garner or lose depending on how well it does its job, and the performance criterion is financial. The ongoing process of legitimation, then, operates firm by firm and across firms as a whole. State corporate law facilitates the process without determining the result. It wants managers to succeed and so empowers them. But it anticipates failure when it requires at least one class of shareholders to retain the vote.[7] Financial failure – which delegitimates individual firms and firms generally depending on the scale and context – also tends to prompt additional securities regulation. The venue is the securities regime rather than state law for three reasons. First, failure registers most clearly in stock prices; second, financially embarrassed managers have a tendency to fall out of compliance with the federal mandatory disclosure regime; and, third, charter competition tends to keep the states out of the enforcement business. Contrariwise, the political clout of managers waxes during strong stock markets, facilitating access to Congress and state legislatures for beneficial regulation (or deregulation).

Real-world success and failure thus matter a great deal in corporate law, defining legitimacy. But legitimacy in the higher sense of responsible empowerment matters little; if legitimacy mattered, corporate law would find some plausible way to assign responsibility for corporate externalities. Consider in this regard the law of piercing the corporate veil, which holds out the possibility of assigning responsibility for tortious externalities to the firm's shareholders. These rules make perfect sense when viewed from the point of view of classical doctrinal theory. Limited liability comes with entity status, and can be lost if the shareholders fail to respect the entity's legal earmarks: If the firm is run as an "agent or instrumentality" of its shareholders rather than as a separate entity, the shareholders' limited liability can be lost. Yet, viewing the matter from the point of view of economic substance, agency is what the enterprise is all about. What results is a license to externalize, maintainable by rote observance of formalities. While this outcome is indefensible as a matter of economic theory, the core purposes of capital-raising and freedom of action are much enhanced.

If legitimacy mattered, corporate law would not draw a bright line between insiders and outsiders, disavowing all responsibility for the latter. It would find ways to bring disempowered constituents into the tent. Its refusal to do so dates back at least to *Dodge v. Ford Motor Co.* (1919), the touchstone case enunciating a duty to shareholders over other constituents. Those exceptions that have opened up serve the end of enhancing management's freedom of action rather than the end of integrating corporate governance into the wider social settlement embodied in regulation. Thus do the American Law Institute's (1994, Section 2.01) *Principles of Corporate Governance* describe the firm's objective with the hedged phrase "with a view to enhancing corporate profit and shareholder gain." The hedge permits management to effect distributions within the firm, relaxing the shareholder value norm at the shareholders' expense without imposing duties of social responsibility. The same goes for the corporate charity permission and the admission of constituent interest in takeover defense contexts. These exceptions do implicate wealth redistribution, but only on a spillover basis.

Corporate law's cavalier infliction of tortious externalities and insistence on contract as the means of engagement by outsiders are tolerated only because outside regulation makes significant adjustments to ameliorate socially and economically unacceptable results. Labor, environmental, and consumer protection regulation all serve this end, not to mention the antitrust laws and the tax system. Their common purpose is to contain the discretion vested in managers by corporate law. Outside regulation makes the world safe for the corporate law delegation and thereby makes firms and corporate law legitimate by indirection. This inside/outside settlement dates back to the early 20th century, survived the Depression intact, and today seems more stable than ever.

Still, the system is fully defensible in theory only on the assumption that the backstop regulations adequately protect the outside interests. The assumption remains highly contestable, and so will corporate law's investiture of power to go forth to injure and exploit remain justifiably controversial. It follows that the inside/outside settlement never satisfies observers who seek to integrate corporate law within models of democratic society. Each generation renews the Category 4 debates concerning constituents and responsibility in the teeth of a stable doctrinal settlement that excludes them.

This awkward system can be defended. Contractual norms come to bear first, with caveat emptor looming larger as a positive value than protection of expectations. If one is a constituent who does not enjoy the special protection of one of the supplemental regulatory regimes, caveat emptor is all corporate law holds out to be as it sanctions wealth transfers from outsiders to insiders. Outsiders who do secure contracts but nonetheless emerge with impaired expectations, like employees and senior security holders, find little solace in contract norms. To look at the jurisprudence is to see results obtained through formalistic interpretation of the bargains' contents with no thought of fairness, or, in some cases, even of effectuating the parties' expectations. Formalism prevails, making winners of the empowered and losers of the powerless. The jurisprudence smirks in its complicity. In US corporate law, winning has its privileges and optimality is always Kaldor–Hicks efficient.

The best that can be said about corporate law's insistence on limiting its boundaries to the concerns of insiders is that its coherence is enhanced. Corporate law remains uncluttered with complex instructions that might inhibit freedom of action or have unintended effects, triggering uncertainty. Corporate actors can rely on the division of regulatory function, and things go much more smoothly and cheaply. Meanwhile, the constituents learn that they need to go somewhere other than corporate law for assistance. There is a legitimacy point too. The widespread acceptance of corporate law's lack of evenhandedness does not really follow from deeply held contractarian beliefs and free-market partisanship. What is valued is not the means but the end, and the end is economic opportunity. Corporate law's appeal to wealth creation registers positively in the American polity at some deep level. The median voter accepts a system that aggressively divides winners and losers so long as it identifies with the winners, or at least holds out a hope for a place for her children in the winner's circle.

But the median voter will from time to time make regulatory demands, and now is one of those times. The late-2008 US financial collapse and federal bailout (the "Troubled Asset Relief Program") amount to an external shock to the prevailing regulatory equilibrium. The financial sector for some years has been pursuing high-risk investment and financing strategies, strategies that turned out to be ill-advised when the downside risks were realized in 2007 and 2008. The outside polity then proved unwilling to live with the downside consequences, and the bailout followed. The bailout amounts to an externalization on the public of risks undertaken by financial corporations; the measure of the externality is the eventual net cost to the public. The externality justifies new regulation, certainly for the financial sector and probably more widely for corporations. Contractarian arguments will not suffice to stop it; nor will the interest in protecting management's freedom of action. At the same time, the regulation will be external, following the familiar pattern. The legal corporation will survive substantially intact, as it did during the 1930s.

All of this suffices to put the burden of persuasion on the system's critics, who have never managed to produce an alternative model that surmounts coherence objections and resonates in the context of America's social settlement. The critics seem always to end up in an awkward alliance of convenience with management apologists, taking Dodd's side in the Berle–Dodd debate of 1932 (Berle, 1932; Dodd, 1932). In that famous encounter, two progressives differed on the question as to how society should deal with management power. Dodd modeled managers as statesmen, appealing to their better instincts. Unfortunately for Dodd's case, managers have not hewn to the statesmanlike path. Berle made an agency argument – managers had to be controlled somehow and imposed fidelity to the shareholder interest was the best means to the end. But, as we have seen, corporate law has never accepted that argument as an absolute, lest shareholder control crimp freedom of action. The present financial crisis will not change the pattern of response. Although managers got us into the present mess, taking full advantage of their freedom of action, they did so in pursuit of shareholder value, managing to a stock market that warmly approved their high-risk approach.

## 7. CONCLUSION

The dialectic framework of this chapter's typology implies that the corporate law's theoretical debates do not resolve. Arguments and conclusions are rooted in metapolitical preferences and unverified notions about aligning productivity incentives. The debates will continue to go back and forth along predictable lines until the day we have a verifiable, generally accepted template for a productive governance. But that day lies only in the most visionary of futures. In our context, production, viewed ex-ante, is too uncertain a phenomenon to be directed by some infallible instruction manual. Caution prevails, favoring the inherited legal context and empirical testing in competitive markets.

Meanwhile, dialectic can lead to synthesis, if not in the abstract then in history. Corporate doctrine synthesizes dialectically opposed positions in practice. Famous corporate law cases achieve their high-profile status for the very reason that binary opposites from theoretical debates come to play on their facts. Courts work through the dialectic tensions in situation-specific ways, making no attempt at general theoretical resolution. The process is similar, although more highly politicized, when a proposed regulation of the Securities and Exchange Commission works its way through the notice and comment process. In all lawmaking contexts, the results are highly sensitive to the performance of real world firms. Corporate law thus serves to mediate the disputes of corporate legal theory in specific situations, fixing its attention on the objective of productivity. Verified productive success always controls, whatever its theoretical implications. Contrariwise, when failure leads to externalities, regulation results.

## NOTES

1. For example, in the context of corporate law debates, a morally motivated case for constituent rights will be accompanied by a fully developed consequential case keyed to productivity. However, a given discussant's grounding of a case in economic welfare does not necessarily imply a philosophical attachment to consequentialism.

2. See, for example, theoretical models addressing optimal arrangements for sharing and transferring control between debt and equity interests (Aghion & Bolton, 1992; Dewatripont & Tirole, 1994). See also Jensen and Murphy (2004, p. 15): "[C]onsistent with 'stakeholder theory' value-maximizing firms will be concerned about relations with all their constituencies. A firm cannot maximize value if it ignores the interest of its stakeholders."

3. See, for example, Becht, Bolton, and Röell (2002, p. 58): "It is not possible to conclude on the basis of economic analysis alone that there is a unique set of optimal rules that are universally applicable to all corporations and economies, just as there is no single political constitution that is universally best for all nations."

4. This point originated in Manne (1965).

5. The enabling exception in Delaware General Corporation Law's Section 141(a): "The business and affairs of every corporation organized under this chapter shall be managed by or under the direction of a board of directors, *except as may be otherwise provided in this chapter or in its certificate of incorporation*" (emphasis added) is in fact irrelevant to the governance of large firms.

6. The development of the law of corporate reorganization followed similar lines. Before the Bankruptcy Act of 1934, the federal courts' equity receivership maintained formal fidelity to individual choice even as it sought in practice to facilitate recapitalizations on a "cram down" basis. It took Congressional intervention during the Depression to surmount the conceptual barrier and mandate a majoritarian reorganization regime.

7. Losers in a given firm get a backstop of sorts from the federal bankruptcy regime. But, across bankrupt firms as a whole, the trend over time has been less forgiving.

# REFERENCES

Aghion, P., & Bolton, P. (1992). An incomplete contracts approach to financial contracting. *Review of Economic Studies*, *59*, 473–498.

American Law Institute. (1994). *Principles of corporate governance: Analysis and recommendations*. St. Paul, MN: American Law Institute.

Becht, M., Bolton, P., & Röell, A. (2002). *Corporate governance and control*. ECGI Finance Working Paper no. 02/2002.

Berle, A. (1932). For whom corporate managers are trustees: A note. *Harvard Law Review*, *45*, 1365–1372.

Berle, A., & Means, G. (1991). *The modern corporation and private property* (Revised ed.). New Brunswick, NJ: Transaction Publishers.

Bratton, W. (1992). The economic structure of the post-contractual corporation. *Northwestern University Law Review*, *87*, 180–215.

Dewatripont, M., & Tirole, J. (1994). A theory of debt and equity: Diversity of securities and manager–shareholder congruence. *Quarterly Journal of Economics*, *109*, 1027–1054.

Dodd, E. (1932). For whom are corporate managers trustees? *Harvard Law Review*, *45*, 1145–1163.

Jensen, M., & Meckling, W. (1976). Theory of the firm: Managerial behavior, agency costs and ownership structure. *Journal of Financial Economics*, *3*, 305–360.

Jensen, M., & Murphy, K. (2004). *Remuneration: Where we've been, how we got there, what are the problems, and how to fix them*. ECGI Finance Working Paper no. 44/2004.

Kraakman, R., Davies, P., Hansmann, H., Hertig, G., Hopt, K., Kanda, H., & Rock, E. (Eds). (2004). *The anatomy of corporate law: A comparative and functional approach*. Oxford, UK: Oxford Press.

Manne, H. (1965). Mergers and the market for corporate control. *Journal of Political Economy*, *73*, 110–120.

Nader, R., Seligman, J., & Green, M. (1976). *Taming the giant corporation*. New York, NY: Norton.

## Case

*Dodge v. Ford Motor Co.* (1919). 170 N.W. 668.

# THE SINGLE CONSTITUENCY ARGUMENT IN THE ECONOMIC ANALYSIS OF BUSINESS LAW

David Millon

## ABSTRACT

*The essay points out a common thread that runs through law-and-economics business law scholarship. Working largely independently of each other, economically oriented scholars working in different areas have argued that the law should focus on the interests of a single constituency – shareholders in corporate law, creditors in bankruptcy law, and consumers in antitrust law. Economic analysts thus have rejected arguments advanced by "progressive" scholars working in each of these areas that the law should instead concern itself with the full range of constituencies affected by business activity. The law-and-economics single constituency claim rests in part on skepticism about judicial competence, but the underlying premise is an objection to the use of law for redistributive purposes. The primary value is efficiency, defined in terms of market-generated outcomes. It is argued here that this political commitment implies a strong tendency toward maintenance of the existing distribution of wealth, and that even more importantly, the single constituency claim may actually have redistributive implications. In each of these areas of business law, however, a regressive program favors*

**Law & Economics: Toward Social Justice**
**Research in Law and Economics: A Journal of Policy, Volume 24, 43–60**

**ISSN: 0193-5895/doi:10.1108/S0193-5895(2009)0000024007**

*owners of capital against those who are generally less well off, such as workers and small-business owners.*

## 1. INTRODUCTION

This essay addresses an interesting phenomenon in law-and-economics scholarship in business law, specifically in the areas of corporate, bankruptcy,[1] and antitrust law. In each of these areas, "progressive" scholars have argued that the law should take into account the well-being of a number of constituencies whose interests are affected by business activity. For example, in corporate law, employees have received a great deal of attention, and regard has also been given to creditors, customers and suppliers, and the local communities in which business is conducted. Progressive bankruptcy law scholars have also emphasized employee interests, as well as those of other constituencies who have a stake in a firm's continued existence. So-called populists have argued that antitrust law should promote a range of social and political values through the encouragement of small business and opposition to concentrated production. In contrast, law-and-economics scholars in each of these areas have argued forcefully that the law should promote the interests of only a single constituency: corporate law should focus on shareholders, bankruptcy law on creditors, and antitrust on consumers. Other interested stakeholders should fend for themselves, through contractual self-protection.

These "single constituency" arguments dominate academic discussions of corporate and antitrust law. They are also ascendant in judicial thinking about antitrust and very influential in corporate law. The law-and-economics approach to bankruptcy, though certainly very prominent, has been somewhat less prevalent in the academy and has yet to have a significant impact in the courts.

I will briefly rehearse the arguments that have been deployed on behalf of the single-constituency claim in each of the three areas, indicating questions regarding the arguments' supporting claims. I will then offer some thoughts about what these parallel developments tell us of the underlying assumptions and values of law-and-economics scholarship in business law, specifically that the single-constituency position in each area is based on a commitment to market-generated outcomes, and that the effect is to endorse the existing distribution of wealth. I will also suggest that, though assertedly based on hostility to redistribution, in each case the single-constituency position may indeed have redistributive effects – favoring those who are already relatively well off and disfavoring workers and small business owners.

## 2. THE SINGLE CONSTITUENCY ARGUMENT

### *2.1. Corporate Law*

Prompted by the explosion of hostile takeovers during the 1980s and the dislocations they brought about, a number of scholars challenged the orthodox view that corporate law's sole objective should be to maximize shareholder wealth. So-called "progressive" academics argued that management of target firms should be empowered – or required – to consider the interests not just of shareholders but also of the target's employees, creditors, suppliers, customers, and local communities (e.g., Johnson, 1990, 1992; Johnson & Millon, 1989; Millon, 1988a, 1990, 1991; Mitchell, 1995). The concern was that these nonshareholder constituencies faced the prospect of big losses if the successful bidder were to liquidate the firm or radically cut expenses to pay down the massive debt necessary to finance a successful bid. Some scholars drew on economic ideas to argue for "multi-fiduciary" understandings of management's responsibility that extended beyond the hostile takeover context (e.g., Dallas, 1995; Mitchell, 1990; O'Connor, 1991).

Law-and-economics scholars have rejected these multi-fiduciary models and insist instead that corporate law should privilege the interests of shareholders over those of the corporation's various nonshareholder constituencies. This "shareholder primacy" vision of corporate law is now the orthodox view among corporate law academics, though it certainly is not universally accepted. According to law-and-economics scholars, the theoretical basis for this position stems from the idea of the corporation as a network of contracts among the firm's participants (e.g., Butler, 1989; Easterbrook & Fischel, 1991). Corporate law provides default terms for the contracts among shareholders, management, and the firm's other parties. The justification for the content of corporate law's default terms is their presumptive efficiency. These are the terms that parties are most likely to deem desirable. Including them in corporation statutes eliminates the need to identify and specify them and therefore reduces the costs of contracting.

Most notable of corporate law's default rules is the shareholder primacy principle. Its presumptive efficiency is based on three considerations.[2]

The first has to do with the shareholders' place in the corporation in relation to other participants. As residual claimants, the shareholders' interests in the firm's assets are subordinate to all other fixed claims, including those of creditors and employees (e.g., Butler, 1989, pp. 107–108; Easterbrook & Fischel, 1991, pp. 67–70). A rule that imposes on management the duty to maximize shareholder wealth compensates shareholders for the greater risk they face. It also ensures that management will use its best efforts to generate surplus, which benefits not only shareholders but also fixed claimants, whose prospects of being paid improve with improvement in the corporation's performance. By giving shareholders exclusive powers of control over management, shareholder primacy also places that responsibility with the constituency that has the greatest stake in managerial success.

This argument, often repeated, is in fact quite problematic. As Stout (2002) points out, shareholders are residual claimants only when the firm is in bankruptcy. The rest of the time, management has broad discretion to distribute revenues among the firm's various constituencies, and shareholders will only receive dividends if management decides to pay them. If the claim is that shareholders' well-being depends on whether the corporation is doing well, a similar point can plausibly be made about workers. Although wages might be fixed, various other important interests are not, including the magnitude of retirement benefits, relied-upon expectations with respect to job security and promotion prospects, and understandings regarding working conditions (Greenfield, 1998, pp. 305–307). In these and other respects, workers' fortunes wax or wane according to the corporation's success. Further, employees who have made non-diversified, firm-specific investments of human capital may face significantly greater risk than do shareholders.

Agency cost concerns provide a second basis for the shareholder primacy default rule. That rule is said to be superior to one that would require management to serve the interests of all the firm's constituencies because it provides a single metric and thereby facilitates evaluation of managerial performance (Clark, 1986, p. 20; Easterbrook & Fischel, 1991, p. 38; Jensen, 2001, p. 9; Roe, 2001, p. 2065). In contrast, a multifiduciary approach would result in confusion as corporate management attempts to juggle conflicting interests without the benefit of guidance as to their respective weights. At worst, this approach would provide management with a screen behind which to conceal its own self-serving activities. In any event, judges are ill-equipped to second-guess management because they lack the ability to engage in complex balancing inquiries.

This argument, too, is problematic. In fact, management must serve multiple, potentially conflicting interests even if its only fiduciary obligation is to the firm's shareholders (Macey, 1991, p. 33). Common shareholders do not have monolithic investment horizons, and preferred shareholders, whose claims are typically fixed, have different risk preferences than do common shareholders and resemble creditors in this regard. Judges, too, are in fact quite accustomed to administering legal doctrines that require balancing of conflicting interests.[3]

Finally, law-and-economics scholars argue that the shareholder primacy default rule is efficient because, in contrast to fixed claimants, shareholders and managers are unable technologically to write contracts that specify ex ante all of the affirmative tasks management would need to perform in order to maximize shareholder wealth (Macey, 1991, p. 36). Nonshareholder constituencies, in contrast, may be better able to define negative restrictions on management's ability to engage in opportunistic behavior that threatens the value of their fixed claims. Whether this distinction is accurate may, however, be more problematic than initially appears. It is questionable whether employees and other nonshareholder constituencies can negotiate and draft contractual protections that fully protect them from the various kinds of management conduct that can reduce the value of their claims against the corporation. Bond indentures, which themselves are incomplete in this regard, should not be seen as models for employment contracts.

The law-and-economics model of the corporation thus conceives of the corporation in contractual terms and – though each of its supports is problematic – asserts the efficiency of the shareholder primacy default rule. Shareholder primacy has two components. One identifies the constituency whose interests are to command management's primary attention. The other accords to shareholders ultimate powers of control. This regime thus makes shareholders the sole beneficiaries of fiduciary duties and vests in them alone powers of control over management. Corporate law should have nothing to say to nonshareholder constituencies except the implicit injunction to bargain for protection of their own interests and pursue redistributive agendas through remedies and procedures provided by other bodies of law (e.g., Clark, 1986, p. 30; Hansmann & Kraakman, 2001, p. 441).

### *2.2. Bankruptcy Law*

Progressive bankruptcy law scholars – referred to as "traditionalists" by law-and-economics "proceduralists" (e.g., Baird, 1998) – defend the existing federal bankruptcy reorganization regime's attention to the interests of the full range of constituencies threatened by a firm's failure (e.g., Gross, 1999; Korobkin, 1991; Warren, 1987). Of particular concern are employees who have made significant firm-specific human capital investments or are too old for retraining. Even those who can find new jobs face potentially high transition and psychological costs. Also deserving of regard are customers and suppliers of the distressed firm, communities concerned about the impact on property values of an empty plant, and government entities relying on tax revenues. Continuation of the business thus is a significant priority. Even if dissolution is the eventual outcome, the bankruptcy process has at least provided breathing room for adjustment. Bankruptcy law thus should serve to soften the impact of business failure on those noncreditor constituencies who have an interest in the business' continuation. When designed with this objective in mind, a Chapter 11 reorganization will generally result in devaluation of creditor claims because continuation of a business that cannot be saved reduces the likely payout to creditors.

Law-and-economics scholars see in bankruptcy law a less ambitious, more clearly focused agenda. Federal law supplements state debtor–creditor law by providing a system for orderly adjustment of creditors' claims, who otherwise would find themselves racing with each other to assert claims on the firm's limited assets. In effect, bankruptcy law provides a solution to a collective action problem by specifying an arrangement that the creditors would themselves have agreed to had they been able to negotiate with each other ex ante – the so-called creditors' bargain (Jackson, 1982; Jackson, 1985). The point is to maximize creditors' collective benefits, as defined by their state law-based claims. Bankruptcy law itself confers no substantive rights on creditors or anyone else. Certainly it should not be a vehicle for easing the impact of firm failure on the corporation's various noncreditor constituencies.

A federal bankruptcy regime that reflects the bargain that creditors would have struck among themselves is efficient for them, because a disorderly run on the debtor's assets is costly and any individual creditor's prospects for success are uncertain. A system that maximizes the value of creditors' claims also has the virtue of reducing the cost of credit in comparison to one that sacrifices creditor value in order to protect the interests of the firm's other constituencies (e.g., Rasmussen, 1992, p. 59). Although plausible, this might, however, be flipped on its head: a system that seeks to reduce the costs of firm insolvency borne by the firm's employees should lower the cost of labor, whereas one that prioritizes creditor interests presumably increases labor costs. The cost-reduction argument thus presents a difficult and complex cost–benefit problem that economically oriented bankruptcy scholars have not resolved.

Further, it is said that a federal regime that in effect gives workers rights that they do not enjoy under state debt collection law encourages forum-shopping (Baird, 1987, pp. 825–827). Law-and-economics bankruptcy scholars can see no reason why state and federal law should offer legal regimes that offer different substantive rights to the interested parties. If, however, a "progressive" approach to reorganization is for some reason superior, it is hard to see why it should be rejected simply for the sake of symmetry. One might also argue that the inconsistency between a "progressive" reorganization regime and state debt collection law could be justified because of differences between the kinds of situations that call for large-scale reorganization and more routine debt collection scenarios that do not involve multiple creditor claims on a severely limited asset pool.[4]

Law-and-economics bankruptcy scholars also echo concerns about judicial competence expressed by like-minded scholars in other areas. They are skeptical about the desirability of the judicial discretion necessarily involved in reorganizations that seek to balance the various conflicting interests at stake in a bankruptcy case (e.g., Baird, 1987, pp. 820–821). The argument is repeated despite the pervasiveness of balancing in other areas of law (e.g., Aleinikoff, 1987).

### *2.3. Antitrust Law*

The parallel development in antitrust law is the debate between antitrust "populists" and law-and-economics efficiency proponents. Drawing on the political concerns that animated the Sherman Act (Millon, 1988b), populists have argued that antitrust law should concern itself with more than just consumer welfare and allocative efficiency. According to this view, concentrated economic power corrupts the political process and impedes economic opportunity. Antitrust can promote competition and dispersion of economic power by ensuring that small businesses are able to flourish.

In contrast, law-and-economics scholars insist that consumer welfare is the only appropriate goal for antitrust. Although economically-oriented antitrust scholars may differ on specific questions, all agree that this should be antitrust's objective (Hovenkamp, 2005, p. 31; Posner, 2001, p. ix). Low prices and product innovation, rather than the control of economic power as such, deserve priority over other values, and robust market competition is the best way to ensure that productive resources are put to their highest valued uses. Differences among current economic approaches tend to be based on differing assumptions about the robustness of competition in actual markets, but these differences are not great. Post-Chicago antitrust scholars may part company with their Chicago School predecessors in their greater willingness to favor government intervention to improve competition, but both camps agree about the underlying goal, which is a single-minded pursuit of allocative efficiency in order to maximize consumer welfare, and neither supports aggressive interference with market processes and results (Jacobs, 1995, p. 242). Today's version of the Harvard School shares this conception of antitrust's appropriate goal, differing from the Chicago School only on specific questions of the desirability of legal intervention (Hovenkamp, 2005, pp. 37–38). For all of these economic approaches, protection of small businesses or other "political" values are not part of the equation. Such has been the success of the economic stance that antitrust populism no longer presents a seriously considered alternative in the academy or in the courts.

The law-and-economics approach has been so successful that no one worries much about the embarrassing fact that the populist understanding is much more clearly grounded in the legislative history than is the economic one. Leading scholars acknowledge this fact (e.g., Hovenkamp, 2005, pp. 39–42; Posner, 2001, p. 35), but argue that the spareness of the statutory language and the need for intellectual coherence justify resorting to economic principles. It is also said that judges are ill-equipped to make complex decisions about wealth distribution and so should rely instead on the supposedly more precise prescriptions of neoclassical economic theory (e.g., Hovenkamp, 2005, p. 45). One might ask why judges, who generally lack formal training in economics or sophistication in its application to complex real-world business scenarios, might be thought competent to administer an antitrust regime based on economic principles. Law-and-economics proponents respond to this concern by arguing for reduction of antitrust's role rather than entertaining questions about the value of an exclusively economic orientation.

## 3. UNDERLYING VALUES AND ASSUMPTIONS

In all three of these areas, various visions of social justice have informed efforts to interpret important areas of business law so as to take into account the full effects of economic activity on the full range of affected constituencies. In each case, law-and-economics scholars have rejected such efforts, insisting instead that the law should have a single policy objective, whether that be protection of shareholders, creditors, or consumers. There are some interesting parallels. It is commonly said in each area that courts are ill equipped to juggle the interests of several constituencies or make principled choices among competing values. Law-and-economics proponents in each of these areas also assert that, for instance, corporate law is not the vehicle for promoting employee interests; some other area of the law should be selected instead. However, looking at "the law of business" as a whole (Winkler, 2004), it becomes apparent that law-and-economics scholars actually see no place for employee interests in any of the areas of the law that bear so directly on worker well-being.

The common thread that runs through economic analysis in each of these areas is a foundational commitment to allocative efficiency, the primary value for most mainstream law-and-economics scholars. They therefore start with a fundamental affinity for markets as the best way to see that resources are put to their highest valued uses. This predisposition brings with it a healthy skepticism about governmental regulation, and a basic belief that the law should facilitate voluntary transactions because the parties gain from trade and social welfare is thereby enhanced (at least assuming minimal externalities). The argument assumes that regulations that attempt to improve outcomes for some parties by giving them more than they have realized through bargain must come at the expense of other parties' welfare, so instead of a world of winners, we have one in which some win and others lose, according to metrics devised by the state. This amounts to redistribution, which is, by definition, inefficient. From this objection, it is a short step to lamentations about statism, socialism, and tyranny (e.g., Bainbridge, 1997).

Since, for efficiency proponents, the main goal of law is to facilitate market transactions, corporate law theorists have tried to talk about corporations entirely in terms of contract and of corporate law as a set of default rules that most parties would prefer and that they are free to include or not in the bargains they strike with each other. (The existence of a number of mandatory rules creates a problem for the positive claim but not for the normative one.) Bankruptcy law is conceptualized as a solution to a contracting problem. As such, it is designed to establish the sharing rules that the firm's creditors would have agreed to among themselves if circumstances had not rendered that solution impossible as a practical matter. Antitrust law ends up with little to do except proscribe cartel-type collusion and, perhaps, particularly nasty predatory practices by firms with substantial market power. Most of the time, competition provides the necessary discipline.

If none of these bodies of law is supposed to protect the interests of employees, small business owners, local communities, and others harmed by market activities and effects, all one can say is that these stakeholders must look after themselves, through the bargain mechanism. If workers want security against layoffs, they can buy it, paying for it with lower wages. Small businesses can attempt to ensure their survival by selling things that people want at prices they are willing to pay. Local communities can bargain for a corporation's long-term presence by offering a richer package of tax and infrastructure incentives. In other words, law-and-economics scholarship in the business law area is based on the notion that people are entitled to what they can pay for but no more.

From the law-and-economics perspective, devotion to market-generated outcomes and a limited role for law is greatly appealing. For them, alternative perspectives embrace redistributive agendas administered by state actors whose competence and motives are suspect. Many people have questioned this market-oriented vision of law and social life. For progressive business law scholars, the essential objection is that hostility to redistribution through law and insistence on the notion that people should advance their interests through market transactions represents a profound attachment to the existing distribution of wealth and power. In a world in which one is born into a particular social and economic station, it is very difficult to advance simply through market transactions. Success tends to result from extraordinary talent or industry. Unequal educational opportunities and social barriers tend to limit people's prospects regardless of ambition or work ethic. Although our culture is fond of Horatio Algier rags-to-riches success stories, their very popularity reflects their abnormality. The dominance of the market ensures that most people tend to end up more or less where they started (e.g., The Economist, 2004).[5] Sharp disagreement over the legitimacy of existing inequalities marks the fundamental difference between progressive and law-and-economics scholarship in business law.

## 4. DISTRIBUTIONAL QUESTIONS

More can be said about the single-constituency argument. There is not just a commitment to markets and a limited role for law, with an implicit endorsement of the economic status quo. In each case, the effect of the rules proposed by law-and-economics scholars may be to tilt the playing field in favor of particular groups and at the expense of others. Although ostensibly hostile to redistribution, the economic approach may in fact have that tendency. Redistribution, however, is in an upward direction, a reverse Robin Hood phenomenon.

### *4.1. Corporate Law*

The shareholder wealth maximization norm advocated by law-and-economics scholars can indeed result in benefit to all corporate constituencies. If management is able to increase firm value, shareholders benefit, but so too do various nonshareholder fixed claimants, because the risk of nonpayment is lower than it otherwise would have been. The problem, though, is that the shareholder value injunction is unforgiving, threatening management's job security, and increasing firm value is not easy. Accordingly, management can benefit shareholders not only by increasing firm value but also through opportunistic wealth transfers from nonshareholders to shareholders.

For example, management may cause the corporation to borrow money in order to repurchase the firm's common stock. Shareholders may benefit from this distribution, but existing creditors lose value because the firm's increased leverage increases the risk of default on the corporation's obligations to them. Or, a hostile takeover may reward shareholders with a handsome premium over market price, but the additional cost of paying down the debt needed to complete the acquisition can result in sharp cost-cutting measures, including plant closings and layoffs. For many displaced workers, lost jobs represent the corporation's reneging on implicit promises of long-term employment (Schliefer & Summers, 1987). The increased debt burden will also reduce the value of existing creditor claims. Corporations can also attempt to avoid explicit contractual commitments. For instance, efforts to escape defined benefit–pension obligations also benefit shareholders at the expense of employees. Lost jobs and reduced pensions in turn impose costs on the larger public, which must fund assistance programs through tax payments. Some corporations – Wal-Mart is said to be among them – may deliberately set wages at a low level relying on the existence of government assistance to make up the deficiency (Greenfield, 2007, p. 137). Shareholder profits thus come at the expense of workers and the federal government. Management may also resort to illegal means – such as fraudulent accounting manipulations – to prop up share values. The consequences can be disastrous for workers, as was the case at Enron, where employees lost not only their jobs but also the lion's share of their retirement savings when the house of cards collapsed.

Whether by legal means or not, corporate management has strong incentives to meet the demands of the shareholder primacy principle by maximizing short-term share prices. The commitment of law-and-economics scholars to this principle is assertedly based on a preference for market-based outcomes over legal regulation and as such claims to reject redistributive legal regimes. In fact, however, this model brings with it a built-in tendency for redistribution, not by government but by corporate management serving the interests of shareholders. When employees, taxpayers, and local communities foot the bill, the wealth transfers occur in an upwards, regressive direction.

### *4.2. Bankruptcy Law*

According to law-and-economics scholars, bankruptcy is supposed to maximize the return to creditors in cases of financial distress by providing a collective enforcement mechanism for their nonbankruptcy, state-law based claims on the corporation's assets. Because bankruptcy is supposed to eschew other values and interests, other corporate constituencies get nothing unless they too can assert a state law-based contractual claim. Take the case of employees, for example. If they are owed wages, they are creditors in the same sense that lenders are and will participate in the distribution of the firm's assets as general unsecured creditors. Their primary concern, however, may not be the debtor's performance of past obligations, but rather whether it will honor its commitments in the future. Employees may have reasonable, relied-upon expectations of long-term employment. They may, for example, have made firm-specific human capital investments on the assumption, encouraged by the employer, that they will earn a return on that investment over the long term. Now they are faced with the economic and psychological costs of unemployment and the need to make new investments in job training, relocation, and the like. These losses are genuine consequences of the firm's failure, but, because workers are unable to assert a contractual claim to compensation, they are precluded from participation in the distribution of the firm's assets. Creditor-focused bankruptcy policy thus requires employees to bear the full cost of their own noncontractual losses. In contrast, because most creditor claims are by definition contract-based, they are compensated as fully as possible.

This vision of bankruptcy policy – which as yet has not taken hold in the courts – implies a particular approach to allocation of the costs of firm failure. Rather than attempting to spread these costs equitably among the business' various participants, creditors alone are supposed to share the firm's remaining assets. Severance payments or training and relocation benefits for employees are unavailable unless based on existing contractual obligations. Even efforts to continue operations for a time so as to soften the impact of failure on employees and local communities are illegitimate if collapse is inevitable because such efforts devalue creditor claims. The result is a different kind of distributive impact. Rather than taking from some constituencies to give to another, here the question is who should bear a larger share of the costs of firm failure. Law-and-economics bankruptcy scholars in effect argue that creditors should be protected against such costs to the greatest extent possible. Noncreditors, therefore, suffer at their expense.

### *4.3. Antitrust Law*

The law-and-economics approach to antitrust may also have significant distributive effects, though here the primary beneficiaries are not the constituency – consumers – that antitrust is supposed to protect. They are instead the owners of large businesses, who have benefited from changes both in the conception of antitrust's purpose and its enforcement. As in corporate and bankruptcy law, the economic approach favors the owners of capital over the interests of other constituencies affected by business activity.

In accordance with the Chicago School critique, courts since the 1970s have overruled a number of cases that had denounced various business practices as per se illegal, holding that they should be evaluated under the context-specific rule of reason instead. These include certain vertical restraints,[6] expulsion of trade association members,[7] and a manufacturer's acquiescence in a retailer's demand that it terminate a rival selling below the manufacturer's suggested retail price.[8] These changes reflect developments in economic theory suggesting that certain practices once condemned as per se illegal, may, in some circumstances, have a procompetitive explanation. Chicago School scholars would in many cases have preferred a rule of per se legality (e.g., Posner, 1981), but in practice the rule of reason may amount to the same thing because rule-of-reason cases are almost impossible to prove (Hovenkamp, 2005, p. 8; Posner, 2001, p. 31). In effect, then, the turn to a more nuanced analysis probably results in nonliability for some instances of anticompetitive conduct. Although a rule of reason approach may make sense according to economic theory, practical realities thus result in an underinclusive legal standard in place of per se rules now deemed to be overinclusive because they cannot be justified economically.

In other areas, courts have formulated tests that may be underinclusive according to economic theory, but, nevertheless, are thought to be desirable in order to avoid vexing problems of administrability. For example, economic theory teaches that under some circumstances above-cost pricing may be predatory. Nevertheless, courts have formulated rules requiring proof of below-cost pricing. This approach is justified because a more elaborate inquiry into whether a firm's pricing policy is aggressively procompetitive, rather than anticompetitively predatory, is too complex a task for a court to perform competently (Hovenkamp, 2005, pp. 48–49).

There is an irony here. It is now widely believed that economic analysis is the only legitimate methodology for making sense of antitrust law and policy. At the same time, however, there is great skepticism about the ability of judges and juries to understand and apply unfamiliar economic ideas to complex market scenarios, where they have no choice but to rely on conflicting expert opinions that may appear to be equally plausible. Consequently, it is argued that courts should either apply relatively clear, readily administrable rules, even if they are underinclusive, or else engage in an open-ended, wide-ranging inquiry into the particular facts of a case, even if the result is a burden that a plaintiff is unlikely to be able to bear. From this perspective, even if the result is underenforcement, that is tolerable because care must be taken to avoid an excessively zealous regime that would deter procompetitive behavior. In addition, it is a core tenet of the economic approach that, generally speaking, market forces tend to correct anticompetitive practices anyway, so the social costs of such practices are likely to be short-lived.

What this means in practice is that the turn to a focus on consumer welfare leaves small businesses without the protections that an earlier understanding of antitrust sought to achieve. This is an explicit objective of the economic approach's rejection of earlier "political" understandings of antitrust. However, even conceived of in narrow consumer-welfare terms, the economic approach may have problematic distributive implications. Anticompetitive practices that in the past would have been condemned may now escape unscathed because doctrine now defines liability more narrowly or because of practical difficulties of proof. In this respect, antitrust enforcement can be seen as underinclusive. Because of its underinclusiveness, corporations and their shareholders will, in at least some cases, be able to engage in and get away with anticompetitive conduct. This can include efforts to impede rivalry, exert leverage on upstream and downstream counterparties, and extract above-cost prices from consumers. Law-and-economics partisans insist that competition will eventually prevail and that a more interventionist approach to antitrust enforcement would be too costly, but small business owners and consumers will pay a price. A market-based antitrust policy centered on consumer welfare and hampered by practical concerns about administrability may thus end up allowing some firms and their shareholders to reap rewards that truly competitive markets or a more aggressive antitrust policy would preclude. Here again, the single-constituency focus, committed to market outcomes, ends up having redistributive consequences. The difference, though, is that the asserted beneficiaries of antitrust law – consumers – do not benefit from this redistribution. As in the cases of corporate and bankruptcy law, it is the owners of capital who are the winners.

## 5. CONCLUSION

A fundamental objection to the law-and-economics approach to business law is its hostility to redistributive legal structures. As long as efficiency is defined in terms of voluntary exchange, weaker, less economically powerful members of society will be left to protect themselves through contract and will always be disadvantaged in that enterprise. Law is needed not just to facilitate market exchange, but also to remedy its shortcomings. Legislators understand this idea well and have enacted laws in each of these areas that implicitly reject the markets-only approach of law-and-economics partisans. In the corporate law area, state statutes (Millon, 1991), as well as some important judicial decisions,[9] endorse a multifiduciary conception of management's responsibility. The legislative history of the bankruptcy code reveals clearly that Congress supported reorganization under Chapter 11 in large part so that firms in financial distress could continue to operate without job losses and other social costs (Warren, 1987, p. 788). Even efficiency proponents admit that none of the antitrust statutes was enacted to promote consumer welfare. Instead, Congress seems to have had in mind fundamentally political concerns about the threats posed by economic concentration to individual opportunity and liberty and conceived of dispersed, balanced economic power as the best way to meet those threats. Despite these political realities, law-and-economics scholars now dominate academic discourse in each of these three areas. Their influence on the development of antitrust law and, to a lesser extent, corporate law has been substantial.

Economically oriented scholars in each of these areas have done more than just argue against legal rules that interfere with market processes and outcomes. They have also claimed that in each area the law should concern itself with the interests of a single constituency. Asserting the primacy of a single constituency in each appears to do more than just leave disfavored constituencies to their own devices. It may also enhance the relative position of already privileged constituencies – investors, lenders, large corporations – at the expense of workers and consumers. So, although claiming to be neutral with respect to distributional questions, the economic analysis of business law may actually have a significant redistributive tilt, one that leans in a regressive direction.

## NOTES

1. In the bankruptcy area, the focus is on corporate insolvency regulated under chapters 7 and 11.
2. Older property-based arguments in favor of shareholder primacy (e.g., Friedman, 1970) have been superseded because, under the contractarian model, it no longer makes sense to refer to shareholders as "owners" of the corporation and therefore entitled to management's special regard (e.g., Bainbridge, 1997, p. 863, n. 22).
3. For a critical evaluation of the widespread use of balancing in U.S. constitutional law, see Aleinikoff (1987).
4. It should be noted that the "vertical" forum-shopping concern is not present in corporate law, which is largely governed by state law, or antitrust, which is primarily a federal matter. To the extent there are conflicts between state and federal law in these areas, the preemption principle resolves the conflict.
5. Attachment to private ordering may do more than simply reinforce the economic status quo. In the aggregate, market transactions between parties with unequal resources may over time actually exacerbate existing inequalities because relative wealth confers bargaining power in particular transactions (e.g., Greenwood, 2001, pp. 822–824).
6. *State Oil v. Kahn* (1997) (maximum resale price setting); *Continental T.V., Inc. v. GTE Sylvania, Inc.* (1977) (vertical territorial division).
7. *Northwest Wholesale Stationers, Inc. v. Pacific Stationery & Printing Co.* (1985).
8. *Business Electronics Corp. v. Sharp Electronics Corp.* (1988).
9. *Unocal v. Mesa Petroleum Co.* (1985, pp. 954–955).

## ACKNOWLEDGMENT

The author is grateful to Josh Fairfield for his thoughtful suggestions.

# REFERENCES


Aleinikoff, T. (1987). Constitutional law in the age of balancing. *Yale Law Journal, 96*, 943–1005.

Bainbridge, S. (1997). Community and statism: A conservative contractarian critique of progressive corporate law scholarship. *Cornell Law Review, 82*, 856–904.

Baird, D. (1987). Loss distribution, forum shopping, and bankruptcy. *University of Chicago Law Review, 54*, 815–834.

Baird, D. (1998). Bankruptcy's uncontested axioms. *Yale Law Journal, 108*, 573–599.

Butler, H. (1989). The contractual theory of the corporation. *George Mason University Law Review, 11*, 99–123.

Clark, R. (1986). *Corporate law*. Boston, MA: Little, Brown and Co.

Dallas, L. (1995). Working toward a new paradigm. In: L. Mitchell (Ed.), *Progressive corporate law* (pp. 35–65). Boulder, CO: Westview Press.

Easterbrook, F., & Fischel, D. (1991). *The economic structure of corporate law* (pp. 38, 67–70). Cambridge, MA: Harvard University Press.

Friedman, M. (1970). The social responsibility of business is to increase its profits. *New York Times Magazine*, September 13, p. 32.

Greenfield, K. (1998). The place of workers in corporate law. *Boston College Law Review, 39*, 283–327.

Greenfield, K. (2007). *The failure of corporate law: Fundamental flaws, progressive possibilities.* Chicago, IL: University of Chicago Press.

Greenwood, D. (2001). Beyond the counter-majoritarian difficulty: Judicial decision-making in a polynomic world. *Rutgers Law Review, 53*, 780–853.

Gross, K. (1999). *Failure and forgiveness: Rebalancing the bankruptcy system.* New Haven, CT: Yale University Press.

Hansmann, H., & Kraakman, R. (2001). The end of history for corporate law. *Georgetown Law Journal, 89*, 439–467.

Hovenkamp, H. (2005). *The antitrust enterprise: Principle and execution.* Cambridge, MA: Harvard University Press.

Jackson, T. (1982). Bankruptcy, non-bankruptcy entitlements, and the creditors' bargain. *Yale Law Journal, 91*, 857–907.

Jackson, T. (1985). Translating assets and liabilities to the bankruptcy forum. *Journal of Legal Studies, 14*, 73–114.

Jacobs, M. (1995). An essay on the normative foundations of antitrust economics. *North Carolina Law Review, 74*, 219–266.

Jensen, M. (2001). Value maximization, stakeholder theory, and the corporate objective function. *Journal of Applied Corporate Finance, 14*, 8–21.

Johnson, L. (1990). The Delaware judiciary and the meaning of corporate life and corporate law. *Texas Law Review, 68*, 865–936.

Johnson, L. (1992). Individual and collective sovereignty in the corporate enterprise. *Columbia Law Review, 92*, 2215–2249.

Johnson, L., & Millon, D. (1989). Missing the point about state takeover statutes. *Michigan Law Review, 87*, 846–857.

Korobkin, D. (1991). Rehabilitating values: A jurisprudence of bankruptcy. *Columbia Law Review, 91*, 717–789.

Macey, J. (1991). An economic analysis of the various rationales for making shareholders the exclusive beneficiaries of corporate fiduciary duties. *Stetson Law Review, 21*, 23–44.

Millon, D. (1988a). State takeover laws: A rebirth of corporation law? *Washington and Lee Law Review*, *45*, 903–934.

Millon, D. (1988b). The Sherman Act and the balance of power. *Southern California Law Review*, *61*, 1219–1292.

Millon, D. (1990). Theories of the corporation. *Duke Law Journal*, *1990*, 201–262.

Millon, D. (1991). Redefining corporate law. *Indiana Law Review*, *24*, 223–277.

Mitchell, L. (1990). The fairness rights of corporate bondholders. *New York University Law Review*, *65*, 1165–1229.

Mitchell, L. (Ed.) (1995). *Progressive corporate law*. Boulder, CO: Westview Press.

O'Connor, M. (1991). Restructuring the corporation's nexus of contracts: Recognizing a fiduciary duty to protect displaced workers. *North Carolina Law Review*, *69*, 1189–1260.

Posner, R. (1981). The next step in the antitrust treatment of restricted distribution: Per se legality. *University of Chicago Law Review*, *48*, 6–26.

Posner, R. (2001). *Antitrust law* (2nd ed.). Chicago, IL: University of Chicago Press.

Rasmussen, R. (1992). Debtor's choice: A menu approach to bankruptcy. *Texas Law Review*, *71*, 51–121.

Roe, M. (2001). The shareholder wealth maximization norm and industrial organization. *University of Pennsylvania Law Review*, *149*, 2063–2081.

Schliefer, A., & Summers, L. (1987). *Hostile takeovers as breaches of trust*. Working Paper no. 2342. National Bureau of Economic Research.

Stout, L. (2002). Bad and not-so-bad arguments for shareholder primacy. *Southern California Law Review*, *75*, 1189–1209.

*The Economist*. (2004). Ever higher society, ever harder to ascend. *The Economist* (December 29), 22–24.

Warren, E. (1987). Bankruptcy policy. *University of Chicago Law Review*, *54*, 775–814.

Winkler, A. (2004). Corporate law or the law of business? Stakeholders and corporate governance at the end of the century. *Law and Contemporary Problems*, *67*, 109–133.

## Cases

*Business Electronics Corp. v. Sharp Electronics Corp.*, 485 U.S. 717 (1988).

*Continental T.V., Inc. v. GTE Sylvania, Inc.*, 433 U.S. 36 (1977).

*Northwest Wholesale Stationers, Inc. v. Pacific Stationery & Printing Co.*, 472 U.S. 284 (1985).

*State Oil v. Kahn*, 522 U.S. 3 (1997).

*Unocal v. Mesa Petroleum Co.*, 493 A.2d 946 (Del. 1985).

# CORPORATE LAW AND THE RHETORIC OF CHOICE

Kent Greenfield

## ABSTRACT

*Rhetorically, the notion of choice has always been a powerful one in politics and law. This chapter is intended to offer a note of caution about its use. Despite its progressive hue of individual freedom, the rhetoric of choice increasingly tends to be a notion used to defend and uphold existing matrices of economic and social power. This is because the rhetoric of choice is an excellent way to support existing power relationships. The assertion that people acting within such power relationships are simply choosing their current situation undermines efforts to change those relationships. The powerful stay powerful; the weak stay weak. This is true in a number of areas, from discussions about school vouchers, to debates about tort reform, to the disagreements surrounding the regulation of pornography.*

*The dependence on choice rhetoric also exists in corporate law, where the school of thought currently dominant in corporate law doctrine holds that the corporation is best seen as a voluntary arrangement among all the various stakeholders of the corporation. The rhetoric of choice is thus a powerful tool to fight against any reform of current relationships within the corporation that would embolden and empower stakeholders*

**Law & Economics: Toward Social Justice**
**Research in Law and Economics: A Journal of Policy, Volume 24, 61–89**

**ISSN: 0193-5895/doi:10.1108/S0193-5895(2009)0000024008**

*traditionally left out of the corporate power structure. Those involved with the corporation, whether shareholders, employees, or communities, have chosen their position, and thus should not complain when they do not receive more than what they explicitly contracted to receive. In this way, the notion of choice is used to bolster a view of corporate law that protects those already within the corporate power structure and excludes important stakeholders from corporate decision making. The rhetoric of choice is used in the same way in corporate law discourse as it is used elsewhere by the right – to justify or bolster existing matrices of economic and social power.*

## 1. INTRODUCTION

For progressives, a dedication to liberty has often meant a respect for, and protection of, individuals' right to make choices for themselves. When one hears about "the right to choose," the progressive fight to protect a woman's right to an abortion is the example that will leap most quickly to mind, but the concept of choice is broader. Choice has also been an important theme in progressive struggles against poverty as well as discrimination on the basis of race, sex, and sexual orientation. Women deserve the choice as to whether to terminate pregnancy; poor people should be given greater opportunities, and thus more choices, in their lives. Race-based animus, like animus based on sex or sexual orientation, is wrong in part because it limits the choices of the victims of such discrimination.

Historically, the respect for individual choice has been a significant, if not essential, part of modernity, a part of history's march from feudalism's dependence on status to modernity's dependence on contract (Coquillette, 2004).[1] It is a part of – perhaps the most crucial aspect of – modernity's respect for the autonomy and dignity of the individual (cf. Nozick, 1974). Choice is a powerful notion not only in legal and political theory but in political practice as well. Simply framing a political issue as an issue of choice is a very powerful and successful persuasive technique, especially in the United States.

Rhetorically, choice has always been a powerful notion in politics and law. This chapter is intended to offer a note of caution about its use. Despite its progressive hue of individual freedom, choice tends (perhaps increasingly) to be a notion used to defend and uphold existing matrices of economic and social power. This is true in a number of doctrinal areas, but especially so in corporate law, where the idea of choice is the defining principle of that slice of mainstream corporate law doctrine and scholarship based on neoclassical economics. There, the notion of choice is used to bolster a view of corporate law that protects those already within the corporate power structure and excludes important corporate stakeholders from corporate decision making.

This chapter explores the use of choice rhetoric in a number of legal and political debates, including those surrounding issues of school vouchers, pornography, tort reform, regulation, and civil rights. Using insights gained from this analysis, this chapter then criticizes the use of parallel choice rhetoric used in corporate law scholarship and doctrine. The chapter begins by describing how notions of choice have been used in political and legal debates over the past century or so. Choice rhetoric can be used to support or undermine the status quo, and although it is used in both ways in any given historical moment, trends can be highlighted. For example, the *Lochner* era was characterized by the use of choice rhetoric to support the then-existing economic power. After the New Deal era and into the middle part of the 20th century, the left was able to use the rhetoric of choice as an important aid in its efforts for civil rights, economic rights, and abortion rights. In the last quarter of the 20th century, the political right again seized on choice rhetoric, most prominently in the law and economics movements but also in other areas of politics and law. The rhetoric of choice is now perhaps the most powerful tool the right can bring to bear in fighting for regulatory efforts as diverse as school vouchers and tort reform, because the rhetoric of choice is an excellent way to support existing power relationships. The assertion that people acting within such power relationships are simply choosing their current situation undermines efforts to change those relationships. The powerful stay powerful; the weak stay weak. All those involved have chosen their current position, and their choice should be respected.

This chapter argues that in corporate law, too, the rhetoric of choice has been a powerful tool, especially within the contractarian school of thought that views the corporation as a "nexus of contracts" freely entered into by the corporation's many constituents. The school of thought currently dominant in corporate law doctrine holds that the corporation is best seen as a voluntary arrangement among all the various stakeholders of the corporation. The rhetoric of choice is thus a powerful tool to fight against any reform of current relationships within the corporation that would embolden and empower stakeholders traditionally left out of the corporate power structure. The rhetoric of choice is used in the same way in corporate law discourse as it is used elsewhere by the right – to justify or bolster existing matrices of economic and social power.

## 2. THE RHETORIC OF CHOICE IN CURRENT DEBATES

Consider the following apparently disparate political issues:

*School vouchers*. Those supporting school vouchers argue that the state should subsidize the educational choices of students. Vouchers represent an amount of money the state will contribute to the school a student chooses to attend. Each student receives a portable voucher; whether the student goes to a private or public school, in a local neighborhood or far away, the voucher can be used to defray the cost of going to that school. Voucher advocates argue that giving students this freedom to use public money to pay for school enlarges the range of choice available to students. This enlargement of choice is important for all, but especially important (as the argument goes) for students from low-income families and from neighborhoods with poor neighborhood schools.[2]

*Tort reform*. For the past few years, congress has been struggling with so-called "tort reform" – statutory limitations on the types of personal injury law suits that can be brought and on the amount that juries can award a successful plaintiff. The general debate on tort reform has focused on medical malpractice, but there have been more particularized efforts to protect fast food companies and gun manufacturers as well. With regard to medical malpractice, a leading argument in favor of tort reform is that patients should not be able to sue for injuries suffered in medical procedures that they *choose* to undergo, knowing their inherent risks. With regard to fast food companies and gun manufacturers, Congress has recently been considering bills barring suits from people claiming harm by the companies' products.[3] The statute protecting fast food companies, called the "Personal Responsibility in Food Consumption Act," was explicitly based on the notion that customers who choose to eat fast food should not be able to seek redress for harm that befalls them from that choice.[4]

*Pornography*. In debates about the regulation of pornography and sex work more broadly, one of the most powerful arguments in favor of decriminalization is the notion that the women involved in such work deserve to have their choices respected. As Sylvia Law writes, some feminists "see the freedom to explore sexuality and to recognize women as sexual agents as a central tenant and energizing, organizing principle of the women's liberation movement of the late twentieth century" (Law, 2000, p. 540). Or as Alan Wertheimer writes in a related context, sexual consent should be respected even within contexts of inequality. "I do not doubt that women sometimes agree to sexual relations that they would reject under different or more just or equal background conditions. But we do not enhance their welfare or their autonomy by denying the transformative power of their consent" (Wertheimer, 2003, p. 191).

Many other current debates seem to center on the concept of choice. For example, with the perceived need for additional security, the law surrounding "consensual" searches continues to evolve,[5] and by some accounts an increasing proportion of police oversight is based on consent.[6] Similarly, issues of gay rights depend increasingly on whether sexuality is seen as a preference or an orientation dictated by heredity.[7] Likewise, arguments in favor of the privatization of Social Security, the issue on which President George W. Bush chose to spend much of his political capital at the beginning of his second term, were based in large part on the attraction of offering a greater range of investment choices to those wanting to plan for their retirement (Bush, 2005; Caffrey, 2005, p. K1; Toner, 2005, p. A16).

There are additional examples of the invocation of choice arguments at the level of political theory. In democratic societies, the "consent of the governed" has been a concept that has long won adherents. Rousseau (1762, p. 109), for example, argued that "residence constitutes consent," meaning that anyone who chooses to live within a jurisdiction can be considered to have agreed to whatever laws that jurisdiction puts forth. This stance remains the theory behind electoral politics: if your candidate does not win, you still have to obey the laws until you get another chance to vote. This is the high theory behind the old bumper sticker saying "America: Love It or Leave It." It is also the concept behind an exchange in an episode of "30 Days," a television program on the FX network where an individual must live for 30 days in an uncomfortable situation that challenges his or her beliefs. In one episode, an atheist lived with an evangelical Christian family. The atheist invited the family to a meeting of other nonbelievers, who talked about their offense at having "In God We Trust" on United States currency and coins. The evangelicals' response was, "I guess it doesn't bother me that it's on the money. If it bothers you, move" (30 Days, 2006).

A similar view on choice has been expressed by one of the nation's leading conservative constitutional law scholars, Steven Calabresi. He has written that the gay rights issue should be handled by having gays and lesbians "who wish to escape moral opprobrium" move to "secular" cities, whereas "Americans of faith" should "form and live in communities" where they can discriminate openly. Channeling Rousseau, Calabresi (2004, p. 1123) suggests that "[t]hose who choose to live in a part of the country where their views on homosexuality are in the minority should learn to gracefully put up with a prevalence of opposing views."

What unites each of these debates is the centrality of the rhetoric of choice. *How* it is used, however, differs in various contexts. In some situations, public policy arguments are made that purport to build and expand choice (school vouchers, Social Security privatization). In others, the arguments are in favor of greater protection for existing choices, or in favor of recognizing the right to make certain choices (sex work, pornography). In the largest category, arguments are made that people should be held accountable for their choices under the existing legal or political framework (gay rights, tort reform, religious establishment).[8]

The power of choice as a rhetorical tool is striking in each of these situations, even though in the end its use is seemingly contradictory. In some cases, additional choice is an aspiration and it is argued that the choices available now are not sufficient; we should use the law to add choices. In other situations, even if existing choices are narrow and constrained, the arguments are made in favor of recognizing the rights of the choosers to make those very choices. In still other situations, choices are seen less as a right than as an act for which one must take responsibility, even if the choices are constrained and limited.

What explains the use of choice as a rhetorical tool in each of these public policy debates? Furthermore, what do they have to do with corporate law? Let us look deeper.

## 3. THE RHETORIC OF CHOICE IN REGULATORY BATTLES

The use of the rhetoric of choice is not a new phenomenon. On occasion, it is used to hold the line against regulatory protection. At other times, it is used to argue in favor of such protection. Perhaps the most famous example of using choice rhetoric as an obstacle to regulatory protection is the early 20th-century case of *Lochner v New York*. The use of choice rhetoric to support regulatory protections is a newer phenomenon.

### *3.1. Lochner: A Case Study in Using Choice to Protect the Status Quo*

Despite its progressive hue, the notion of choice is often touted to justify the status quo. This is Calabresi's tactic when he argues that gay men and lesbians should choose not to live in cities where the majority population discriminates against them. It is similarly the tactic applied by evangelicals in their conversations with atheists described above. An excellent way to support the existing framework of laws and regulation, whatever they are, is to argue that people have already voluntarily subjected themselves to it. Whatever mix of rights and obligations that already exists has been chosen, which offers the concomitant legitimacy that comes with choice. Moreover, the argument is made that within a given set of legal rules, one's actions within that framework constitutes a free choice to accept whatever outcomes are created by those actions.

This tactic has typically been used by the right, since it is extremely powerful in defending the status quo and opposing progressive movements calling for change in that status quo. Progressives fighting the injustice that occurs within the status quo must either argue that people are not really making the choices that they seem to be making, that the choices made do not reflect the true preferences of the actors, or that the choices should not be respected. But these counter-arguments find little traction in a political and social culture that revels in individualism. As George Annas (1998, p. xi) has written in the context of medical consent (but which applies more broadly): "Because of the high value Americans place on liberty and autonomy, and because it supports market values, choice rhetoric has assumed such prominence in public discourse that merely labeling something as a "choice" has a tendency to arrest conversation and prevent more than superficial analysis of the nature of the choice in question."

Perhaps the most famous use of the choice frame in opposing regulatory protections is its use in the Supreme Court's so-called *Lochner* era, which lasted for 50 years or so from the latter part of the 19th century till the New Deal. During that time, the Supreme Court routinely struck down economic regulations as violations of freedom of contract. The freedom of contract – really a principle of freedom of economic choice – was seen as a value protected from governmental attack. Any regulation of economic life that constrained choice was constitutionally suspect. As the Court said in *Lochner* itself, the decision juxtaposed the right of the state to regulate with the right of the workers to *choose* the conditions of their job.

> [W]hen the state ... has passed an act which seriously limits the right to labor or the right of contract in regard to their means of livelihood ... it becomes of great importance to determine which shall prevail – the right of the individual to labor for such time as he may choose, or the right of the state to prevent the individual from laboring ... (Lochner, 1905, p. 54)

This notion of choice was not very robust, of course, in that it ignored the constraints faced by the workers in the contracting process. Few would seriously contend that it is much of a choice when the two alternatives are to work in unsafe conditions for 80 or more hours per week or to have yourself and your family go hungry because of lack of money. But the absence of real alternatives did not much bother the Court, nor did it concern the laissez-faire theorists of the time. As long as government was not skewing the choices of the parties to a contract, the differences in bargaining power, or the dearth of alternatives for one party or the other, did not vitiate the sanctity of the choices, in fact, made.

The *Lochnerian* assumptions about choice in economics paralleled those of Rousseau in politics or Calabresi with regard to gay rights. What exists is chosen. *Lochner* went further, in the sense that the market was considered to be natural and given, so that anything that occurred within it won the imprimatur of consent. The market was free; whatever happened in it was chosen, and choice was liberty to be protected by the Constitution (Sunstein, 1993, pp. 45–62).

The Court did not begin to question its notion of choice until the principles of laissez-faire economics themselves came under attack during the New Deal. The New Deal constituted a sea change in economics, law, and politics. The intellectual giants of the era saw that the so-called "free market" was a creature of politics and law.[9] But they also operated on the basis of a new insight about choice, namely that the market was *not* an area ruled by choice. Rather, it was an area dominated by coercion – the coercion of the marketplace – which forced people to sell their labor in horrid conditions in order to house, feed, and clothe themselves and their families.[10] New Deal theorists recognized that choice in the narrow, limited sense, which had been protected by the *Lochner*-era Court, was not only inconsistent with economic well-being but also inconsistent with the nation's aspirations to improve the lot of citizens most in need. Government assistance was necessary to make real choices available.[11] This was the exact insight later used by civil rights leaders calling for government assistance to end *de facto* segregation as well as private prejudice in the marketplace.

### *3.2. Using the Rhetoric of Choice in Support of Regulatory Protections*

The second way the rhetoric of choice is used is as a part of an argument *in favor of* adjustments in the regulatory or legal framework. Here, the typical move is to argue for the expansion of choice, an especially powerful strategy in United States politics because of its connection, as mentioned above, with individualism and freedom. For several decades, choice rhetoric was used primarily by those on the left. The New Deal insights – that government was necessary in order to build the conditions necessary for choice and opportunity to flourish – were expanded beyond issues of economic rights and applied to assist movements for civil rights and eventually abortion rights.

In the initial desegregation battles, choice rhetoric was a powerful tool in casting doubt on state laws and private policies requiring the separation of people based on race. Students in some areas of the country were not allowed into their schools of choice based on their race. Some people were not allowed to enter their local public swimming pool because of their race, or to eat or work where they wished, or to purchase houses in the areas where they wanted to live. All these prejudices resulted in, or were embodied by, restrictions on the choices of racial minorities. Some of these restrictions, for example, school segregation, arose as a function of laws that explicitly limited the choices of racial minorities about, for instance, the schools available to their children. Others, such as the limitation on the range of choices arising from discrimination in employment and housing, arose out of the *absence* of laws offering meaningful regulation of other private parties – usually whites – who were restricting market choices because of racial animus.

Changes in laws were thus seen as the answer to the restriction on choice. The end of segregation *de jure*, limiting choice, clearly required a change in law. But the end of segregation *de facto,* which limited choice just as much, required a change in law as well. Even though laws such as the Civil Rights Act (1964) and the Fair Housing Act (1968) nominally consisted of limitation on the choices of certain market actors (such as employers, shopkeepers, and home sellers) to discriminate, such laws were seen as important components of a *protection* of choice. Government guarantees were necessary in order to protect individuals' choices that otherwise would have been restricted by the so-called "free market." The market was a source of coercion, and government assistance was required to be free of it.

The language of choice was even more pronounced in the abortion rights battle, and its use was intentional. Historian Rickie Solinger traces the use of the word "choice" in the abortion context to a 1969 decision by the National Abortion Rights Action League (NARAL) to name their first national action "Children by Choice" (Solinger, 2002, pp. 4–5). "Choice" was, in effect, being market-tested as the watchword of the movement (Wood, 2006). And in his opinion for the Supreme Court, Justice Harry Blackmun picked up on the choice language in *Roe v. Wade* (1973) itself. Choice rhetoric thus became the way to talk about a very difficult subject without alienating moderates. "Many people believed that 'choice' – a term that evoked women shoppers selecting among options in the marketplace – would be an easier sell" (Solinger, 2002, p. 5).

Interestingly, both sides in the abortion debate used choice rhetoric. In the *Roe v Wade* (1973) oral argument, the assistant attorney general who argued in support of Texas's abortion prohibition suggested that the real choice was made at the time Roe (Norma McCorvey) became pregnant and stated, "Now I think she makes her choice prior to the time she becomes pregnant. That is the time of the choice ... Once a child is born, a woman has no choice; and I think pregnancy makes her make that choice as well" (*Roe v. Wade*, 1973, *transcript*, 1971). In direct response, Justice Stewart added another take on choice, saying, "Maybe she makes her choice when she decides to live in Texas" (*ibid.*). It is not clear from the transcript whether this latter comment was intended to be sarcastic; indeed, Justice Stewart voted with the majority in *Roe*. But it is notable that Stewart's likely sarcasm is the exact argument used by Stephen Calabresi with regard to gay rights.

Note that in the abortion debate, the use of choice rhetoric was used most successfully in service of the de-regulatory move – to strike down prohibitions on abortions. Once the movement required affirmative regulatory assistance, however, choice rhetoric became less available, and political and legal momentum lagged earlier than it had in the civil rights movement. For example, when Congress restricted the use of Medicaid and other federal monies from being used to pay for abortions, it was not seen as a restriction on choice but instead a recognition of the notion that taxpayers should not be forced to pay for procedures that they found abhorrent (Coats, 1996; *Harris v. McRae*, 1980, p. 309). In *Harris v. McRae* (1980, p. 309), with the Supreme Court case upholding the restriction, Justice Brennan's dissent criticized the Court for failing to recognize that the government's "denial of public funds for medically necessary abortions ... serves to coerce indigent pregnant women to bear children that they would otherwise elect not to have" in part because they did not adopt restrictions. His argument that the *absence* of affirmative funding amounted to coercion of women to continue pregnancies failed to resonate with most Americans. A poll more than a decade after the decision indicated that over 70% of Americans people supported prohibiting the use Medicaid monies to pay for abortions.[12]

Note, however, that Brennan's argument in *McRae* was probably correct as a matter of fact. Merely lifting prohibitions on abortion allows for choice for some, but for many women who needed abortion the so-called choice would only be made real if they could use public funding to pay for it. Government assistance was necessary to support genuine choice, just as in the civil rights struggle. Such arguments, however, failed to carry the day in the abortion debate.

Compare the above examples with the current push for "school choice." This is an effort to enlist the assistance of public funds to enable children to attend public *or* private schools. The effort of the school choice movement mirrors the goals of both the civil rights movement and the abortion movement to enlist affirmative government assistance to make the choices sought in those movements genuine possibilities. Not surprisingly, advocates of school choice make explicit their similarity with the civil rights movement, where the efforts to enlist government support were successful, at least early on. According to one school-choice advocate, "Parental educational choice is an historical movement destined to succeed, powered by the same moral imperatives which made the *civil* rights movement's success inevitable" (Byrne, 1999).

## 4. THE RETURN OF CHOICE ON THE RIGHT: CHOICE IN CORPORATE LAW

The successful capture of choice rhetoric by the left did not last long. Perhaps because choice rhetoric was not as easily applicable, public support for "second stage" efforts in the civil rights movement, such as affirmative action and "forced" busing, waned. Similarly, as mentioned above, public funding for abortions – necessary to make the promises of *Roe* a reality – was not provided, in part because many taxpayers felt that public funding meant that they would be *forced* to pay for abortions (notably the opposite notion of choice).

The economic promises of the New Deal were also under attack. Ronald Reagan gained widespread public acclaim for his deregulatory appeals, saying that regulation was constraining America rather than liberating it.[13] Concurrently, neoclassical economics, with its lionization of individual choice and aversion to government regulation, came back into vogue in law schools – under the guise of the Law and Economics movement – and to some extent in economics departments. Although the focus on choice in the decades between the New Deal and the Reagan era had been a part of the civil rights and women's rights movements, the Law and Economics movement adopted the notion of choice as a key rhetorical and theoretical tool, transplanting it from its civil rights context back into its *Lochner*-era usage.

Although a fixation on neoclassical law-and-economics has weakened over time in most legal disciplines, the field of corporate law developed into, and remains, one of its bastions within the legal academy.[14] The primary way neoclassical economics has projected itself within corporate law is through the assertion that corporate law is "contractarian." But the notion of contract utilized is quite narrow, depending on a very simplistic notion of choice.[15]

The scholars who popularized the contractarian model of corporate law made the notion of choice central to their argument. University of Chicago professor Daniel Fischel (1982, pp. 1273–1274) argued in one of his first descriptions of the nexus-of-contracts version of corporate law that "[b]ecause the corporation is a particular type of firm formed by individuals acting *voluntarily* and for their mutual benefit, it can far more reasonably be viewed as the product of private contract than as a creature of the state." The implications of this view are well known. Corporate constituencies are assumed to be best able to determine their mutual rights and obligations by way of voluntary arrangement. Corporate law should thus provide "off-the-rack" rules that are primarily enabling (rather than prescriptive) and that can be easily contracted around (Easterbrook & Fischel, 1991). Law should not dictate the details of the obligations among the parties because each party is assumed to know her own interests and to protect them best through bargaining and exchange. In this way, the argument goes, developments in corporate charters and, indeed, in corporate law, will trend toward efficiency, because inefficient arrangements will cause participants in those arrangements to change the terms of the bargain over time in order to avoid losses.

Moreover, because people know and protect their own interests, terms of the corporate "contract," whether in charters or in state incorporation statutes, are correctly "priced" through an efficient capital market. The fact that the terms all have a price associated with them means that the contractarians can call the complete contract "consensual" in that any shareholder who buys the security can be said to have agreed completely to the contract. "All the terms in corporate governance are contractual in the sense that they are fully priced in transactions among the interested parties" (*ibid.*, p. 17). This view of corporate law, then, depends fundamentally on the notion that the participants in the corporate contract are economically rational actors, and are *choosing* to take part in the corporate form exactly as they find it. This mimics Rousseau, in that agreeing to participate within an existing legal regime is taken to constitute choice to abide by whatever happens.

Importantly, corporate law adopts the fiction that shareholders make exactly this type of decision about every stock they own. Because shareholders can learn about companies from information freely available and can sell stock in a fluid securities market, it is assumed that those who hold a company's stock voluntarily accept the risk/return ratio of that security. If the stock tanks, then the shareholder cannot blame anyone but him- or herself. Even if no actual shareholder is as informed as the theory would have it, the theory wins out. These fictions allow corporations to be characterized as voluntary, consensual organizations. In Easterbrook and Fischel terms, "the corporation is a voluntary adventure" (*ibid.*, p. 12).

Contractarian thought found traction within the courts early on, where it was used to endorse a very pro-management view of fiduciary duty. Shareholders were the principals who contracted with management to run the company. The arrangement was voluntary, so law did not need to step in to vary the terms of the deal.[16] Perhaps the best statement of this assumption appears in Judge Winter's famous opinion in *Joy v. North*, (1982), one of the earliest articulations of the contractarian model within the context of a case. Explaining why shareholders should not be able to win a suit brought against negligent directors alleging they breached their fiduciary duty to shareholders, Judge Winter argued that shareholders had *chosen* to take the risk of directors' negligent behavior. "Shareholders to a very real degree voluntarily undertake the risk of bad business judgment" (*Joy v. North*, 1982, p. 885). How had they expressed their choice? By buying the stock. As Judge Winter stated,

> Investors need not buy stock, for investment markets offer an array of opportunities less vulnerable to mistakes in judgment by corporate officers. Nor need investors buy stock in particular corporations. In the exercise of what is genuinely a *free choice*, the quality of a firm's management is often decisive and information is available from professional advisors. Since shareholders can and do select among investments partly on the basis of management, the business judgment rule merely recognizes a certain voluntariness in undertaking the risk of bad business decisions. (*ibid.*, emphasis added)

Notice that the assumption of choice implicit in *Joy* goes beyond even that which the *Lochner* Court made in the employment context, which Calabresi recently made with regard to gay rights, and which Rousseau made with democratic theory. *Joy* is famous, and appears in many corporate law casebooks, in part because it expresses a new and aggressive view of judicial deference to managerial decisions. The question of what the shareholders had agreed to – i.e., the level of fiduciary duty contained in the corporate "contract" between shareholders and management – was the question to be *answered* by the case. Judge Winter answered it by simply noting that the shareholders had purchased stock. Of course, if one were to take the contractarian notion of choice seriously, one would have to determine at least that the legal rule was so deferential when shareholders bought the stock, and that they actually voluntarily subjected themselves to it. But *Joy* did not ask the question of what the shareholders really chose. Although the *Lochner* Court, Calabresi, and Rosseau only go so far as to assume that individuals' decisions within a legal framework constitutes a meaningful choice to subject themselves to those rules, Winter assumed that shareholders' "choices" in purchasing stock constituted a voluntary subjection to a legal framework that had not yet been clearly articulated.

Also problematic is the fact that the assumption about consent and voluntariness within corporate law extends beyond shareholders. Everyone else involved in a company – from creditors to employees, from customers to communities – is also assumed to be consenting to their involvement in a meaningful way. This is what the law-and-economics scholars mean when they say a corporation is a "*nexus* of contracts." Everyone else connected to the firm – creditors, communities, workers, the government – is voluntarily so connected. No one is being coerced. If the parties dislike the terms of the "contract" between themselves and the company, they can leave. Not only can shareholders sell their shares, but employees can quit, managers can find a different company to manage, suppliers can sell their goods elsewhere, creditors can sell their bonds. Communities, we shall presume, can kick the corporation out or refuse to allow it to do business.[17]

This leaves the corporation completely able to disregard any putative obligation that is not explicitly set out in contract, regulation, or common law.[18] According to Fischel (1982, p. 1271), corporations should not be held accountable to society in addition to ways explicitly set out in the corporate "contract" because doing so would "disrupt the *voluntary* arrangements that private parties have entered into in forming corporations." Corporations should not be asked to look after the needs of their employees either, since workers "must look to their contractual rights rather than invoke fiduciary claims" (Easterbrook & Fischel, 1982, p. 91). Further, if employees bargain for a certain contract with only limited job security protection, "they ought not grumble if they are held to their bargains when business goes bad. Each investor must live with the structure of risks built into the firm ... it is all a matter of enforcing the contracts. And for any employee ... that means the explicit negotiated contract" (*ibid.*, p. 37).

Moreover, the absence of protections within the labor contract does not mean, according to contractarians, that workers are unable to bargain for those protections. "Rather, the absence of contractual protections ... may simply reflect the fact that [non-shareholder] constituencies are unwilling to pay for such protection in the form of lower wages" (*ibid.*, p. 36). In other words, if workers wanted to be the beneficiaries of management's fiduciary duties, they would simply bargain for such a contractual benefit. Because they have not chosen the protections, they must have chosen the lack of protection. We should respect their choice.

This is a return to *Lochner*, if only within corporate law. The contract is available to all; protections are there for those who negotiate for them; the market protects those who choose to protect themselves. People should be held responsible for the choices they make.[19]

## 5. EVALUATING CHOICE

The fixation on choice within corporate law is derived from a set of beliefs about individual autonomy and behavior. The assumption is that people actually *choose* – which is taken to be a mental decision of some kind usually followed by some kind of physical manifestation of that decision. This is the same assumption made throughout neoclassical economics, and it is worth examining.

Indeed, the notion of choice remains central to neoclassical economics' "rational actor" theory. Individuals are assumed to act in a way—by choosing behaviors, products, everything – that maximizes their own welfare (Thompson, 2000). As each person acts as to maximize his or her own welfare, the exchanges that occur will inevitably make all parties to voluntary deals better off. Economics thus recommends that individuals are given as much freedom to choose (and to contract) as possible, because with such freedom to choose comes not only individual benefit but social benefit as well.

But of course the economist's version of "rationality" is not particularly robust. It does not require an inquiry into the substance of any choice. Economists determine what is rational by observing what people actually *do*. This determination turns on an assumption about choice: what is chosen is by definition rational, because if it were not they would choose to do something else.

The problem with this assumption, of course, is that if the economists are correct, then there is no way to observe a person acting irrationally, or making a poor choice (unless he or she is actually crazy). Viewed in this light, rationality is something that humans share with lower animals. Judge Posner (1986, p. 15) admits in his Law and Economics text that "it would not be a solecism to speak of a rational frog." Rationality, in the economists' view, is something that could be used to describe the decisions of a frog in deciding which lily pad to sit on.

So, the economists' "rational" choice does not mean much, since there is *some* element of choice in virtually every human act. Even someone who signs a contract with a gun to his head is making an economically rational choice – it is more beneficial to sign even a bad contract than to be shot in the head.[20] Economists are assuming that the entire human situation is characterized by rational choice, and that laws and regulations should be made on that assumption. But if rational choice does not in fact exist, then economics is fundamentally flawed.

The rational actor theory has been the subject of myriad attacks. So-called behavioral economics has been especially influential in the last decade or so, deconstructing the rational actor theory using insights from psychology, which provide an account of human behavior that is more sophisticated than typically used in economics. These more sophisticated models of human behavior take into consideration, for instance, bounded rationality and bounded willpower, as well as a richer definition of self-interest (Jolls, Sunstein, & Thaler, 1998). Study of actual humans (rather than the so-called rational humans of economic theory) shows that choices are malleable and easily manipulated – human preferences can be created and destroyed. Choices, behavioral economists assert, are not so rational after all, and more and more research is showing just that.

For example, studies show that more choice sometimes makes people *less* happy (which is irrational from an economic point of view). In a study that examined the marketing of jam, one store offered a number of jams to taste and choose from, whereas a different store offered only a few jam choices (Schwartz, 2005, pp. 19–20). When offered more choices of jam, people made *fewer* purchases of jam. What is more, when offered more choices, buyers were *less* happy with the purchases they did make.

There are additional examples that relate to the concept of "anchoring." Research has shown that consumer choice for an item is affected drastically by the other items ("anchors") offered around it. For example, when someone decides how much to spend on a new suit, the prices of suits they *will not* buy affect their decisions about suits they *will* buy. As Barry Schwartz describes in *The Paradox of Choice*, in a fancy department store displaying suits costing over $1500, an $800 pinstripe may seem like a bargain, and will likely be purchased, but in a store where most suits cost less than $500, that same $800 suit will seem extravagant, and will probably be left on the shelf (*ibid.*, pp. 61–62). Another example comes from a catalog of high-end kitchen equipment offering a bread maker for $279. Sometime later, the catalog added a deluxe version for $429. The catalog did not sell many of the expensive ones, but the sales of the $279 version almost doubled (*ibid.*).

Traditional theory would predict that rational actors would be unaffected by extraneous information, such as the price of a product that is not purchased. But as a matter of fact, people's choices can be manipulated in predictable ways, and marketers take advantage of these "irrationalities" all the time.

The rationality of choice also depends on the ability of people to know and predict their own preferences. Efficient outcomes occur only if the choices made in fact increase utility. If the actual results of an exchange do not map very well onto what was expected, then efficiency will not correlate very well with choice, either. Worse, if utility is only randomly associated with choice, then one cannot be sure that respecting choice will have any connection with utility (or happiness) at all.

Indeed, the studies that are relevant here suggest that humans have a difficult time anticipating what will make them happy in the future. This is in part based on yet another problem with how humans process information – that many people cannot even correctly keep track of what made them happy in the past. This is because the human brain collapses past experiences and stores them as memories in ways that distort their accuracy. According to some studies, humans remember past experiences by condensing them to their salient elements, which tend to be whatever was best or worst about the experience, and whatever happened first and last (*ibid.*, p. 49; Gilbert, 2006, pp. 202–205). This makes a significant difference in how people make choices, since their choices about the future are inevitably based on their poor memories of past choices. Thus, if their memories are not accurate reflections of how they felt in the past, then their choices will lead to poor results even by their own assessment.

The most colorful example of this difficulty comes from a study of patients undergoing colonoscopies (Schwartz, 2005, p. 50). The painful procedure entails a physician manually inserting a probe into the colon. The procedure is painful throughout, but when the doctor manipulates the probe it is particularly so. In the study, the doctors removed the probe from some patients as soon as the procedure was done. For other patients, the doctor would leave the probe motionless inside the colon for additional 20 seconds. Although painful, these last 20 seconds were less painful than the earlier part of the procedure. This latter group of patients thus endured more total time with a probe inside their colon, and the total amount of pain they suffered was greater than the first group by any objective or subjective measure. The remarkable finding from this study was that the latter group of patients, who had undergone more discomfort and a longer procedure, *remembered* less discomfort than the first group (*ibid.*). Their memories were influenced less by the aggregate amount of discomfort than by what they felt during the last 20 seconds. This is more than just an esoteric point from medical research. Those who remembered less discomfort (even though they had actually suffered more) were *more willing to return for annual screenings*.

There are literally thousands of similar studies showing that people are not as economically rational as the rationality theory would assume. Authority, marketing, memories, and lack of information clearly affect people. People act out of altruism and spite. People misremember their pasts and do not accurately predict their futures.[21]

All this is to say that people's actual choices are hardly a reliable method by which to make economic judgments, even if efficiency is our only or primary goal. Even if the notion of choice continues to have power in political discourse, its explanatory power in economics is undergoing a withering attack. The important point here is that many traditional law-and-economics scholars do not seem to realize this, and most of those who do not realize this seem to work in the area of corporate law.

If choice has such limited use in actuality, why is it used so often at the level of rationale and justification, whether in politics or in legal doctrine? And why is it that we see it now, perhaps more than ever, in debates ranging from school vouchers to corporate law?

One hypothesis can be ventured: despite its limited value in explaining anything, choice is *very* powerful as a rationale brought to bear in defense of the status quo or in order to bolster existing power and wealth matrixes. Socially, economically, and politically, Americans are returning to a *Lochnerian* era, where a fixation on choice protects the prerogatives of the already privileged party. The rhetoric of choice and contract protects the existing power dynamic and economic status quo.

Recall the earlier arguments about school vouchers, tort reform, pornography, gay rights, and the like, and how the rhetoric of choice was used to protect existing power dynamics. With regard to school vouchers, studies are beginning to show that school "choice" does not benefit the less well-off among us by actually giving them more educational opportunities. Rather, it merely reduces the costs of private schools for those who already go to private schools (Schiller, 2001, p. 2; Lips & Jacoby, 2001, p. 8; Murphy, Nelson, & Rosenberg, 1997, p. 16). Children from disadvantaged communities end up staying in the same schools from where they started, but with less public money at their disposal because a portion of public education funds now flow to private schools. Children who started out with more opportunity get even more choice. If true, this trend will exacerbate existing educational inequality (Chemerinsky, 2003; Green, 2002).

With tort reform, the mantra of personal responsibility is used to focus attention on the actions of those who suffer harm caused by certain products or services. As individuals' decisions to undergo the surgery or eat the Big Mac become the focus, attention is shifted away from the decisions of those who manufacture those products or provide those services, even if those decisions are negligent or reckless toward the possibility of harm arising from those products. This adjustment in public attention has the effect of insulating the corporate decision makers from liability and shifting the cost of injuries away from corporations and onto customers, patients, or other tort victims.

The same is true about the other examples mentioned at the beginning of this chapter. Respect for the choices of sex workers shifts attention away from the constraints under which those choices are made, and makes into an afterthought the culpability of the (mostly) men who take advantage of the availability of sex work. And although there are reasonable grounds for disagreement on the point (Law, 2000), the wide availability of pornography and sex work would seem to underscore the existing status quo of sex relations rather than undermine it (MacKinnon, 1993).

Even in many of the current civil rights battles, choice rhetoric is used as a way to maintain the status quo. In the debates about gay rights, for example, the rhetoric of choice is used in two ways to justify the existing status quo of discrimination on the basis of sexual orientation. If sexual orientation is a choice, then many people on both sides of the debate seem to assume that the grounds for protection against discrimination are less than they would be if sexual orientation is immutable. This argument mimics the arguments made in constitutional law equal protection cases relating to race and sex discrimination. In part because neither race nor sex is a matter of choice, statutes referencing such classifications are deemed constitutionally suspect. But the problem arises when these assumptions are transplanted into the arguments about discrimination based on sexual orientation. Many people on *both* sides of the debate seem to assume that if sexual orientation is not a function of choice then it might be protected; if it is a matter of choice then it is not.[22] And note that for some, discrimination against LGBT (lesbian, gay, bisexual and transgendered) people may be appropriate even if sexual orientation *is* immutable, since the choice of where to live is still a choice. If Calabresi is right, the mere choice of living in a jurisdiction where being gay is unprotected constitutes a choice to be subject to such discrimination.

The same thing happens in corporate law.[23] Government should not step in to adjust corporate governance, because doing so would upset voluntary arrangements. If management chooses to lay off employees or close a factory, the employees have no reason to complain unless they have explicit job protection provisions written into their contract (cf. *Local 1330, United Steel Workers v. United States Steel Corp.*, 1980). They chose to take on the risk of job loss. If the management acts negligently and hurts the financial fortunes of the company, the employees and shareholders cannot complain since they voluntarily chose to run the risk of mismanagement (cf. *Joy v. North*, 1982). Communities that offer millions of dollars in tax breaks to entice companies to locate there or stay in place have no recourse if the company takes the money and leaves. They chose to give the money, and if the community wanted to protect itself it should have done so through contract (*Ypsilanti Charter Township of Ypsilanti v. General Motors Corp.*, 1993).

But of course depending on explicit contract as the only method of recourse or self-protection is hardly a neutral principle. Parties to contracts only get the protection that they are able to pay for. One receives only the protection that one's market power can seize. If you are a community struggling to maintain yourself, an employee who cannot easily pick up and move to the next town or state or country; or a minority shareholder whose voting power is nonexistent, then contract law does not offer many protections. One must look for recourse to other areas of law – to areas of law that use principles of fiduciary duty or some other source of obligation. But if the only law available is based on contract, then we are back at square one, with the powerless unable to improve their lot. They cannot choose to do better unless another party chooses to allow them to do so. So in corporate law as elsewhere, the rhetoric of choice is a powerful tool to protect existing market power.

What bears attention, however, is that the fixation on choice is increasingly being used throughout politics and law for the same ultimate purpose: to maintain existing economic and social power. If the status quo is deserving of defense and congratulation, then legal doctrines recognizing choice are the way to go. If not, we need to find a better way, and not just in arguments about school vouchers, tort reform, gay rights, and pornography, but in corporate law as well.

## 6. BEYOND CHOICE

Where does this take us? I must be much more tentative in my prescriptions than in my descriptions, but I am beginning to believe that we are on the cusp of a new stage of legal and political development over the issue of choice and contract. We are about to move from mere choice to something else, and the move may be analogous to similar historical developments in the civil rights movements to protect people from discrimination based on sex and race.[24]

The move looks like this: the focus on choice in the contexts mentioned in this article is something like formal neutrality in constitutional law and political philosophy. As in many first-generation civil rights movements, the emphasis is on formal equality: remove legal impediments that apply to a certain group. "Do not allow the law to impose special disabilities on us. At least allow us to be formally equal. At least allow us to choose, engage in contracting as any other person would be allowed to do."[25]

But we have recognized in constitutional law and political philosophy that formal neutrality, over time, simply replicates existing power relationships. Formal neutrality removes legal impediments, but it does not redress inequalities.[26] *A focus on choice does the same thing; it gives everyone the same right to be acted on by others and by the market.*[27]

Over the course of the 20th century, we learned this truth with regard to economic choice, and race and sexual discrimination. Mere choice, in the simple, neoclassical, Posnerian frog sense, does not help much if one does not have meaningful alternatives, sufficient information, and adequate resources.[28] The New Deal embodied a notion that economic choice needed substantive support; the civil rights movements learned the same lessons, even if they were less successful in winning the public policy changes necessary to make the choices real. We need to keep these insights in mind even now, especially with the rhetoric of choice spreading throughout politics and law.

How can we make these insights accessible? One idea is to make a conceptual shift, distinguishing between choice and something more robust. Perhaps we could use the term "consent" to identify the more meaningful notion. Although choice is something even a frog can do, it takes a human to consent. The notion of consent takes into account the quality of knowledge and information available; the existence of alternatives; the oppressiveness or lack thereof of the situation. We know something of what consent looks like; our intuitions are that it should indeed be respected. The distinction may resonate with people and make it easier to challenge the choice rhetoric that has become so pronounced.[29]

Moving from choice to consent would mean that we would be especially skeptical of areas of law founded on choice alone, instead of consent. Moving from choice to consent would encourage us to build capacity for consent (in our children, in our schools, in our workplaces, in our laws) rather than respecting mere choice. Moving from choice to consent would mean that we should use metrics for policy other than simple unconsidered preferences. Moving from choice to consent would make us quite wary of areas of our lives where our choices and preferences are manipulated.

We would recognize that choice cannot be our touchstone. It purports to explain and excuse everything; but in fact it explains nothing. It is used, cynically, to justify the existing balance of power. As George Annas (1998, p. xv) has said, "[All this is] not to say that choice is bad – only that limited, illusory, or coercive choices do not deserve to be honored with liberty rhetoric or taken seriously ... In America, when we are told of something new that is proposed because it will increase choice and control, we should all ... dig deeper to try to discover what's really at stake."

## NOTES

1. Coquillette (2004, pp. 473–474) excerpts Sir Henry Maine's 1864 treatise *Ancient Law*, which says, "There are few general propositions concerning the age to which we belong which seem at first sight liked to be received with readier concurrence than the assertion that the society of our day is mainly distinguished from that of preceding generations by the largeness of the sphere which is occupied in it by Contract ... Not many of us are so unobservant as not to perceive that in innumerable cases where old law fixed a man's social position irreversibly at his birth, modern law allows him to create it for himself by convention."

2. See Parents for Choice in Education (n.d.) ("School choice can be best defined as empowering parents to select the educational environment they feel is best for their child. In other words, *school choice is parental choice*. Some families are already able to exercise school choice simply because they have the resources to move to the neighborhood of their choice or to pay private school tuition. Families that do not have these same resources can only exercise choice through the use of different school choice tools, such as vouchers and tuition tax credits.") (emphasis in original).

3. Protection of Lawful Commerce in Arms Act, Section. 397, 109th Cong. (2005) (enacted as Pub. L. No. 109–92 (codified at 15 U.S.C. Section 7901)); Commonsense Consumption Act of 2005, S. 908, 109th Cong. (2005) (introduced on Apr. 26, 2005); Protection of Lawful Commerce in Arms Act, H.R. 800, 109th Cong. (2005) (introduced on Oct. 26, 2005); Personal Responsibility in Food Consumption Act of 2005, H.R. 554, 109th Cong. (2005) (passed by the House of Representatives on Feb. 2, 2005).

4. For an excellent analysis of the role of choice in the tort reform battle, with special attention paid to the problem of obesity and fast food, see Benforado, Hanson, and Yosifon (2004).

5. See *Schneckloth v. Bustamonte* (1973) (discussing value of searches based on consent); *Georgia v. Randolph* (2006) (discussing role of consent in search of house when one resident consents and the other objects). It is worth noting that the entire field of search and seizure law depends, in a sense, on choice. A search occurs only when an individual's reasonable expectation of privacy has been violated.

See, e.g., "[A] Fourth Amendment search occurs when the government violates a subjective expectation of privacy that society recognizes as reasonable." *Kyllo v. United States* (2001) (citing *Katz v. United States* (1967) (Harlan, J., concurring)). In many cases, this inquiry turns on whether a person has chosen to subject him- or herself to public view or to put him- or herself in the position where he or she knows he or she has no expectation of privacy. The cases are abundant. See, e.g., *Dow Chemical Co. v. United States* (1986) (holding that photographing an industrial complex with a precision aerial mapping camera is not a search); *United States v. Taketa* (1991, p. 667) ("[v]ideotaping of suspects in public places, such as banks, does not violate the fourth amendment" because there is no expectation of privacy in these places); *United States v. Gonzalez* (2003) (mailroom of a public hospital); *Thompson v. Johnson County Community College* (1996) (security personnel locker area of a community college); *United States v. Lopez* (1984) (public street); *United States v. Bifield* (1980) (gas station); *State v. Augafa* (1999) (public street); *State v. Henry* (2002) (public restroom).

6. See Simmons (2005, p. 773) ("Over 90% of warrantless police searches are accomplished through the use of the consent exception to the Fourth Amendment."); Strauss (2001, p. 214) ("Although precise figures detailing the number of searches conducted pursuant to consent are not – and probably can never be – available, there is no dispute that these type of searches affect tens of thousands, if not hundreds of thousands, of people every year."); Whorf (2001).

7. See, e.g., Editorial (July 2, 2006), "The freedom to be gay", *L.A. Times*, p. M4; Angier (1993, p. A24).

8. See Benforado et al. (2004, p. 1802) ("dispositionism [the belief that people's own choices determine their behavior] has had and continues to have an immense effect on both the framing and resolution of virtually every major social policy debate, from affirmative action to standardized testing, from gun control to school 'choice,' and from gay rights to the war on terrorism.").

9. For a review of that analysis, see Sunstein (1993, p. 50) ("The law created property and contract rights, and the law imposed various limits on those rights. Market wages and market hours were in this sense a creation of law, not of nature, and not of laissez-faire.").

10. See *ibid.* (pp. 48–49) ("If coercion and law were seen there [in the market], regulation would be a justified corrective. The same principle that doomed slavery could also call for government assistance against the forms of coercion that drive people to take menial jobs at trivial pay, or that force people to work sixty hours per week if they are to work at all."). The most influential piece from the time is likely Hale (1923).

11. See Sunstein (1997, p. 320) (discussing Franklin Roosevelt's "Second Bill of Rights," which included "the right to a useful and remunerative job," "the right to earn enough to provide adequate food and clothing and recreation," "the right of every family to a decent home," "the right to adequate medical care," and others).

12. A CBS/New York Times poll in 1993 indicated that 72% of Americans did not want their tax dollars to pay for abortions (David Ellerbrock, 1995; *Health Reform at Risk—Coverage of Abortion Under National Healthcare Policy*, 1993).

13. See Fukuyama (2008) (calling "financial deregulation" a Reagan-era "article of faith"); Horwitz (1991, p. 264) ("The Reagan Administration came to power in

1980 on a program of reducing the size of government and getting government out of the economy").

14. See Greenfield and Nilsson (1998) (arguing that corporate law is the "closest living relative" of classic utilitarianism); Arlen, Spitzer, and Talley (2000) (Corporate law is an "intellectual bastion of economic conventionalism").

15. For a more in-depth discussion of the underlying assumptions of main stream corporate law scholarship, particularly that the correct view of corporate law is one based on private, voluntary contracts, see Greenfield (2006, pp. 29–37).

16. See generally Mitchell and Mitchell (2006, p. 101) (explaining how agency law depends on notions of choice).

17. Cf. Macey (1991, pp. 42–43) (arguing that even though other non-shareholder stakeholders can protect themselves through contract, communities cannot; the remedy for them is through appeal to "local and state government for redress").

18. Actually, Fischel and Easterbrook (1982, p. 1177, n. 57) famously wrote that corporations should not even be required to obey laws, as long as the expected penalties for breaking the law are lower than the expected benefits from disobedience: "(M)anagers not only may, but also should, violate the rules when it is profitable to do so." For a critique, see Greenfield (2006, ch. 4).

19. It is important to note the irony here. This view of corporate law fits within the current fixation on choice and personal responsibility, but only if one ignores one of the fundamental characteristics of the corporate form: limited liability. The protection of shareholders from liability arising from the acts of the corporation may make sense for a number of reasons, perhaps most clearly as a straightforward subsidy for businesses organizing themselves in the corporate form. But it can hardly be squared with the rhetoric of personal responsibility, since it is the exact opposite.

20. In fact, rational choice theorists would also assert that taking a bullet instead of signing a contract would *also* be rational, if that is what one observes. If it were not rational, the person would not have chosen it.

21. For an excellent review of these studies in a very readable form, see Gilbert (2006).

22. Though there are exceptions, many people on both sides of the debate on gay rights tend to make the immutability assumption (Balog, 2006; Pickhardt, 1998). This is an extremely problematic assumption, however. See generally Richards (1999). Even if one's decision as to sexual orientation is undetermined by genetic makeup, it may nevertheless be the kind of choice that is deserving of not only political protection but heightened constitutional protection as well. For further discussion, see Smith (2005), Marcosson (2001), and Halley (1994) (arguing that litigation over sexual orientation should not rely on the immutability of sexual orientation). Cases that try to come to terms with this problem include *Nabozny v. Podlesny* (1996) (holding that high school students who were homosexual, regardless of whether it is a choice or not, could pursue claims for a violation of equal protection against school administrators who were deliberately indifferent to harassment and beatings inflicted on the students); *Montgomery v. Indep. Sch. Dist. No. 709* (2000) (holding that a student who was harassed and beaten on the basis of his perceived sexual orientation could proceed with an equal protection claim, regardless of whether he is a member of a specially protected class or not); *Tanner v. Oregon Health Sciences Univ.* (1998) ("cases make clear that immutability—in the sense of inability to alter or change—is

not necessary"); *High Tech Gays v. Defense Indus. Sec. Clearance Office* (1990) (applying rational basis review to a policy that discriminated on the basis of sexual orientation because "[h]omosexuality is not an immutable characteristic; it is behavioral and hence is fundamentally different from traits such as race, gender, or alienage, which define already existing suspect and quasi-suspect classes").

23. For another excellent analysis of this point, see Greenwood (2005).

24. For a more robust treatment of this point, see Greenwood (2003).

25. *Civil Rights Act of 1866* ("All persons within the jurisdiction of the United States shall have the same right in every State and Territory to make and enforce contracts, to sue, be parties, give evidence, and to the full and equal benefit of all laws and proceedings for the security of persons and property as is enjoyed by white citizens, and shall be subject to like punishment, pains, penalties, taxes, licenses, and exactions of every kind, and to no other."). See also Justice Clarence Thomas's dissent, quoting Frederick Douglas, in *Grutter v. Bollinger* (2003), the case upholding college admissions policies that consider race in order to promote a diverse student body: "[I]n regard to the colored people, there is always more that is benevolent, I perceive, than just, manifested towards us. What I ask for the negro is not benevolence, not pity, not sympathy, but simply justice. The American people have always been anxious to know what they shall do with us... I have had but one answer from the beginning. Do nothing with us! Your doing with us has already played the mischief with us. Do nothing with us! If the apples will not remain on the tree of their own strength, if they are worm-eaten at the core, if they are early ripe and disposed to fall, let them fall! ... And if the negro cannot stand on his own legs, let him fall also. All I ask is, give him a chance to stand on his own legs! Let him alone! ... [Y]our interference is doing him positive injury." What the Black Man Wants: An Address Delivered in Boston, Massachusetts, on 26 January 1865, reprinted in 4 The Frederick Douglass Papers 59, 68 (J. Blassingame & J. McKivigan eds. 1991) (emphasis in original), quoted in *Grutter v. Bollinger* (2003) (539 U.S. 306, 349–50 Thomas, J., dissenting).

26. See Greenfield (2006, p. 18) ("The most profound difficulty in the enabling account [that corporate law simply enables parties to the corporate contract to dictate their own relationships] is the assertion that the corporate contract optimizes the interests of the various parties to the deal. Because law is supposed to stand aside, any contract that results from a negotiation depends upon the power of the parties going into the negotiation. The resulting contract defining the terms of corporate governance thus mirrors the preexisting market power of the various parties. To say that a contract optimizes the interests of the parties may be true in that it allows the parties to improve on what would be their lot without such a contract. But it is emphatically not the case that all contracts are fair, just, supportive of human dignity, or consistent with the interests of society as a whole."

27. As Anatole France (1894, p. 95) observed: "The law, in its majestic equality, forbids rich and poor alike to sleep under bridges, to beg in the streets, and to steal their bread."

28. See Benforado et al. (2004, p. 1797) ("While the law sometimes recognizes a concept of 'imperfect information' there is no similar concept of 'imperfect autonomy.' We see 'free choice' or 'no choice' and nothing in between. And yet 'imperfect autonomy' is the reality of our predicament.").

29. This shift in terminology would only work if "consent" is indeed considered more meaningful than choice. In present usage, this may or may not be the case. In some situations, the term "consent" does not connote the robust level of agency I want to propose. For example, in the area of so-called consensual searches under the Fourth Amendment, there is no requirement at all that the person "consenting" to a search even be aware that the search can be refused (*Schneckloth v. Bustamonte*, 1973), and there is no requirement that the situation itself be free of coercive elements (*United States v. Drayton*, 2002) (search deemed consensual even though conducted in a bus with an armed police officer at the front and rear of the bus and another bending over passenger requesting search). Outside the Fourth Amendment context, however, the term "consent" does imply a level of information and understanding that is worth building on. Consider the requirements for consent in the context of medical care, for example, which urge doctors to make sure the patients consenting to treatment have a level of understanding and knowledge before making a choice (Annas, 1998).

## ACKNOWLEDGMENTS

Thanks are given to Sean Glasheen and Rebecca Kiselewich for excellent research assistance. This chapter benefited greatly from responses from participants at the Seattle University School of Law Conference on Economics and Social Justice, September 29, 2006, as well as from the faculty of Western New England College School of Law, where a work-in-progress paper on a related topic was presented. Thanks also go out to the students from two most recent Elements of the Law seminars, both of whom focused on the notion of choice and consent.

## REFERENCES

30 Days, Atheist/Christian. Aired on the FX network, originally broadcast August 9, 2006.

Angier, N. (1993). Study of sex orientation doesn't neatly fit mold. *New York Times*, July 18, p. A24.

Annas, G. J. (1998). *Some choice: Law, medicine, and the market*. New York: Oxford University Press.

Arlen, J., Spitzer, M., & Talley, E. (2000). *Endowment effects, other-regarding preferences and corporate law*, April 21 (draft). Olin Working Paper no. 00-2 2.

Balog, K. (2006). Equal protection for homosexuals: Why the immutability argument is necessary and how it is met. *Cleveland State Law Review*, *53*, p. 557.

Benforado, A., Hanson, J., & Yosifon, D. (2004). Broken scales: Obesity and justice in America. *Emory Law Journal*, *53*, p. 1645.

Bush, G. W. (2005). Strengthening social security for the 21st century, February. Available at http://www.whitehouse.gov/infocus/social-security/200501/socialsecurity.pdf

Byrne, C. A. (1999). School choice is civil rights issue of new century. *The Sun*, July 8. Available at http://www.acton.org/ppolicy/education/theology/new_century.html

Caffrey, A. (2005).Can you manage your own money? Amid push to privatize social security, many in US admit they're daunted or don't know investing basics. *Boston Globe*, April 3, p. K1.

Calabresi, S. G. (2004). Lawrence, the Fourteenth Amendment, and the Supreme Court's reliance on foreign constitutional law: An originalist reappraisal. *Ohio State Law Journal*, *65*, p. 1123.

Chemerinsky, E. (2003). Separate and unequal: American public education today. *American University Law Review*, *52*, p. 1474.

Coats, D. (Senator). (1996). Statement of Senator Coats. *Congressional Record*, 142 Cong. Rec. S10245, 10277.

Coquillette, D. R. (2004). *The Anglo-American legal heritage* (2nd ed.). Durham, NC: Carolina Academic Press.

David Ellerbrock, D. (1995). Unfair health insurance. *The Daily Collegian Online*, March 20. Available at http://www.collegian.psu.edu/archive/1995/03/03-20-95tdc/03-20-95dops-letter-1.asp

Easterbrook, F. H., & Fischel, D. R. (1982). Antitrust suits by targets of tender offers. *Michigan Law Review*, *80*, p. 1177, n. 57.

Easterbrook, F. H., & Fischel, D. R. (1991). *The economic structure of corporate law*. Cambridge, MA: Harvard University Press.

Fischel, D. R. (1982). The corporate governance movement. *Vanderbilt Law Review*, *35*, 1273–1274.

France, A. (1894). *The red lily*. (Stephens, W., Trans., 1921). New York, NY: John Lane.

Fukuyama, F. (2008). The fall of America, inc. *Newsweek*, October 13. Available at http://www.newsweek.com/id/162401/output/print

Gilbert, D. (2006). *Stumbling on happiness*. New York, NY: Random House/Knopf Publishing.

Green, S. K. (2002). The illusionary aspect of "private choice" for constitutional analysis. *Willamette Law Review*, *28*, 557–560.

Greenfield, K. (2006). *The failure of corporate law*. Chicago, IL: University of Chicago Press.

Greenfield, K., & Nilsson, J. E. (1998). Gradgrind's education: Using Dickens and Aristotle to understand (and replace?) the business judgment rule. *Brooklyn Law Review*, *63*, p. 799.

Greenwood, D. (2003). Gendered workers/market equality. *Texas Journal of Women and the Law*, *12*, p. 323.

Greenwood, D. (2005). Markets and democracy: The illegitimacy of corporate law. *University of Missouri-Kansas City Law Review*, *74*(1), p. 41.

Hale, R. (1923). Coercion and distribution in a supposedly non-coercive state. *Political Science Quarterly*, *28*, p. 470.

Halley, J. E. (1994). Sexual orientation and the politics of biology: A critique of the argument from immutability. *Stanford Law Review*, *46*, p. 503.

Health Reform at Risk – Coverage of Abortion Under National Healthcare Policy – Editorial. (1993). *Commonweal*, July 16. Available at http://findarticles.com/p/articles/mi_m1252/is_/ai_14061944

Horwitz, R. B. (1991). *The irony of regulatory reform: The deregulation of American telecommunications* (p. 264). New York, NY: Oxford University Press.

Jolls, C., Sunstein, C., & Thaler, R. (1998). A behavioral approach to law and economics. *Stanford Law Review*, *50*, p. 1471.

Law, S. A. (2000). Commercial sex: Beyond decriminalization. *Southern California Law Review, 73*, p. 540.
Lips, C., & Jacoby, J. (2001). The Arizona scholarship tax credit: Giving parents choices, saving taxpayers money. *The Cato Institute/Policy Analysis*, September 17, p. 8. Available at http://www.cato.org/pubs/pas/pa414.pdf
Macey, J. R. (1991). An economic analysis of the various rationales for making shareholders the exclusive beneficiaries of corporate fiduciary duties. *Stetson Law Review, 21*, 42–43.
MacKinnon, C. (1993). *Only words*. Cambridge, MA: Harvard University Press.
Marcosson, S. (2001). Constructive immutability. *University of Pennsylvania Journal of Constitutional Law, 3*(April), p. 646.
Mitchell, L., & Mitchell, D. T. (2006). *Corporations: Cases and materials*. Durham, NC: Carolina Academic Press.
Murphy, D., Nelson, F. H., & Rosenberg, B. (1997). The Cleveland voucher program: Who chooses? Who gets chosen? Who pays? *American Federation of Teachers*, 16. Available at http://www.aft.org/research/downloads/charter/ClevelandVoucherProgram.pdf
Nozick, R. (1974). *Anarchy, state, and Utopia*. New York, NY: Basic Books.
Parents for Choice in Education. (n.d.). School choice info/frequently asked questions. Available at http://www.choiceineducation.org/schoolchoice_faq.php
Pickhardt, J. (1998). Choose or lose: Embracing theories of choice in gay rights litigation strategies. *New York University Law Review, 73*, 928–952.
Posner, R. A. (1986). *Economic analysis of law* (3rd ed.). Little, Toronto, ON: Brown and Company.
Richards, D. (1999). *Identity and the case for gay rights*. Chicago, IL: University of Chicago Press.
Rousseau, J. (2005 [1762]). *The social contract*. Raleigh, NC: Hayes Barton Press.
Schiller, Z. (2001). Cleveland school vouchers: Where the students come from, policy matters, September, p. 2. Available at http://www.policymattersohio.org/pdf/ClevelandVouchers.pdf
Schwartz, B. (2005). *The paradox of choice: Why more is less*. New York, NY: HarperCollins.
Simmons, R. (2005). Not "voluntary" but still reasonable: A new paradigm for understanding the consent searches doctrine. *Indiana Law Journal, 80*, p. 773.
Smith, J. B. (2005). The flaws of rational basis with bite: Why the Supreme Court should acknowledge its application of heightened scrutiny to classifications based on sexual orientation. *Fordham Law Review, 73*, p. 2769.
Solinger, R. (2002). *Beggars and choosers: How the politics of choice shaped adoption, abortion, and welfare in the United States*. New York, NY: Macmillan/Hill and Wang.
Strauss, M. (2001). Criminal law: Reconstructing consent. *Journal of Criminal Law and Criminology, 92*, p. 214.
Sunstein, C. (1993). *The partial constitution*. Cambridge, MA: Harvard University Press.
Sunstein, C. (1997). *Free markets and social justice*. New York, NY: Oxford University Press.
Thompson, R. B. (2000). Teaching business associations: Norms, economics and cognitive learning. *Georgia Law Review, 34*, p. 1000.
Toner, R. (2005). It's 'private' vs. 'personal' in debate over Bush plan. *New York Times*, March 22, p. A16.
Wertheimer, A. (2003). *Consent to sexual relations*. Cambridge, UK: Cambridge University Press.

Whorf, R. H. (2001). Consent searches following routine traffic stops: The troubled jurisprudence of a doomed drug interdiction technique. *Ohio Northern University Law Review*, *28*, p. 21.
Wood, S. (2006). On language: Choice. *BITCHfest*, 144–147.

## Laws and Statutes

Civil Rights Act of 1866, 42 U.S.C. Section 1981 (1866).
Commonsense Consumption Act of 2005, Section 908, 109th Cong. (2005).
Fair Housing Act, 42 U.S.C. Section 3604 (1968).
Personal Responsibility in Food Consumption Act of 2005, H.R. 554, 109th Cong. (2005).
Protection of Lawful Commerce in Arms Act, H.R. 800, 109th Cong. (2005).
Protection of Lawful Commerce in Arms Act, Section 397, 109th Cong. (2005).
Title VII of the Civil Rights Act of 1964, 42 U.S.C. Section 2000e-2 (1964).

## Cases

*Dow Chemical Co. v. United States*, 476 U.S. 227 (1986).
*Georgia v. Randolph*, 547 U.S. 103 (2006).
*Grutter v. Bollinger*, 539 U.S. 306, 349–50 (2003).
*Harris v. McRae*, 448 U.S. 297 (1980).
*High Tech Gays v. Defense Industrial Security Clearance Office*, 895 F.2d. 563 (9th Cir. 1990).
*Joy v North*, 692 F.2d. 880 (1982).
*Katz v. United States*, 389 U.S. 347 (1967).
*Kyllo v. United States*, 533 U.S. 27 (2001).
*Local 1330, United Steel Workers v. United States Steel Corp.*, 631 F.2d. 1264 (1980).
*Lochner v. New York*, 198 U.S. 45 (1905).
*Montgomery v. Independent School District No. 709*, 109 F. Supp. 2d 1081 (D. Minn. 2000).
*Nabozny v. Podlesny*, 92 F.3d 446 (7th Cir. 1996).
*Roe v. Wade*, 410 U.S. 113 (1973).
*Schneckloth v. Bustamonte*, 412 U.S. 218 (1973).
*State v. Augafa*, 92 Haw. 454 (Haw. 1999).
*State v. Henry*, 151 Ohio App. 3d. 128 (Ohio App. 2002).
*Tanner v. Oregon Health Sciences Univ.*, 157 Or. App. 502 (Or. App. 1998).
*Thompson v. Johnson County Community College*, 930 F. Supp. 501 (D. Kan. 1996).
*United States v. Bifield*, 498 F. Supp. 497 (D. Conn. 1980).
*United States v. Drayton*, 536 U.S. 194 (2002).
*United States v. Gonzalez*, 328 F.3d. 543 (9th Cir. 2003).
*United States v. Lopez*, 585 F. Supp. 1400 (D. Conn. 1984).
*United States v. Taketa*, 923 F.2d. 665 (9th Cir. 1991).
*Ypsilanti Charter Township of Ypsilanti v. General Motors Corp.*, 506 N.W.2d. 556 (Mich. Ct. App. 1993).

# FAITH BASED INVESTING: ARE SHARES ENTITLED TO THE RESIDUAL?*

Daniel J. H. Greenwood

## ABSTRACT

*Shareholder dividends are "rents": they are paid out of a producer's surplus that, in a fully competitive market, would not exist. In any market system, no one has a right to rents. Why, then, do shareholders receive dividends? Most likely, share gains have been the result of the usefulness of the share-centered ideologies in justifying a tremendous shift of corporate wealth from employees to an alliance of top managers and shareholders. This alliance now shows signs of breaking down, as the managers learn they no longer need the ideological cover. Standard accounts conceal the struggle over corporate surplus and the weakness of shareholder claims to appropriate it. Recognizing that distribution of corporate surplus is a political struggle is the first step towards a less ideologically blindered discussion of how that struggle ought to be structured.*

* This chapter is a heavily revised version of Greenwood (2006).

**Law & Economics: Toward Social Justice**
**Research in Law and Economics: A Journal of Policy, Volume 24, 91–130**

**ISSN: 0193-5895/doi:10.1108/S0193-5895(2009)0000024009**

# 1. INTRODUCTION

Everyone knows that shares receive dividends because they are entitled to the residual returns of a public corporation. Everyone is wrong.

Basic principles of market competition, applied to the actual law of corporations, sharply contradict the conventional wisdom. First, shareholders are not residual claimants in any legal or economic sense so long as the corporation remains in existence. Second, standard economic theory implies that shareholders should receive dividends only under noncompetitive conditions, and not often even then.

Standard accounts elide the problem by a number of mutually contradictory rhetorical tropes, each seeking to portray payments to shareholders as philosophic entitlements or market necessity. None stands up to serious questioning. Instead, payments that corporations make to shareholders result from the then-current economic and political power of the stock market and, especially since the taming of the hostile takeover market, from ideological victories in a multilateral struggle over corporate surplus. Shareholder returns depend on shareholder power – both the soft power of ideology and the hard power of law and the legally structured market – at least as much as on underlying business success.

Moreover, the struggle is largely over rents – the surplus generated by the corporation itself. Accordingly, if the current results are unattractive, we can change the rules, modify the power of the various players, or seek to persuade them to accept different views of their ethical rights and obligations with no efficiency implications.[1] The distribution of rents matters: if corporate returns go to shares, we may generate more investments but we definitely end up with far more inequality, short-term outlooks, and tolerance of anti-social externalization; if returns go to top managers, we reward entrepreneurialism but invite corruption; if returns go to rank and file employees, they are shared most widely but there may be a cost in lost flexibility; if returns remain inside the corporation, they may contribute to growth or simply subsidize slack. But nothing in the nature of the corporate form requires that the current distribution be viewed as a sacred entitlement or a necessary consequence of our way of life.

# 2. THE ECONOMICS OF DIVIDENDS

On the standard economic view, shareholders contract to receive corporate profits, which are the same as the residual, that is, what is left over after all contracting parties have been paid their contract amounts (Brealey & Myers, 1996, p. 364). This account is quite problematic.

Public shareholders are perfectly fungible providers of the most perfectly fungible of commodities in our most competitive of markets. In a competitive market, the price of a commodity should be its marginal cost. Accordingly, shareholders should expect to be paid no more than the marginal cost to the firm of retaining them. But corporate law provides that shareholders have no right to corporate distributions at any given time – shareholder contributions are permanent capital that the firm may retain without further payment for as long as it deems appropriate. The marginal cost of existing shareholders is therefore zero, and that should be the price they can command in a competitive capital market.

Focusing instead on product markets, we reach the same conclusion. In fully competitive product markets, any firm that paid shareholders a current return would be uncompetitive: its costs, and therefore its prices, would be higher than those of competitors that defer shareholder payouts. In less competitive product markets, a firm might have disequilibrium or monopoly profits. Still, it need not give them to shareholders at any given time. In a system of rational maximizers, dividends would always be paid tomorrow, and tomorrow would never arrive. Accordingly, under standard economic pricing theory shareholders should expect no return.

Shareholders in public firms have no contractual or other legally enforceable right to any payment at all. The corporation, acting by board decision, determines in its discretion whether and when to pay dividends or otherwise transfer funds to shareholders. Thus, dividends bear a certain resemblance to bonuses or tips – an after-the-fact payment enforceable only by custom, not law. Traditional tips, however, occur in personal service markets where repeating personal relationships and reputational concerns can enforce after-the-fact payments without recourse to contract; bonuses, similarly, occur in multi-period markets where bonus payers have incentives not to renege because disappointed recipients will quit (and employees have sufficient market power to be willing to accept the risk that they will be fired without full payment). In contrast, shareholders are both fungible and anonymous. Standard explanations for the stability of tips or bonuses will not work in this context. Instead, the usual economic models predict that dividends as known should not exist.

Shareholders of closely held corporations, unlike publicly held ones, actually control the firm and, like real owners, can use that power to simply take any corporate surplus (disequilibrium profits) that may exist. Therefore, closely held firms do not present the full dividend puzzle. In the era of hostile takeovers, public shareholder returns were based primarily on the threat that shareholders would sell the company to a private owner. When public shareholders had the power to force managers to accept takeovers, managers had to treat public shareholders *as if* they had the powers of a dominant owner because otherwise they would sell to someone who *would* have those powers (Greenwood, 1996). Today, however, takeovers are quite difficult without the consent of incumbent boards. To explain the continued high returns to public shareholders, we must look to ideology: shareholders receive returns, in large part, because corporate decision makers think that they ought to.

The following sections explain these claims in detail.

### *2.1. Defining Profit*

The conventional claim is that shareholders are entitled to the corporation's profit, but profit is an ambiguous term. For current purposes, the accounting definition is circular; the claim must rely, instead, on the economic understanding.

By accounting convention, profits are the difference between a corporation's income and expenses, but accountants label dividends and similar payments to shareholders (e.g., stock buybacks) as distributions of profit rather than corporate expenses.[2] In this trivial sense, of course, shareholders necessarily receive the residual (or at least part of it) by definition: accountants classify any corporate proceeds that go to shareholders as residual, but call sums committed to any other participant expenses. On this definition, the standard view is just a claim that shareholders are entitled to receive whatever shareholders receive.

The standard economic understanding of profit is more useful here. Accounting profits are a measure of what remains in the firm or is distributed to shareholders in any given period. In contrast, economic profits measure the surplus the firm has created, regardless of whether that surplus is retained or to whom it is distributed. The concept should be familiar to all lawyers who deal with closely-held businesses: economic profit is what we have in mind when we talk about closely-held firms subject to the corporate income tax lowering their taxes by paying out profits to their shareholder/owner in the form of rent, interest, or wages rather than dividends.

Economic profit is usually defined as the difference between the lowest expenses the corporation would have had if it paid the lowest (quality adjusted) market price for its inputs, and the income it would have had if it had charged the highest (quality adjusted) market price for its output. Defined in the subjunctive in this way, economic profit is the profit the firm could make, given its skills, technology, and competitors. It represents the pool of funds that can be given to any corporate participant without threatening the viability of the firm – not only shareholders, but other investors, suppliers, employees, taxing authorities or consumers.

Thus, the economic concept clarifies the standard view. Rather than an empty claim that whatever shareholders receive should be labeled profit, it is a falsifiable claim that corporations do, or should, distribute the difference between the price they could charge and the costs they must pay – their economic profit – to shareholders rather than to any other corporate participant. That is, the standard view is a claim that employees, suppliers, and debt holders should be paid as little as possible, and customers charged as much as possible, in order to maximize the amount available for distribution to shareholders.

On the economic definition of profit, it should be clear that, contrary to accounting convention, only some payments to shareholders should be called profit. Conversely, some payments to other corporate roles or factors of production should be considered distributions of profit rather than costs. In free markets, factors of production will participate in the firm only if they are paid to do so. Accordingly, payments to any factor must be classified as costs to the extent that they are necessary to purchase the asset or service needed. For these purposes, capital – whether contributed to the firm in the form of equity or debt – is no different than labor or raw materials. The firm must pay if it is to attract the financing it needs – whether it pays in the form of interest, dividends, promises of future capital gains, or (as sometimes happens in closely-held corporations) more imaginative ways.

One part of what accountants call profit, then, must be reclassified as a cost and not considered part of the residual at all. Normal returns to capital – the market cost of capital adjusted for the risk associated with the particular investment – are a cost of doing business just like wages or raw materials. Any payment or distribution the firm must make to attract and retain the capital the firm needs is a cost, not profit.

Conversely, whenever any factor of production is paid more than necessary – whether that payment is called wages, bonus, interest, dividends, stock buy-back, loan, rent, price, featherbedding, sloth, or even green cheese – the unnecessary payment should be considered a distribution of economic profit. Indeed, even if the firm lowers its prices below the market clearing price, that forgone profit should be viewed as a distribution of economic profit to consumers.

Once it is clear that the claim that "shareholders are entitled to the residual" is a claim that shareholders are entitled to economic profits, we can begin to see the full difficulty of the conventional wisdom. As shown later, from an economic perspective it is hard to see how such a deal could be made in a competitive market. From a legal perspective, it is hard to find any evidence that such a deal has been made. Normatively, the claim that such a deal should be made defies ordinary understandings of the morals of the marketplace. The only reasonable conclusion is that if in fact shareholders do receive the residual, or part of it, it must be by a combination of firm monopoly power in the consumer market and shareholder ideological power inside the firm. The next sections consider these perhaps surprising claims seriatim.

### *2.2. In Competitive Markets, the Firm Cannot Charge for Shareholders' Contribution*

In competitive markets, competition reduces prices to marginal cost (Coase, 1960). That means that at equilibrium, the residual – the surplus created by the corporation – goes to consumers, not shareholders. Even if competition does not preclude the corporation from seizing the residual, economic profits are disequilibrium rents. No one has a pre-legal claim on rents in a capitalist market. Thus, any claim that shareholders are "entitled" to the economic profits must be based on some identifiable aspect of their legal rights, not somehow inherent in the nature of the corporation.

#### *2.2.1. At Equilibrium, Economic Profit Goes to Consumers*

Corporations exist when they are able to organize employees, capital, and other resources to produce a product or service for less than the highest price consumers are willing to pay. Economic profit – the difference between the firm's marginal cost and the marginal consumer's reservation price – is the social value the firm creates. Economic profits are rents, in the standard sense of a surplus that is available to be distributed to any participant without affecting the use of real resources. Standard economic theory predicts that, normally, rents should be competed away as prices adjust to the marginal cost of efficient producers. In other words, in fully competitive markets at equilibrium, the residual – the economic profit – goes to consumers. In less competitive markets, the firm may be able to retain part of the rents or other firm participants may succeed in appropriating them.

Ordinarily, no firm participant has a special claim to being the source of the corporate surplus. On the one hand, each participant needs the firm: if a given participant did not, it would be able to produce goods or services without incurring the firm's organizational, decision-making, and bureaucratic costs, and, because its costs would be cheaper, would quickly drive the firm out of business (Coase, 1937, p. 386). On the other hand, each of the firm's participants is likely to be a "but-for" cause of the surplus: if the firm did not need them to produce its product, why would it retain them? Thus, the very existence of the firm is evidence that any residual it creates must be credited to the entity itself rather than any participant or factor of production taken separately. Capital without labor would be as barren as the reverse.

The law recognizes this fundamental unity of the firm in two important ways. First, it assigns ownership of the economic profit to the firm itself in the first instance. Thus, contract, property and tort law each treat the corporation itself as a legal person, meaning that the corporation, not any of the humans or roles associated with it, is liable for its obligations and entitled to the proceeds of its sales. Second, the law defers to internal corporate decisions regarding allocation of the surplus. The authorized corporate decision-making body – the board – is entitled to decide what contracts to enter into and how to use corporate resources under the broad umbrella of protection of the business judgment rule. Courts rarely intervene in the firm's own decision-making to protect or promote particular visions of corporate purpose or interests of particular firm participants. The upshot is that, as a matter of law, the firm – not its shareholders, employees, or other participants – owns and controls the firm's surplus until the firm decides to dedicate it to some particular purpose.

Although the firm is the creator and the owner of the surplus, it will be unable to retain it in a competitive market. Instead, competition should drive prices down to no higher than the marginal cost of the next-to-lowest cost producer. Under competitive conditions, the surplus created by the corporation goes entirely to customers, not shareholders.

Of course, this does not mean that shareholders should earn nothing. Shareholders, like any firm input, will refuse to contribute unless they expect to be paid as much as they can command elsewhere, namely, the normal returns to capital. Thus, at first glance, we should expect shareholders to receive at least a normal return.

In competitive markets, normal returns should also be the most shareholders can charge. If they try to charge any more, corporations seeking capital will go elsewhere. Moreover, any corporation that agreed to pay capital – a fully fungible commodity – more than normal returns would have above-market expenses and be forced to charge above-market prices. Its competitors in the consumer market, paying only the market cost for capital, would quickly drive it out of business.

In short, as a first approximation, shareholders should expect to earn neither more nor less than a normal return, which, in turn, should be just the marginal cost of capital. Shareholders should expect no economic profit or residual at all. Instead, the simplest model of market dynamics suggests they will receive just the part of accounting profits that the economic conception views as a mislabeled cost.

*2.2.2. Shareholder Contributions to the Firm Are a Sunk Cost That Should Not Be Reflected in Competitive Prices*

For firms operating in even moderately competitive markets, there is an additional barrier to being able to distribute surplus to shareholders. Standard price theory holds that in a competitive market, the firm should be able to command a price equal to the marginal cost of production (Coase, 1946, p. 169). But normal returns to capital are an average cost, not a marginal cost. As explained below, the marginal cost of shareholder capital contributions is zero. As a result, firms in competitive markets should not be able to include even normal returns to capital, let alone economic profits, in their prices. Shareholders in competitive product markets should expect no returns at all (and, foreseeing this, should decline to become shareholders in the first place).[3]

The marginal cost of shareholder capital is zero because of the legal rights public shareholders have or, rather, do not have. Other capital suppliers have clear rights to require the firm to pay them. Sole proprietors can put money into or take money out of the business largely at will, limited only by fraud and fraudulent conveyance rules. Controlling shareholders in closely held corporations have almost the same rights as sole proprietors, providing they follow formalities designed to make clear the boundaries between firm and personal funds. Partners have the inalienable right to end the enterprise or to unilaterally withdraw their capital, even in violation of agreements they have made (Uniform Partnership Act, Sections 31, 38). Lenders and bondholders have contractual rights to interest payments and to return of their capital on a certain date.

In contrast, public shareholders have no right to interim payments, no date on which their capital is to be returned, no right to withdraw their capital, and no right to force the firm to wind up, liquidate, or sell at any fixed time.[4] Dividends are after-the-fact payments made at the discretion of the corporation. As a matter of law, only the board, acting for the corporation as a whole and restrained by its fiduciary duty to the corporation, has the right to transfer corporate funds to shareholders, whether by dividend or otherwise, but it has no obligation to do so at any time (Del. Code Ann. tit. 8 Section 170; compare Blair and Stout (2001, pp. 403, 406)). Similarly, directors must initiate any decision to liquidate or sell the firm.[5]

Individual shareholders may "exit" by selling their shares, but the seller is paid by the buyer, not the firm: the original capital contribution remains with the firm. Instead of the contract rights of creditors or the control rights of owners, public shareholders have only a collective political right to elect the board (but not to restrict its discretion to act in the best interests of the firm) that is virtually meaningless so long as the firm remains public.[6]

To be sure, popular ideology and occasional courts hold that the firm is supposed to earn a return for shareholders at some point (see, e.g., *Dodge v. Ford Motor Co.*, 1919). But a corporation has no legal obligation to pay a dividend or equivalent at any given time and shareholders have no legal right to force it to do so.[7] The firm can always defer dividends to a later date and the final distribution, like the messianic age, can remain always tantalizingly close without ever actually arriving. This right to delay means that in any given time period, the firm always has the right to continue to use capital contributed by shareholders without paying for it. Thus, the marginal cost to the corporation of shareholder capital is zero.

Under standard price theory, prices match marginal – not average – costs at equilibrium in competitive markets. The reason is simple. Any firm that attempts to raise its prices to generate funds to pay shareholders will be underbid by competitors that defer paying shareholders. To retain customers, all firms will be forced to reduce their prices to their marginal costs, which do not include paying shareholders in the current period. Since marginal costs are lower than average costs, all firms in competitive markets can expect to run an economic loss at equilibrium (which accounting conventions will record as a less frightening break-even), and shareholder returns will have to wait until a future that will never arrive.

In short, in competitive product markets, corporations will not be able to charge anything at all for their use of shareholder capital. They should, therefore, have great difficulty paying shareholders a normal return, let alone residual or economic profits. Of course, to the extent that shareholders can predict this in advance, they will simply decline to invest in the first place. Standard price theory ineluctably predicts that public stock markets should rarely coexist with competitive product markets.

### *2.2.3. Residual Retained by the Firm or Distributed to Firm Participants, Including Shareholders, Must Be Disequilibrium Returns to Innovation or Monopoly*

Looked at another way, if the firm does have a residual (in the sense of economic profits) to give to shareholders, then it must be charging more than its marginal cost. In turn, this means that it must not be selling a commodity in a fully competitive market at equilibrium. This could be because of the innovativeness or efficiency of the firm: if the corporation is able to produce at a lower cost or higher quality than its competitors, it can earn more than a normal return until they catch up. Alternatively, the ability to charge more than marginal cost could be the result of longer-lasting sources of pricing power: cascades or network gains in which consumers find benefits in using the same product as other consumers (Arthur, 1990)[8]; increasing returns to scale that make the largest producer also the most efficient (Chandler, 1990, pp. 56–58); legal monopolies such as patent, copyright, or trademark protection; or even simple anti-trust violations.[9]

If, on the other hand, competition prevails, the entire surplus created by the firm will go to consumers and the firm's inputs, including shareholders, will earn no more than their cost at the margin. The airline industry may be an example: constantly hovering at the edge of bankruptcy, as a group the companies in this highly competitive industry probably have earned no returns for shareholders since deregulation.

## *2.3. Rational Maximizers Will Not Give Corporate Surplus to Shareholders*

In the real world, consumer markets often are not fully competitive, many products are not commodities, and firms often are able to charge more than marginal cost, thus covering their average costs and even earning disequilibrium economic profits. Not coincidentally, many publicly traded companies fit into these categories. Some, such as Proctor & Gamble and Wal-Mart, are mass producers with increasing returns to scale that allow the largest producers to earn economic profits because their size gives them lower marginal costs than their competitors. Others benefit from network effects that make their product more useful than those of competitors, like Microsoft or Disney, or have legal monopolies of nonfungible trade secrets, trademarks, patents or copyrights, like Coca-Cola, Nike and most pharmaceutical and chemical companies.

These economic profits are rents: disequilibrium profits from monopoly or innovation that can be distributed to any participant in the system without efficiency implications.

Shareholders, however, are perfectly fungible providers of the most perfectly fungible of commodities in our most competitive of markets. A firm paying shareholders for providing capital has no reason to pay more than a competitive price for their product, even if the firm makes super-competitive returns (Greenwood, 2004, p. 818). If shareholders attempted to charge more, corporations would simply look elsewhere for capital (by finding new shareholders, borrowing, or using internally generated funds).

Moreover, as corporate finance theorists normally assume, the returns capital commands should be a function of the nondiversifiable risk it assumes – which is another way of saying, again, that the price of capital is set in an anonymous market, independent of the (fully diversifiable) risk of success or failure of a particular firm. In other words, the price of capital – the normal return that firms must pay to attract the capital they need – should be equal to the marginal cost of producing it, not to its productivity in a particular context.

Accordingly, even if the firm has disequilibrium or monopoly profits, shareholders should not have market power to charge the firm any part of them. Conversely, it is hard to see why corporations – our epitome of rationality – would voluntarily pay more than the market price. Rational maximizers do not give free gifts.

The second puzzle, then, is why the shareholders in a publicly held firm should expect to receive the corporation's returns to innovation and monopoly rents even when there is a residual. Real owners (including the shareholder of a close corporation) can simply take the residual; creditors may be able to contract to receive it. Public shareholders can do neither.

Conventional wisdom conflates public shareholders with "owners" of the firm and simply assumes that, as owners, they can, or should be able to, appropriate the corporation's surplus. The next sections explain why public shareholders should be seen, like other investors, as fungible sellers of fungible capital that should receive no more than the market price for their product.

### *2.3.1. Fungible Capital Should Command Only Commodity Prices*

A firm can obtain capital from three basic sources: retained earnings, debt, and equity. Companies with investment opportunities can finance them internally by using economic profits – that is, by charging consumers more than they must and paying suppliers, bondholders, shareholders, executives, other employees, or the public fisc less than they could. Alternatively, they can borrow from banks or sell bonds, in effect renting capital. Finally, companies can issue equity, buying permanent capital by granting the rights of stock ownership.

Modern finance theory, at least since Modigliani and Miller's indifference theorem, teaches that that the three sources of capital are entirely comparable and largely fungible (Modigliani & Miller, 1958, pp. 261–297). If the financial markets were fully competitive and fully informed, competition and arbitrage would assure that the risk-adjusted price of capital would be the same regardless of its legal characterization as retained earnings, debt, or equity. The firm would pay the same risk-adjusted equilibrium cost for capital regardless of which source it tapped.

In the real world, of course, financial markets are rarely at equilibrium, and even if they were to hit that magic point, no one would know. Accordingly, the theoretical insight that the different sources of capital are fundamentally the same has the paradoxical real world consequence that investors and corporations alike focus their energies on finding the differences that remain. From the firm's perspective, there is only one: price.[10] Corporate finance teaches corporate executives that their job is to maximize corporate returns by obtaining capital for the firm at the lowest possible cost; thus, firms will switch from debt to equity, for example, depending largely on which market is offering money for a lower price.

If the sources of capital are interchangeable, however, the position of shareholders is quite strange. On the corporate finance view, all they are is sellers of cash and, perhaps, some risk-bearing services.[11] But capital is a highly fungible commodity. If one supplier seeks to charge more than the going rate, corporations can switch to another. Equity capital competes directly with debt. If shareholders were to attempt to charge more than lenders, firms presumably would shift from equity to debt by issuing more debt and using the proceeds to buy back stock, as is done in a leveraged buy-out. Conversely, if equity capital appears to be charging less than debt capital, we would expect firms to increase their purchases of equity, for example, by going public or issuing additional stock and using the proceeds to pay down debt.

In short, just like sellers in a competitive market, shareholders should be able to charge no more than the cost of the commodity they have to sell. In the case of stock sales directly by the corporation, this would be the general cost of money – at equilibrium, the same amount the firm would pay bondholders or bank lenders. Lenders receive a fee (interest) that is closely related to the general cost of producing money (i.e., general interest rates), adjusted to reflect the expected risk of the particular firm. They do not expect to participate in extraordinary firm earnings, except perhaps to the extent that such earnings reduce risk for which the creditors have already been compensated. In a competitive capital market, firms should refuse to sell stock if shareholders demand any more than the normal return lenders would receive.

Once stock is issued, however, the shareholder's position worsens. Current shares represent a past service – capital transferred to the firm when the share was originally purchased from the firm. Since shareholders have no right to reclaim the capital represented by their shares, they are contributing no ongoing service. As seen in the previous section, past services should be insufficient to even claim a normal return, let alone any share of the economic profit.

In the end, firm participants can obtain more than the marginal cost of their contribution only if they themselves have some sort of disequilibrium or monopoly power. Public shareholders – because they are fully fungible providers of a fully fungible commodity in a highly competitive market – are the *least* likely firm participants to have that kind of power. Thus, even when firms have the market power to charge more than marginal cost so that they can earn economic profits, it is hard to see how shareholders would have the market power to seize them.

### *2.3.2. What Have You Done for Me Lately?*

Firms are best thought of as a system of ongoing, continuously renegotiated relationships. In any given period, contracting parties have a contractual right to receive the payments they negotiated for in the earlier period. Over time, however, the important determinant of what each corporate participant receives is not past contract but current market strength.

Thus, for example, most employees have at-will contracts. An at-will contract can be terminated at any time for any reason. This right to terminate means that contractual terms are always subject to renegotiation – at any given time, the contractual period has always just ended. Friction aside, then, contractual terms in the current period should always be a function of market conditions in the current period. Other firm participants are in similar positions. If a supplier has a contractual right to a payment that is no longer justified by current market prices, the corporation will quickly find an alternative supplier, and past contractual rights will, at most, govern past relationships. If interest rates drop, the firm will replace its past loans with newer ones reflecting current interest rates.

Even if a particular corporate participant has obtained contractual protection against such renegotiation – for example, employees who have won long-term contractual protection for their pensions or against layoffs or bondholders with long-term guarantees of interest rates – the protection is likely to be meaningful only to the degree that the firm can escape market competition. If the firm fails to renegotiate long-term contracts to reflect current market conditions, its competitors will. In even moderately competitive markets, customers will find an alternative supplier providing similar goods at better prices or better goods at similar prices. Either the legacy contracts will be breached, or the legacy firm will fail. In either case, long-term contracts collapse into spot markets.

Consider the history of the steel, automobile, or airline industries. In each case, the leading companies made extensive promises to employees to pay benefits in the future – pensions, medical insurance, employment through recessions, increasing pay with seniority. Presumably, the firms received current benefits: they paid employees less than they would otherwise have had to because of these promises. But when the time comes for the company to pay for these past benefits, it has a problem – any new competitor automatically has lower costs, even if it is using the same technology, the same knowledge, the same capital, the same employees, and even the same promises (so long as they have not yet matured).

The old company must run faster than its younger competitors just to stay in the same place. Sometimes, organizational stability, smarter design, or locked-in customers will allow it to do that. But if the newcomers also have disruptive technology (as in the steel industry), or if technical innovation means that work forces are shrinking so that promises to past employees become a larger part of current costs (as in the auto industry, and, indeed, most US factory-based production), or if the new company is successfully able to imitate the older one (as regularly happens to airlines), or worse yet able to provide a better product through better design sense, technical proficiency or managerial skill (as in the car industry), the old contracts are not going to be worth much. If the firm is to remain competitive, it must find a way to renege on its past promises. If the contractual beneficiaries are able to insist on their legal rights, the older firm will have higher costs, and in a reasonably competitive market, the effect of these costs will be to drive it out of business, or at least into bankruptcy where courts will allow it to reform contracts to reflect current market conditions. And as the new firms mature, they too will be forced to renege on their promises by newer firms making newer promises for more distant futures.

In short, any time a firm participant forces the firm to pay above (current) market prices for (current) services – or any price at all for past services, no matter how legitimate the legal claim – the economic effect is to give the firm a cost that competitors do not have.[12] At this point, a new company – even with no additional skill or technical improvements, and, if it can find someone willing to accept its word, even making the same long term commitments – can out-compete the old one. Mobile factors of production such as capital, executives, and the most productive employees will shift to the new one, while the old one is left with the least mobile participants and they, in turn, are left with claims against a failing entity.

Shareholders present the same issue as legacy cost employees, but more so. Like employees with future expectations, shareholders make their contribution in one period and expect to be paid at a later time. Firms that actually pay, then, will automatically be at a cost disadvantage relative to younger firms that do not yet have to pay or relative to older ones that find a way to renege on similar past promises.

The problem is worse for shareholders, however, because unlike employees, shareholders are entirely fungible with no continuity advantages to offer. Experienced employees may learn the idiosyncrasies of the company's technology and bureaucracy, the special needs of customers or how to get the most out of suppliers. They may be better able to make the incremental improvements that characterize progress in many fields or better able to maintain old machines or long-standing relationships. These bodies of hard and soft knowledge can be hard for an upstart to recreate. Where this is so, an older company may be able to maintain competitive costs with a newer one despite legacy promises. Moreover, employees are real people who often will have to build real lives in reliance on the promises the firm has made. Some managers may feel moral, if not legal, obligations to meet those obligations even if market pressures push them to breach. Shareholders, in contrast, represent nothing more than past cash investment. If a new firm can obtain capital more cheaply than the old one, there is no possibility of an offsetting legacy advantage stemming from continuity. Nor do shareholders have the human faces of betrayed employees: most shareholders are just pools of funds. Managers who have learned to resist the moral pull of employee claims are unlikely to be much moved by shareholder claims.

The consequence should be clear: like retirees and unionized workers in older manufacturing industries, shareholder claims are a cost without a current benefit. Managers in even a semi-competitive environment will feel compelled to reduce these costs to the maximum extent possible. Trained to view equity capital as largely interchangeable with retained earnings and borrowed money, corporate managers should look askance as shareholder claims to the residual: in a capitalist economy, no one has a right to rents, and commodity providers are never entitled to more than the cost of replacing them. If shareholders seek current payments for past services, the rational manager's first response will be to just say no.

### *2.3.3. Waiting for Messiah*

Managers, however, have a better option. Instead of rudely telling shareholders to get lost, they can politely tell them to wait their turn. The result will be the same.

One of the core doctrines of corporate law is that the managers have no obligation to maximize shareholder returns in any particular time frame (Stout & Blair, 2006). The rational managerial response to shares, then, is to promise great returns in the future. *Later*, we should see managers promising, they will pay huge dividends; *now*, they need to use shareholder contributions in order to grow the company.[13] Later, however, as every procrastinator knows, need never arrive (Utset, 2003). As in Red Queen's contract, it's "jam to-morrow and jam yesterday, but never jam to-day" (Carroll, 1871, p. 53).

More generally, shares represent a promise that maximizing investors should view with extreme skepticism: "purchase our equity when we are starting up and have many investment opportunities, and we will pay you dividends later, at a time we determine in our sole discretion, when we lack sufficient opportunities and no longer will have any need of you or your money." If investors accept this promise, firms should respond by selling as much equity as they possibly can and then constantly deferring the date on which the promised dividend payout actually occurs. They may also investigate whether these investors would be interested in purchasing a famous bridge or two. Rational investors, however, should see that a promise to pay dividends tomorrow, with no guarantee that tomorrow will ever arrive, is a promise that is unlikely to generate much value. Therefore, they should decline to invest based on it. In turn, rational corporations should see that rational investors are not going to trust them and should see no point in even making the offer.

Were the stock market and corporate issuers to behave according to rational maximizing principles, no dividends would be paid to public shareholders even when less than fully competitive markets allowed the firm to earn a surplus. Anticipating this, potential public shareholders would decline to invest in initial offerings. The initial public offering (IPO) market ought to fail in a classic market for lemons. Secondary markets for shares, in turn, ought to trade at extremely low prices, reflecting the low probability of passive investors receiving any returns. The only successful offerings, the model predicts, would be firms with a dominant shareholder and a credible promise to treat public, passive shareholders equally with the insider.

## *2.4. Alternative Explanations for Dividends within the Economic Model*

IPOs, however, do exist. Something, then, is wrong with the theoretical picture. Either investors and managers are systematically irrational, investing based on faith that the normal rules of capitalist behavior will be suspended for their benefit, or the economic theory is not capturing the true dynamics. In the next subsections, some attempts to rescue the maximizing economic theory are explored, before concluding that the theoretical problem requires moving to a different paradigm altogether.

### *2.4.1. Dividends as Reputational Investments*

If shares have neither the legal right to current dividends nor the market power to demand them, perhaps firms simply give them out as appreciation for past services rendered. Dividends, in other words, perhaps should be seen as a form of corporate charity or a type of tip, analogous to the pre-ERISA[14] common law understanding of pensions.

Rational profit maximizers, like difficult relatives, do not give free gifts. Seeming gifts always have strings attached. As seen earlier, corporate managers are trained to maximize profits and, at least when they are operating within the corporate finance framework, to view equity as simply a cost like all others. If equity is just another cost, there is no reason to give shareholders any more than they are legally entitled to (for past services) or have the market power to demand (for present and future services). As stated before, shareholders have no legal right to payment for past or present services. Thus, within the rational maximizer model, payments to shareholders must be made in order to induce future services.

Perhaps, then, corporations pay dividends in order to entice investors to purchase stock in future offerings, much as maximizers are said to tip in order to enhance their reputations with dates or waiters.[15] But end game problems should make this reputation rationale collapse in the corporate context even if it works in the restaurant business.

If people tip mainly to purchase a reputation, presumably they would free ride when they could do so without consequence – they would leave no tip when eating alone out of town. Most people do not seem to do that, suggesting that the tip story does not work even its home territory (Kahneman, Knetsch, & Thaler, 1986).

If dividends are tips, the free-riding problem should be even worse. First, managers should recognize that paying dividends to ease future stock offerings is rational only if the firm intends to make such an offering in the future. Moreover, given the short job tenure of participants on both sides of this game – both top management positions and Wall Street have notoriously high turnover – managers should assume that any reputation they purchase by paying dividends will have a quite brief half-life. Accordingly, if the firm is not planning to issue equity in the relatively *near* future, it has an incentive to cash in on its past reputation by ceasing to pay dividends.

Second, recognizing that firms may act in this manner, investors should heavily discount any promises to pay dividends after the point at which the firm is not in dire need of new equity capital.

The explanation of dividends as tips, then, predicts that firms ought to issue dividends when they need capital at the *beginning* of their life cycle, and then *reduce* them as they mature. Moreover, investors, understanding that dividends are paid in order to attract future capital rather than to compensate past purchasers, should be willing to invest only if the company looks likely to need to attract future equity investors, and should price shares based on the assumption that all returns will come early on. In almost the exact opposite of conventional "life-cycle" theory, investors would expect that once firms can internally generate adequate investment capital, they will stop paying dividends.

These predictions bear a certain resemblance to some parts of the private equity start-up market, where investors expect to cash out quickly, but none whatsoever to the public stock market. If investors viewed public stocks in this fashion, prices would be low indeed. The theory that dividends are tips or reputational investments to induce future stock purchases fails.

### *2.4.2. Going Private*

Rational maximizer models, as seen before, suggest that publicly traded corporations should always defer dividends to a future period that never arrives, and that shareholders, anticipating this behavior, should be unwilling to invest in publicly traded equities. The model, then, predicts that the public equity markets will fail. Instead, firms should raise capital by borrowing, because lenders, unlike equity holders, have legally enforceable rights to returns.

However, public corporations need not remain public. The possibility of going private may add some otherwise unobtainable value for the public shareholders. That is, shareholders may expect not dividends but a final payment when the company goes private. If this expectation is rational, it would explain why investors are willing to become shareholders (although it still leaves dividends prior to the going-private payment somewhat mysterious).

*2.4.2.1. Closely Held and Family-Dominated Firms.* The shareholder of a closely held corporation has a dramatically different bundle of rights than shareholders in public firms. In public firms, elected directors make major firm decisions in accordance with their views of the *interests* of the corporation and its shareholders.[16] In contrast, in closely held firms, the *will* of the sole shareholder controls – not someone else's views of its or the firm's interests. Interests are replaced by will in two ways. First, the board serves solely at the shareholder's pleasure and thus must respond to its will: a sole shareholder can call, without board approval, a shareholder meeting at which it is the sole voter and at which it may appoint or dismiss directors without cause or reference to elected terms of office.[17] Second, a sole shareholder is not constrained by the directors' fiduciary duties, except in the most extraordinary circumstances: generally, the sole shareholder would be the only person with standing to invoke these standards.[18] The only meaningful restraint on the sole shareholder using the firm as it wishes is the alter-ego doctrine – it must respect the formal separateness of the corporation if it wishes to retain protection against the firm's creditors in the event of insolvency. This rarely will be a substantive restraint.

A shareholder with this degree of control is fairly called an "owner" of the firm. Like other owners (but unlike shareholders of a publicly traded corporation), it has the power to do with the corporation what it will, including operating it in the way it wishes, determining business plans without regard to the views of others, and, most importantly for present purposes, simply taking any surplus the corporation may generate. This shareholder receives a dividend because it chooses to, not because it can bargain for it (assuming the firm has the market power necessary to generate a surplus in the first place).

Similarly, even when there is more than one shareholder, a dominant shareholder with enough votes to elect its delegates to the board of directors (even by a plurality) has a degree of control that the shareholders of a public firm lack. With control comes attributes of ownership. Like a real owner, a dominant shareholder need not contend that it is morally entitled to appropriate the surplus, beg for tips, or assure the firm of its future usefulness. If the firm has the market power to generate a surplus, a controlling shareholder can use its control to take it.

To be sure, unlike a sole shareholder, controlling shareholders are limited by shareholder and board fiduciary duties.[19] But those duties are silent with regard to struggles over firm surplus between shareholders as a group and all other firm participants and roles – under current law, fiduciary duties do not restrain a board or a controlling shareholder from allocating all or any fraction of the firm surplus to shareholders as a group. The law is somewhat more protective of minority shareholders. Most importantly, shares of the same class must be treated equally – if the controlling shareholder declares a dividend on its shares, it must pay the same dividend on shares of the same class held by others.[20]

The upshot is that passive shareholders may actually be better off in a firm with a dominant shareholder than in a classic Berle and Means firm, particularly if control is in the hands of a family and the family chooses to allow outsiders to purchase shares with the same dividend rights as those held by the family. American conventional wisdom is skeptical about family-controlled publicly traded corporations, fearing that the insiders will take too much of the firm value in roles that do not require them to share with outsiders – for example, by hiring themselves on above-market terms or using company resources for personal consumption. In contrast, in many other countries, most publicly traded firms are family controlled. The reason may be that even if the family takes a disproportionate part of the returns to shareholding, it also has the power to ensure that there are returns to shareholding in the first place. Passive shareholders, then, simply tag along, assuming that dividend-seeking family members will have influence beyond that granted by the statutes and cases. Still, if investors in Google expect that owners Sergey Brin and Larry Page (or their heirs) will find it in their personal economic interest to declare dividends, they must be taking a long view indeed. For the foreseeable future, Google's controlling shareholders should be able to consume all they want without sharing the company's largess with the public shareholders.

*2.4.2.2. Leveraged Buyouts and Private Equity.* Family-owned firms combine the ancient problems of aristocracy and capital accumulation. On the one hand, inheritance is an ineffective system for finding talented and skilled leaders, and on the other, few families have enough assets to finance a large modern organization. Modern closely held firms usually take a completely conventional approach to the first problem: they are managed by professionals chosen and supervised in more or less the same way as classic Berle and Means firms. As to the second problem, they have been reluctant to abandon the real advantages of diversification and cheap capital that public investors can provide. Accordingly, in the modern era, leveraged buyouts (LBOs) and private equity firms have sought to solve the dividend puzzle without returning to the feudal era, and specifically without depending on individual or family owners.

In a leveraged buyout, a firm converts most of its equity into debt. Often the limited amount of equity left is transferred in large part to the professional managers. The upshot is that the company is closely held, but the investors remain public, relabeled debt holders rather than shareholders. Private equity firms function in much the same way: they raise their own capital from their own passive equity investors and in the debt markets, from more or less the same pools of funds that finance the public equity market and the debt market that underpins LBOs, and use those funds to take companies private, often causing the company to issue still more debt in the process and usually with the same transfer of equity in the underlying operating company to incumbent managers.

For current purposes, the common elements between these ways of financing firms using bank or publicly held debt are more important than the differences. In each case, the operating firm remains under institutional – not family – control, generally with the same professional managers that it had prior to the transaction. In each case the professionals usually receive a significant part of the remaining equity, which (depending on the details of the deal) may offer the possibility of vastly higher returns than professionals have traditionally been able to command. The new executive compensation schemes appear to have the possibility of higher volatility as well, but in practice that possibility seems to materialize only rarely.

Significantly, the vehicles change the firm's relationship to the public capital markets in similar, and similarly limited, ways. In each case, widely held equity is replaced by almost as widely held debt. The debt market, to be sure, is less liquid and more institutionalized than the equity market. But in each case, the investors are largely institutions with expertise in investing rather than operating – both the former stockholders and the new debt holders are from Wall Street rather than Main Street, specialists in gathering financial assets from the public and deploying them in the capital markets rather than in actually running businesses. And in each case, the investors remain passive, with no effective means of control over the corporation.

Even when buyout or private investment firms exercise control over the managers of the underlying corporations, nothing fundamental has changed. Even Berle and Means corporations have division heads whose autonomy is limited by the presence of superior officers; the LBO and private equity firms, like the head office of the conglomerates they are descended from, merely add another layer of professionals policing professionals. In short, even after the LBO or private equity buyout, the investors remain basically passive pools of retirement and endowment funds, and the company remains basically run by professional managers.

Passive debt investors are more or less the same as passive equity investors, and the capital they provide to the firm is more or less interchangeable, with one major distinction. Unlike equity, debt has legally enforceable rights to specified returns at specified times and therefore has a positive marginal cost.

At first glance, that debt investors have enforceable rights to tangible, time-bound returns might seem to solve the dividend puzzle (where, as described above, rational firms would never distribute dividends and thus rational investors would never invest). Firms that pay interest, unlike firms that pay dividends, are legally bound to pay, and so public investors can invest based on reason and not faith alone.[21] One might imagine, then, that the public equity market was an oddity, a speculatively driven moment between debt-dominated public markets (the 19th century railroads, the post-World War II boom), and a return to debt-dominated public markets through LBOs and private equity. The Japanese and German systems, which have often seemed anomalous to American observers in their dependence on bank financing, would instead appear as paradigms of dependence on debt. It would become clear that at least over the long run, we differ not because of our deeper stock markets but because of our deeper, and less bank-dominated, debt markets.

But the world is not that simple. So long as the equity market does not collapse, a debt-financed firm in a competitive market will face competitors that remain equity financed. They should have lower marginal costs (since in any given period they need not pay for their equity capital) and therefore be able to out-compete debt-financed firms. Thus, it is not immediately obvious how debt-financed firms survive the absence of a collapse of the equity market.

Most explanations of the LBO phenomenon have assumed that LBOs compete by being more efficient. Proponents have pointed to the strong incentives on managers, particularly if they hold some of the highly leveraged stub stock. As a stick, they must generate enough cash flow to pay the debt or face bankruptcy and the possibility of disgrace or displacement. As a carrot, if they generate cash flow beyond the claims of the debt, it rapidly increases the value of their stockholdings.

Unfortunately for this explanation, the basic problem remains that LBO firms must pay for their capital, whereas the dividend puzzle is precisely that equity markets appear willing to provide capital for free. It is hard to see why the LBO structure's more expensive capital and closer supervision by the capital markets would increase innovation. Similarly, neither the carrot nor the stick appears potent enough at the margin to transform managers. Even CEOs without equity stakes are a well-paid and hard-working crowd. The marginal carrot here seems unlikely to strongly motivate dedicated professionals to work harder still – but it does offer those CEOs who are most motivated by their own personal wealth a multitude of new opportunities to extract existing corporate assets instead of working harder to grow them for others. The stick seems equally inadequate: modern bankruptcy reorganization has functioned more often as a business-planning tool than as a disgrace for managers or an existential crisis for the firm.

Increased debt, then, seems unlikely to make firms more efficient. Instead, the key power of debt lies in redistribution. Debt-financed firms may be able to deliver more of the firm's surplus to investors. First, as is well-known, debt financing allows the corporation, in effect, to repeal corporate income tax, shifting to investors corporate resources that otherwise would have gone to the public. Corporate income tax is levied on corporate income, defined more or less along the lines of accounting profit. Dividends are deemed to be paid out of income; interest, in contrast, is deemed to be an expense that reduces income. Thus, if the firm is generating a surplus and retains it or pays it to investors in the form of dividends, it must pay income tax on it. If it pays the same surplus to investors in the form of interest, the payments reduce its net income and avoid corporate income tax.[22] Money that is not paid in income taxes is available for other firm purposes or participants.

The tax story can be generalized. High leverage increases the value of the firm to investors (shareholders plus debt holders) primarily because it is a useful tool for convincing other firm participants to reduce their claims on the corporate pie – redistributing rather than creating wealth. In equity-financed firms, if investors seek a larger share of corporate returns, they must ask employees to take less: "You need to work harder for less pay so that the company will make higher profits so it can voluntarily pay higher dividends." This is a tough position to justify – the cause of upward redistribution does not commonly inspire idealistic sacrifice. Employees are likely to resist, if not by strikes then at least by turnover, slowdown, and reduced morale.

However, in a debt-financed firm, the company can go to the same employees with a very different claim: "If we don't make our interest payment, our corporate survival is at stake. It is time for all members of the team to pitch in." Pulling together for the good of the team is much more inspiring than "reverse Robin Hood." Firms struggling to stay out of bankruptcy may well be able to convince employees to work harder for less – or, if they do end up in reorganization, be able to enlist the court's assistance. But the substance of the two programs is the same. Investors are taking a larger part of the corporate pie, leaving less for everyone else.

*2.4.2.3. The Power of the Credible Threat.* If dominant shareholders or high interest debt-holding investors can simply take the surplus, then the value of company stock (even when passively held) potentially includes the possibility that the company will be sold to a dominant shareholder or levered up. A decade or two ago, most theorists looked to this market for corporate control to solve the problems of passive shareholders.

The intuition was that if managers do not act to maximize surplus and distribute that surplus to shareholders, the company will be worth more held privately than held publicly. Consequently, managers of public companies will face a stark choice. Either they operate the company as if it were already private, or its stock price will decline to the point where arbitrageurs will seek to profit by buying at the low public price and forcing the company to go private or lever up so they can sell at the higher private price. At equilibrium, the public stock market should converge on private market values and managers of public firms should behave as if they were under the supervision of dominant shareholders. In short, the threat that public shareholders might sell control to a dominant shareholder that *would* have effective ownership rights paradoxically can force managers to act as if the public shareholders also were owners, even without the sale ever taking place.

In the heyday of the market for corporate control, in the late 1980s, this picture bore a strong resemblance to reality.[23] The market for corporate control forced managers to act in the interests of the stock market as mediated through the price of the shares. The threat of a junk bond-financed buyout offer ensured that even less leveraged companies shifted company resources to capital from other participants. The actual shareholders, to be sure, had no more authority, power, or legitimacy than in the initial descriptions above, but the stock *market*, by its power to set the price of the company's stock lower than its value in the private or leveraged market, could coerce managers into giving the shares the surplus.

However, the Poison Pill and the "just-say-no" defenses largely emasculated the market for corporate control.[24] It no longer seems powerful enough to solve the dividend puzzle. Shareholders have never had the power to sell the company; the board must first negotiate and approve any potential deal.[25] Nor does fiduciary duty give shareholders significant additional rights – Delaware reviews board decisions regarding when or whether to put a company up for sale with the usual deference given to all other board decisions under the business judgment rule. Boards, not courts, shareholders or contracts, determine the time frame within which corporations operate.[26] Hostile takeovers worked by stepping out of this framework. Instead of selling the company, shareholders sold their shares (and votes) to a buyer which could then control the firm's internal political process, electing a board that would do its bidding. The Poison Pill, its statutory equivalents and the judicial approval of "just say no" defenses eliminated this end-run. With the new legal rules in place, sales of control blocks of shares are governed by basically the same rules as sales of the company – as a practical matter, both require advance approval by the board prior to shareholder action. Accordingly, just as the board may decide to defer dividends to a future that need never arrive, so too may it defer changes in control indefinitely, largely independent of shareholder or substantive judicial views.

Under this legal regime, the market for corporate control replicates the dividend puzzle rather than solving it. If managers choose not to privatize or lever, shareholders have no way of making them do so. If managers decide that privatization is in their own interest, they can count on shareholder support at a low price (since shareholders, as a group, are trapped in the company and, as seen earlier, their rational expectations as public shareholders are quite low, they should be happy to sell their limited birthrights for relatively cool messes of lentils). Consequently, the primary beneficiaries of the threat of privatization or levering should be those in control of the transaction: top managers and directors.

In short, if shareholders had the right to force companies to go private or buy them out, we would expect them to use those rights to appropriate the bulk of the corporate surplus. Corporate law has not given shareholders those rights at any time in the modern era. For a brief moment in the 1980s, however, outside arbitrageurs had a relatively unfettered right to buy control blocks of stock and thus control of companies without the consent of the incumbent management. This meant, in effect, that the force of the stock market as a whole – not the corporation's own shareholders – drove the sale of public corporations, because the stock market as a whole determines stock price, and thus made it economically worthwhile, or not, for the arbitrageurs to act. This active hostile market for corporate control could coerce corporations into acting in the interests of the stock market. With the demise of the hostile takeover, however, arbitrage to move a company into the private or highly leveraged markets is possible only with consent of the incumbent managers, and thus one would expect those managers, who in any event are less fungible than shareholders, to obtain the bulk of the proceeds. Even the possibility of going private is not enough to make it likely that public shareholders will earn a return.

## 3. BEYOND MARKET RATIONALITY

We have seen that the legal rights of public stockholders make it quite unlikely that rational public shareholders would expect to earn even a normal return, let alone a share of the corporation's surplus. In markets characterized by economic rationality, shareholders should expect to earn a return only in two scenarios: either in the presence of an active market for hostile takeovers, or in family-controlled companies where not all family members are employed, family ties prevent the insiders from rationally maximizing their own interests without regard for the interests of their relatives, and public shareholders hold stock with rights tied to the rights of the noninsider family members. The latter may be a caricature of the public markets in Canada, Italy, and Korea; the former is a simplified picture of the United States in the boom of the late 1980s. In the vast American investments of the 19th century the public participated, as predicted by these models, largely as debt-holders, not through the stock market. But the modern era American stock market simply defies these predictions.

The stock market is perhaps the economic sector that is closest to the economic model's assumptions of anonymity, absence of outside commitments or values, and maximizing behavior. If it cannot be explained by the rational maximization model, then perhaps it is time to turn to more complex models.

One possibility is that shareholders receive dividends because it is right and just that they do so. The rational actors of economic models are not moved by ideological or moral claims, but real people are. If shareholders have a strong pre-legal moral claim to the residual, even rational actors might expect to receive the residual because of the power of morality, even without help from market, law, or raw power. Perhaps, then, the stock market functions because shareholders have a fundamental justice claim, or believe that others believe they do.

In my view, the normative claim of shareholders to the residual is weak as a rational matter, but powerful as a matter of sociological ideology. Thus, though it is implausible that shareholders receive (or expect to receive) the residual because it *is* just that they do so, it seems likely that the system functions at least in part because many people *believe* that it is. This section, then, explores faith-based economics – the possibility that the market depends on a nonrational belief that dividends will be paid that is strong enough to override rational maximizing behavior, game-theoretical strategies predicated on assumptions that others will behave in a rationally maximizing way, and serious attempts to think about what capitalist (or more general) norms actually require.

### *3.1. Moral Rights*

Moral claims to economic product can stem from a number of sources: creation, need, equity, settled expectations or ownership, contract or agreement, or simple power are perhaps the most likely. None work for passive public shareholders, who did not create the corporate surplus, are poor proxies for the neediest, have not been robbed or defrauded, have neither agreement nor established property rights granting them the surplus, and need ideological justifications precisely because they lack actual power.

If corporate surplus is returns to innovation, surely the party with the strongest claim is the innovators. Often, it will be difficult to tell which corporate participants are the sources of innovations, particularly when the innovations themselves are the product of the collective enterprise rather than individual initiative. Still, passive shareholders, as the purely fungible providers of a purely fungible commodity, are the least likely candidate. Capital is an important contribution to every enterprise, but it is rarely innovative. If the corporate surplus is instead the result of situational or other monopoly, the moral claim of shareholders is even weaker. No one has a pre-legal entitlement to economic rents in a capitalist system.

Moral claims based in need, equity, or settled expectations fare no better than claims based in creation. Shareholders are poor candidates for paternalistic intervention to change the results a free market would generate. First, roughly one quarter of shares are held by extremely wealthy individuals and families and another half are owned by institutions. These shareholders are quite capable of defending their own interests. Second, even smaller shareholders, who may have difficulty bargaining on their own behalf, benefit from the ample protections of a highly sophisticated market, powerful and sophisticated intermediaries and advisors, and the extensive consumer protection and truth in labeling provisions of the federal securities regime. Finally, investment capital is fully mobile and therefore should be able to bargain quite effectively against other corporate participants, most of whom (especially the human employees) suffer from varying degrees of lock-in. Leaving a job is always somewhat traumatic, involving at a minimum changing communities and patterns of life even if not uprooting spouse and children. Finding an alternative IPO or other passive investment is hardly in the same category.

Shareholders, then, should have few claims beyond their actual contractual rights: the right to receive whatever distributions the company makes to them whenever it decides to make them; the right to vote on a basis of one vote/one share for the ultimate corporate decision-makers; and the right to transfer stock, with the associated collective ability to drive the stock price down to the point where the directors may see advantages to going private. As seen earlier, standard economic rational maximizer models cannot explain how those rights can generate shareholder returns.

### *3.2. The Power of Words*

Moral claims need not be correct to be powerful. They need only persuade, and the persuasion need not be logically defensible. If directors are persuaded that shareholders ought to be treated as if they were owners, trust beneficiaries, principals or contractual insurers with an inexplicably favorable deal, they may conclude that shareholders' claim to the surplus is just and right.

The metaphors of ownership and property rights, agency, trust and contract are pervasive in corporate law discourse and management training alike.[27] These metaphors fail as serious attempts to analyze either law or market. But their failure as analysis is, in the end, the best indication of their power. They are not descriptions of the workings of the market, but rather moralistic calls to action; their importance lies in their uniformly pre-Copernican placement of shareholders at the center of the corporate universe.

Ironically, the central pillar of the shareholder value maximization principle is its demand that directors refuse to act as the self-interested, amoral, rational maximizers of economic theory. Instead, it teaches them, they should be a peculiar sort of altruist, working only to maximize the "well-being" of a self-interested, amoral, uncommitted but not particularly rational stock market.

More ironically still, this reverse-Rawlsian altruistic demand that managers promote the interests of the best-off also turns out to be the best available justification for managers helping themselves to an ever larger share of the corporate pie. Shareholder returns are the ideological price managers pay in order to defend the otherwise indefensible: fiduciaries using their trust to enrich themselves.

But this game will not last forever. The more managers are able to pay themselves, the less they look like fiduciaries and the more they look like entrepreneurs or owners. If they are ever able to convince themselves or us to see them in that light, I suspect all the metaphors of shareholder ownership and managerial altruism will fade away, leaving the moral claims of shareholders as weak as their legal ones.

These counter-intuitive contentions are now examined more closely.

### *3.2.1. The Problem of Paying Managers as Fiduciaries*

From one perspective, corporate managers are capitalist free agents who contract with the firm in an arms length transaction governed by the "workaday … morals of the market place" (*Meinhard v. Salmon*, 1928, p. 464). In this role, they are entitled, indeed expected, to sell their work for the highest price they can get. But once hired, corporate managers, including CEOs, are agents of the firm, required by the fiduciary norms of agency law to set aside their own interests and work instead for the interests of the firm.

Directors are not agents – on the contrary, board decisions are acts of the principal itself. But they too have a fiduciary duty to act in the interests of the firm that closely resembles the duty of an agent. Taken seriously, this duty of loyalty also requires "not honesty alone, but the punctilio of an honor the most sensitive" pursuant to which "thought of self was to be renounced, however hard the abnegation" (*ibid.*, pp. 464, 468).[28]

The conflict between these two norms – one praising the self-centered maximizing behavior postulated in simple economic models and ordinarily seen only in sociopaths, and the other requiring extreme altruism of a degree that would qualify the self-abnegating practitioner for sainthood were the goal less mercenary – pervades corporate law (Greenwood, 2004, p. 825). The conflict is most obvious, perhaps, in the question of CEO pay.

If the CEO is working in the interests of the firm and has "renounced all thought of self" why is he paying himself so much? The duty of loyalty means that a faint odor of impropriety necessarily emanates from every CEO pay package, demanding explanation and justification.

For many years, corporate leaders resolved the tension by emphasizing that they were public servants, stewards of the enterprises that provide America's jobs and drive our economy, and thus, like all public servants, entitled to a reasonable professional income. This justification, however, lost its usefulness when CEO perquisites broke ranks with the professions. Democratic leaders are entitled to a decent living. Deriving enormous wealth from a position of stewardship, however, is usually more associated with dictatorship and corruption (Greenwood, 2008).

Beyond the basic requirements of fiduciary duty, moreover, most companies require a degree of employee loyalty to survive and prosper. Employee loyalty, in turn, is best encouraged by appealing to team spirit – convincing the employees that the company's interest is their interest. But the rapidly increasing income and status gaps between CEOs, as team captains, and their employees, as team players, is obviously destructive of *esprit de corps*. A certain degree of egalitarianism is essential to create the sense that "we are all in this together." As a result, any credible organizational theory will have difficulty justifying vast pay or prestige gaps between leaders and those led within an organization.

Relatedly, our publicly traded corporations are bureaucracies, and any bureaucracy is limited by its ability to process information up and down its hierarchy. Vast social gaps between the decision-makers at the top and the actors at the bottom predictably lead to bad decisions and poor implementation. No doubt, there are leaders who are so smart and so charismatic that they can successfully lead without communication from those below them, but they are exceptions. This is why we expect egalitarian capitalist economies to outperform dictatorial ones and why we expect generals who lead from the midst of democratic armies to defeat emperors who rule from distant palaces. Astronomical CEO salaries, prima facie, should look like dereliction of duty if the core of the CEOs duty is to rally the troops or listen to them (assuming the relevant troops are the employees).

### *3.2.2. Appropriating Surplus and the Duty of Loyalty*

Share-centered ideologies do not solve these real sociological problems. Shifting from institutional views to a share-centered view does, however, conceal them.

If the corporation is understood as its shareholders, then managers can reasonably compare their share of the corporate pie to shareholder returns rather than employee pay. A different team means a different comparison group. As leaders of an institution, they were implicitly entitled to be paid as sophisticated professionals, more than but in the same general range as the rest of the bureaucracy. But if the corporation *is* its shareholders and its purpose is returns to shareholding, then managers, as leaders of the pursuit of profit, can reasonably claim a percentage of profits – a far larger sum.

Moreover, if the corporation is its shares, then it is not its employees. One thinks differently about motivating outsiders than insiders, looking less to loyalty and more to carrots and sticks. If the employees are outsiders, then it will seem more reasonable to motivate them by the stick of fear of firing, on the one hand, and on the other, by the carrot of a competitive tournament in which individual executives are motivated to compete against each other in order to win the grand prize. On the view of the firm as fundamentally a team of employees, high CEO pay is likely to look like a sign that the leaders are betraying the team by corruptly lining their own pockets, and thus as an invitation to similar behavior throughout the organization. But if individual executives are seen, instead, as competitors to be motivated by a prize if they win the game, then higher pay for the incumbent CEO looks less like misappropriation of corporate assets and more like a stronger motivation to his subordinates.

Furthermore, if the central problem of corporate leadership is not overcoming the bureaucratic problems of communication but rather assuring that CEOs have common interests with shareholders, then high CEO pay can appear as a solution instead of a central part of the problem. High pay, after all, will make CEOs more like capitalists than employees, and high pay tied to stock returns will do so even more. Pay them enough, and perhaps they will begin to feel the difference between themselves and their subordinates, creating exactly the break in empathy that is necessary for a regime that motivates by threats of layoffs and competitions in which only a few can win. Make them rich enough, and they may begin to think of the company in the risk-neutral manner of diversified portfolios.

For each of these reasons, the share-centered view of the corporation justifies high CEO perquisites. CEOs thus have a tremendous incentive to accept and promote the share-centered metaphors: in the share-centered corporation, they are doing their duty by making themselves into the new American aristocracy.

The share-centered ideologies can be psychologically useful even beyond justifying high CEO pay. For directors and managers, they appear to solve the biggest conundrum of their position. Fiduciary duties are owed to the firm itself. But firms are not preexisting natural entities endowed by our Creator with unalienable Rights and self-evident interests. Rather, the very fiduciaries who are charged with working in its interest also may set and reset the firm's boundaries, members, goals, and purposes, thereby defining what it is and what its interests might be even as they aim to serve them. Directors and managers who attempt to think seriously about their responsibilities will discover that far from being "firm" the object of their fiduciary duty is much like the poet's description of Oakland: there is no there there (Stein, 1937, ch. 4). The share-centered ideologies replace this dizzying indeterminacy with easily understandable and calculable directions: maximize the returns of an imaginary, undiversified stock investor with no commitments to firm or society beyond the stockholding itself. Easy answers are often wrong, but ease alone can make them attractive.

Finally, so long as investors believe that they are entitled to the corporate surplus, they are likely to expect that they will receive it, and so long as they expect to receive it, they will value stocks as if they were going to receive it. In turn, as Miller and Modigliani correctly pointed out, if shareholders will ultimately receive the surplus, they should be indifferent as to when they receive it. Even if dividends or other distributions are deferred, some other investor should be willing to purchase the stock based on expected future distributions – and the stock market, collectively, can go up based on new investor savings and expected profits rather than actual distributions. The perpetual motion machine is in the short-term interest of every decision maker in the game.

### *3.2.3. Where Shareholder Returns Come from*

The short answer to the puzzle of shareholder returns, then, is this: shareholders receive returns because investors, directors, and CEOs believe they are entitled to them.

The underlying faith in the rightness of operating the corporation for the shares is not based on any compelling economic, moral, or legal argument. However, CEOs who consciously or unconsciously need a justification for seizing a significant part of the corporate surplus for themselves find the share-centered metaphors of the corporation more comfortable than the alternatives.

CEOs, unlike shareholders, have actual economic and political power in the corporation. They use that power to pay dividends and otherwise act to keep stock prices relatively high because the share-centered ideology tells them they should. They subscribe to the share-centered ideology because it offers the best available justification for their own perquisites. Meanwhile, investors, believing that they will get the corporate surplus in the end, act in a way that makes it largely irrelevant that they are only partly receiving it in the meantime.

Outside the chief executive's office, the share-centered metaphors also have some appeal: they offer an explanation of a world that would otherwise seem unfair, exploitative, anti-democratic, and dysfunctional. If corporations exist for the sake of their shareholders, then perhaps their employees, customers, and neighbors have no legitimate complaint when they are treated as no more than means to an end that is not their own. And if one is being treated that way, it may be more appealing to have an explanation than simply a simmering sense of injustice.

Cynically, simplistic, unprofessional, and uninteresting as this explanation is, it must be a major part of the truth. The great secret of the manager–shareholder conflict at the heart of corporate law is that, conflicts notwithstanding, the shareholder-centered view unites managers and shareholders to shift the corporate surplus from all the other corporate participants. Only then do the arguments over the spoils begin.

In the end, both the political and the market power of public shareholders are quite limited. Most politics is by informal persuasion, in the shadow of the law, the barrel of a gun, or the power of the electorate. In public corporations, shares have votes, but anonymous, transient, unorganized, and fungible shareholders have little connection with the actual institutional firm.

The basic protection shareholders have today is the principle that all shares must be treated equally when a dividend is declared and the assumption that stockholding managers will, in the end, want to issue dividends – both to extract larger sums from the corporation than they feel they can award themselves in salary and to maintain the value of their own stock or options. That said, when managers determine that their interests are no longer aligned with the other shareholders, there will not be much the outside shareholders can do about it.

And in the end, managers are likely to find that the public stock market has outlived its usefulness. The share-centered ideologies taught CEOs to treat the actual human beings with whom they work as mere means to an end, as tools to be exploited in the cause of profit maximization. But the only justification this ideology offers for why managers, who have trained themselves to betray the people with whom they work, should then altruistically turn their gains over to market abstractions, is a mélange of metaphorical claims that shareholders own the company.

Top managers largely control the corporation. They have now established that, unlike other employees, they are critical to the corporation's success and that corporate profits should be viewed as their own marginal product, entitling them to be paid (in the interest of shares) like entrepreneurs. In short, they have the control that characterizes owners, they perform the basic ownership function of making critical decisions, and they take a large part of the residual. For at least two decades, top managers have regularly used their control of the corporation to make themselves shareholders, thus giving themselves the ideological mantle of owners entitled to appropriate the corporate surplus, instead of mere officeholders able to do so. Not surprisingly, the premiums offered to the public shareholders to approve these transactions have decreased over time. The remaining issue is how much longer it will take to find a new language in which to discuss still-public corporations, allowing top managers to take the surplus without paying to take the company private.

## 4. CONCLUSION

Shareholders are not entitled to the residual by law, justice, nature, or even economic bargains and incentives. Accordingly, shareholder expectations of returns are more fragile than generally assumed, the economic consequences of changes in shareholder rights probably would be less than generally assumed, and there is no reason to think that the current distribution of corporate surplus is more or less efficient than alternative ones.

Instead, the struggle for the corporate surplus – the residual – is a political struggle over economic rents. No party has any special claim to them precisely because the surplus would not exist but for the contribution of all the claimants. From an economic perspective, the shareholders, as fully fungible providers of a fully fungible commodity, have a weaker claim than most. From a political perspective, the power of the shareholder claim depends on the power of the shareholder role, which, as we have seen, is more limited than a casual student of corporate governance literature might imagine.

The key weapons the shares have are two. First, they have an ideological claim to entitlement, founded in the metaphors of ownership, contract, and agency.[29] The claim embodies its own critique: it is only because public shareholders are *not* owners or principals and do *not* have legal rights to corporate residual that their defenders feel the need to so strenuously insist that they are and do. In the end, the claim that shares ought to be treated as if they had more rights then they do is simply a demand for reverse Robin Hood upward redistribution of wealth.

Second, in recent decades top management has found the rhetoric, and sometimes the reality, of share-centeredness useful for its own purposes. Managers, nearly everyone agrees, are fiduciaries for the corporation with no independent claim to ownership or entitlement. So long as this remains the law and the social understanding, CEOs must justify their actions as being on behalf of the corporation, not themselves. The share-centered views of the corporation conveniently rationalize high CEO pay and perquisites – if CEOs are major shareholders, they are more likely to think like shareholders than like employees. Moreover, by viewing the stock market rather than the bureaucracy as central to corporate life, the share-centered metaphors distract attention from the ineffectiveness of our modern CEO aristocrats and their failure to create decent jobs at decent wages.

The theory of economic determinism failed in the communist regimes. It fares no better in the capitalist ones. In the end, we must decide through politics, not economics, how much power we wish to give to the stock market, how much to democratic processes, and how much to leave to unguided professionals in semi-autonomous quasi-private organizations. The distribution of the surplus is part of the issue, but the more fundamental issues are how we want our public corporations to operate, towards which goals, and with what relationship to the people who make them up. So far, the defense of the share-centered corporation has proceeded mainly by invoking rhetorical claims to a shareholder supremacy that simply does not exist. But metaphors of ownership or agency are no substitute for social analysis – the question is not whether shareholders "are" owners of the corporation, but whether pretending they have so much power in the corporate governance structure is good for society as a whole.

The alliance of convenience between CEOs and the stock market has proven only partially productive, creating cheap goods but failing to produce enough good jobs outside the upper echelons. The metaphors of share ownership have obscured the real world power structures. The academic task is, first, to fully elucidate the false metaphors, and second, to shift the debate's imagery to metaphors that illuminate instead of concealing. The political task is to find a model which produces wealth for all, not just a small elite; which promotes decent work places and productive careers, not just consumers' playgrounds; and which respects our ecosphere, not just a narrow vision of the econosphere.

# NOTES

1. "Rents," as the term is used in economic analysis, refer to disequilibrium surplus that can be distributed to any participant without changing the underlying use of resources. Any payment to a factor of production in excess of its marginal cost, which is what it would receive in a fully competitive market, is a rent – a value transferred to one party without the other one getting something equal in return. Conflicts over rents involve attempts to appropriate existing resources rather than developing new ones. On the concept of "rents" as used in the public choice and law and economics literature, see, for example, Sachs and Warner (2001), Buchanan, Tullock, and Tollison (1988), McChesney (1987), and Kelman (1988, p. 227) (describing rent-seeking, when it is worthy of condemnation, and ambiguities in concept).

2. Legal "surplus" is closer to accounting profit than economic surplus or residual (Del. Code Ann. tit 8 Section 154).

3. Compare Warren Buffet's famous investment advice to invest only in companies with a "franchise" – by which he means some ability to charge more than the commodity price.

4. As Blair and Stout (2001) point out, this is one of the key benefits of the corporate form.

5. See Del. Code Ann. tit. 8 Sections 141, 203; *Smith v. Van Gorkum* (1985) (holding that directors may not delegate determination of whether to sell company to shareholders); *Paramount v. Time* (1989) (court may not "substitut[e] its judgment as to what is a 'better' deal for that of a corporation's board").

6. When shareholders can threaten credibly to take the company private, the situation changes. See Section 2.4.2.

7. See, for example, *Paramount v. Time* (1989) ("The fiduciary duty to manage a corporate enterprise includes the selection of a time frame for achievement of corporate goals. That duty may not be delegated to the stockholders.").

8. Even where there is no obvious advantage to standardization, it still often remains more important to go to the same movies, listen to the same music, wear the same clothes, or join the same club as our peers than it is to find the best of those products. See, for example, Hansmann (1980, p. 892) (describing this phenomenon in the context of country clubs). When a cascade occurs, the producer of the favored product may be able to charge monopoly prices despite the existence of competitors. Even if the competing product has similar technical specifications, without the customer base, it cannot provide true substitutability.

9. Micklethwait and Wooldridge (2003) (describing J. P. Morgan's attempts to raise prices above marginal cost by suppressing "ruinous competition").

10. The discussion may seem slightly strange to readers used to thinking of investors as buyers of securities rather than sellers of capital. From that perspective, the product – the securities – is not quite as fungible. Securities vary not only in price but in expected return, risk, legal and market enforceability, time frames, and so on. But the inversion of perspectives changes nothing fundamental. For securities buyers, firms appear mainly as bundles of risk and return, and portfolio theory teaches that bonds and stocks are just different ways to allocate proceeds from the same pool. As Modigliani and Miller teach, the firm's ability to generate returns to capital is fundamental; its division of (economic) profit between different securities is merely contingent.

11. Theorists have contended that shareholders provide risk-bearing services to the firm, absorbing short-term business shifts that are more expensive for other, less diversified, corporate participants to bear. I find this claim somewhat implausible – dividends generally seem to be more stable than employment, not less as ought to be the case if the stock market were in the insurance business. But for current purposes, we can accept the claim and note that nowhere else in the economy do insurers expect to share in extraordinary profits earned by the insured. Risk-bearing services, even if rendered, do not change the analysis in the text.

12. The problem is a variant of the well-known market for lemons issue (Akerlof, 1970).

13. See, for example, Lowenstein (1991, p. 125) (describing instances in which managers did not pass on economic profits to shareholders, but instead used them to expand, diversify, etc.).

14. Employee Retirement Income Security Act.

15. The real explanation of tips starts with recognizing that people are not normally maximizers. However, shareholders, most of which are institutions under strong market pressures to short-term profit maximization, are far more likely to maximize than human beings. Within maximizing theory, the economics of tips is a well-known mystery, since rational maximizers presumably would free-ride, at least when they do not expect to return to the restaurant or need to impress a date. See, for example, Kahneman, Knetsch, and Thaler (1986).

16. *Aaronson v. Lewis* (1984): "A cardinal precept of the General Corporation Law of the State of Delaware is that directors, rather than shareholders, manage the business and affairs of the corporation."

17. See, for example, Del. Code Ann. tit. 8 Section 228 (right of shareholders to act without a meeting by unanimous consent); Section 141 (k); (removal of directors without cause); Section 109 (right of shareholders to amend bylaws); Section 141 (b) (right of corporation to modify the size of its board by bylaws).

18. In contrast, in public corporations, courts may impose their own view of the "real" interests of shareholders or the corporation instead of the expressed will of actual shareholders, individually or collectively. See *Dodge v. Ford Motor Co.* (overruling majority shareholder's view of dividend policy), *State ex rel. Pillsbury v. Honeywell* (1971) (declaring actual views of actual shareholder irrelevant); *Paramount v. Time* (1989) (ignoring expressed views of majority of shares); *Revlon v. MacAndrews & Forbes* (1986) (holding that corporation must act in interests of "shareholders" imagined to have no interests beyond their shareholdings); *Unocal Corp. v. Mesa Petroleum Co.* (1985) (holding that some shareholders are less equal than others). See generally, Greenwood (1996).

19. So long as there are minority shareholders with standing to bring complaints of breach of fiduciary duty, there will be judicially imposed limits on the ownership rights of the dominant shareholder. The board of directors has a fiduciary obligation to act in the interests of the corporation, and dominant shareholders may have fiduciary obligations to minority shareholders. However, these fiduciary duties are limited by the business judgment rule; courts remain quite deferential to the internal corporate decision-making processes so long as dominant shareholders and their boards respect corporate formalities.

20. But see *Unocal Corp. v. Mesa Petroleum Co.* (1985) (allowing discrimination against particular shares based on the identity of their owner as "greenmailer").

21. The difference between debt and equity should not be overexaggerated. The contract's right to interest is limited to company assets. Debt investors, thus, must persuade themselves that the company will be able to repay its debts when due. For long-term debt, this may be almost as much a leap of faith as equity investment. It is relatively easy for managers to choose, for example, to make short-term gambles, knowing that they will be able to appropriate gains (as pay or other perquisites) while imposing losses on debt-holders (or, as regularly happens in financial crises, the taxpayers).

22. Taxation at the investor level may create countervailing pressures. However, many of our largest investors are tax insensitive (e.g., retirement plans, endowments, mutual funds).

23. See note 1.

24. Del. Code Ann. tit. 8 Section 203 (statutory pill); *Moran v. Household Int'l* (1985) (upholding pill); *Paramount Communications, Inc. v. Time Incorporated* (1989) (upholding just say no).

25. Del. Code Ann. tit. 8 Section 141 (powers of board); *Smith v. Van Gorkom* (1985) (holding that board must exercise its fiduciary duty to determine whether sale of the company is in its best interests prior to allowing shareholders to vote), ratified and modified by Del. Code Ann. tit. 8 Section 146 (permitting board to agree to allow shareholders to vote with a recommendation that they reject should later developments cause it to reverse its initial approval).

26. *Paramount Communications, Inc. v. Time Incorporated* (1989) (upholding the right of board to determine the time frame in which the company operates). I oversimplify, of course. Once the company is up for sale or the board takes targeted defensive measures, judicial scrutiny increases, although it remains largely procedural. See, for example, *Omnicare, Inc. v. NCS Healthcare, Inc.* (2003) (fn. 36–40) (emphasizing that even an "enhanced scrutiny" of the "reasonableness of the substantive merits of the board's actions" is largely procedural – devoted to establishing the "adequacy of the decision-making process" and evaluating the merits only to determine if they were "within a range of reasonableness" "in the context in which action was taken.").

27. For preliminary discussions of the metaphors of corporate law, see Greenwood (2005b); Greenwood (2004, Parts IV.A, IV.B.3); Greenwood (2005a).

28. The duty of loyalty clearly bars corporate fiduciaries from promoting their own interests at the expense of the corporation's. Cardozo notwithstanding, however, corporate law's duty of loyalty is quite a bit weaker than the equivalent duties in trust law or governmental civil service norms, let alone the punctilio of an honor most sensitive. Nepotism, conflicts of interest, and even what Boss Tweed unsuccessfully defended as "clean graft" typically are permitted in the corporate sector, at least with adequate disclosure and approval by disinterested parties. See *Bayer v. Beran* (1944) (allowing the corporation to hire the CEO's spouse so long as the corporation was no worse off than if it had hired a third party); Del. Code Ann. tit. 8 Section 144 (2006) (regulating ratification of interested transactions). This rule is often an appropriate response to information problems: insiders may be willing to provide better terms than could be had in arms length transactions and apparently corrupt transactions may have benefits that are not obvious to outsiders. However, the information problems are identical in the public sector and, indeed, seem

more likely to be correlated to scale than business form, so the explanation does not justify the difference between public sector and corporate norms. More likely, the acceptance of nepotism in the corporate world is a reflection of the survival of the personalized norms of feudal loyalty (epitomized in modern law in the property right to be idiosyncratic and the employer's right to fire at will), while the public sector has more completely adopted the market and bureaucratic norms of anonymity reflected in notions of single price, careers open to talent, equality before the law, and anti-discrimination law.

29. See note 28.

## ACKNOWLEDGMENTS

Special thanks to Dean Kellye Testy, Dana Gold and the Seattle University School of Law for organizing the conference where this chapter was first presented, and to Bill Bratton, Tim Glynn, Kent Greenfield and fellow participants for their helpful comments.

## REFERENCES

Akerlof, G. A. (1970). The market for "lemons": Quality uncertainty and the market mechanism. *Quarterly Journal of Economics, 84*, p. 488.

Arthur, B. (1990). Positive feedbacks in the economy. *Scientific American, 92*(February).

Blair, M., & Stout, L. (2001). Director accountability. *Washington University Law Quarterly, 79*, pp. 403, 406.

Brealey, R. A., & Myers, S. C. (1996). *Principles of corporate finance* (5th ed.). New York, NY: McGraw-Hill.

Buchanan, J., Tullock, G., & Tollison, R. (1980). *Toward a theory of the rent seeking society*. College Station, TX: Texas A & M University Press.

Carroll, L. (1871). *Through the looking glass and what alice found there*. London: The Macmillan Company.

Chandler, A. D., Jr. (1990). *Scale & scope: The dynamics of industrial capitalism*. Cambridge, MA: Harvard University Press.

Coase, R. H. (1937). The nature of the firm. *Economica, 4*, p. 386.

Coase, R. H. (1946). The marginal cost controversy. *Economica, 13*, p. 169.

Coase, R. H. (1960). The problem of social costs. *Journal of Law and Economics, 3*, p. 1.

Greenwood, D. (1996). Fictional shareholders: 'For whom is the corporation managed,' Revisited. *Southern California Law Review, 69*, p. 1021.

Greenwood, D. (2004). Enronitis: Why good corporations go bad. *Columbia Business Law Review, 2004*, pp. 773, 818.

Greenwood, D. (2005a). Introduction to the metaphors of corporate law. *Seattle Journal for Social Justice, 4*, p. 273.

Greenwood, D. (2005b). Markets & democracy: The illegitimacy of corporate law. *University of Missouri-Kansas City Law Review*, *74*, p. 41.

Greenwood, D. (2006). The dividend puzzle: Are shares entitled to the residual? *Journal of Corporation Law*, *32*, 103–159.

Greenwood, D. (2008). The puzzle of private equity: The rape and pillage problem. *Brooklyn Journal of Corporate, Financial and Commercial Law*, *3*, p. 92.

Hansmann, H. (1980). The role of nonprofit enterprise. *Yale Law Journal*, *89*, pp. 835, 892.

Kahneman, D., Knetsch, J. L., & Thaler, R. (1986). Fairness as a constraint on profit seeking: Entitlements in the market. *American Economic Review*, *76*(4), 728–741.

Kelman, M. (1988). On democracy-bashing: A skeptical look at the theoretical and "empirical" practice of the public choice movement. *Virginia Law Review*, *74*, p. 227.

Lowenstein, L. (1991). *Sense and nonsense in corporate finance*. Reading, MA: Addison-Wesley.

McChesney, F. (1987). Rent extraction and rent creation. *Journal of Legal Studies*, *16*, p. 101.

Micklethwait, J., & Wooldridge, A. (2003). *The company: A short history of a revolutionary idea*. New York, NY: Modern Library.

Modigliani, F., & Miller, M. (1958). The cost of capital, corporation finance, and the theory of investment. *American Economic Review*, *48*(3), 261–297.

Sachs, J. D., & Warner, A. M. (2001). The curse of natural resources. *European Economic Review*, *45*, p. 827.

Stein, G. (1937). *Everybody's autobiography*. London: William Heinemann Publishing.

Stout, L., & Blair, M. (2006). Specific investment. *Journal of Corporate Law*, *31*, p. 719.

Utset, M. (2003). A theory of self-control problems and incomplete contracting: The case of shareholder contracts. *Utah Law Review*, *2003*, p. 1329.

## Laws and Statutes

Del. Code Ann. tit. 8 Sections 141, 144, 154, 170, 203, 228.

Uniform Partnership Act (U.P.A.) Sections 31, 38.

## Cases

*Aaronson v. Lewis*, 473 A.2d 805, 811 (Del. 1984).

*Bayer v. Beran*, 49 N.Y.S.2d 2, 10 (N.Y. Sup. Ct. 1944).

*Dodge v. Ford Motor Co.*, 170 N.W. 668 (Mich. 1919).

*Meinhard v. Salmon*, 164 N.E. 545 (N.Y. 1928).

*Moran v. Household Int'l*, 500 A.2d 1346 (Del. 1985).

*Omnicare, Inc. v. NCS Healthcare, Inc.* (Del. 2003).

*Paramount v. Time*, 571 A.2d 1140 (Del. 1989).

*Paramount Communications, Inc. v. Time Incorporated*, 571 A.2d 1140 (Del. 1989).

*Revlon v. MacAndrews & Forbes*, 506 A.2d 173 (Del. 1986).

*Smith v. Van Gorkom*, 488 A.2d 858 (Del. 1985).

*State ex rel. Pillsbury v. Honeywell*, 191 N.W.2d 406 (Minn. 1971).

*Unocal Corp. v. Mesa Petroleum Co.*, 493 A.2d 946 (Del. 1985).

# CORPORATE SOCIAL RESPONSIBILITY: LESSONS FROM THE SOUTH ON LAW AND BUSINESS NORMS

Claire Moore Dickerson


## ABSTRACT

*Corporate social responsibility describes the role that society expects of business organizations. Because it is difficult to see societal norms in one's own society, comparative law can help us increase the salience of those norms in our own community. Looking at how a set of business laws uniform across 16 West and Central African countries lives in one of the member states, Cameroon, we see that society expresses its norms not only when behavior tracks the positive law, but also, and very importantly, when it diverges from that law. After studying examples of divergence in the South, specifically in the African country Cameroon, the chapter turns to the North. Using the United States as the illustration, and focusing on the role of business entities, the chapter identifies ways of opening the discussion among all political constituents, even those outside the traditional business community.*


**Law & Economics: Toward Social Justice**
**Research in Law and Economics: A Journal of Policy, Volume 24, 131–157**

**ISSN: 0193-5895/doi:10.1108/S0193-5895(2009)0000024010**

# 1. INTRODUCTION

Among legal professionals, a discussion of the corporation's role in society focuses on applicable laws. That is not surprising: we tend to value our own stock-in-trade. Law professors question the appropriateness of corporate governance statutes by considering what managerial behavior they encourage, and activists bring suits to attack specific provisions they consider nonproductive. These efforts come both from the left and the right, and they confirm the importance of national laws.

That, at least, is how things look from the North. In Cameroon, where I spent three months in the course of two years, I explored the limits of national laws' usefulness in influencing business organizations. Business in the South can take shape relatively untrammeled by business laws, but research in Cameroon confirms that business does get done. This research reveals three fundamental concepts. First, corporate social responsibility is deeply political. That is, society's determination of the role that corporations are to play within that community is political. Typically, the desired role falls somewhere along a spectrum that at one end allocates all interests to owners, a model often called "shareholder primacy," and at the other end allocates those interests across a wider range of stakeholders, including some combination of employers, suppliers, customers, and sometimes even some portion of the local community.

Second, corporate governance standards embedded in the business laws have a limited ability to channel corporate behavior, especially in the face of divergent cultural norms. These points of divergence appear when there is persistent disobedience of legal norms or when players are systematically behaving "better" than the legal standard requires. The third basic concept is that these behaviors help reveal the cultural norms that undergird the relevant community's true understanding of corporate social responsibility.

A comparative study finds parallels in the North, specifically in the United States: corporate social responsibility is a political phenomenon; corporate governance laws implement the corporate social responsibility norm and simultaneously both influence and are defined by that overarching norm. Because the split between national laws and applicable culture is not as marked in the North as in the South, corporate governance laws in the United States do tend to implement, and thus to reflect, the applicable corporate social responsibility norm. Where, instead, corporate governance laws diverge from behavior, corporate social responsibility is again highlighted by the dissonance.

These are not surprising conclusions, but the comparative study reveals with particular force the unreliability of national law to any effort to modify corporate social responsibility, unless the effort is focused on areas of divergence. This chapter will accordingly look for and at divergence between law and social norms.

Finally, the study suggests that national law, even when weak or countercultural, can still play a role as vocabulary and forum for discussing both corporate social responsibility and corporate governance. Because business in the South is often not conducted in corporate form, I am using the terms "corporate social responsibility" and "corporate governance" to apply to any business enterprise, whatever form it takes.

## 2. SOUTH: CORPORATE SOCIAL RESPONSIBILITY, CORPORATE GOVERNANCE, AND THE REALITY OF OHADA'S BUSINESS LAWS

The starting point of the comparative study is a review of specific, national business laws applicable in the South. The focus of this analysis is a system of business laws operational in West and Central Africa.

### *2.1. OHADA: Political Tool on a Developing Economy's Small-Scale Map*

In 1993, the political authorities of 14 West and Central African states signed a treaty ("OHADA Treaty") to create a regime whose center point is a uniform system of laws; there now are 16 state parties to the treaty. Pursuant to that treaty, the eight uniform laws already adopted under OHADA, the first of which came into effect in 1998, are automatically part of each contracting state's internal laws (OHADA Treaty and Uniform Acts [UAs]).[1] The laws and the institutions that make them are collectively called (in English) the Organization for the Harmonization in Africa of Business Laws, or "OHADA."[2]

Importantly, pushed by a very difficult economic climate and facilitated by highly centralized political systems, the contracting parties adopted OHADA for the articulated purpose of increasing investment, and in particular foreign investment (Dickerson, 2005, p. 20, note 3). If OHADA increases the predictability of commercial transactions, it will reduce the foreign investors' transaction costs and thus increase the host country's attractiveness as a center for investment.

All but two of the current members of OHADA are former French colonies and therefore had been applying old versions of French law before the advent of OHADA; the eight OHADA uniform acts are influenced by modern French law. Because the governments' expressed first line of attack was to encourage foreigners to invest, they sought a system that would be familiar to business people from the North. The goal was to reassure investors about the predictability of legal protections.

On the practical level, OHADA does start with an advantage: as local legal professionals confirm, the terms and provisions of its uniform acts are more readily available than were many of the prior laws. Although the OHADA uniform acts are not "codes" in the sense of the French Civil Code, they are simple and straightforward on the whole, making the laws remarkably accessible in an environment where it has been difficult even for local legal professionals to know what the law is. Where internet databases are beyond reach, the principal source for all eight uniform acts is a single volume roughly the size of a thick paperback, containing both text and scholarly commentary. Further, the OHADA acts' uniformity magnifies the benefits of accessibility: what legal professionals and business people learn in one OHADA country applies to the other contracting states.

In addition to the business laws, OHADA provides various supranational institutions, including a legislature and a court. The legislature, the Council of Ministers, is made up the contracting states' justice and finance ministers. The supranational court, the Common Court of Justice and Arbitration ("CCJA"), receives appeals from the contracting states' second-highest national courts on matters relating to OHADA law (OHADA Treaty, articles 13–16). The CCJA's decisions are published both on paper and on the internet,[3] thereby introducing some transparency from the top and simultaneously protecting the laws' uniformity of interpretation and application. This is the juridical context of OHADA law (Dickerson, 2005).

Although the contracting states collectively took a bold step by signing the OHADA Treaty, even on a small-scale map that covers a large area in little detail, there are both practical and conceptual issues. By definition, the OHADA regime is a transplant from the North, and as such its authenticity is automatically in doubt (Berkowitz, Pistor, & Richard, 2003, pp. 185–186; Teubner, 1998, pp. 14–32; Watson, 1996, pp. 339–340, 346–351). Or, more precisely, an observer cannot be certain how the law will present when it is actually put into operation. That we will see clearly when we move to the detailed, large-scale image and study how the law functions on the ground.

We can, however, glean at least the publicized intention of the finance and justice ministers when, functioning as the legislative Council of Ministers, they adopt specific provisions of the uniform acts.

For example, the uniform act on commercial law has provisions concerning commercial leases that include terms relatively favorable to the lessee (Teghen, Registrar-in-Chief, Limbe Court, 2005). Interestingly, foreign investors historically have tended to rent rather than own. Thus, these provisions in the local context do indeed appear favorable to the classic foreign direct investor, which serves OHADA's stated goal of promoting foreign investment.

If that is the appearance, the reality of course depends on how well the lease terms are enforced. That, in its turn, depends on the government's willingness to allow causes of action to go forward. As a practical matter, the answer is at least partially political. Local professionals complain that recovery pursuant to the OHADA insolvency law is dangerously favorable to debtors, which is surprising given that foreign direct investors tend to be creditors. The political reality, however, can be at odds with the law's precise wording – even in the case where the foreigner in fact is a debtor. For example, legal professionals report an instance in which the government protected foreign capital by blocking law suits against a foreign debtor, because even the concededly pro-debtor language of the law was deemed to offer the foreign debtor insufficient protection. The case, much talked about in legal circles, involves a Cameroonian bank whose Cameroonian judgment creditor sought to reach assets in the bank's account at the central bank. The local legal professionals assert that foreign interests behind the central bank teamed with the Cameroonian bank to petition the government, which then interceded to prevent execution of the judgment. The government knew how to protect the foreign direct investor, unimpeded by local laws.

Although the government's demonstrated leanings in favor of foreign direct investment does not necessarily describe the role of the corporation, or more generally the role of business in society, it may hint at what the government excludes from a definition of corporate social responsibility. Even if the purpose of business organizations in the South is broadly defined to encourage, and therefore to protect, foreign direct investment, that is not necessarily incompatible with a norm to protect certain domestic sectors or certain resources, including human resources. Transparency and predictability of enforcement would continue to encourage foreign direct investment even if the government imposed some standards. Thus, a government that to all evidence protects foreign business entities' investments but not their own host-country workers defines by its behavior a pro-capital, anti-labor role for business organizations. Its national laws may appear to guarantee workers' rights, but if the political will to enforce them is lacking, the laws are, as a functional matter, nonexistent.

OHADA offers a doctrinal understanding that corporate law supports at least some rights of workers; the issue is how to convince governments to respect and enforce their own laws. Scholarly writings describe the overarching standard of performance for OHADA corporations as "*intérêt social*," a French conception inherited through OHADA law. This principle, variously translated as "social interest" or "corporate interest," charges the corporation to take into account the entire interest of the corporation (Koné, 2003, pp. 16, 18–19; Paillusseau, 1967). In the absence of any special arrangements, multinationals investing in the OHADA territory will be subject to the principle of corporate interest because the company law provides that a foreign business with its statutory headquarters in an OHADA country must operate through or reconstitute as a domestic company (UA Company Law, article 120).

Where the corporate-interest norm does apply, it is not yet clear whether OHADA will lean toward the minimum view that describes the corporate interest as, essentially, the owners' interest, or toward the broadest view that would include not only owners but also employees, suppliers, customers and, ultimately, the entire community affected by the business. Given that developing countries in general and Cameroon in particular have systematically adopted every international treaty on human rights – far more than has the United States – it is unlikely that the OHADA countries will officially endorse the minimum standard. Assuming, then, for the sake of argument, that OHADA will end up in the middle of the range, at least the employees would likely be included. This outcome would be consistent with currently existing OHADA uniform acts, including the insolvency law that requires payment of employee-wages before obligations to secured creditors (UA on Insolvency and Collective Procedures, article 166). A yet broader conception of corporate interest would include natural resources and the environment within the class of interests to be respected.

Especially because OHADA is uniform across a significant portion of West and Central Africa, corporate interest as the definition of corporate social responsibility could be an important tool in the globalizing economy: by respecting this norm, the governments could present a united front and perhaps begin to influence multinational behavior at least on their own soil. That would be a convincing use of national laws to start patterning businesses to recognize constituencies other than their owners.

Favoring local constituencies could even be an astute political move for the local governments: most shares of foreign multinationals are not held by citizens of the OHADA contracting states and, therefore, are not part of the governments' electorate. Neither is preferring the local to the foreign necessarily utopian. Since the beginning of this century, South Africa has protected its citizens by using the World Trade Organization's agreements and its own courts, coupled with an effective public relations campaign, to shame multinational pharmaceutical companies into reducing the price of the anti-HIV/AIDS drugs (Dickerson, 2002, p. 1439). Cameroon, as a member of the WTO, could follow this same path, and then enforce in favor of employees and against the multinationals' subsidiaries the OHADA understanding of corporate interest.

As is the case for creditors and lessees, however, reality in the OHADA territory is, instead, determinedly pro-foreign investor. As a practical matter the governments appear to favor foreign interests. In Cameroon, for example, legal professionals pointed to no example of the government wielding the protections of the WTO agreements in favor of its citizens. Thus international norms are not applied to protect local citizenry against foreign commercial interests. Further, foreign-owned businesses are systematically granted waivers from the obligation to domesticate their corporations, thus depriving the local citizenry both of the protection of OHADA's corporate-interest norm, and of the power of OHADA's uniformity. Consequently, despite favorable laws and the practical power of a highly concentrated executive branch, there is no clear evidence that the Cameroonian government or its counterparts in other OHADA contracting states have encouraged foreign multinationals to soften their focus on short-term market incentives in favor of local long-term interests.

### *2.2. OHADA: Practical Application on the Large-Scale Map*

At the large-scale level, the level where domestic businesses operate, OHADA functions at its most practical. So long as the businesses are small enough, they are allowed to do what comes naturally with relatively little governmental intervention other than the inevitable taxation. The political reasons for the government to sacrifice workers' rights or environmental protection in exchange for foreign direct investment are less salient here because the stakes for the government do not seem as high. Other governmental effects, however, are felt. For example, there are difficulties in forming official business entities because of lengthy and expensive procedures – largely revenue measures implemented by rafts of mandatory forms. The World Bank in its "Doing business in 2004: Understanding regulation" (World Bank, 2003, pp. 86–87) had suggested more generally that French-based systems tend to be more highly regulated and therefore more of a drag on the economy than are common-law legal systems. This suggestion has been challenged (Acemoglu, Johnson, & Robinson, 2001, pp. 1383–1384; Beck, Demirgüç-Kunt, & Levine, 2003, pp. 138–137; Dickerson, 2005, pp. 30–39; Rajan & Zingales, 2003). Nevertheless, prodded by the World Bank, the Cameroonian government has begun to address these transaction costs, at least optically. This is an important point: OHADA does not regulate the formation of business entities, except to require a filing with the official registry (UA Company Law, article 98). The larger governmental structures matter, but OHADA company law focuses on the obligations of management – on corporate governance – and not on implementation. By the OHADA Treaty, the contracting parties determined at the outset the extent of OHADA's incursion into their sovereignty, and the treaty does not authorize OHADA to dismantle and rebuild the national structures such as the governmental agencies that control formation of business organizations, or the customs or tax systems, or the national judicial regimes.

What OHADA does provide are clear, accessible business laws and some top-down transparency that, together, may have a positive impact within the existing governmental structures. What, then, does OHADA say about corporate governance?

### *2.2.1. OHADA's Provisions Relating to Corporate Governance*

OHADA company law constrains management through rigorous disclosure rules and minimal use of general standards. The uniform act does prohibit management from abusing rights, and it does expressly specify that neither majority nor minority owners, now in a quasi-management role, are to abuse their power (UA Company Law, articles 130, 131). Nevertheless, the thrust of the law is to demand disclosure, and to do so by using formal structures and rules rather than standards. For example, OHADA provides a centralized registry and insists on publication of essential filings. These requirements are serious: organizational forms that otherwise shelter owners from liability will lose that ability if they fail to register and publish constitutive documents as required by company law (UA Company Law, articles 29, 110, 385).

Business-organization forms that do not offer owners the protection from limited liability, too, must file with the registry. This requirement applies even to sole proprietors: any natural person who is active in business as statutorily defined is obliged to file as a "trader" ("*commerçant*"). OHADA law specifies the rights and obligations among such traders.[4] Even the business organization that arguably operates most like a general partnership, the "*société à nom collectif*," can be formed only by a filing with the registry, and its owners must be "traders," thus requiring double disclosure (UA Company Law, article 270).

But the registry does much more than publish extensive and detailed filings of organizational documents. It also centralizes information concerning a business's operations. For example, various forms of secured interests are recorded in the registry; and national law can constitute the record book for real estate mortgages, too (UA Security Law, articles 72, 102, 122). In this way, too, the structure forces disclosure.

OHADA was drafted with the recognition that management must monitor the corporation and ties the results of the monitoring to the disclosure obligations. Again, the mechanism is a combination of rules and structures: for on-going operations over a specified size, official statutory auditors impose and enforce both monitoring and disclosure (UA Company Law, article 694). These auditors have an affirmative duty to monitor the business's financial health and to warn – by disclosure – if it is in imminent danger (UA Company Law, articles 150, 153, 157). The auditors are highly regulated and very constraining.

For a transplanted legal system, especially one seeking uniformity across a large region, this relatively mechanical and detailed approach to disclosure may well be sensible: standards are slippery in any context but, as we will see, especially when not home-grown. To be sure, the uniform acts as drafted do make a real effort to appreciate realities in the region and to be practical. These uniform acts are Northern in inspiration and form, but they recognize that a developing economy has relatively few large businesses and thus relatively little in the way of separation of ownership from management (Berle & Means, 1932). OHADA company law thus expressly authorizes even the analogue to the corporation ("*société anonyme*"), a business form that can be used for a public as well as a private company, to have a single owner.

OHADA's company law further explicitly contemplates the use of a single manager – who may or may not be the owner – to exercise the combined functions generally allotted to the Board of Directors on the one hand, and senior management on the other, so long as the company has three or fewer shareholders (UA Company Law, articles 385, 494, 495). This looks like a recipe for malfeasance as it permits a total separation of ownership from management; anecdotally, however, the reality is less sharp. First, single-owner firms typically rely on owner-management, as one would expect. Second, we will see that the corporation is thus authorized to mimic a plausible structure for a limited liability company. For a closely held firm that does to some degree separate ownership from management, three owners and, for example, a single manager may be a corporate novelty in historical terms, but the structure is similar to other business forms.

*2.2.2. As Applied, OHADA's Influence is Limited*

The modernity and sophistication of OHADA laws are impressive. The rub, however, is that even at the conceptual level a law focusing on management and governance provides incomplete information about the larger principle the scheme intends to advance. Saying that managers cannot abuse their power does not specify whether the applicable definition of "corporate interest" obligates management to consider employees as well as owners.

Further, because a developing economy has an extensive informal sector, even law as well-drafted and comprehensive as the OHADA uniform acts will reach only a portion of active businesses, namely its formal economy. By 2003, Cameroon's formal economy was estimated to contribute less than half of the country's gross domestic product and create fewer than 20 percent of new jobs (AfDB & OECD, 2003, p. 101). The question, then, is where to find the Cameroonian definition of the overarching principle, the definition of what we call corporate social responsibility, as applied to all businesses. We have seen that the government, from the top, has expressed that business would favor foreign direct investment. We have also seen that, in general, the government's behavior is consistent with the view that business law's role is to attract that kind of investment, and not necessarily to conform to the legal notion of "corporate interest." The direct impact of formal business laws in Cameroon is limited by the relatively modest reach of the formal economy, and the boundary between formal and informal is difficult to identify since many businesses ostensibly in the formal economy have a presence in the informal one. Nevertheless, domestic business operations can reveal the local conception of corporate social responsibility, that is, the purpose for a business form.

This analysis will focus on closely held businesses because, in part, there are very few publicly held local businesses in the region. The primary public market, located in Abidjan, Côte d'Ivoire, has only 46 listed companies (BRVM, 2006). The reason is also in part that these few public companies are aberrational not just because of their infrequency, but also because they tend to exist as a result of privatization, not of entrepreneurial efforts (Lavelle, 2001, pp. 722–723). Consequently, they are likely to have retained close ties to the government, and managerial behavior will not necessarily reflect purely business motives and norms.

Further, the businesses must have an effective separation of ownership from management before we can see whom the governance norms, in fact, protect. If there is no separation of management and ownership theoretically the principles of corporate social responsibility still apply, but missing will be the internal conflict that helps reveal why businesses behave as they do. What then, is the evidence of the actual behavior of corporations and other business organizations in a developing country like Cameroon? When below the political radar, how do they behave? The critical understanding is that business is done with little support from or interference by business law.

This does not mean that that law is irrelevant, nor does it mean that the law lacks sophistication or elegance. Whatever the limit of the laws' influence, people do sue, and from discussions with legal professionals, they do so with an expectation of vindication that sounds familiar to Northern ears. At the same time, there are issues with the judicial system, as confirmed when a former president of the Cameroonian bar announced in a speech at a convocation of lawyers that he looks forward to a time when what an attorney knows will be more important than whom the attorney knows. Lawyers admit quite openly that certain judges can be influenced, although they prefer not to offer the bribe themselves (instead, they have the clients do so). There are, of course, thoroughly incorruptible judges and lawyers, but the pressure is significant, and the consequence for the legal system is unpredictability. This limits the impact of any law, including OHADA.

Transparency is limited, too. As previously noted, any case involving OHADA laws decided in national courts and appealed above the intermediate appellate level must go to the CCJA instead of to the national supreme court. The decisions of the CCJA are published and each decision does refer to its history in the lower (national) court. This guarantees at least some measure of transparency. However, for a multiplicity of reasons having to do with the cost of appeals and the unwillingness of the national supreme courts to relinquish all cases concerning business issues, the CCJA sees only a small fraction of all disputes decided under OHADA law and, consequently, its published decisions only scratch the surface of OHADA jurisprudence.

Decisions that do not rise to the CCJA are not uniformly accessible, and even if technically published they are not distributed as widely as the legal professionals would wish, further limiting transparency. Remarkably too, the editor of a privately published volume containing the prior year's cases decided in Anglophone Cameroon noted that he and his co-editors had not included all decisions, as they had judged some so aberrational as to be inexplicable on the basis of legal analysis. It is perplexing to have the private editor of cases decide which ones to publish – it is as though West Publishing selected the cases it considered defensible and refused to publish the others. The editor's behavior underscores the tension between the system in theory and that in practice: everyone lives with the knowledge of endemic corruption, and even efforts to attenuate its impact can exacerbate the judicial system's unreliability.

Failure of transparency thus decreases confidence in the judicial system and also certainly makes it harder to predict the level of consistency of enforcement. Nevertheless, sometimes the law on the ground is on the contrary predictable, but not in a way that reduces transaction costs. For example, we saw that the OHADA system requires substantial disclosures through its registry. From the outset, the drafters had anticipated that the registry would be fully computerized, and funds have begun to flow to that end. Work is beginning on this project, and when completed the registry will be a source of significant information.

For the moment, however, the reality is different. A visit to an office of the registry, housed at a trial-level court, reveals a complete lack of computerization, but this does not inevitably mean that the retrieval and indexing system must be wholly unsuited to the purpose. Over the centuries, legal systems have devised effective ways of filing and indexing manually, but instead the clerk showed me volumes with information entered on a purely chronological basis, with no cross-indexing. She told me that a potential creditor would probably not be allowed to review the registry directly, but would have to rely on the clerk's office. Presumably the employees of the clerk's office have less incentive than would the creditor to effect a thorough search of the books. This means that a creditor seeking to learn the identity of a particular company's managers, and the extent and source of what are its existing secured borrowings, will very likely be unable to locate the information even if it has been filed with the registry as required (UA Commercial Law, articles 27, 28; UA Company Law, articles 13, 97, 397; UA Security, articles 73, 102). As a practical matter, today essential information will be predictably unavailable to a potential creditor deciding whether to lend, and to an existing creditor trying to recover on a loan, even when the information technically is public.

Because the laws are weak, we cannot assume that OHADA's definitions of corporate governance, let alone its "corporate interest" conception of corporate social responsibility, are respected. Neither an analysis of the uniform acts' texts nor a study of case law will reliably reveal how businesses operate because we cannot know to what extent the laws are enforced. Consulting with business people and their lawyers, however, offers some insight.

*2.2.3. Businesses in Operation*

Consider, first, classic governance problems. A company, substantial by local standards, has a traditional chief as its managing director. The chief, when I interviewed him, would not tell me the exact ownership structure, but he did indicate that there are other owners, all members of the extended family, and that the formal structure of the business is the analogue to the limited liability company. When I asked him about constraints on him as a manager, he said that if he were suddenly to drive a better car or wear a better suit, he would be stopped in the street by the investors. He indicated that he would fear for his life. Whether or not he was exaggerating the likely consequences, he expressly recognized a constraint on his behavior as manager (Dickerson, 2007, pp. 201–202; Interview conducted by Dickerson on October 16, 2005, in SW Province, Cameroon).

But on the other hand, exclusive of self-dealing, the managing director possesses to all appearances extraordinary authority. The other owners are often referred to as "sleeping partners," using the venerable term for limited partners. In limited liability company terms, he is a member–manager and the others are merely members. This is a familiar structure in the North, too, but the significant point is that when culture diverges from the legal norms embedded in the transplanted, North-inspired laws, in the South cultural realities trump the form. The person who actually is dominant will be the most active, whether a general partner surrounded by limited partners unable to act without serious cost, or a limited liability company's owner, surrounded by other owners. Members of limited liability companies indicated that, at least in certain circumstances, all owners expect the senior person, typically a man, to run the business and distribute what it earns as he sees fit. This is the managing director's responsibility as well as his authority.

The governance requirement actually applied is largely compatible with the Northern expectations of OHADA laws, but includes considerable culturally based flexibility concerning distribution of largess. As the chief made clear, self-dealing is inappropriate, but Northern definitions of self-dealing have narrowed senior management's discretion in a way that the chief's discretion is not. To all evidence, the chief's obligation is to a range of constituents wider than the technical owners and agents of the formal business entity. One way to view this is to appreciate that the traditional chief wears two hats, but that although he may not enrich himself, he also may not be required – or expected – to adhere rigidly to the boundaries that separate a traditional chief from a chief executive officer, when identifying the persons to whom he owes a duty.

If this example shows cultural norms stretching the Northern conception embedded in the transplanted statute, even more surprising to a Northerner would be the example of culturally approved behavior diametrically opposed to applicable, formal business law. Consider the following story, narrated to me by two lawyers in Cameroon. An uncle had taken a sibling's son under his wing and had gone into semi-retirement, leaving the nephew to manage the business. By doing this, the uncle transferred management to his nephew, while keeping all ownership rights.

His uncle out of the way, the nephew took assets from his uncle's business and used them to establish his own operation. The nephew did this without informing his uncle, and the new business prospered. Assuming that (as is likely) the uncle's business had been formed as the analogue to our limited liability company, under OHADA law the nephew's conduct is impermissible as an abuse of rights. Depending on local law – OHADA leaves application of criminal law to the national regimes – the activities may also be theft. Nevertheless, when the uncle found out, he did not accuse the nephew of betrayal. Nor did he merely tolerate the illegal behavior out of a sense of family loyalty. Instead, the uncle affirmatively approved of his nephew's behavior and was proud that his nephew had so efficiently managed family assets.

Yet more than in the example of the traditional chief, here the nephew's management role as understood by the uncle is fundamentally irreconcilable with the OHADA text. This is not a question of margins. The simplest explanation is that in the eyes of the uncle and of his nephew, the relevant business was not limited by the boundaries determined by the official form of the uncle's business. If that is true (as it appears to be), then the nephew's behavior – in the context of this accreted appreciation of the business form – is compatible with OHADA and similar Northern norms. Now the nephew is managing the family business's assets so as to increase its value for all constituents, not just his uncle. Once again, culture determines that the official, statutorily mandated boundaries are permeable and that the real boundaries include a larger activity than that of the statutory business organization alone.

Both the example of the traditional chief and that of the nephew express divergence between classic Northern governance norms and actual, locally approved behavior. The approved behavior reflects a broader, community-based understanding of the business entity's role than that woven through the Northern-inspired laws. When business people operate in an arena sheltered from the government's enforcement powers, the actually approved standards of corporate governance reveal a relatively stakeholder understanding of the business entity's role in society. Put differently, the conception of corporate social responsibility is on the stakeholder end of the stakeholder–shareholder primacy spectrum.

At this point, it may be tempting to conclude that business laws, and specifically OHADA's laws, are largely irrelevant. Certainly, even very well-situated personages pay scant attention to the laws. The general manager of one of Cameroon's largest companies could not tell me the actual business form of his organization. His in-house lawyer knew, but had not realized that by failing to file with the official registry, the company's owners would not benefit from limited liability that the business form otherwise offered. These are well-educated, successful, motivated people; the business was simply large enough and well enough connected to the government that formal niceties were inconsequential.

In the vineyard of legal practice, however, many lawyers, judges and legal academics display impressive knowledge of the OHADA laws and a sincere commitment to developing a predictable, clear legal system. University-organized conferences draw significant audiences. Two dozen lawyers who had organized a workshop under the auspices of the University of Buea on OHADA laws in their own town later gave up two days of work and traveled seven hours by bus each way to attend a similar workshop organized by the bar association of another region. The courts closed down for the day so that all lawyers and judges could attend. At the last of the series, in yet another locale, businessmen who learned about the workshop by a live radio broadcast joined the assembly unbidden. Law matters because of the structure that it is capable of providing even when its reality does not match its potential. For all the impediments to full implementation of the OHADA laws, they offer a way to talk about what business means: they are both a vocabulary and a forum for the discussion. In this way, even when the law casts only a faint shadow, it can still have an effect on social norms and, ultimately, on the understanding of both corporate governance and corporate social responsibility.

## 3. NORTH: CORPORATE SOCIAL RESPONSIBILITY, CORPORATE GOVERNANCE, AND THE REALITY OF BUSINESS LAWS

### *3.1. Law as Political on the Small-Scale Map of a Mature Legal Environment*

In the North, and more particularly in the United States, business laws are not so quickly labeled as political. Nevertheless, we recognize their political nature from the argument that Delaware's legislative and judicial pronouncements are shaped by the desire to keep the federal government from preempting corporate law. This is at least one reason why Delaware does not complete the race to the bottom, and does not favor management over shareholders yet more (Bebchuk & Hamdani, 2002). We appreciate that the federal government is not uniformly pro-shareholder either: it sought to favor management against aggressive shareholders by restricting class actions when this type of litigation fell into political bad odor (Securities Litigation Uniform Standards Act of 1998, 2006). A different kind of political kabuki is the network of high-level contacts between captains of industry and senior politicians. Recent examples have included chief executive officers becoming U.S. Secretaries of the Treasury and even Vice President, and at the beginning of this decade the alleged close ties between high-level politicians and the chief executive of the now-iconic Enron.

The influences on the whole seem opportunistic and principally to favor a perception of short-term political advantage. Some protect shareholders; some protect management; some seem even more narrowly focused on self-interest. None have the broad sweep of the top-down political interference found in Cameroon. A fundamental difference between that country and the United States is that the latter has a mature market for business laws that is relatively difficult for the government to manipulate. Thus, in the United States, changes in the law tend not to be as radical, and even if the pendulum swings sometimes to the advantage of managers and sometimes to that of shareholders, the reality lies toward the midpoint between those two constituencies. Corporate law is outside all broad social discussions, including any questioning about business's impact on the larger community.

A contrary example proves my point. The political machinery rarely steps into the corporate arena to protect constituencies other than shareholders or managers. Post-Enron public outrage was not enough to trigger Congressional response to manager malfeasance; it took WorldCom's debacle six months later to generate corporate legislation, which, at least in passing, addresses the interests of employees, a nonshareholder, nonmanager constituency. And indeed, the Sarbanes–Oxley Act's protection for employees is quite limited: the primary provision that affirmatively seeks to constrain management activity harmful to employees prohibits senior management of a public corporation from trading during a blackout period when nonmanagement employees cannot trade (Sarbanes–Oxley Act of 2002, Section 306). This is a bit roundabout as a political statement despite the electorate's drumbeat of outrage, but it underscores that the political dance in the United States truly is almost exclusively between shareholders and senior management. It certainly does not have the reach and flair of adopting an entire legal system to attract foreign direct investment.

### *3.2. Law on the Small-Scale Map of a Mature Legal System*

If this is the scene at the highest political levels, what is the picture from the business-law trenches? From the ground up, using the same technique of looking at the law as written and the law as it works in practice that we applied to Cameroon, the challenge is to glean from the law and from behavior a practical understanding of corporate social responsibility as reflected in corporate governance norms.

We all know the general assumption that shareholder primacy controls in the United States. If, as Milton Friedman said, corporate social responsibility means increasing profits available to shareholders, a properly designed system of corporate governance will encourage that outcome (Friedman, 1970, p. 32). The constraints on managerial behavior are – or should be – an implementation of the applicable principle of corporate social responsibility. If, in its turn, business conduct conforms to the corporate governance norms incorporated in the legal system, the actual behavior will also be consistent with shareholder primacy.

Inevitably, this analysis is impressionistic, but the choice of example is intended to be better than random. Just as the Cameroonian illustrations are salient because they are counterintuitive in the context of the formal legal structure, I search for civil disobedience in the United States business community's corporate sector, because such locations already evidence divergence from the law as written; thus there, further movement may be possible.

#### *3.2.1. Northern Law below the Overtly Political Radar*

*3.2.1.1. Doctrinal Northern Norms.* In the United States, the obligations of managers and of controlling shareholders are largely left to common law principles of fiduciary duty. Meaningful disclosure to the shareholders and the public does not depend on structures. Like the OHADA register, our states' secretaries of state do accept and file certificates of incorporation, but these public documents are meager indeed and typically include no information about management or about the actual as opposed to potential ownership structure. This public filing also contains no information about the business's financial status. Statute and regulation do not mandate that closely held businesses have auditors, not even for businesses that are very large.

To be sure the market – often in the form of lenders – will demand that the company have audited financials, but that is a private matter.

Meantime, states continue to reduce management's fiduciary obligations. This trend affects even the obligations that benefit owners, ostensibly the constituency favored under the shareholder-primacy paradigm. Specifically, in the near-corporate environment, certain state statutes permit noncorporate business forms to reduce the owners' fiduciary protection against management excess (Miller, 2004, pp. 1611, 1639–1640). This change affects the limited liability company and a type of partnership used in the world of private equity, although this context clearly is one of significant separation of ownership from management. As a practical matter, however, investors routinely resist the lowering of protections as long as they can.

After a time, however, the outcome is similar to the example of the Cameroonian traditional chief. In the United States, the investors in venture capital funds at the outset enforce their pro-shareholder industry norms even though the business forms offer a pro-management alternative. A difference, of course, is that in Cameroon the manager is in the cultural driver's seat, although in the United States' venture capital industry, at least at the very beginning of a fund, the investors, not the fund managers, set the terms. Once the US business is off the ground, however, managers do begin to take over. As the separation of management from ownership becomes more extreme, the pro-shareholder standards increasingly are not fully available. In the United States, we have neither the rules nor the structures to mandate disclosure and monitoring for most closely held businesses. Thus, for a private company in the United States, the articulated norm is shareholder primacy, but in practice owners have to fight management for their rights.

The emphasis on monitoring and disclosure is quite different for public companies, and for the moment the trend is for more of each, with the Sarbanes–Oxley Act being a relatively recent and much-discussed constraint on management. Fiduciary concepts, too, play an important role for public companies in balancing management authority and shareholder interest. Sometimes the courts apply state fiduciary principles to mandate management disclosure, care, and loyalty (*Smith v. Van Gorkom*, 1985; *Sinclair Oil Corp. v. Levien*, 1971). Sometimes the courts apply federal analogues, including prohibition against insider trading, to realign the relationship between management and shareholders (*SEC v. Texas Gulf Sulfur Co.*, 1969; *United States. v. O'Hagan*, 1997).

*3.2.1.2. Divergence in the Mature Legal System.* Since the legal system in the United States applicable to business is relatively mature, a lack of cases likely indicates compliance rather than widespread civil disobedience. In contrast, a significant number of cases, especially after repeated litigation in an area of law or after a series of high-profile government actions on a subject, suggest that the social norms in the business community are at odds with the formal law. The schematic can be summarized as follows. First, behavior that society recognizes as meeting a "higher" standard than the minimum generally mandated by law can reveal a divergence between law and social norms. Although perhaps counterintuitive, as illustrated below, this form of divergence can give rise to litigation. Second, in situations where companies engage in behavior that society at best tolerates, but that is undeniably "lower" than the minimum legal standard, litigation also can result.

The first form of divergence between law and behavior concerns socially laudable acts that under the relevant legal regime are no worse than legally questionable. Consider again the Cameroonian traditional chief whose fellow-owners apparently expected him to use some firm assets to care for nonowners, thus suggesting that the fellow-owners' consent was at least in the context somewhat explicit. In the United States, similarly, we have business people who not only comply with corporate law mandates, but exceed the minimum requirements. A very famous example is found in Stewart Macaulay's study of Wisconsin businessmen who, driven by concern for their reputations outside the firm, failed to cause their businesses to extract from every contract the last ounce of legal rights. These businessmen may have moderated their behavior in part also because of the likelihood of continued future dealings with the parties with whom their businesses had contracted. (Macaulay, 1963, p. 63; Axelrod, 1984, pp. 10–11). Together, these social influences led the managers to cause their business entities to behave in a cooperative manner not merely permitted by contract law, but also rising well above the minimum standard of good faith in performance and enforcement (Restatement (2d) Contracts, Section 205).

Under corporate law, however, this reputational effect creates tension: is the manager giving the company's supplier a break not required by contract to improve the manager's standing in the local society? Or does the manager advance the argument that cooperative behavior today will create benefits for the corporation in its future relations? The answer to these questions signals whether the manager views the "over-generous" behavior as a violation of a fiduciary obligation but continues nevertheless, or whether the manager believes the behavior to be permitted. In a situation without the potential of a long-term iterative relationship, I witnessed the chief executive officer of a public company refuse to have his corporation seize on a poorly drafted contract clause. Both parties remembered what had been intended, but his shareholders could have argued that he breached his fiduciary duty to them by not forcing the advantage. This CEO behaved in a way that the larger society might well applaud, but that is very close to the line of behavior prohibited by corporate law and, depending on the circumstances, may well be on the wrong side of that line. Another example is Aaron Feuerstein, CEO of Malden Mills: although not a sole shareholder, to all appearances he decided without consulting the minority owners that the company would pay the employees while the mill was being rebuilt after a devastating fire (Nohria, Piper, & Gurtler, 2003; Teal, 1996). The most famous case focused on legally misguided but arguably "good" acts is *Dodge v. Ford Motor Co.* (1919) in which Henry Ford, a dominant but not sole shareholder, testified that he wanted the company to curb excess profits in order to be able to better the lives of the company's employees. However disingenuous Henry Ford's testimony may have been, it offers yet another example of ostensible do-gooding forbidden by business law (*Dodge v. Ford*, pp. 683–684).

The technical analysis, of course, is that under a narrow, traditional definition of the U.S. business form, the shareholders are the manager's only legitimate master. The fear in business law, as in trust law, is that a manager will not be able to choose wisely between two masters: self (or community) and shareholders (Scott, 1967, Section 1). If the boundaries are relaxed, the manager's sole master, like that of the traditional chief, is the local community. The social and legal norms are reconciled.

At the other end of the spectrum are acts that are at best tolerated and are clearly in violation of positive law. The Cameroonian analogue is the nephew taking the corporate opportunity, although there the nephew's behavior was more than merely tolerated. In the United States, there is an area of law under the general rubric of corporate governance that continues to produce a seemingly endless stream of litigation: insider trading. Despite consistent government opposition to insider trading for three-quarters of a century, and despite increasingly vigorous government objection to the practice over the past 40 years, cases keep appearing. Polls report that people admit being in favor of insider trading for their own benefit (Bainbridge, 1995, p. 1242). Sometimes big fish get caught, but often it is relatively little fish, indicating that the pro-insider trading norm permeates society.

Clearly, society has not internalized this version of protecting actual and potential shareholders from management and related self-dealing. In fact, the principal difference between the uncle in Cameroon and the insider trader in the United States is that an insider trader is not openly applauded;

nevertheless, the public perception is no worse than wry recognition. When Martha Stewart was accused of insider trading, the media repeatedly reported the charges incorrectly, focused intensely on alleged character flaws, and generally revealed more schadenfreude than outrage.

Despite the government's efforts to change the public's mind by very public shaming of very public managers, the problem persists. As a matter of social norms, perhaps Henry Manne was right to question the US laws condemnation of insider trading (Bainbridge, 1995; Manne, 1966). But what does that say about the concept of shareholder primacy? Scholars may try to explain their defense of insider trading by demonstrating that it does not hurt and may even benefit shareholders, thus showing that the public's tolerance of the practice is at least not inconsistent with the principle of shareholder primacy. The people who actually engage in the behavior, however, are almost certainly not thinking at that level. From their perspective, they are merely taking advantage of an opportunity. It would be silly not to; maybe it is their due.

Like the Cameroonian nephew, the insider traders are reconfiguring the business entity to reflect social realities in opposition to legal norms. Very big players who happen to be managers may represent management triumphing (for a time) over shareholders, but small players are much closer to employees taking office supplies as a kind of self-help extra compensation.[5] Viscerally, we in the United States easily label the Cameroonian nephew's behavior a breach of fiduciary duty and taking of corporate opportunity; however much we may decry insider trading on an intellectual level, the polls and the stream of cases do suggest that here our outrage is more hypocritical. Insider trading is a form of civil disobedience, but not to all evidence politically motivated.

### *3.2.2. Definition of Business Organization*

As we saw in the discussion of Cameroonian business, a related question concerns the precise definition of the relevant business organization. In the examples from the South, the actual as opposed to formal business entity is the family, broadly defined.

We in the North know the classic answer to a question about the identity of a business form. What the comparative analysis invites us to recognize is that the relevant community may reach well beyond the formal borders of the business entity. By unwinding Coase's view of the firm as a nexus of contracts and recognizing that real, long-term, relational contracts can create a functional firm just as notional contracts can, we recognize the modern reality (Coase, 1937; Jensen & Meckling, 1976). A business that relies on outsourcing is more than its core functions; it includes its suppliers and even some of its customers (Dickerson, 1998). The corporation at the center of the network of contracts and other relationships is the "hub." This corporation's management manages the entire extended firm, and will be concerned with its shareholders, of course, but also with the extended firm's constituent parts. This is not formally a duty by law except to the extent that the contractual relation creates an obligation, and the actual managerial attention can be explained by the managers' desire to maximize the profits for hub shareholders. Nevertheless, the practical reality is that the hub's management fixes its attention not only on its own shareholders, but also on other constituents.

In the Cameroonian examples, applying the social understanding of the business entity's boundaries showed that the managers' behavior actually was in line with the Northern principles embedded in the OHADA business laws. In the United States, the resolution is not so neat. Social norms do not necessarily explain why certain managers behave to a higher standard than the applicable minimum legal requirement, or why a significant number of managers systematically violate a legal standard whose enforcement is well publicized. The comparative analysis, however, does underscore three important points.

First, the underlying social as opposed to legal relationships in Cameroon are affective. In the United States, the hub's connection to those at the outsourced reaches of the larger business entity is contractual and even less rich than are the connections among the people within the core. For the hub, the purpose of the purely contractual (even if relational) connections with the constituents on the spokes is precisely to increase the possibility of acting adversarially. The purpose of that structure is to squeeze the constituent suppliers, for example, and to be able to cut them off when a better opportunity arises.

Second, this same adversarial environment is at the bottom of insider trading. In both contexts, an opportunity is a good one only when there is someone from whom to take it. The behavior depends on the existence of an "other" and, thus, is consistent with conceptualizing a business entity as a series of real contracts. Thus, the clearly illegal behavior from the examples of insider trading is driven by motives that destroy community, even though the behavior is only mildly socially transgressive. Contrast this with the Cameroonian nephew's effort to build community.

Third, the example of United States managers who perform in a socially laudable manner but at some risk of legal liability underscores how the narrow legal definition of business, the narrow limited categories of persons to whom the manager owes a positive duty, is incompatible with community building. Contrast that with the traditional chief's broad sense of social responsibility.

## 4. CONCLUSION: IMPLICATIONS OF THE COMPARATIVE ANALYSIS

I started this analysis, prompted by discussions concerning how to promote a more progressive vision of corporate social responsibility in the United States. In the room were both scholars and activists. The scholars mostly listened, a bit wearied by a battle long fought without visible progress. The activists focused on what particular law they would next attack in an effort to change specific managerial behavior with the hope that the managerial class would ultimately internalize new and different norms.

What the comparative analysis teaches is that the changes have to be social first. To be sure, this is a big enough issue that all efforts, including those more narrowly focused on legal analysis, can have an impact. But the efforts are for the purpose of influencing the social norms.

The analysis also reveals that law will have limited effect where the contrary social norms are deeply entrenched. We saw that the OHADA business laws will inevitably have to be interpreted so as to be consistent with existing cultural norms. Similarly, the best opportunity to shape the concept of corporate social responsibility is to start a dialogue at precisely those points where the current law diverges most sharply from social norms.

In the past, I have assumed that standards like fiduciary obligations will be a way of opening corporate governance, and thus corporate social responsibility, to take the larger community into account. However, this approach has become increasingly unlikely to succeed as Delaware has cut back on those duties. With respect to noncorporate business forms, Delaware statutes now permit substantial opting out of fiduciary duties (Del. Code. Ann. tit. 6, Section 15–404, 2005 (partnerships); Del. Code. Ann. tit. 6, Section 18–1101, 2006 (limited liability companies)). With respect to corporations, Delaware courts have edged toward increasing management's focus on shareholders, especially, of course, in the context of takeovers (*Unocal Corp. v. Mesa Petroleum Co.*, 1985; *Revlon v. MacAndrews & Forbes Holdings, Inc.*, 1985).

Nevertheless, perhaps the law can provide a forum for true discussion of the issue if we demonstrate how these standards of corporate conduct can be socially costly. Simultaneously, I wonder whether the political result will, instead, be a further focusing of the duties on the narrow interests of shareholders. Perhaps the most fruitful approach is to consider why do-gooding where social standards are higher than legal standards can lead to legal liability. Why should fiduciary duty, historically based in moral assumptions, constrain behaviors applauded in nonfiduciary arenas? This is a throw-back to Austin's Scott's (1967) discussion of a fiduciary's duty when subject to more than one master; identifying and considering the relative importance of the various potential masters would be a way of bringing the legal obligations in line with social norms.

The other take-away from this analysis is that it may be time to open a real conversation about insider trading. Why it is that this behavior, long condemned, is socially tolerated at all levels of society? Insider trading is different from other illegal behaviors that continue despite legal prohibition, for example, theft or murder, in that those crimes are socially unacceptable. Even outside the world of corporate scholars and activists, actors on both ends of the political spectrum should be willing to engage this topic. The outcome of such a discussion is, of course, unclear. But the outcome of not launching this discussion is a continuation of the dominant paradigm.

## NOTES

1. On October 17, 2008, the Council of Ministers approved the first amendment to the OHADA treaty; as of March 4, 2009, it is currently circulating among the member nations for signature. As of March 4, 2009, the West African OHADA contracting states are Benin, Burkina Faso, Côte d'Ivoire, Guinea, Guinea-Bissau, Mali, Niger, Senegal and Togo, and the Central African contracting states are Central African Republic, Chad, Cameroon, Comoros, Congo, Equatorial Guinea and Gabon. The uniform acts cover the following disciplines (in order of adoption): company law and economic interest groups; general commercial law; law of security interests and other encumbrances; simplified recovery procedure and methods of execution of judgments; bankruptcy and insolvency law; arbitration law; accounting law; and law on transport of goods by road. As this book goes to print, a UA on Cooperative and Mutual Companies is scheduled to be presented for adoption by the Council of Ministers at the meeting scheduled for April 2009. Other UAs are currently in the drafting stage.

2. In the original French: "l'Organisation pour l'Harmonisation en Afrique du Droit des Affaires."

3. The official site of OHADA's executive branch, the Permanent Secretariat, is www.ohada.org. A private website is as of the date of this writing more complete. See www.ohada.com, See also www.juriscope.org

4. "Trader" is too narrow a translation but nevertheless the common one. UA General Commercial Law, articles 2–7, 19 (definition of "*commerçants*" and stipulation of obligation to file with the register); article 202 (contracts under this UA apply only to "*commerçants*").

5. Scholars suggest that one of insider trading's most famous apologists, Henry Manne, was instrumental in launching what became the shareholder-primacy school (Blair & Stout, 2006, p. 724). This indicates that insider traders respect at least one applicable legal norm (shareholder primacy) as they violate another (insider trading). In either event, both the large and the small traders conform to – and help create – the pro-trading social norm.

## REFERENCES


Acemoglu, D., Johnson, S., & Robinson, J. A. (2001). The colonial origins of comparative development: An empirical investigation. *The American Economic Review, 91*, 1371–1401.

AfDB, & OECD. (2003). African Economic Outlook, Cameroon. Available at http://www.oecd.org/dataoecd/12/59/2498098.pdf.

Axelrod, R. (1984). *The evolution of cooperation*. New York, NY: Basic Books.

Bainbridge, S. W. (1995). Incorporating state law fiduciary duties into the federal insider trading prohibition. *Washington and Lee Law Review, 52*, 1189–1269.

Bebchuk, L. A., & Hamdani, A. (2002). Vigorous race or leisurely walk: Reconsidering the competition over corporate charters. *Yale Law Journal, 112*, 553–615.

Beck, T., Demirgüç-Kunt, A., & Levine, R. (2003). Endowments and finance. *Journal of Financial Economics, 70*, 137–181.

Berkowitz, D., Pistor, K., & Richard, J.-F. (2003). The transplant effect. *American Journal of Comparative Law, 51*, 163–203.

Berle, A. A., Jr.., & Means, G. C. (1932). *The modern corporation and private property*. New York, NY: Commerce Clearing House.

Blair, M., & Stout, L. (2006). Specific investment: Explaining anomalies in corporate law. *Journal of Corporation Law, 32*, 719–744.

Bourse Régionale de Valeurs Mobilières ("BRVM"). (2006). Sociétés Cotées. Available at http://www.brvm.org/fr/documentation/societes.htm

Coase, R. H. (1937). The nature of the firm. *Economica, 4*, 386–405.

Dickerson, C. M. (1998). Spinning out of control: The virtual organization and conflicting governance vectors. *University of Pittsburgh Law Journal, 59*, 759–804.

Dickerson, C. M. (2002). Human rights: The emerging norm of corporate social responsibility. *Tulane Law Review, 76*, 1431–1460.

Dickerson, C. M. (2005). Harmonizing business laws in Africa: OHADA calls the tune. *Columbia Journal of Transnational Law, 44*, 17–73.

Dickerson, C. M. (2007). The Cameroonian experience under OHADA: Business organizations in a developing economy. *Business and Society Review, 112*, 191–213.

Friedman, M. (1970). The social responsibility of business is to increase its profits. *New York Times*, September 13, Section 6, p. 17.

Jensen, M., & Meckling, W. (1976). Theory of the firm: Managerial behaviour, agency costs and ownership structure. *Journal of Financial Economics*, *3*, 305–360.

Koné, M. (2003). *Le nouveau droit commercial des pays de la zone OHADA: Comparaisons avec le droit français*. Paris, France: LGDC.

Lavelle, K. C. (2001). Architecture of equity markets: The Abidjan regional bourse. *International Organization*, *55*, 717–742.

Macaulay, S. (1963). Non-contractual relations in business: A preliminary study. *American Sociological Review*, *28*, 55–67.

Manne, H. G. (1966). In defense of insider trading. *Harvard Business Review*, *44*, 113–122.

Miller, S. K. (2004). The role of the court in balancing contractual freedom with the need for mandatory constraints on opportunistic and abusive conduct in the LLC. *University of Pennsylvania Law Review*, *152*, 1609–1659.

Nohria, N., Piper, T., & Gurtler, B. (2003, 2006). *Malden mills (A)*. Boston: Harvard Business School Publishing.

Paillusseau, J. (1967). *La société anonyme: Technique d'organisation de l'entreprise*. Bibliothèque de droit commercial. Paris: Sirey.

Rajan, R. G., & Zingales, L. (2003). The great reversals: The politics of financial development in the twentieth century. *Journal of Financial Economics*, *69*, 5–50.

Scott, A. W. (1967). *The law of trusts*. Boston, MA: Little, Brown & Co.

Teal, T. (1996). Not a Fool, Not a Saint. *Fortune 201*, November 11 1996. Available at 1996 WLNR 4989923.

Teghen, R., Registrar-in-Chief, Limbe Court. (2005). Interview, October 31.

Teubner, G. (1998). Legal irritants: Good faith in British law or how unifying law ends up in new divergences. *Modern Law Review*, *61*, 11–32.

Watson, A. (1996). Aspects of reception of law. *American Journal of Comparative Law*, *44*, 335–351.

World Bank. (2003). *Doing business in 2004: Understanding regulation*. Oxford University Press.

## Laws and Statutes

Del. Code Ann. tit. 6, Section 15-404 (2005) (partnerships)

Del. Code Ann. tit. 6, Section 18-1101 (2006) (limited liability companies)

OHADA Treaty and Uniform Acts. Available at http://www.ohada.com

Sarbanes–Oxley Act of 2002, Pub. L. No. 107-204, 116 Stat. 745 (codified in scattered sections of 11, 15, 18, 28, and 29 U.S.C.).

Securities Litigation Uniform Standards Act of 1998, Pub. L. No. 105-353, 15U.S.C., Section 77p (2006); Exchange Act, Section 28(f), 15 U.S.C., Section 78bb(f) (2006).

## Cases

*Dodge v. Ford Motor Co.*, 170 N.W. 668, 684 (Mich. 1919).

*Revlon v. MacAndrews & Forbes Holdings, Inc.*, 506 A.2d 173 (Del. 1985).

*SEC v. Texas Gulf Sulphur Co.*, 401 F.2d 833 (2d Cir. 1968), cert. denied, 394 U.S. 976 (1969).
*Sinclair Oil Corp. v. Levien*, 280 A.2d 717 (Del. 1971).
*Smith v. Van Gorkom*, 488 A.2d 858 (Del. 1985).
*United States v. O'Hagan*, 117 S. Ct. 2199 (1997).
*Unocal Corp. v. Mesa Petroleum Co.*, 493 A.2d 946 (Del. 1985).

# SECTION B
# SEEKING SOCIAL JUSTICE THROUGH LAW AND ECONOMICS

# THE DISCOURSE OF "CONTRACT" AND THE LAW OF MARRIAGE

Thomas W. Joo

## ABSTRACT

*Marriage is often compared to a "contract." This analogy purports to proceed from a settled concept called "contract," under which legitimate obligations derive from consent. The analogy creates confusion when applied in the legal context. In law, "contract" refers to a broad category of legal obligation. Many legal theorists believe "contractual" enforceability* should *be based solely on consent. But as a matter of positive legal doctrine, consent is neither necessary nor sufficient to establish enforceability. A contract's enforceability also depends on its relationship to public welfare.*

*Thus the "contract" analogy does not constitute a legal* justification *for an approach to marriage based solely on the consent of the parties. It merely expresses a normative* preference *for a consent-based approach. The chapter illustrates this point using examples of current marriage-related issues, such as covenant marriage, prenuptial agreements, and same-sex marriage.*

## 1. INTRODUCTION

The discourse of "contract" is increasingly imported into other sub-fields of the law. This chapter attempts to model this rhetorical practice using the

**Law & Economics: Toward Social Justice**
**Research in Law and Economics: A Journal of Policy, Volume 24, 161–187**

**ISSN: 0193-5895/doi:10.1108/S0193-5895(2009)0000024011**

contractual discourse about marriage law as an example. Commentators frequently use analogical reasoning to argue that the law governing marriage and related issues should be, or should not be, like the law of contracts. But the discussion takes too narrow a view of the meaning of contract. Both supporters and opponents of a "contractual" approach to marriage law tend to use "contract" to signify a market-libertarian normative view about the role of bargaining rather than to refer to the actual, more complex nature of contract law.

In legal terminology, a "contract" is a legally enforceable promise.[1] The enforceability of contracts is based in large part – but not exclusively – on voluntary bargaining and mutual assent. Thus the theory and doctrine of contract law struggle with the tension between liberty and enforceable obligation. Although the legal definition focuses on enforceability, neoclassical economists use the term "contract" to refer to voluntary, reciprocal relationships, without regard to their legal enforceability.[2] And while the neoclassical economic model does not concern itself with enforceability, neoclassical law-and-economics theory (L&E) tends to assume (often implicitly) that the allocational efficiencies attributed to voluntary bargains constitute a normative basis for their legal enforceability. But even though the L&E position is nominally concerned only with the instrumental goal of efficient allocation, it of course draws rhetorical strength (intentionally or not) from notions, embedded in legal culture and in our political culture more generally, of "freedom of contract" as a categorical good. Long before L&E, the 19th century "Classical" school of contract law also based its theory of enforceability on voluntary mutual assent, based in part on early concepts of efficiency but also on ideological commitments to individual liberty.

While the Classical model has a long historical pedigree, Realist and post-Realist notions of "contract" subsequently asserted that the concept is descriptively far more complex and normatively contested. Some commentators continue to argue as a normative matter that enforceability should be based primarily on voluntary assent, but many others disagree. Moreover, there is further disagreement over the importance of voluntary assent as a descriptive matter of contract doctrine. Under the "objective theory" of contract formation, for example, assent turns on one's words and actions, not only one's subjective state of mind. As explained in the Second Restatement of Contracts, contract formation normally requires a "manifestation of assent," but "[t]he conduct of a party may manifest assent even though he does not in fact assent." (American Law Institute, 1981, Sections 17(1), 19(3).)

Furthermore, courts are often called on to solve contract disputes over issues the parties' agreement does not address. This typically occurs when contract language is ambiguous, or the parties face a contingency that the contract language does not contemplate. If contract law were truly dependent on the parties' mutual assent, courts would have no basis on which to resolve such disputes. In such situations, however, courts routinely construct and enforce so-called "hypothetical bargains": terms the parties never explicitly or implicitly agreed on. Under this theory, the court purports to determine what the parties *would have* agreed to had they considered the issue now in dispute. Of course, such hypothesizing has a subjective aspect to it. As Charny (1991) observes, a court taking this approach makes assumptions (typically unspoken) that may conceal normative biases (pp. 1815–1817). A court typically attempts to simulate the bargain that would have been reached by "reasonable" or "rational" parties. Although this purports to be an objective standard, it is of course likely to reflect the normative biases of the court (Joo, 2002, pp. 797–798).

Voluntary assent is not only unnecessary to support contractual obligation, but also insufficient. Many kinds of voluntary bargains are not enforceable contracts, such as those that lack consideration, are unconscionable, or violate public policy.

## 2. METAPHOR: TARGET, SOURCE, SCHEMA

Many areas of social life, such as marriage, are analogized to contract. Such analogies are often defended as rationalizing, or attacked as coarsening, our view of marriage. The effect of such analogies on our views of contract is less commonly considered. As suggested earlier, "contract" is a contested concept. Consistently equating it with marketist ideology may or may not change our views of marriage, but is likely to affect our understanding of contract.

Analogical reasoning purports to take one concept (such as marriage) and measure it against another concept (such as contract). Cognitive scientists refer to the first concept as the "target domain" and the second as the "source domain" (e.g., Lakoff, 1993). For analogical reasoning to work as advertised, the target and source must be relatively fixed concepts. But the legal notion of "contract," like any other complex intellectual construct, legal or otherwise, is a capacious, internally conflicted, and much-contested concept. When a source domain like "contract" is contested, the analogical reasoning process requires the simultaneous, reflexive redefinition of *both* the target and the source domains.

As a non-legal example of this process, consider the common characterization of sound as a "wave." This draws an analogy between the behavior of sound and the behavior of the surface of water. To say sound is analogous to a wave requires us to do a lot of abstraction: emphasize and reify "core" properties of sound and water waves – periodicity, refractability, reflectability – and abstract away (ignore) a lot of "trivial" characteristics – waves are wet, but not sound; you can surf on waves, but not on sound. This process of abstraction – of core qualities – creates a "schema": a superordinate ideal category, *wave*, which includes both water waves and sound, but is really neither.[3] This capacious concept of *wave* probably did not exist until the analogy was drawn. Moreover, it now affects our idea of what is the "essence" of the original concept, a water wave: it is not the wetness or surfability, but the periodicity. This essentialization has redefined our idea of "wave" such that we do not even think of "sound wave" as a metaphor: we say sound (and light, and earthquakes, and many other things) *is* a wave, and that has come to be meant as a literal statement, because "wave" has come to refer to a technical abstraction rather than a watery phenomenon. Similarly, the contract metaphor has changed the meaning of "contract" from a set of shifting, contested real-world legal practices to a rule-bound theoretical abstraction.

As the earlier example suggests, the cognitive scientists' model of analogical reasoning has often been used to analyze scientific reasoning. According to this model, analogical reasoning is used as a heuristic to build a descriptive and predictive model of, for example, how sound behaves. In applying this concept to the history of science, Gentner and Jeziorski (1993) distinguish the analogical metaphors that dominate modern science from figurative metaphors like those seen in literature.[4] Analogical metaphors are highly structured mappings made up of tight, one-to-one correspondences. Analogies attempt to rely solely on the mapping to make their arguments. Figurative metaphors are looser and draw less on logic than on "extraneous associations." The earlier example of sound as wave qualifies as an analogy because it is made up of one-to-one correspondences between the target and source domains. Gentner and Jeziorski argue that analogy is more logically sophisticated and useful as a scientific heuristic.

Gentner and Jeziorski also argue that analogical metaphors are more rhetorically powerful than figurative ones. This of course is a subjective assessment. Moreover, it varies according to context. For Gentner and Jeziorski, the context was the development of the scientific method: specifically, how plausible, testable hypotheses are generated. In law and policy, where empirical testability is not always paramount, and ideological commitments are closer to the surface, figurative metaphors may have greater power. The life of the law, after all, has not been based on logic.

Although cognitive scientists like Gentner and Jeziorski tend to think of "analogical" and "figurative" metaphors as two different kinds of rhetorical devices, they are better described as two ends of a spectrum with all metaphors actually falling somewhere in between. Any figurative metaphor is based on at least some direct mapping of characteristics, and, moreover, any analogical metaphor will invoke some "extraneous associations." The author of the metaphor is likely to consider rhetorical effect when choosing the source domain, and tailor the source and target schema accordingly. In law or any other innately political area, that redefinition is driven in large part by the author's pre-existing normative agenda.

In any case, these choices will evoke "extraneous [that is, non-analogical] associations," regardless of the author's intent. Any existing source domain has connotations beyond the author's control that will influence the audience's experience of the metaphor. Analogical connections between contracts and marriage, for example, will gather rhetorical strength from the positive cultural and ideological associations between "contract" and liberty and free markets whether or not the analogy is intended to take advantage of such "extraneous associations."

Scientists are no more immune than others to bias in their choices about domain and schema construction. Scientific theories derived from analogies, however, are subject to empirical falsification. Some legal analytical projects are falsifiable: for example, attempts to predict how a law will affect a measurable phenomenon (such as crime or pollution), or to predict how the law will treat a new issue based on an analogous past issue. But, of course, lawyers more typically use analogies to support normative positions: how the law *should* treat a new issue based on an analogous past issue. For example, a lawyer might argue that marriage is like a contract, and contract law tends to implement the intent of the parties; thus marriage law *should* also implement the will of the parties.

Of course this kind of normative "theory" is not subject to falsification. It may open inquiry into policy effects, but empirical data on policy effects is distinct from normative positions about what policy effects are desirable. That is, normative "theories" are ultimately not theories at all, but rather statements of preference. Thus it is pointless to debate whether such "theories" are "accurate." Indeed, because analogy is not clearly superior to figurativeness in legal argument, and because there are probably no pure analogies in law, it is pointless to debate whether a theory is a "correct" application of analogical reasoning, as opposed to figurative argument. Rather, it is more useful for the audience to identify the author's various rhetorical devices and ask why they are, or are not, convincing.

Furthermore, the audience should recognize that while a metaphor's express purpose may be to advance arguments about the target, these arguments are based on assumptions about the source. It is particularly important to identify and examine these assumptions when the source domain is a contested and normatively freighted one, such as contract. Metaphor remakes both the target and source domains to create a new, overarching schema that purports to describe both, but in fact may be a normative prescription for both. Thus, the metaphorical use of contract discourse to debate policy regarding marriage is not just a heuristic for analyzing marriage, but an exercise that may reshape our notion of "contract."

## 3. R AND K: TWO CONSTRUCTIONS OF THE SOURCE DOMAIN "CONTRACT"

The contract metaphor in marriage law illustrates the redefinition of target and source. When imported into other legal domains, "contract" is consistently used to stand for the libertarian model of contract. That is, calling something a "contract" asserts that it is the product of mutual assent *and* that this assent gives it legal legitimacy. Such a model, the so-called "contractarian," or "nexus of contracts" model, served as the foundation of contemporary corporate law theory, and has been highly influential on legal doctrine. In its strongest form, laid out most comprehensively by Easterbrook and Fischel (1991), this view holds that a corporation is nothing more, and nothing less, than a series of voluntary bargains, or "contracts," among economic actors such as shareholders, management, creditors, and employees. As William Bratton argues in this volume, empirical research has undermined the assumptions of the nexus-of-contracts model. Nonetheless, old models die hard.

Like a corporation, a marriage is often analogized to a "contract" by courts and legal theorists. Libertarian advocates of private ordering argue that the terms of an intimate relationship (including, but not limited to, the terms of dissolution) should be set by the parties and not by the state. Weitzman (1981, pp. 227–254), for example, argued that couples should be allowed to use private ordering to vary the terms of, or even as a complete substitute for, the legal status of marriage. The law has come to accept this view to some extent, as shown by the legal recognition of prenuptial agreements and separation agreements.

Libertarian advocates of private ordering in the marriage context typically use contract discourse to justify parties' broad right to set the terms of their relationship. As Weitzman (1981, p. 231) put it, "The belief that individuals should have the freedom and privacy to arrange their personal affairs as they wish (as long as they do not endanger others) is fundamental to the philosophy of those who advocate intimate contracts." Communitarians respond that this contract analysis is inappropriate because marriage implicates concerns about the family unit and the social fabric, whereas contract focuses solely on individual liberty (e.g., Regan, 1999; Brinig, 2000). Despite their differing normative stances, both these arguments proceed from the same descriptive model of "contract," which emphasizes the libertarian aspect of contract and downplays the obligatory aspect. Although liberty may support freedom to set the terms of an intimate relationship, obligations to society and third parties suggest that there should be limits on that freedom. Libertarian marriage theorists, like contractarians, downplay the contested nature of the "contract" concept. Communitarian marriage theorists do the same: rather than argue for an expansive notion of contract, they argue that marriage should not be thought of as "contract" at all because – like libertarians – they believe that contract analysis precludes the consideration of anything but the individual interests of the contracting parties.

Libertarian theorists recognize that legal policy toward marriage has an impact on social welfare, of course, but they tend to argue that a policy favoring private ordering is the best way to increase social welfare as well as the welfare of the parties (e.g., Weitzman, 1981, pp. 237–239). Whether free bargaining leads to efficient outcomes is open to dispute. Moreover, even assuming that it does, whether any given bargain is in fact "free" is debatable. Efficiency may be compromised, and the freedom of bargaining called into question, by a host of factors, such as transaction costs, disparities in bargaining power and access to information, or the simple fact that real bargaining parties are less-than-rational actors. The dispute over the efficiency of bargaining begs the question, what exactly is "efficient"? Do concepts of economic efficiency describe social optimality? Although the quest for "efficiency" is routinely portrayed as normatively uncontroversial, there are, of course, competing definitions of "efficiency" (e.g., the Pareto and Kaldor-Hicks models) that reflect different views about the normative significance of the distribution of gains and losses.

Contract law and theory struggle with these issues. The contract *analogy*, however, ignores this struggle. By calling an aspect of marriage – say, a prenuptial agreement – a "contract" and implying that this proves its enforceability, the analogy takes for granted the economic efficiency and libertarian legitimacy of "contract." This practice also entrenches the notion that the concept of "contract" is (and should be) concerned only with efficiency and liberty. But the grounds for contractual enforceability – that is, the reasons why the law deems some relationships enforceable and not others – are far more complex. By holding up "contract" as the antithesis of "law," both libertarian and communitarian theorists miss the fundamental fact that so much of what we call "contract" law is in fact "regulatory" law (Braucher, 1990). As will be explained later, rights and obligations in contracts (like those in other areas of law, including marriage) in fact derive from communitarian normative commitments *as well as* from libertarian ones. They are also influenced by other normative concerns, such as moral and policy judgments, and practical considerations like public choice pressures, path dependency, and the like.

The use of contract rhetoric in debates over marriage law and policy illustrates the tension between, and conflation of, the two faces of contract: liberty and obligation; or put differently, private ordering and state mandate. This sheds light on not only the meaning of marriage and divorce, but also the contested meaning of "contract." Further, it tells us a great deal about the business of analogizing among legal concepts and the process of analogical legal reasoning generally.

Fig. 1 is a modest attempt at illustrating the relationship between liberty and obligation in contract doctrine and theoretical discourse. In traditional legal parlance, a "contract" is a legally enforceable promise. In Fig. 1, this is represented by "K," the white oval. Some, but not all, Ks arise by mutual assent. Anglo-American political discourse, however, often essentializes "contract" as a domain defined exclusively by mutual assent. Ironically, academic lawyers also take this approach, although it is inconsistent with positive contract law. Call this R, for "relationship" (based on mutual assent). In Fig. 1, R is represented by the dark gray box.

As noted earlier, both communitarian and libertarian commentators on marriage see the source domain, "contract," in terms of voluntary, mutual assent when they use (or reject) contract as a metaphor for marriage. Neoclassical economists also use "contract" in this sense, and thus neoclassical law-and-economists have also adopted it. But the multiple meanings of "contract" generate confusion. Even if practitioners of L&E mean only to refer descriptively to the voluntary nature of "R" when they

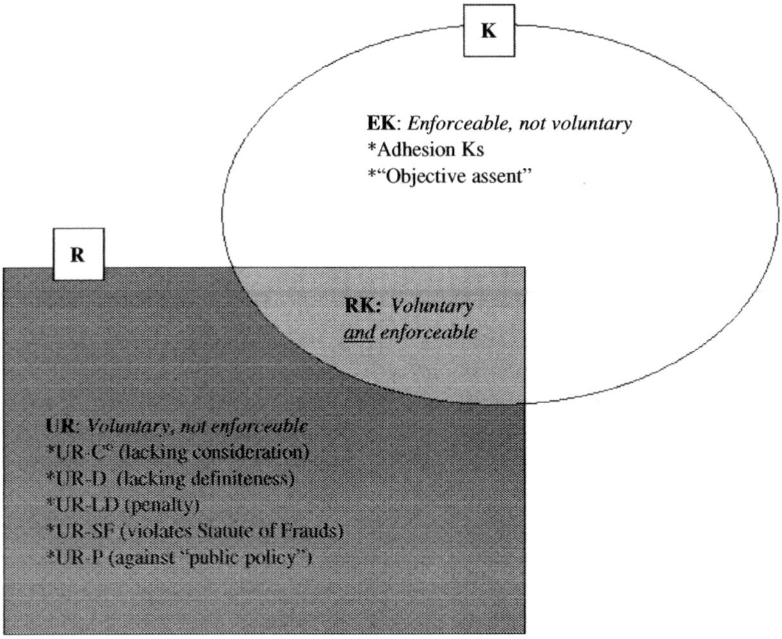


*Fig. 1.* The R–K Overlap.

use the word "contract," the term evokes "extraneous associations" of legal enforceability (K) as well as libertarian legitimacy.

The implication is that a "contract" is RK: an agreement that is voluntary *and enforceable on the basis of its voluntary nature*. As Fig. 1 indicates, however, R and K overlap, but only incompletely. Some agreements are indeed enforceable and voluntary. But even though the enforceability of contracts is typically said to derive from mutual assent, voluntariness is in fact neither necessary nor sufficient for enforceability under positive contract law. That is, some things are both Ks (enforceable obligations) and Rs (voluntary agreements), but not all Rs are Ks, and not all Ks are Rs. In Fig. 1, EK = that part of K that does not overlap with R (i.e., obligations that are *enforceable* despite the lack of voluntary assent); UR = that part of R that does not overlap with K (i.e., undertakings that are voluntary but *unenforceable*); and RK = the overlap (i.e., obligations that are both voluntary and enforceable).[5]

The incompleteness of the overlap indicates a simple descriptive truth, but one often ignored by libertarian contract theorists and neoclassical economists: there is a difference between mere "agreements" (R) and enforceable "contracts" (K), and it is law, not the parties, that draws the distinction (Braucher, 1990). Nonetheless, "contract" metaphorists tend to ignore the existence of UR and EK.

Again, voluntariness is neither necessary nor sufficient for enforceability. Enforceability derives from other factors as well. Contract doctrine may classify an R as UR for a number of reasons: because it lacks consideration (–C°), definiteness (–D), or in some cases a writing (–SF) (Statute of Frauds), or because it imposes a penalty on breach, in violation of the doctrine of "liquidated damages" that allows only compensation, not penalty, as a remedy for breach (–LD). Thus some agreements are voluntary but unenforceable, represented in Fig. 1 by UR, the non-overlapping portion of the square.

Rs may also fall into UR because they conflict with public policy (UR-P). First-year law students typically memorize mutual assent, consideration, definiteness, and (sometimes) writing as the four requirements of contractual enforceability. But even agreements that satisfy all those elements can be declared unenforceable by courts (and legislatures) based on their incompatibility with "public policy." Thus there is in effect a required "fifth element" of enforceability: compatibility with public policy, or P. As Eisenberg (2001) points out, "social welfare" is an important consideration in the enforceability of contracts. In this respect, "contract" law has significant "regulatory" aspects (Braucher, 1990). One may disapprove of that fact normatively, and the precise extent of it is open to descriptive dispute, but the existence of P as a factor in enforceability is clear, and is clearly not a trivial or marginal aspect of K.

The most obvious example is courts' refusal to enforce bargains whose subject matter is illegal, such as a promise to pay commercial bribes in violation of a statute (*Sirkin v. Fourteenth St. Store*, 1908). But courts also invoke subjective interpretations of public welfare to invalidate or restrict contracts that violate no laws, such as liability waivers and promises to refrain from business competition (*Tunkl v. Regents of University of California*, 1963; *Hopper v. All-Pet Animal Clinic*, 1993). Courts also invoke public welfare to invalidate contracts that are said to encourage divorce: for example, a contract in which a married man promised stock to a woman in exchange for her promise to marry him if he obtained a divorce (*Reynolds v. Estate of Reynolds*, 1976).

Similarly, on the level of theory, even the preference for "freedom of contract" in neoclassical economics derives from a utilitarian theory of collective social welfare, not from a categorical preference for individual freedom per se. Under this view, individuals are rational actors whose private bargains allocate resources to those who value them most, thereby maximizing overall social welfare (Barnett, 1986).

To restate part of the earlier discussion in this new terminology, libertarians often argue that "contract" is a normatively proper analysis because a marriage is descriptively an R and "contract" encompasses only RK: an obligation that is enforceable according to the will of the parties. Communitarian critics of this view implicitly accept that "contract" means RK. They disagree with libertarians only on normative grounds: that is, "contract" is an unacceptable standard for enforcing marital obligations because it fails to consider P. Both normative positions fail to see that they share a narrow view of "contract" that does not conform to the notion of "contract" in legal doctrine. Normatively, mutual assent may be a fine argument for enforceability, but as a positive matter, it is neither necessary nor sufficient. K does not ignore P; it *requires* P.

In their insightful treatment of marriage as a "relational contract," Scott and Scott (1998) take a more nuanced approach to the contract metaphor. They recognize that contractual freedom consists not merely of license, but also the freedom to enter into binding commitments. Moreover, they present a descriptive model of "contract" that distinguishes between R and K, and describe marriage as having elements of both. In their view, a marriage is for the most part what I call a UR – a voluntary commitment that the law will not enforce. The commitments are "enforced" by non-legal institutions such as economic incentives, norms within the relationship, and community norms. The law's refusal to enforce the marriage vows provides the most obvious evidence of this theory. Legal enforcement, or K, plays a role, albeit a limited one: "policing massive defections from the cooperative norm and ... resolving economic and parental claims upon termination of the marriage (when the extralegal incentives to cooperate are greatly diminished)." Scott and Scott also acknowledge that neither contract law nor marriage law serves the will of the parties exclusively; both impose some mandatory rules that limit party autonomy. And they recognize that at least some of these rules reserve for the state the right to veto certain bargains on substantive grounds. That is, P plays a role and can trump the will of the parties. For example, "[s]ome bargains – such as contracts of enslavement – are faulty regardless of whether the bargaining process was rational" (pp. 1257–1258).

Following this multilayered portrait of contract as the source domain, however, Scott and Scott's analogy to marriage as the target focuses almost exclusively on the R-aspect of contract. This is clear from the fact that their analysis is structured around a hypothetical bargain between two prospective spouses. Despite their acknowledgement of P, Scott and Scott explain the state's limited role in the marriage relationship as the likely outcome of a hypothetical bargain between rational prospective spouses. Most such parties, Scott and Scott predict, would consider both legal and non-legal methods of enforcement, but would "not *agree* to legal enforcement of the terms of the marital bargain … unless formal sanctions would provide a more efficient substitute for, or a complement to, informal normative sanctions" (p. 1294). That is, the law's refusal to enforce the terms of the marriage vows is proper because it is what the *spouses* would want, not because such deference is good for society generally. Similarly, although they incorporate legal enforceability into their model of contract, they see it as an exercise of individual freedom motivated by self-interest and not as an obligation imposed by society: "autonomous individuals frequently will *pursue their own ends* by voluntarily restricting their future freedom through enforceable legal commitments to others" (p. 1232).

## 4. EXAMPLES OF RK AND EK ISSUES IN MARRIAGE

As argued in the previous section, assent is neither necessary nor sufficient for contractual enforceability. Nonetheless, assent certainly can contribute to enforceability as a doctrinal matter. And moreover, assent is popular and culturally powerful as a basis for a normative theory of contract or marriage. But even conceding the importance of assent, outward manifestations of assent to a relationship do not necessarily constitute a meaningful voluntary undertaking of its terms; this is true in more conventional contract settings and is particularly true in the marriage setting as explained later. Furthermore, despite the increased recognition of private ordering, some agreements purporting to supplement or supplant marriage remain unenforceable. Some commentators and courts argue that this is problematic because marriage and related agreements should be treated "like contracts." But in fact the application of "special" scrutiny to some marriage-related agreements is perfectly consistent with the general contract law principle that enforceability requires P.

The argument that R is sufficient for the enforceability of the terms of marriage does not derive from contract doctrine as source domain. Rather, it is a normative argument for enforceability based on liberty rather than obligation. Thus the use of R as a metaphor for the enforceability of marriage terms is not really an argument for *why* marriage law should be libertarian; rather, it is merely a restatement of an exogenous normative preference for liberty over obligation. This, of course, does not detract from the normative propriety of this preference, but neither does it support it.

### *4.1. "I Do" as Assent*

It is common to refer to spouses as having "agreed" to the background rules of marriage. Because the law tends not to intervene in the relationship during the term of a marriage, the relevant background rules consist primarily of the rules governing divorce. The well-known problems with form contracts apply here: parties' lack of knowledge of terms and their lack of choice of forms call into question whether they have knowingly and willingly assented to the form terms.

Legal scholars from the Left have criticized the fact that couples wishing to marry have traditionally had no choice but to submit to the sexist and heterosexist background terms of marriage law. In my terminology, they were subject to those terms as a matter of state-imposed obligation (EK) and not as a matter of choice (R). Weitzman (1981) argued for "contract" (i.e., RK) as a potential cure for this lack of choice: partners should have the power to choose through private ordering to alter the default terms of marriage or even supplant the legal status of marriage completely. Weitzman argued not only for contractual variations of the marital property regime, but also for the recognition of contracts establishing relationships for which marital status is unavailable, such as same-sex couples and relationships involving more than two people. If couples have the option of replacing background rules with their own, custom-tailored rules, rational behavior theory predicts that the marriage is more likely to be based on *actual*, subjective assent, which generate a welfare-enhancing bargain. Parties can use the opportunity to spell out and agree to their own terms. And because parties that do not design their own terms voluntarily forgo the choice to do so, submitting to the default regime constitutes assent to the default terms of background law. According to Weitzman, contract "accords couples the freedom and privacy to order their personal relationships as they wish."

Fineman (1995) has taken the preference for private ordering one step further. She argues that state-sanctioned marriage is irreparably broken, and the patriarchal model of the family it perpetuates outmoded, as shown by the soaring rate of divorce and the increase in families headed by single women. Thus Fineman argues that state-sanctioned default marriage terms should be abolished, and intimate relationships should be privately ordered (pp. 228–230).

In recent decades, the law has indeed moved toward a larger role for private ordering. The most obvious example is the increased recognition of prenuptial and postnuptial agreements that vary the background regime of property division in the event of divorce. The role of contract to define the terms of marriage may go beyond marital property issues. The Uniform Premarital Agreement Act (1983), adopted in about half of U.S. jurisdictions, also recognizes prospective spouses' right to contract with respect to "any other matter, including their personal rights and obligations, not in violation of public policy or [criminal] statute" (Section 3(8)). In addition, courts also recognize at least some agreements that define the rights and obligations of partners who are not married; this occasionally includes same-sex partners for whom marriage is not an option (one example, *Crooke v. Gilden*, is discussed later).

By the late 20th century, all states had adopted so-called "no-fault" divorce regimes, in which a spouse may seek divorce without alleging fault on the part of the other spouse. The increased ease of divorce generated opposition from the Right, which triggered a statutory development known as "covenant marriage." Interestingly, whereas the public discourse critiquing no-fault divorce is typically couched in communitarian terms about protecting culture and morality ("family values"), the statutes are steeped in the terminology of assent.

The first "covenant marriage" statutory scheme was enacted by Louisiana in 1997; Arizona and Arkansas subsequently enacted similar laws.[6] Although the covenant marriage movement is rooted in cultural conservatism,[7] the Louisiana statute avoids references to marriage as a social institution and instead conforms to the prevailing assent-centered discourse about marriage. A covenant marriage is both more difficult to enter into and more difficult to exit than a conventional marriage. Louisiana requires a couple wishing to enter into a covenant marriage to sign an affidavit affirming that they have received premarital counseling from member of the clergy or a marriage counselor Louisiana Revised Statutes Annotated (La. R.S.A., 2008, Section 9:273(A)(2)(a)). As directed by the covenant marriage statute, the Louisiana Department of Justice has produced an informational pamphlet for prospective covenant spouses that is available to clergy and counselors (La. R.S.A., 2008, Section 9:309). In addition, the couple must make the following recitation, rich with references to informed assent:

> We do solemnly declare that marriage is a covenant between a man and a woman who agree to live together as husband and wife for so long as they both may live. We have

> chosen each other carefully and disclosed to one another everything which could adversely affect the decision to enter into this marriage. We have received premarital counseling on the nature, purposes, and responsibilities of marriage. We have read the Covenant Marriage Act, and we understand that a Covenant Marriage is for life. If we experience marital difficulties, we commit ourselves to take all reasonable efforts to preserve our marriage, including marital counseling.
>
> With full knowledge of what this commitment means, we do hereby declare that our marriage will be bound by Louisiana law on Covenant Marriages and we promise to love, honor, and care for one another as husband and wife for the rest of our lives. (La. R.S.A., 2008, Section 9:273(A)(1))

A covenant marriage is, in fact, not necessarily "for life," but termination is more difficult than in a standard Louisiana marriage. If the spouses later wish to divorce, they may apply for divorce only "subsequent to obtaining counseling" (La. R.S.A., 2008, Section 9:307). Moreover, to obtain divorce without proof of fault, spouses in a covenant marriage must live apart continuously for two years (La. R.S.A., 2008, Section 9:307(A)(5)). In a non-covenant marriage, a no-fault divorce requires only a 180-day wait (Louisiana Civil Code Annotated, 2008, article 102).

Scott (1994) has eloquently defended covenant marriage on classical liberal terms. The covenant marriage option, she argues, enriches liberty because "autonomous individuals often will pursue their life plans by voluntarily undertaking legally enforceable commitments to others" (p. 720). That is, a comprehensive freedom of contract requires offering the option to voluntarily bind oneself. The statute does not mandate more restrictive divorce laws, but offers covenant marriage as a less easily terminable option. In non-covenant jurisdictions, prospective spouses have only one off-the-rack option: marriage that is relatively easily terminable by no-fault divorce. The statute also addresses the prospective spouses' knowledge of the terms of the marital "contract": it requires not only premarital counseling, but also multiple affirmations that the spouses in a covenant marriage understand the meaning of their undertaking.

Thus both Left and Right use liberal notions of autonomy to argue for expanded choice with respect to the terms of marriage. But the fact that spouses are free to craft tailored terms or choose from an array of state-provided forms does not necessarily mean that the choice is a meaningful, informed one. Parties may not even understand the complex default regime or their right to contract around it, and even those who do may lack the means or sophistication to create contracts that opt out of defaults. These generic, and oft-repeated, objections to the rational-actor model of contracting have special significance in the marital context, where we expect the parties to act in accordance with love, and not on rational reflection.

At least one empirical study supports this intuitive notion. Baker and Emery (1993) surveyed individuals who had recently applied for marriage licenses. The subjects knew very little about the terms of the "contract" they were "assenting" to: "The respondents' knowledge of the terms of the marriage contract as embedded in divorce statutes was only slightly better than chance." (p. 441). The subjects had a fairly accurate understanding of the statistical likelihood of divorce and its economic consequences. But despite this knowledge, they were systematically overoptimistic about the likelihood that *they* would get divorced, and about what *they* were likely to get in terms of alimony and custody should they get divorced. Similar surveys administered to law students as part of the same study suggest that increased knowledge of the divorce statutes does not correct this over-optimism.

In sum, regardless of their knowledge of the likelihood of divorce and of the legal consequences of divorce, the individuals surveyed seemed to believe that this information simply did not apply to them. Louisiana's covenant marriage law apparently attempts to insure that a commitment is truly voluntary by requiring both education and multiple explicit manifestations of informed assent. This attempt may prove fruitless, however. Parties to a marriage do not calculate its net benefits, or even make a conscious decision to disregard its risks; rather, they have an inability – perhaps endemic to the marriage context – to appreciate the risks. Baker and Emery predict that due to this cognitive bias, "Individuals will rarely engage in private ordering (prenuptial contracts) at marriage, and attempts to increase public knowledge of the legal terms of the marriage contract are not likely to be effective" (p. 448).

Assent to background divorce law inferred from silence, and even express contracting around defaults may appear to indicate R, but may actually be EK in R's clothing: the terms are enforceable *despite* the lack of meaningful mutual assent.[8] This suggests that neither the categorical libertarian value of self-determination nor the consequentialist notion that market transactions generate efficiency supports the enforceability of marriage or tailored, "contractual" alternatives thereto.

### *4.2. Unenforceability on Policy Grounds*

Some courts and legislatures are concerned that parties (overwhelmingly women) who give up statutory marital property rights under prenuptial agreements do so under pressure or without full knowledge of what they are giving up. Thus some jurisdictions have tried to protect these parties by adding additional requirements for enforceability, such as full disclosure of assets or access to outside legal advice. For example, in California, a prenuptial agreement cannot be enforced against a party unless she or he had independent legal counsel at signing (California Family Code, 2004, Section 1612(c)). Ohio requires, among other things, "full disclosure, or full knowledge and understanding of the nature, value and extent of the prospective spouse's property" (*Gross v. Gross*, 1984).

Other jurisdictions, however, reject this special scrutiny of prenuptial private ordering. The Supreme Court of Pennsylvania, for example, upheld a prenuptial agreement on the precept that "[c]ontracting parties are normally bound by their agreements, without regard to whether the terms thereof were read and fully understood and irrespective of whether the agreements embodied reasonable or good bargains" (*Simeone v. Simeone*, 1990). The court explicitly rejected the "old rule" of special scrutiny for prenuptials. According to the court, the old rule was based on a lack of respect for women's ability to make informed, voluntary choices.

Despite the disparity in the rules and their assumptions about human nature, note their fundamental normative similarity: both purport to make the will of the parties the first priority of the law. But contract law does not focus solely on the parties' will: it prohibits the taking of unfair advantage in the bargaining process precisely to protect parties' autonomy and dignity. And because the definition of "unfairness" varies according to the context of the case, declaring that prenuptials shall be treated "like contracts" merely begs the question of whether they should undergo special scrutiny before enforcement; it does not answer it. Indeed, recall in *Simeone*, the Pennsylvania case that upheld a prenuptial as a "contract," the court observed that "contracting parties are *normally* bound by their agreements," clearly acknowledging that courts may refuse to enforce some agreements.

The *Simeone* court criticized the rule of special scrutiny on the ground that it was based on an assumption that women were categorically weak parties in bargaining. The court stated uncontroversially, that, "women nowadays quite often have substantial education, financial awareness, income, and assets." Thus the court refused to make an inquiry into the fairness of the prenuptial agreement, and announced a new rule to that effect. But while the court was correct to point out that a woman's bargaining position is not always inferior to a man's, it did not consider whether *this* woman's bargaining position was inferior to *this* man's, such that she might have entered into an oppressive contract in violation of P. When Catherine Walsh married Frederick Simeone in 1975, he was a 39-year-old neurosurgeon with assets of at least $300,000, and she was a 23-year-old nurse. Catherine challenged a specific technical provision of the prenuptial agreement – her relinquishment of her statutory right to alimony during the litigation – on the ground that she did not have legal advice before signing. But the court, adopting a narrow view of "contract" and a blanket generalization about the relative power of women and men, refused to inquire into the relative power of Catherine and Frederick. This is not to say that the court's decision was wrong, but that its insistence that the court must enforce the agreement according to its terms because it was a "contract" is not an argument, but a conclusion. Courts do not need to make sexist, paternalistic generalizations to inquire into the fairness of a contract. As the concurring justice pointed out, whatever the normative propriety of gender equality, women in fact regularly receive unfair terms in contract contexts (p. 168).

As discussed earlier, however, public policy, or "P," is a significant element of contract analysis. Dissenting in *Simeone*, Justice McDermott argued for a more searching review of the prenuptial agreement, but adopted the majority's limited view of contract: "I am not willing to believe that our society views marriage as a mere contract for hire ... Our courts must seek to protect, and not to undermine, those institutions and interests which are vital to our society" (p. 168). That is, rather than arguing for greater scrutiny on the ground that P is an aspect of contract enforceability, Justice McDermott argued that the court had to reject a contract analysis in order to consider the state's policy interest in marriage.

More specifically, the "special" scrutiny of contracts between intimates is not "special" to the prenuptial context, but rather an inherent aspect of contract law. In *Bratton v. Bratton* (2004), the Tennessee Supreme Court held that postnuptial agreements [9] are not prohibited per se by public policy. "Generally, postnuptial agreements will be treated in the same manner as antenuptial and reconciliation agreements. That is to say, they should be interpreted and enforced as any other contract" (p. 600). But the *Bratton* court went on to acknowledge that even "normal" contract doctrine requires a court to make fact-specific inquiries about the assent process and to reject agreements that are the product of overreaching. A contract may be unenforceable if it was the product of "undue influence." (Farnsworth, 1999, pp. 273–274). The relationship between the contracting parties – marriage being only one example – is relevant in this regard

> While it is lawful and not against public policy for husband and wife to enter into such contracts, yet they are not dealing with each other as strangers at arm's length. [...]

> Transactions of this character are scrutinized by the courts with great care, to the end that no unjust advantage may be obtained by one over the other by means of any oppression, deception, or fraud. Courts of equity will relieve against any unjust advantage procured by any such means, and less evidence is required in such cases to establish the fraud, oppression, or deception than if the parties had been dealing at arm's length as strangers. . . . (*Bratton v. Bratton*, p. 601, quoting *In re Estate of Edwin Gab*, 1985, p. 926)

Such a demanding, relationship-specific inquiry need not uniformly favor women, as the majority assumed in *Simeone*. *Bratton* relied in part on such an inquiry to deny a divorcing wife's attempt to enforce a postnuptial agreement against her former husband. The court stated that if she had promised to stay in the marriage, that did not constitute consideration for the postnuptial terms, because it was in effect a threat to leave him and thus constituted coercion (p. 603).

Ertman (1996) has argued that contract law has progressive potential for marginalized sexual minorities. Sexual minorities are frequently treated as criminals, but seek to eventually reform the law to protect their identity as a right. Ertman argues that the legal recognition of consensual intimate relationships as contracts constitutes an intermediate stage toward such reform. Her ambivalence about this stage is reflected in her apt term for it: "contractual purgatory." One of Ertman's examples is instructive. In *Crooke v. Gilden* (1992), Gilden sought to enforce an agreement that gave her half ownership of a home originally owned by her lesbian partner Crooke. The consideration recited in the contract was "mutual contribution toward improvement of the real estate and sharing of expenses and assets." Crooke argued that the agreement was unenforceable because the actual consideration for the property interest was their lesbian relationship. Under Georgia law, "[a] contract to do an immoral or illegal thing is void" (Official Georgia Code Annotated, 1982, 12-8-1), and Georgia law at the time outlawed consensual "sodomy" (Official Georgia Code Annotated, 1982, 16-6-2)[10]. The trial court refused to order specific performance of the contract on the ground that "an 'illegal and immoral' relationship between the parties constituted an implicit part of the consideration for the contract." (p. 646).

The Georgia Supreme Court rejected Crooke's argument, however. The consideration recited in the contract was perfectly legal, the court held, and "the parol evidence admitted demonstrates that the alleged illegal activity was at most incidental to the contract rather than required by it" (p. 646). As Ertman points out, although the decision gave legal recognition to a same-sex couple's property arrangement, it hardly put their relationship on equal dignity with a heterosexual one. Indeed, the court reached its result only by marginalizing the central fact of the lesbian relationship, thus suggesting that in the future, such arrangements would fare best if the parties' keep their sexual identities closeted.[11] Nonetheless, "contractual purgatory is perhaps a haven where the alternative is damnation to criminalization, or no recovery at all" (Ertman, 1996, p. 1139).

Note that by referring to "contractual purgatory" as a step forward (albeit a limited one) Ertman is referring to a state in which a court *enforces* a same-sex relationship under contractual principles. The mere *application* of contractual principles is not necessarily a step forward. Contract law is not inherently progressive. A law that uniformly required all voluntary, bargained-for property agreements to be enforced according to their terms would arguably be a progressive step for gay relationships; at least it would have the virtue of formal equality. But contract law contains no such rule. As so clearly stated in Georgia law, contractual principles empower judges to strike down freely bargained-for agreements on public policy grounds. This power is quite broad: independent of the statute that made the lesbian relationship illegal, the court could have struck down the agreement on the far more subjective basis that the relationship was "immoral."

In short, the (somewhat) "progressive" results of "contract" cases like *Crooke* do *not* flow inexorably from contract doctrine, which very clearly empowers judges to use their discretion in subordinating ways as well as progressive ones. "Progressive" results in contract cases are the work of judges who choose to exercise their discretion in progressive ways.[12] Removing this discretion is not necessarily a solution. As Ertman points out, strict enforcement of private ordering can also be either progressive or subordinating, depending on the context; for example, married women tend to be better served by default marital property rules than by prenuptial agreements (pp. 1119–1120). "Private law" lacks transformative potential without changes in "public law" – that is, the progressive potential of R depends on our understanding of P. This is reflected in federal civil rights law, which both requires formal racial equality in the right to contract and prohibits racially discriminatory refusal to contract.[13]

The role of P is further demonstrated in the controversy over whether a state that does not recognize gay marriages should recognize gay marriages from out-of-state. Although the Constitution requires that each state give "full faith and credit" to the laws of other states, the Supreme Court has developed a "public policy exception" to the rule. Under the rule, when State A does not wish to recognize State B's law, State A needs only a minimal connection to the case ("minimum contacts," in the jargon) to justify applying its own law in the interests of the local public. When State A invokes the "exception," a reviewing court will not evaluate whether A's interest in the case outweighs B's interest in having its law recognized in State A. Opponents of gay marriage thus argue that a state need not recognize gay marriages performed in other states (e.g., Myers, 2005). However, at least one prominent commentator (Kramer, 1997) has argued that the public policy exception should be unconstitutional. Whether it is desirable for a state to have the power to refuse to recognize same-sex marriages from other states is well beyond the scope of this chapter. But as a matter of current doctrine, it appears that states do have this power.

Thus there is no politically neutral approach to the interstate recognition question. A state's refusal to recognize gay marriages based on the public policy exception would obviously be a statement of normative disapproval of gay marriage. Because a state is not required to recognize out-of-state gay marriages, however, recognizing gay marriages is necessarily a normative statement of approval of same-sex marriage as well, and not just a neutral, mechanical result dictated by R. That is, a non-Massachusetts court's decision to recognize a Massachusetts same-sex marriage would not be a mere recognition of the parties' "freedom of contract," or a mandatory application of full faith and credit. Because the court *has* the power to reject out-of-state marital "contracts" on policy grounds, the choice not to do so would be a normative finding that the state has no interest against gay marriage greater than its interest in freedom of contract.

The public policy rule is typically referred to as an "exception" to the rule of Full Faith and Credit, and not as a core aspect of the doctrine. This implies that it is an extraordinary power granted to protect local policy from contrary out-of-state policy. But as discussed earlier, courts (and of course legislatures) have the power to invalidate *local* contracts on policy grounds as well as foreign ones. Thus *any* decision to enforce a K requires the state to both consider "freedom of contract" *and* make policy evaluation about the substance of the agreement. For example, many states used to categorically refuse to enforce prenuptial agreements or recognize "palimony" arrangements – both of which are "contracts" which at least ostensibly satisfied all the requirements for enforceability save one: in the state's view, they undermined the public policy interest in traditional marriage. If nonconformity with P makes an agreement unenforceable, then any recognition of an agreement as a K must also be an implicit recognition that it complies with P (more specifically, that any negative public policy impact that enforcement would cause has less weight than the negative impact on freedom of contract that non-enforcement would cause).

## 5. CONCLUSION

Contract is sometimes said to be "colonizing" other discourses. This process is not just a competition among sub-fields of law and politics, but also part of the contest over what we mean by "contract." My aim is not to advocate for or against the contractarian approach to marriage and related issues, but to show that it is not really an argument. It reduces to a normative commitment – just as a "social justice" agenda does.

A metaphor by its nature takes only part of the nominal source, essentializing it into a narrowed "source domain." Thus a metaphor that compares marriage to "contract" refers to something narrower and tidier than the multifaceted and contested concepts of contract law. The source domain and the target define a schema that is supposed to encompass both. Thus the metaphor does not just illuminate the target: it replaces the unruly nominal source called "contract" with a tidier schema, which appropriates the name "contract." At every step, this process is influenced by, if not motivated by, normative attitudes toward what elements (i.e., voluntariness) are essential to defining the source domain and which are merely incidental (i.e., public policy). Thus the metaphor is not an argument, but simply a restatement of the initial normative preferences.

I do not mean to argue that because contract has regulatory and communitarian aspects, marriage law should be regulatory and communitarian. To do so would simply be to engage in the same kind of normative restatement I have described, with only the initial normative bias changed. The extent to which "contract" law is regulatory as opposed to deferential varies from context to context. Thus even if there is any sense to arguing that marriage law should be regulatory because a marriage is like (or is) a contract, that tells us precisely nothing about just *how* regulatory the law should be.

I do not even mean to argue that a "contract" discourse focused on K is normatively superior (or inferior) to one focused on R. By arguing that contract can be essentialized to R, the debate over marriage in contract terms not only affects our notion of marriage, but also contributes to the construction of a "contract" schema focused on R. Other sub-fields of the law, most notably corporate law, are also participating in this process (Joo, 2002). Importing "contract" discourse into other sub-fields under the unexamined, and often unspoken, postulate that "contract" means R spreads and solidifies that postulate, effacing the notion of "contract" as K. My point here is not to show that the R-centric contract schema is "wrong." Rather, my purpose is to analyze the rhetorical tools used to construct it. This should achieve two purposes: first, setting the stage for a more open and informed assessment of the normative prescriptions made in the name of "contract," and second, prompting an appreciation of the interaction between source and target in analogical reasoning.

While this second point may seem an obscure and abstruse ivory-tower concern, it has significant implications for legal discourse in the interest of social justice. That is, although the debate is nominally about marriage, the use of "contract" to mean "liberty" in this context (and others) reinforces the libertarian aspect of "contract" in public discourse and erodes the obligatory aspect. Compare, for example, Elizabeth and Robert Scott's use of the contractarian metaphor with Lenore Weitzman's. Weitzman argued that "freedom of contract" requires the law to allow couples to opt out of the existing marriage and divorce regime and choose less restrictive, more easily terminated relationships. Similarly, Scott and Scott (1998) use the same "freedom of contract" idea to advocate for the availability of expanded choice. But they argue for the option of a marriage "form contract" that is *more* restrictive with respect to divorce. They argue that freedom of contract requires the law to allow couples to opt out of the relatively permissive no-fault divorce regime and opt into one in which divorce is more difficult to obtain. "[C]ontract," they argue, "offers an attractive autonomy-based alternative to ... a status-based regulatory scheme that would impose coercive constraints on divorce" (p. 1231). By "contract" they mean offering covenant marriage as an alternative "form contract."

Both Weitzman, on the one hand, and Scott and Scott, on the other, equate "contract" with voluntary individual choice. But this commonality stands in tension with their obvious normative preferences about marriage – Weitzman's in favor of easier terminability and Scott and Scott's against it. That is, they have clear normative preferences about results, but present their arguments in terms of "neutral" freedom of choice terms.[14] As a result, Weitzman and Scott and Scott focus on the individual's freedom of choice. They choose not to argue that flexibility might be good for third parties and society generally – *and* that that might be just as consistent with "contract."

Is terminability/non-terminability good for third parties, such as children, the public purse, or social health generally? On termination, does the parties' choice of termination rules yield results that are substantively fair to the parties as well as socially constructive? These questions, the kind of questions asked by "social justice" advocates, are not relevant to R, but are of course relevant to K.

If pressed, most contractarian marriage theorists would probably concede that by "contract" they mean a normative vision of individual liberty and not a description of existing contract law. But the terminology obscures this fact, and gains rhetorical power from the "extraneous associations" of the term "contract." Although the rhetoric focuses on R, a "contract" also implies K, an arrangement that is stronger than a mere voluntary promise (which we all know are regularly broken with impunity). I do not mean to engage the normative question of whether liberty should be the organizing principle of relationships – whether obligation should derive only from choice. I merely want it to be understood and evaluated as a normative argument, and not to be mistaken for a settled rule of positive law. The contractarian position is not normatively "neutral" in contrast to a political "social justice" agenda: it is an equally political and normative view, which should be debated as such.

## NOTES

1. Restatement 2d of Contracts, Section 1.
2. See, for example, Hart (1989, p. 1764, note 30).
3. The "sound as wave" example and the concept of "schema" are borrowed from Holyoak and Thagard (1995, p. 24). I use this example and analyze the schema concept in greater depth elsewhere. See Joo (2002).
4. I take some liberties with the terminology here. Gentner and Jeziorski actually distinguish between two classes they call "analogies" and "metaphors," whereas other commentators call both types of mappings a subset of a larger class called "metaphors." I favor the latter approach, and thus use the term "analogical metaphor" where Gentner and Jeziorski use "analogy" and "figurative metaphor" where they use "metaphor."
5. As in any model, of course, the distinctions between categories are exaggerated for effect; in reality the boundaries are fuzzier than the geometric diagram suggests.
6. Louisiana Revised Statutes Annotated (La. R.S.A.) 9:272-275.1, 9:307-309 (2008); Arizona Revised Statutes Annotated, Sections 25–901 to 25–906 (2007); Arkansas Code Annotated, Sections 9-11-801 to 9-11-808 (2008).
7. Prof Katherine Shaw Spaht, who was actively involved in the drafting of the Louisiana statute, describes covenant marriage as a "safe haven" for cultural conservatives who wish to opt out of "the post-modern, dominant culture" (Spaht, 2005, p. 628). While this argument is consistent with liberal notions of autonomy, Spaht's view of marriage is clearly not libertarian: she condemns the U.S. Supreme Court's *Lawrence v. Texas* decision for placing consensual homosexual conduct within the scope of Fourteenth Amendment liberty and suggests that *Lawrence* threatens the institutions of marriage and the family. According to Spaht, "such autonomy creates anarchy" (p. 626). Further, she echoes communitarians' disdain for the concept of marriage as a narrow libertarian "contract": "Covenant spouses defer to marriage, an abstraction representing a third party to the marriage itself, rather than view marriage as a loose union of two radically autonomous selves acting always in each person's own self-interest ... " (p. 628).

8. Sophisticated, normatively loaded arguments have been made that "objective assent" is equivalent to meaningful assent (e.g., Barnett, 1992). But the very fact that such arguments are necessary should establish that objective and subjective assent are not identical, regardless of whether they are functionally equivalent. The Restatement of Contracts recognizes this fact in distinguishing between a "manifestation of assent" and assent "in fact." See Restatement 2d of Contracts, Section 19(3), discussed earlier at page 3.

9. Postnuptial agreements, like prenuptial agreements, prescribe the division of marital property in the event of divorce, but are signed after entering into marriage.

10. *Crooke* was decided in 1992, six years after the U.S. Supreme Court had held Georgia's anti-sodomy statute constitutional as applied to consensual homosexual sex in *Bowers v. Hardwick* (1986) and 11 years before the Court subsequently overturned *Bowers* in *Lawrence v. Texas* (2003).

11. In fact, neither the majority nor dissenting opinion dared speak the name of the allegedly "illegal or immoral" consideration. Leonard (2000, pp. 456–457) explains that it was a lesbian cohabitation, and that Crooke's "illegal or immoral" argument was based on Georgia's anti-sodomy statute.

12. They may also be the result of judicial overreaching. By stating that the relationship was merely "incidental," the *Crooke* court arguably pushed the limits of its appellate role by revisiting the trial court's reading of the evidence, not its application of the law. Further, at least according to the dissent, the court took up this argument on its own motion; Gilden did not advance it (p. 647).

13. According to a federal statute, 42 U.S.C., Section 1981, "all persons ... shall have the same right ... to make and enforce contracts ... as is enjoyed by white citizens." In *Runyon v. McCrary*, 1976, the U.S. Supreme Court established that this law prohibits private parties from discriminatory refusal to contract.

14. Recall also the contrast between the cultural-conservative origins of covenant marriage and the libertarian language of the Louisiana statute. See note 7, earlier.

## ACKNOWLEDGMENTS

The author would like to thank the Center on Corporations, Law & Society at the Seattle University School of Law, Dean Kellye Testy and Dana Gold, Director of the Center. This research was supported by a grant from the UC Davis School of Law (Dr. Martin Luther King, Jr., Hall).

## REFERENCES

American Law Institute. (1981). *Restatement of the law, second: Contracts 2d.* St. Paul, MN: American Law Institute Publishers.

Baker, L., & Emery, R. (1993). When every relationship is above average: Perceptions and expectations of divorce at the time of marriage. *Law and Human Behavior*, *17*, 439–450.

Barnett, R. (1986). A consent theory of contract. *Columbia Law Review*, *86*, 269–321.

Barnett, R. (1992). The sound of silence: Default rules and contractual consent. *Virginia Law Review*, *78*, 821–911.

Braucher, J. (1990). Contract versus contractarianism. *Washington and Lee Law Review*, *47*, 697–739.

Brinig, M. (2000). *From contract to covenant: Beyond the law and economics of the family*. Cambridge, MA: Harvard University Press.

Charny, D. (1991). Hypothetical bargains: The normative structure of contract interpretation. *Michigan Law Review*, *89*, 1815–1879.

Easterbrook, F., & Fischel, D. (1991). *The economic structure of corporate law*. Cambridge, MA: Harvard University Press.

Eisenberg, M. (2001). The theory of contracts. In: P. Benson (Ed.), *The theory of contract law* (p. 261). Cambridge, UK: Cambridge University Press.

Ertman, M. (1996). Contractual purgatory for sexual marginorities: Not heaven, but not hell either. *Denver University Law Review*, *73*, 1107–1168.

Farnsworth, E. (1999). *Contracts* (3d ed.). New York, NY: Aspen Law & Business.

Fineman, M. (1995). *The neutered mother, the sexual family, and other twentieth-century tragedies*. New York, NY: Routledge.

Gentner, D., & Jeziorski, M. (1993). The shift from metaphor to analogy in western science. In: A. Ortony (Ed.), *Metaphor and thought* (p. 447). Cambridge, UK: Cambridge University Press.

Hart, O. (1989). An economist's perspective on the theory of the firm. *Columbia Law Review*, *89*, 1757–1774.

Holyoak, K., & Thagard, P. (1995). *Mental leaps: Analogy in creative thought*. Cambridge, MA: MIT Press.

Joo, T. (2002). Contract, property, and the role of metaphor in corporations law. *UC Davis Law Review*, *35*, 779–818.

Kramer, L. (1997). Same-sex marriage, conflict of laws, and the unconstitutional public policy exception. *Yale Law Journal*, *106*, 1965–2008.

Lakoff, G. (1993). The contemporary theory of metaphor. In: A. Ortony (Ed.), *Metaphor and thought* (p. 202). Cambridge, UK: Cambridge University Press.

Leonard, A. (2000). Chronicling a movement: 20 years of lesbian/gay law notes. *New York Law School Journal of Human Rights*, *17*, 415–564.

Myers, R. (2005). The public policy doctrine and interjurisdictional recognition of same-sex marriages. *Ave Maria Law Review*, *3*, 531–548.

Regan, M. (1999). *Alone together: Law and the meanings of marriage*. New York, NY: Oxford University Press.

Scott, E. (1994). Rehabilitating liberalism in modern divorce law. *Utah Law Review*, *1994*, 687–739.

Scott, E., & Scott, R. (1998). Marriage as relational contract. *Virginia Law Review*, *84*, 1225–1334.

Spaht, K. (2005). Covenant marriage seven years later: Its as yet unfulfilled promise. *Louisiana Law Review*, *65*, 605–634.

Weitzman, L. (1981). *The marriage contract: Spouses, lovers, and the law*. New York, NY: Free Press.

## Laws and Statutes

Arkansas Code Annotated (2008).
Arizona Revised Statutes Annotated (West 2007).
California Family Code (West 2004).
Louisiana Civil Code Annotated (West 2008).
Louisiana Revised Statutes Annotated (West 2008).
Official Georgia Code Annotated (Michie 1982).
Uniform Premarital Agreement Act (National Conference of Commissioners on Uniform State Laws 1983).

## Cases

*Bowers v. Hardwick*, 478 U.S. 186 (1986).
*Bratton v. Bratton*, 136 S.W.3d 595 (Tenn. 2004).
*Crooke v. Gilden*, 414 S.E.2d 645 (Ga.1992).
*Gross v. Gross*, 464 N.E. 2d 500 (Ohio 1984).
*Hopper v. All-Pet Animal Clinic*, 861 P.2d 531 (Wyo. 1993).
*In re Estate of Edwin Gab*, 364 N.W.2d 924 (S.D. 1985).
*Lawrence v. Texas*, 539 U.S. 558 (2003).
*Reynolds v. Estate of Reynolds*, 230 S.E. 2d 842 (Ga. 1976).
*Runyon v. McCrary*, 427 U.S. 160 (1976).
*Simeone v. Simeone*, 581 A.2d 162 (Pa. 1990).
*Sirkin v. Fourteenth St. Store*, 108 N.Y.S. 830 (App. Div. 1908).
*Tunkl v. Regents of University of California*, 383 P.2d 441 (Cal. 1963).

# BEHAVIORAL BIOLOGY, THE RATIONAL ACTOR MODEL, AND THE NEW FEMINIST AGENDA

June Carbone and Naomi Cahn

## ABSTRACT

*This chapter incorporates gender consciousness into critiques of the rational actor model by revisiting Carol Gilligan's account of moral development. Economics itself, led by the insights from game theory, is reexamining trust, altruism, reciprocity, and empathy. Behavioral economics further explores the implications of a more robust conception of human motivation. We argue that the most likely source for a comprehensive theory will come from the integration of behavioral economics with behavioral biology, and that this project depends on the insights from evolutionary analysis, genetics, and neuroscience. Considering the biological basis of human behavior, however, and, realistically considering the role of trust, altruism, reciprocity, and empathy in market transactions requires a reexamination of the role of gender in the construction of human society.*

*First, we revisit Gilligan, and argue that her articulation of relational feminism faltered, in part, because she could not identify the source of the stereotypically feminine. Second, we consider the ways in which the limitations of the rational actor model meant that law and economics could also not resolve the relational concerns that Gilligan raised. Third,*

**Law & Economics: Toward Social Justice**
**Research in Law and Economics: A Journal of Policy, Volume 24, 189–235**

**ISSN: 0193-5895/doi:10.1108/S0193-5895(2009)0000024012**

*we discuss the rediscovery of gender that is emerging from the gendered results of game theory trials and the new research on the biological basis of gender differences. Finally, we conclude that incorporating the insights of this new research into law and the social sciences will require a new methodology. Instead of narrow-minded focus on the incentive effects in the marginal transaction, we argue that reconsideration of stereotypically masculine and feminine traits requires an emphasis on balance.*

## 1. INTRODUCTION

Law and the social sciences are on the brink of a paradigm shift. For the past half century, imperial economics and the rational actor model have dominated academic discourse. The model's simplifying assumptions that bracketed distributions of wealth and entitlements, assumed that preferences were exogenously determined, and maintained that individuals acted to maximize their own self-interest provided a powerful research tool. Although economists have always recognized that the model did not accurately describe human motivation, and whereas subsequent models selectively relaxed the original assumptions, the basic model generated predictions about the potential impact of proposed policies and served to explain the limitations of command-control economics as communism and socialism appeared to run their course. With the "fall of the wall," Fukuyama's celebration of "The End of History," and globalization, the final triumph of decentralization, autonomy, and markets appeared at hand.

Rather than assure the continued dominance of rational actor methodology, however, the very success of deregulation and decentralization is insuring its demise. The most interesting issues of the day, which once focused on the structure of government, are today more focused on the creation of markets and the role of culture. How do societies manage the transition to freer markets and decentralized decision-making? What is the minimum infrastructure necessary for a well-functioning society? Why do some cultures, even within the same society, prosper more readily than others? And perhaps most critically, how do societies instill habits of honesty and trustworthiness that even Richard Posner (1998) sees as enhancing the efficiency of markets?

In addressing these issues, more complex models of human motivation are critical. Economics itself, led by the insights that have come from game theory, is increasingly focused on examination of trust, altruism, reciprocity, and empathy (Goodenough, 2008). Behavioral economics, which has been defined as "the combination of psychology and economics that investigates what happens in markets in which some of the agents display human limitations and complications," attempts to systematically address the limitations of rational actor assumptions (Jolls, Sunstein, & Thaler, 1998). Jolls et al. (1998) observe that the "unifying idea in our analysis is that behavioral economics allows us to model and predict behavior relevant to law with the tools of traditional economic analysis, but with more accurate assumptions about human behavior, and more accurate predictions and prescriptions about law." As the number of exceptions to the assumptions of rationality have multiplied, and as the issues of the hour make the exceptions as, if not more, important than the rules, a multitude of disciplines have joined the behaviorists in proposed alternative theories of human motivation (Prentice, 2003).[1]

These efforts – cumulatively – are on the brink of dethroning the rational actor model altogether for a more robust theory of human motivation. We argue that the most likely source for a new comprehensive theory is based on the integration of behavioral economics with behavioral biology, and that the success of this project, in turn, depends on the integration of the insights that come from evolutionary analysis, genetics, and neuroscience. Other work, and particularly Owen Jones's careful and comprehensive scholarship (Jones & Goldsmith, 2005), lays out the promise of behavioral biology for law. In this chapter, however, we will place these developments within biology and economics in a framework that shifts the focus of legal discussion from the limitations of the regulatory state to the creation of institutions, private and public, that effectively serve to instill norms and coordinate human activity. In the process, we will argue that the new paradigm and the research agenda that accompanies it will be greatly enriched by a reconsideration of the importance of feminism.

"Homo economicus" (Prentice, 2003),[2] that is, the simplified rational actor, maximizes utility by focusing on a relatively narrow definition of self-interest, one largely defined in terms of material well-being (see Posner, 1980; Kronman, 1980).[3] If there is to be an alternative paradigm, it is likely to come from behavioral biology, which starts with Darwin's assumption that any adaptation that provides a better chance of replication is likely to perpetuate itself (Jones, 1997; Dawkins, 2006). This analysis provides information about the differing motivations that explain behavior which go beyond assumptions concerning self-interest. Although the foundational concept of the "selfish gene" might appear to support the rational actor, evolutionary theory has explored the impact of culture on both the genetic and behavioral levels as well as the short- and long-term implications of acting "selfishly" (Dawkins, 2006). Indeed, evolutionary analysis addressed the issues that arise from altruism decades before behavioral economics, incorporating William Hamilton's idea of "inclusive fitness" into basic theories of natural selection in the 1960s (Hamilton, 1964),[4] and Robert Trivers's (1972) theories of "reciprocal altruism" and parental investment in the 1970s.[5] Tooby and Cosmides (1992) extended evolutionary analysis not just to physical innovations or observable behavior, but to the operation of the mind itself, finding that the complexity of the mind is as based in natural selection as is the complexity of the physical body.[6]

Moreover, although the rational actor model treats human motivation as a black box and looks for "revealed preferences" only through the physical manifestations of behavior, developments in neuroscience make possible a more sophisticated understanding of how individuals reach decisions (Jones & Goldsmith, 2005). Contemplating the use of neuroimaging techniques that distinguish between dilemmas that engage the portion of the brain associated with reason versus those engaging the areas that mediate emotion, Jedidiah Purdy (2006, p. 3) observes that, "[l]ike alchemists who dreamed of finding an elixir of life and mystics who labored to see the face of God, investigators now speak of 'seeing utility.'" Even the rational actor model becomes a different beast with the ability to define utility with greater precision.

Finally, advances in genetics have themselves produced a greater appreciation of the role of culture in shaping human preferences. As Jones and Goldsmith (2005) report:

> human behavior, it turns out, is even more complex and more interesting than commonly supposed ... [G]enes do not alone determine behavior, for experience and culture exert important and strong influences. Yet brains are not blank slates on which culture can inscribe anything with equal ease, for genes affect learning and contribute to cultural patterns common to the species. All human behavior reflects the intersection of genes, environments, developmental history, and the evolutionary processes that built the brain to function in the ways it does. This means that the human organism is neither genetically determined nor environmentally determined, but rather possesses multiple potentials that arise through successive interactions of genes and environments.

For example, studies that establish genetic predisposition to depression nonetheless show that depression may not occur in the absence of a major triggering event (Caspi et al., 2003). Conditions in utero that, in turn, reflect the mother's status and well-being, and cultural transmission that primes brain pathways also affect the expression of genetically transmitted traits.

In the new world of biology, nature and nurture are inextricably intertwined (Ridley, 2003).

Taken together, these and other developments in behavioral biology offer a comprehensive new approach to human behavior and motivation. Although the new paradigm has not yet completely emerged, we believe that the new, biologically based methodologies will offer a foundation for a progressive agenda that focuses more directly on how the interaction of humans influences the well-being of societies. This new paradigm offers the potential of a fuller, richer, more complex understanding of why individuals actually behave in ways that not only advance narrow self-interest, but also sacrifice self-interest in ways that advance the greater good. It must account not just for preference manifestation, but also for preference shaping. Realizing the promise of this new paradigm, however, will require reconsideration of the role of gender.

Evolutionary analysis, if it has any coherence, does so because of its focus on reproduction. Reproduction necessarily involves the combination of male and female, and behavioral biology often begins with differences in gender strategies, as Trivers's theory of parental investment suggests. Add neuroscience: if we peer into people's brains, we are likely to discover that gender matters, that there is a correlation between these different gendered evolutionary strategies, different brain development, and different contemporary behaviors. Moreover, a greater understanding of genetics is likely to produce not only more information about sex-linked characteristics, but also greater study of what determines conditions in the mother's uterus that prime fetal development and the role of maternal bonding and transmission of values that activates or suppresses genetic predisposition. It is impossible to discuss biology without considering gender.

Of course, addressing gender explicitly raises fears that male and female will be defined in terms of essentialist qualities, and that the historic discrimination against women in accordance with the gender stereotypes of the day will be reinforced. Although we believe that the new biology distinguishes between differences in observed preferences and differences in the capacity to master complex tasks, we also believe that the multiple risks that come from stereotyping are real. Although we cannot let the threat of stereotyping affect our acquisition of knowledge, we must acknowledge the threat and confront it.

In this chapter, we will not attempt either to fully articulate the new paradigm or to fully describe the new biological techniques we believe will contribute to it. Instead, we will incorporate gender consciousness into critiques of the rational actor model by revisiting Carol Gilligan's critique of

Lawrence Kohlberg's account of moral development. This effort will provide a lens on the relationship between the demise of the rational actor, the rise of the new paradigm, and feminism. In the process, we wil argue that Gilligan's articulation of relational feminism, whereas it rests on many of the attributes that behavioral biology and economics also emphasize, faltered, in part, because Gilligan could not identify the source of the stereotypically feminine values she wished to revalue. Second, we will consider the ways in which the limitations of the rational actor model mean that law and economics also could not resolve the relational concerns that Gilligan raised. Third, we will discuss the shift across disciplines that has made the social meaning of Gilligan's critique more salient. This shift should prompt reconsideration of Gilligan's project of revaluing "feminine" concern about relational values as a necessary counterpoint to the "masculine" inclination to create hierarchies and to overemphasize material advantage. This idea of balance, opposed to maximization or conflict, may be an essential element of the new paradigm.

## 2. RELATIONAL FEMINISM REVISITED

Kate Bartlett defined feminism in 1990 as "asking the woman question" or identifying "the gender implications of rules and practices which might otherwise appear to be neutral or objective."

Initially, this produced a focus on equality: inclusion of women on the same terms as men. The focus soon moved to consideration of the ways in which women's perspectives differed from men's. Women in rape cases, for example, asked, "why the defense of consent focuses on the perspective of the defendant and what he 'reasonably' thought the woman wanted, rather than the perspective of the woman and the intentions she 'reasonably' thought she conveyed to the defendant" (Bartlett, 1990). As a result of the changed perspectives, rape laws changed and, indeed, Michigan eliminated the consent issue altogether, whereas other states revised what had been immunity to charges of rape within marriage (Chamallas, 1988). These reforms occurred partly because the articulation of women's perspectives altered perceptions of justice for men as well as women, and partly because the inclusion of women in political and legal circles changed the balance of power.

Feminist concerns quickly shifted, however, from easily remedied examples of formal inequality to circumstances in which men and women's situations were not the same. Consider, for example, the issue of pregnancy discrimination. The Supreme Court held that, since only women become pregnant and not all women do, differences in the treatment of pregnancy from other medical conditions were not "sex discrimination" (*General Electric Co. v. Gilbert*, 1976). Congress responded by amending Title VII to bar discrimination in employment on the basis of pregnant status (Becker, Bowman, & Torrey, 2001). Feminists of the time argued that gender equality and full social inclusion required not just equal treatment, but consideration of the ways in which women differed from men, and inclusion of "feminine" as well as "masculine" values in the definition of the common good.

Carol Gilligan galvanized this discussion with her 1982 book, "In a Different Voice." In that work, she criticized the research of Harvard developmental psychologist Lawrence Kohlberg. Building on Piaget's development theories, he had constructed six stages illustrating the development of moral judgment on the basis of an empirical study of 84 boys whose development he followed over the course of 20 years (Gilligan, 1982).[7] Gilligan used the application of Kohlberg's theories to two prototypical 11-year-olds, Jake and Amy, to capture Kohlberg's psychologists' failure to value the "relational caring voice" stereotypically associated with women.

Kohlberg had presented his test subjects with the following dilemma:

> In Europe, a woman was near death from a very bad disease, a special kind of cancer. Doctors thought that there was one drug that might save her. It was a form of radium that a druggist in the same town had recently discovered. The drug was expensive to make, but the druggist was charging ten times what the drug cost him to make. He paid $200 for the radium and charged $2,000 for a small dose of the drug. The sick woman's husband, Heinz, went to everyone he knew to borrow the money, but he could get together only about $1,000, which was half of what it cost. He told the druggist that his wife was dying and asked him to sell it cheaper or let him pay later. But the druggist said, "No, I discovered the drug and I'm going to make money from it." Heinz got desperate and broke into the man's store to steal the drug for his wife.
>
> Should the husband have done that? Was it right or wrong? (Gilligan, 1982)

Jake constructs the dilemma, as Kohlberg did, as a conflict between the value of Heinz's wife's life, and the value of the property to the druggist (Gilligan, 1982). He sees the issue "sort of like a math problem with humans," with only one possible solution (*ibid.*). At 11, he is confident of his answer. He believes in the power of logic. He uses a hierarchical approach to select one value over another. And since his answer is rationally derived, he assumes that anyone else would reach the same conclusion, and that a judge "would also consider stealing to be the right thing for Heinz to do," and that the judge would thus give him a light sentence (*ibid.*).

Amy, also 11 and planning to become a scientist, took a different approach to the dilemma. She saw it as "a narrative of relationships that extends over time" (Gilligan, 1982). In contrast with Jake's confidence, she seems evasive and unsure. She considers the effect on the wife if Heinz were to be imprisoned and unable to care for her. She would encourage Heinz to go back and try to change the druggist's mind. She holds to the idea that it is wrong both to permit the wife to die, and for Heinz to have to steal. Although she enjoys solving the question posed, which asked her to justify *Heinz's* behavior, Amy is puzzled by the druggists' indifference. Her firmest conclusion is that if Heinz were to persist, he would eventually find a way to persuade the druggist to provide the drug (Gilligan, 1982). If this were a law school exam, Jake would earn a higher grade than Amy, and for similar reasons, including his greater willingness to answer the question posed, he ranks more highly on Kohlberg's test of moral development (Hartwell, 1995).

Gilligan objected to the higher rank given the "ethic of justice" that valorized hierarchical thinking over the "ethic of care" that paid more attention to relationships. Her critique, with its contrast of "webs" and "ladders," inspired a firestorm of reaction (Abrams, 2001). It also generated a new wave of feminism that sought to identify and revalue the traditionally feminine and traits associated with women across a wide variety of fields. In addition, the discussion amplified an emerging debate between communitarians and libertarians. Feminists joined communitarians such as Michael Sandel in identifying liberalism with an impoverished conception of individual actors that celebrated independence at the expense of connection. The new movement identified women's perspectives with greater emphasis on human relationships, and greater concern for the emotional quality of human interactions (West, 1988).

Following Gilligan, a generation of relational feminists celebrated connection, care, and context, examining the relationship between the individual and her location within a larger society. Relational feminism sought to explore the internal construction and parameters of particular relationships, as well as the place those relationships occupy in the external world. It emphasized the development of values that would serve as an alternative to hierarchy and competition. The concept of connection became an important touchstone for both "cultural" and radical feminists. As Robin West explains, "Underlying both radical and cultural feminism is a conception of women's existential state that is grounded in women's potential for physical, material connection to human life, just as underlying both liberal and critical legalism is a conception of men's existential state that is grounded in the inevitability of men's physical separation from the species" (West, 1988, p. 14). This "physical, material" connection symbolizes the ability of women to focus on relationships.

Connection is, of course, not a monolithic concept, and it inherently encompasses principles of empathy and intimacy. Through empathy, we can "understand [ ] the experience or situation of another, both affectively and cognitively" (Henderson, 1987, p. 1579). Empathy allows us to draw on our own experiences so that we can understand, and thus feel connected to, others.

Although Gilligan's contributions to developmental psychology are undeniable, and whereas the influence of relational feminism remains strong in fields such as education, relational feminism soon foundered on two issues that divided feminists: is the relational critique Gilligan championed in fact about gender differences, and if it is, what is the source of the differences? Many feminists attacked the idea of gender essentialism, that is, the claim that women share "essential" qualities that distinguish them from men, or common experiences that give all women similar perspectives (Abrams, 2001).[8] Indeed, researchers have questioned whether what Gilligan observed is about gender at all. Subsequent studies, for example, administered Kohlberg's questions to larger groups without necessarily finding that boys and girls answered the questions differently (see Tavris, 1992; Friedman, Robinson, & Friedman, 1987; Thomas, 1986; Walker, 1984; Rothbart & Albert, 1986; Ford & Lowery, 1986).[9]

Gilligan, however, never claimed that she was describing women's distinctive qualities; she only wanted to revalue those associated with the stereotypically feminine. This nonetheless left open the source of the stereotypes. A famous exchange between Gilligan and Catharine Mackinnon illustrates the dispute:

> *Gilligan*: Your definition of power is his definition.
>
> *Mackinnon*: This is because the society *is* that way, it operates on his definition, and I am trying to change it.
>
> *Gilligan*: To have her definition come in?
>
> *Mackinnon*: That would be a part of it, but more to have a definition that she would articulate that she cannot now, because his foot is on her throat.
>
> *Gilligan*: She's saying it.

> *Mackinnon*: I know, but she is articulating the feminine. And you are calling it hers. That's what I find infuriating.
>
> *Gilligan*: No, I am saying she is articulating a set of values which are very positive.
>
> *Mackinnon*: Right, and I am saying they are feminine. And calling them hers is infuriating to me because we have never had the power to develop what ours really would be. (Gilligan, 1985)[10]

Mackinnon concluded that even if Amy's responses can, in fact, be linked to a distinctive women's perspective, there is no reason to believe that the views "are theirs," that is, that they represent the authentic views of women. She argued that women may have learned to value care because caring for men was what men valued, and that to emphasize women's orientation toward care without emphasizing the context of the constraining social construction in which it emerged was an "insult to [women's] possibilities" (Abrams, 2001). Following the attacks on Gilligan, feminism fractured. It placed greater emphasis on Mackinnon's power analysis than on Gilligan's ethic of care, and on identifying women's diverse perspectives than on defining a common agenda (*ibid.*). Although Gilligan's method – giving voice to the girls in her interviews and linking their views to the developmental steps in moral reasoning – made sense in the context of her field, it did not provide a satisfying way to address relational issues across the academy.

At the end of day, although relational feminists retained their conviction that women's ability to connect should receive equal weight with men's preferences for separation and hierarchy, they could not ultimately answer the question whether these differences are nature or nurture – whether the ethic of care arose from women's innate character or simply reflected values developed because men had "their feet on women's throats" (Abrams, 2001).[11] And, to the extent that relational feminism reinforced the association between women and care – rather than the promotion of alternative values – feminists then feared it would be used to undercut women's other claims for equality.

## 3. THE RATIONAL ACTOR MODEL IN FEMINIST CONTEXT

If Gilligan could not ultimately identify the source of the relational values associated with the stereotypically feminine, neoclassical economics marginalized or bracketed relational concerns (Carbone, 1990).[12] Neoclassical economics has long rested on the rational actor model; that is, predictions of human behavior that assume that people act rationally "to maximize their utility according to their preferences," that their preferences are exogenous, information and transactions are costless, and markets work perfectly (Dau-Schmidt, 1997). These assumptions, which expressly exclude consideration of the feedback loops that occur when preferences depend on the reaction of others, give neoclassical economics its predictive power. The assumptions also make law and economics a double-edged sword for feminists; the rational actor methodology is as least as impoverished as Kohlberg's model in dealing with Amy's relational concerns, but it does not hesitate to explain Amy's lack of power or earning capacity in terms of her "revealed preference" for an ethic of care.

Let us return to the example of Heinz and the druggist. Kohlberg used the example to chart the progression of moral reasoning. A neoclassical economist would use the example to predict behavior. If Heinz is assumed to act "rationally," the economist would predict that he is likely to steal the drug *if* he values the possibility of saving his wife's life more than the negative consequences of stealing the drug. The economist's evaluation of Heinz's preferences would take them as exogenously determined and stable over time; Crespi (1997b) explains that for economists to treat preferences as exogenous means that the preferences "are viewed as innate personal characteristics that have a pre-legal, pre-political, acontextual existence, and are not affected by the legal rules that determine people's initial entitlements and govern their conduct." Accordingly, economic models, much like Kohlberg's models of moral reasoning, would approach Heinz's act as independent of Amy's concerns about the wife's reaction to Heinz's possible imprisonment (a contextual factor), or of the law's condemnation, condonation, or mitigation of the act of theft in these circumstances. Indeed, an economist would treat Heinz's act of stealing the drug (since he has already done so in Kohlberg's story) as a revealed preference – a rational Heinz *must* value the drug more than the consequences of the theft if he is willing to steal it.

The neoclassical model uses the same techniques even when the question shifts from the positive (predicting Heinz's behavior) to the normative (determining whether the law should encourage or deter Heinz's theft). To the extent that neoclassical economists propose normative approaches, they tend to advance theories that maximize utility (Dau-Schmidt, 1997).[13] Take the example of a hiker, starving and lost in the woods, who breaks into a privately owned cabin and steals food in order to survive. When charged with breaking and entering, trespass or theft, he claims the defense of necessity. Richard Posner (1998) observes that the necessity defense "will usually succeed if there is a very great disparity between the cost of the crime to the victim and the gain to the injurer." Richard Parry notes that "[a]t least one federal court has expressly declared that necessity is 'a utilitarian defense' based on "maximizing social welfare ... where the social benefits of the crime outweigh the social costs of failing to commit the crime" (Parry, 1999, citing *United States v. Schoon*, 971 F.2d 193 (9th Cir. 1991)). Parry concludes that "this approach, which insists that necessity turns solely on 'avoiding the greatest amount of harm at the least cost,' ... says nothing about the moral desirability of the defendant's choices or conduct ..." (Parry, 1999). David Friedman (2000), however, disagrees, maintaining that the "just" approach and the "efficient" approach often coincide, and that rules promoting efficiency are likely to also produce desirable conduct.[14] After all, our society is hardly likely to conclude that the hiker should starve to death to avoid breaking into the cabin.

Nonetheless, even without taking Parry's concerns into account, a utilitarian calculus does not easily resolve the issue of Heinz and the druggist. Heinz, like the hiker in the woods, is likely to value his wife's life more than avoiding the act of theft, and as the responses to Kohlberg's study suggests, most people are likely to agree with him. Unlike the hiker, however, Heinz has had an opportunity to propose an exchange to the druggist, and the druggist has turned him down. We are not told why. The druggist may have a limited supply of the drug and may prefer the higher (or at least more immediate) amounts other customers can pay. The druggist may have a patent that creates a temporary monopoly and may be convinced that altering the price for one customer will create pressure to reduce the price for many customers who, unlike Heinz, can afford to pay the higher amount. The druggist may dislike or distrust Heinz or may be acting irrationally. The story sets up a market in which the druggist is the only possible supplier; without perfect competition, there is no reason to assume that a Pareto optimal bargain will occur even if one clearly exists.

A court faced with Heinz's prosecution for theft would, therefore, face a dilemma. If it excused Heinz's act, it might encourage others to steal in the face of less exigent circumstances. Indeed, publicly excusing the theft might undermine the strength of the internalized norms against theft, even if there were agreement that this theft is justified. Posner, in adopting a utilitarian approach to the necessity defense, emphasized that the defense was likely to be applied where there was a "*very great* disparity between the cost of the crime to the victim and the gain to the injurer," not just where the gain to the thief outweighed the cost to the victim (Posner, 1998). The necessity defense works only if limited to relatively extreme cases.[15] Uncertainty that it will be applied helps insure that only those facing no real alternatives will act without first exhausting other possibilities.

However, failing to excuse the theft in these circumstances might bring the entire property regime underlying drug sales into disrepute. This example, if it were to turn on the druggist's patent or a monopoly position based on trade secrets, replicates some of the dilemmas underlying pharmaceutical manufacture. The specter of people dying because of their inability to afford a drug that costs little to produce strikes many people as unfair. Extensive scholarship from sociologist Talcott Parsons through Jurgen Habermas (1990) explores the role of legitimacy in holding together parts of society with divergent interests. A group systematically excluded from access to life-saving drugs in the face of an epidemic might view Heinz's conviction for theft as cause for rebellion. The choice of whether to excuse or mitigate Heinz's act of theft might therefore turn, as a matter of policy, on which risk is greater: undermining internalization of the norms against theft by excusing Heinz's flouting of the rules, or calling the legitimacy of the norms into question by applying them in a case in which the druggists' refusal to sell to Heinz's might be perceived as unjust.

In the face of this type of analysis, Kenneth Dau-Schmidt (1997) has called for relaxation of the assumption of exogenous preferences to permit consideration of the role of law in shaping norms, which, of course, in turn affects individual utility. He argues that a major objective of the criminal law, as these examples suggest, is to shape preferences, and any assumption of exogenous preferences is descriptively inaccurate and implicitly promotes the status quo (Dau-Schmidt, 1997). Gregory Crespi (1997b) responded this way:

> Unfortunately, if the exogenous preferences assumption is relaxed, the Chicago School models will no longer be able to provide determinate predictions, since we are as yet unable to formulate precisely when and to what extent our policies will impact preferences... .
>
> We face a difficult choice. We can continue to use restrictive Chicago School models which obscure several crucial questions raised by the fact that many policies do alter preferences: Which preferences should be favored? Which preferences should be disfavored? And what is the appropriate role of the state in shaping individual preferences? Or we can relax the assumptions of our models to allow for endogenous preferences but then find that we are unable either to predict or evaluate the results of our policies. Do we prefer tunnel vision or total blindness?

At the end of the day, the dilemma posed by the question of exogenous or endogenous preferences is not so different from that Gilligan faced. It is obviously correct to observe that the law influences people's values and that

Heinz's decision to steal or not to steal the drug depends in part on the value he places in observing the laws against theft. In addition, whether or not the druggist's motivation for turning down Heinz's proposals affects Heinz's willingness to steal the drug, it certainly affects the perceived legitimacy of a regime that would punish Heinz. Amy's relational concerns are an important component of public policy just as they are an important component of moral development. Crespi's challenge to Dau-Schmidt echoed Mackinnon's challenge to Gilligan: once we acknowledge the salience of these concerns, what framework do we have for evaluating them? How do we know whether they are or should be "hers"? Equally importantly, how do we know whether they should be "ours"; that is, a basis for determining law and policy?

Although law and economics thus offers limited tools for addressing the social meaning of legal rules, it has no difficulty dealing with the differences between Jake and Amy's moral preferences. Let the market decide! Indeed, it is arguable that in the 1990s, the intersection of law and economics and feminism guaranteed the dominance of radical feminism over relational feminism, and the clash between feminism and evolutionary biology delayed the more extensive introduction of biological methods into law and the social sciences. These disputes occurred, in part, because economics, with its bracketing of the initial distribution of resources and emphasis on revealed preferences, assumed that existing gender roles reflected an optimal allocation of responsibilities. If a druggist motivated by the ethic of care (read "female") were to be more likely to value the benefit to Heinz's family over the additional profit she might earn from an alternative transaction, it would simply be an example of the brilliance of the market in action – no matter what the cumulative effect of the positions of female versus male druggists. The justice of the overall result would not be on the table, the collective-action issues (e.g., care-oriented druggists might prefer a norm requiring a shared obligation to assist Heinz) would be marginalized, and the norm-creation process (do druggists develop an obligation to make life-saving drugs available at something less than the full market price?) would be opaque.

In this context, consideration of gender differences, whether innate or culturally constructed, could be hazardous. Gary Becker (1981), for example, in his Nobel Prize winning extension of the realm of economics to the family observed that:

> Although the sharp sexual division of labor in all societies between the market and household sectors is partly due to the gains from specialized investments, it is also partly due to intrinsic differences between the sexes.

> ...[B]iological differences in comparative advantage explain not only why households typically have both sexes, but also why women have usually spent their time bearing and rearing children and engaging in other household activities, whereas men have spent their time in market activities. This sexual division of labor has been found in virtually all human societies, and in most other biological species that fertilize eggs within the body of the female.

The observation triggered in one short paragraph feminist fear and loathing for economics and biology. Here is the seemingly neutral use of economics to justify the world as it is (or more accurately by the time Becker wrote, *was*) on the basis of biology. Becker, ahead of his time on this one, even acknowledged the risk of stereotype threat, and deemed this, too, efficient. He reasoned that "deviant investments (medical education for women?) would presumably be more common if deviant biology (women unable to have children, women unwilling to be homemakers, or women more likely than their husbands to succeed in the medical profession?) were more common – or if it were revealed at younger ages" (Becker, 1981). Given the inability to predict these matters from childhood, Becker argued that it was easier for the utility maximizing parent to simply assume that girls should take home economics, whereas boys study auto mechanics. Different comparative advantages (those trained to be auto mechanics could earn more than those trained to be homemakers) would then translate into advantages from specialization in home and market. It did not matter that Becker bracketed the power structure constraining women's choices and missed the much bigger aspect of specialization transforming women's lives, viz., the much more efficient specialization among women as women moving into the workforce brought home food from McDonald's and hired other women to clean their homes and care for their children (see Carbone, 2000).[16] Economics celebrated the use of biology and equations to valorize the status quo, identifying women with a marginalized ethic of care in the process, even when this novel use of economics was palpably wrong (Fuchs, 1988).[17] In the meantime, they had very little to say about the wholesale change in norms that accompanied the reorganization of women's lives.

## 4. BEHAVIORAL BIOLOGY REVISITED

> Only the most extreme proponents of sociobiology ... would assert that nurturance is or comes to be embodied in a particular portion of the brain.
>
> – Kathryn Abrams (1992)

> Oxytocin is increasingly recognized as important in facilitating bonding between mother and child and between sexual partners ... the role of oxytocin [is] supported by

> experiments with prairie voles, which have "faithful marriages," and montane voles, which do not. When each species received the same amount of oxytocin, they reacted differently, with prairie voles exhibiting "all the characteristic symptoms of monogamy, such as a strong preference for one partner and aggression toward other voles," while the same injections did not affect the behavior of the montane voles.
>
> – Carbone and Cahn (2004)

> What is the promise of neuroeconomics? This nascent field has converted a fast-growing set of laboratory results into an impression of great promise to change our understanding of choice and rationality. Using magnetic resonance imaging (MRI) technology, neuroscientists observe blood flow in the brains of people engaged in familiar tasks of reasoning and choice. The preliminary results already suggest much about which regions of the brain engage in which dimensions of reasoning, choice, and moral judgment. Like alchemists who dreamed of finding an elixir of life and mystics who labored to see the face of God, investigators now speak of "seeing utility." What we have seen only in a mirror darkly, we might now meet vividly and immediately. And in an age when both economics and biology have vast reach and authority in the academy and the larger culture, the analogy to encountering life's essence or God's person might not be altogether far-fetched. For the first time, we could unveil and examine the hidden logic of our lives. This is the promise.
>
> – Jedidiah Purdy (2006)

Fifteen years later, we do have better understandings of the impact of both biology and social construction on the development of sex roles, and of the role that science might play in helping us understand social construction. These insights will come not from discovering a region of the brain controlling nurturance, but as Owen Jones and Tim Goldsmith (2005) emphasize, from "the integrated, interdisciplinary efforts of cognitive scientists, neuroscientists, and evolutionary biologists as well as social scientists in psychology, anthropology, economics, and related disciplines." The use of a broad interdisciplinary approach to address questions long posed by law, economics, and moral reasoning offers to remake what Arthur Leff termed as the choice between "tunnel vision or total blindness" (Crespi, 1997a). These techniques also promise to revitalize relational feminism and to make possible a renewed focus away from individual actors and back toward a more self-conscious understanding of social meaning. To do so, however, will require of confronting – and transcending – the issue of gender.

### *4.1. Feminist Fear and Loathing*

During the same period that Carol Gilligan touched off a wave of excitement about the potential revaluing of the stereotypically feminine, E.O. Wilson set off a wave of revulsion in the same circles with his work on sociobiology. Wilson, whose scientific career focused on the study of ants, argued that the same evolutionary analysis that explained insect evolution could be applied to humans. These evolutionary methods incorporate Charles Darwin's basic insight that "only those traits helping individuals to improve their reproductive success can proliferate" (Jones, 1997).

To understand why Wilson's book on sociobiology was controversial, consider a simplistic application to Heinz and the druggist. To the extent Gilligan claimed that "Amy" was more sensitive to the relational concerns in the story, evolutionary analysis might speculate on the reason why. That speculation is likely to focus on two differences between men and women. First, because women become pregnant and give birth and men do not, women can have fewer offspring than men (Baker, 2000). Second, (and partly as a result of the first), women are more likely to care for children, particularly very young children than men (*ibid.*). Given that women provide the majority of care for children, the children of women more sensitive to their needs are more likely to survive, and thus women are more likely than men to be sensitive to relational concerns.

Feminists were and continue to be extraordinarily wary of such analysis because, as the discussion of Becker's Nobel Prize winning work suggests, such insights play out in the context of a debate between libertarians, who celebrate the results of unregulated market processes as the reflection of women's "revealed" and presumptively authentic preferences, and social constructivists, who see market transactions as the product of the existing allocation of power, and therefore unlikely to maximize either individual (read "women's") happiness or collective well-being. Libertarians, including many of those who embrace the rational actor model, distrust social constructivists because they fear that the emphasis on power authorizes authoritarian countermeasures (e.g., Ridley, 2003).[18]

In a classic debate in the early 1990s, Richard Epstein and Kathryn Abrams explored the implications of biology in exactly these terms. Like Becker, Epstein argued that if there is even a slight predisposition for women to nurture, then it becomes economically rational for women to specialize in nurturing roles. Relying on this analysis, Epstein (1992a, 1992b, 1992c) reasoned that a maternity leave program indicates that social construction is equivalent to "massive coercion by the state in support of dubious schemes of social control that could never earn their place in an open market" (Epstein, 1992a). Epstein argued:

> In occupational categories that are heavily dependent on spatial differences, say, for example, architecture, we should expect to see men, on balance, do somewhat better than

> women in a perfect market because their natural endowments now turn out to be more suitable for the task. But if there are other occupations, such as counseling and guidance, that demand more of the nurturing and intuitive skills associated with the female roles in child rearing, then women should be at a relative advantage to men in seeking these positions ... radical changes in social organization will not obliterate the importance of critical biological differences. (Epstein, 1992c)

In response, Kathryn Abrams observed that it is critical that "gender-specific differences are understood to be complex, changeable phenomena rather than biologically ordained mandates," and that, consequently, Epstein's arguments become even "less clear" (Abrams, 1992). In a hunter-gatherer society, the average man might have an advantage over the average woman in spatial reasoning without necessarily implying either that no woman should pursue a career as an architect, or that the average female applicant would necessary be less successful than the average male applicant in architectural school. For Abrams, the results are a result of conscious social choices critical because of their impact on women's relative standing in society. For Epstein, they are about freely made, "efficient choices"; any more direct intervention to alter the outcomes will be a heavy-handed exercise in futility.

Unsurprisingly, therefore, feminists have met efforts to introduce biological observations into legal discourse with suspicion. Kingsley Browne (1995) charged that, "[i]n contrast to the weighty burden of proof imposed on those urging a biological basis for sex differences in behavior, those arguing that sex differences are socially constructed have borne little burden at all." Richard Epstein (1992c) similarly objected that feminists attempted to treat "social influences dominant to the exclusion of biological ones."[19] Indeed, as we look back to reiteration of generations of debate of nature versus nurture, it is clear that these conflicts reflect more than the level of scientific discourse in the era. David Strauss (1992), writing contemporaneously with Epstein and Abrams, argued that, "people engage in the nature-nurture debate" because it "reflects attitudes. The view that 'it's genetic' goes hand in hand with an attitude that we cannot fight the status quo." Kathy Baker, one of the first legal scholars to explore the intersection between biology and feminism, observed that:

> For years feminists have been describing a world in which sexual violence is pervasive, marriage is a Faustian and dangerous bargain for women, and caretaking is a huge amount of usually unrewarded work. This is the world that the biologists describe also. If the biologist's description is more frightening than the feminist one, it is only because of the common but unnecessary presumption that, because the world *is* that way, it must stay that way. No biologist believes this. (Baker, 2000)

For behavioral biology to escape the Epstein-Abrams gridlock of a decade ago, it has to transcend the debate between biological determination and the clean slate approach of the social constructivists – and in fact it already has. When Kathy Baker states, "no biologist believes this," she is describing a revolution in genetics that promises to dissolve the centuries old dichotomy between nature and nurture. Although evolutionary analysis provides a framework for understanding what we see, behavioral biology, as Jones and Goldsmith emphasize, has become increasingly integrated with modern advances in cognitive psychology, neuroscience and other fields that make it possible to test hypotheses, and in some cases to determine not just correlations with observed behavior, but in some cases causal factors.[20] These new understandings underscore the role of genetic predisposition, not in determining outcomes, but in priming the reactions to environmental conditions. Matt Ridley (2003) writes:

> Genes themselves are implacable determinists churning out utterly predictable messages. But because of the way their promoters switch on and off in response to external instruction, genes are very far from being fixed in their actions. Instead, they are devices for extracting information from the environment. Every minute, every second, the pattern of genes being expressed in your brain changes, often in direct or indirect response to events outside the body. Genes are the mechanisms of experience.

The new biology takes seriously the idea that humans are a social species. The challenge is to explain the genes that allow cultural transmission, that guide the more sophisticated coordination of human behavior (*ibid.*).[21] The new biology has little in common with the blank slate. It is likely to find that women are biologically predisposed to care for children and for that matter, that men better navigate spatial relationships in the open savanna. It nonetheless treats as the far more interesting question how humans coordinate the activities and resources necessary to move from caves to communally constructed log cabins to skyscrapers, and how, within that context, individual roles change. After all, the Dean of the School of Architecture at MIT describes the transformation of her profession from inclusion of a handful of women in the 60s to half of today's classes at many elite schools.[22]

### *4.2. Economics Revisited: The Need for Behavioral Biology*

If economics – and law – are to incorporate insights from biology, they are likely to do so both because of the increased sophistication of behavioral biology and because our understandings of the questions economists pose have changed. Behavioral insights from a multitude of sources – empirical studies as well as biology – have shown the inability of the rational actor model to address the fundamental issues on the horizon. Whether or not true believers in the neoclassical model will change their fundamental approach or simply "tweak" their theories, the model itself is rapidly being supplemented – and supplanted – by alternative approaches (Nelson, 2005; cf Kahneman, 2003).[23]

Indeed, more sophisticated knowledge about behavior is already transforming core theories about democracy and the development of law. Cass Sunstein (2006), for example, has recently called for a "New Progressivism," which builds, in part, on the recognition that whereas command-control economies have been found wanting, so too has laissez-faire economics failed to promote democracy and prosperity in the developing world (Hayek, 1944; Ramirez, 2003).[24] His New Progressivism would respect fundamental rights, promote democracy, and strengthen economic development. At the core of his essay is an effort to incorporate a more sophisticated understanding of human motivation into a redefined role for the state. His vision has three parts, beginning with

> (1) a distinctive conception of government's appropriate means, an outgrowth of the late-twentieth-century critique of economic planning, and (2) a distinctive understanding of government's appropriate ends, an outgrowth of evident failures with market arrangements and largely a product of the mid-twentieth-century critique of laissez faire. (Sunstein, 2006)

The third element then focuses on the role of norms in ordering behavior. Sunstein (2006) emphasizes that social norms, especially when reinforced by government and celebrities, can have a more powerful shaping influence on behavior than government fiat or market incentives taken in isolation. He, therefore, reconsiders the types of legal interventions that can have such effects, suggesting the importance of developing "human capabilities in a way that is alert to the nature of incentives and the role of social norms" (*ibid.*).[25] Sunstein's agenda depends, in turn, on different ways of thinking about law, as well as a more robust understanding of human motivation than the rational actor model can provide.

Dan Kahan (2003), drawing on the insights from game theory, agrees that the role of law, at least in certain settings, should be to shape behavior through its effect on internal rather than external motivation, and that the self-conscious structure of legal institutions matters. Kahan focuses on a central limitation of the rational actor model: the inability to address "collective action" problems. Prisoners' dilemmas games have increasingly focused on the extent to which human behavior, rather than simply narrow self-interest, in fact demonstrates a greater preference for cooperation than the rational actor model might predict. Consider, for example, research experience with the ultimatum game. In the game, one player proposes a division of a given sum of money, which the second player accepts or rejects. If the second player accepts the proposed division, then both players claim their respective shares of the money. If the second player rejects the division, however, the pot of money "dissolves" and neither player takes anything (Purdy, 2006). The rational actor approach suggests that the first player should propose the minimum amount necessary to get the second player to accept, and the second player should accept what is offered because otherwise neither player receives anything. In fact, student subjects most commonly offer 50 percent, and about half the time respondents reject offers below 20 percent (Henrich et al., 2005). Moreover, whereas students' experiences were consistent cross-culturally, studies with hunter–gatherers or nomadic tribes varied. Researchers found that the greater the degree to which subjects participated in market transactions, the more likely they were to offer higher amounts (*ibid.*).

Biology adds further insight. When researchers linked functional magnetic resonance imaging (fMRI) results to experiences with the ultimatum game, they also found distinct brain patterns associated with reciprocity and fairness. In responding to offers perceived as unfair, subjects showed activity in two parts of the brain: the dorsolateral prefrontal cortex (DLPFC), associated with "cognitive processes such as goal maintenance and executive control," and the bilateral anterior insula (BAI), associated with "negative emotional states" such as anger and disgust as well as with sensations of hunger and thirst (Sanfey, Rilling, Aronson, Nystrom, & Cohen, 2003, see also Cohen, 2005). Purdy (2006) reports that "[n]ot only were both regions engaged by unfair offers attributed to human offerors; but activity in the BAI was higher whereas considering offers that respondents rejected than whereas considering offers they accepted" (Purdy, 2006, discussing Sanfey et al., 2003). These findings suggest that the decision to accept an "unfair" offer depends on the balance between the level of anger the offer provokes, and the strength of the cognitive determination to accept it as a matter of self-interest. Purdy concludes that, whereas perceptions of reciprocity and fairness may be widespread, both the strength of the emotional reaction to low offers, and the cognitive willingness to override such reactions may be learned behaviors (Purdy, 2006). Not only are such "preferences" not exogenously determined, they are increasingly within reach of testing and study.

Kahan (2003), acknowledging the ultimatum game results (but writing before the fMRI images became available), emphasized the way such insights change the approach to collective-action problems. He observes that these results show that, first, the assumption that people act to maximize narrow self-interest is not necessarily true, and, second, there is no single equilibrium point toward which human behavior tends to move (*ibid.*). Instead, the results depend on the extent to which the group promotes an atmosphere of trust. Kahan concludes:

> Whereas the conventional logic of collective action counsels the creation of appropriate external incentives, the logic of reciprocity suggests the importance of promoting trust. Individuals who have faith in the willingness of others to contribute their fair share will voluntarily respond in kind. And spontaneous cooperation of this sort breeds more of the same, as individuals observe others contributing to public goods and are moved to reciprocate. In this self-sustaining atmosphere of trust, reliance on costly incentive schemes becomes less necessary. By the same token, individuals who lack faith in their peers can be expected to resist contributing to public goods, thereby inducing still others to withhold their cooperation as a means of retaliating. In this self-sustaining atmosphere of distrust, even strong (and costly) regulatory incentives are likely to be ineffective in promoting desirable behavior.

In other words, Kahan uses the insights of behavioral economics, without biology, to argue for the more self-conscious role of law in norm creation. Strategic intervention affects not just the incentives at the margin for the self-interested utility maximizing actor, but the interaction of the group: in a higher trust society, individuals internalize norms of reciprocity. Their preferences change to place greater value on the esteem in which others hold them, and to exhibit greater concern for avoiding the shame that would follow from the perception that they might be untrustworthy (*ibid.*).[26] These internalized norms, Kahan argues, are more effective in changing behavior, and, in turn, creating higher trust societies, than changes in external incentives. With these insights, legal scholars shift their focus from the marginal incentive effect of legal rules to the design of institutions.

Purdy, arguing that neuroscience will be critical to the next stage of economics, goes beyond Kahan to maintain that precisely what neuroeconomics offers is the ability to test the results of cultural norms or other interventions that may alter the balance between cognitive and emotional brain reactions. He explains that, "the contribution of neuroeconomics is that economic self-interest and the reciprocity characteristic of trust have different correlates in the brain, and may well express distinct and potentially competing motivational systems. If this is true, then those *who design legal systems* should be alert to both the benefits of consonance between the systems and the hazards of bringing them into conflict" (Purdy, 2006). Chorvat and McCabe (2004) observe along the same lines that: "If [government] can frame violations of its rules as defections from social norms, they are more likely to be punished and often private punishment is enough to enforce this obligation. To the extent that society is able to frame defection as cheating and invoke social sanctions, enforcement will become easier."

Sunstein issued his challenge for the creation of a new "progressive agenda"; Chorvat and McCabe write within a tradition closer to the neoclassical school. Together with Kahan and Purdy, however, they all approach the application of behavioral biology to law in terms of legal interventions that consciously interact with social norms. Law, economics, and behavioral biology are all turning away from models that assume narrow self-interest to broader consideration of cooperation, trust, reciprocity fairness – and the idea of morality (for more extensive examination of these issues, see Zak, 2008).[27]

### *4.3. Moral Development in Behavioral Context*

If there is anything that serves to coordinate human behavior, it is the instillation and reinforcement of norms. Kohlberg's research focused on a systematic effort to understand the process of developing moral values, a critical component of norm institutionalization. Accordingly, the new biology may affect our understanding of Kohlberg at least, as much if not more, than our understanding of Gilligan. Kohlberg made two claims: that moral reasoning was a cognitive process, and that his stages of moral development were universal in the sense that individuals in different cultures necessarily moved through the different stages sequentially (that is, from stage one to stage two to stage three without skipping from stage one to stage three). Both claims have been called into question.

Kohlberg attempted to test the cross-cultural applicability of his theory by repeating the studies in different cultures. Testing in Mexico, Taiwan, Turkey, Israel, the Yucatan, Kenya, the Bahamas, and India, he generally found the same stage sequence, with a greater percentage of some societies reaching the higher stages than others (Crain, 1985). Later studies have suggested that only stages one through three are consistently cross-cultural (Ma, 1984; see also Snarey, 1985).[28]

More recent studies have attempted to isolate the factors that produce higher versus lower scores in different cultures on Kohlberg's measure of ethical reasoning.

A study that compared Australian and Chinese auditors, for example, found that the Australians scored higher on Kohlberg's tests than did Chinese from either the mainland or Hong Kong. The authors suggest that, "[h]igher ethical reasoning scores are consistent with societies whose values are classified by individualism, small power distance, short term orientation and strong uncertainty avoidance," and conclude that because Australian and Chinese culture differ on such measures, Kohlberg's test is unlikely to produce the same results in comparable populations (Tsui & Windsor, 2001; see also Al-Shebab, 2002; but see Ma & Cheng, 1996, finding closer cross-cultural results). These findings suggest that culture may well prime the cognitive frameworks for moral choice.

This type of study, however, is limited to the use of surveys that measure the articulation of reasons for moral decision-making. They cannot test ethical behavior, nor can they identify the source of cultural differences beyond the terms of ethical discourse in different communities (compare, e.g., Nisbett & Cohen, 1996).[29] In contrast, Harvard's Cognitive Evolution Laboratory attempts to chart the actual process of moral decision-making by combining the type of moral dilemmas Kohlberg posed with fMRIs that identify the parts of the brain involved. Joshua Greene, an assistant professor of psychology involved in the studies, hypothesizes that emotional and "cognitive" factors compete for the control of behavior, and that different problems may trigger competing subsystems in the brain.

To test these theories, the Harvard lab uses the "trolley" dilemma. In this problem, the researchers ask:

> A runaway trolley is headed for five people who will be killed if it proceeds on its present course. The only way to save them is to hit a switch that will turn the trolley onto an alternate set of tracks where it will kill one person instead of five. Should you turn the trolley in order to save five people at the expense of one? Most people say yes. (Greene, Sommerville, Nystrom, Darley, & Cohen, 2001)[30]

Now, consider Greene's second dilemma, the footbridge problem:

> Once again, the trolley is headed for five people. You are on a footbridge over the tracks next to a large man. The only way to save the five people is to push this man off the bridge and into the path of the trolley. Is that morally permissible? Most people say no. (Greene et al., 2001)

Greene considers how to reconcile the different results. Using purely utilitarian reasoning, both examples involve sacrificing one person to save five. But in the second, the actor must physically push a person to his death. Greene hypothesizes that the internalized restraints on such conduct involve different areas of the brain than the process of determining whether to throw a switch that will less directly produce someone's death. His fMRI analyses, in fact, show that subjects considering the first trolley car example were more likely to engage the areas of the brain involved in working memory (i.e., the parietal lobes and the middle frontal gyrus) and higher cognitive function (Greene et al., 2001). In contrast, the example involving pushing the fat man off the bridge activated areas of the brain associated with emotion (*ibid.*). Greene hypothesizes that the different results arise because the second example triggers a response from the parts of the brain regulating emotions that overrides the utilitarian calculus produced by the parts of the brain governing cognition and working memory. He concludes that these differing responses may also correspond to utilitarian versus deontological approaches in philosophy (see Greene, 2007, see also Greene, 2002).

Greene suggests further that the involvement of different brain areas may explain some of the anomalies Kohlberg discovered in his own tests. In examining college students, Kohlberg found that students he had identified as stage five moral reasoners on one test performed at stage two on a subsequent test. Yet, Kohlberg identified stage two with young children displaying a naively egoistic world view, and his approach to developmental stages maintained that once an individual moved on to a higher stage, there should be no return to the earlier forms of expression (Greene, 2002; see also Fishkin, 1984). The results may be explained, however, by the existence of two different systems, with the stage five reasoning produced by the cognitive system and the stage two results produced by the emotional system.

These results provide new tools in addressing normative issues. Greene emphasizes that his use of fMRIs produces a positive description of the operation of the brain, not endorsement of one normative conclusion over another (Greene et al., 2001; see Greene, 2007).[31] But he clearly believes that the results have implications for implementing normative propositions. Take, for example, the punishment that the criminal law might impose on Heinz. The standard economic approach, using utilitarian reasoning, might recommend the punishment that would provide optimal deterrence in the future. Conversely, a retributivist approach would consider the extent to which Heinz's act deserved punishment. Greene cites a series of studies that show that, in meting out punishment, test subjects are much more influenced by emotional than cognitive factors. It is the level of outrage associated with the criminal act and not the punishment needed to deter that best explained choice of penalty in these studies (Greene, 2007). fMRI studies confirm that the extent of punishment subjects inflict correlates with the degree to which the punishment decision involves the parts of the brain associated with emotion (de Quervain et al., 2004). These results suggest, at a practical level, that a randomly chosen jury is unlikely to inflict a serious penalty on Heinz in accordance with the facts of Kohlberg's scenario unless they feel outrage at Heinz's act, outrage that is unlikely in the absence of betrayal, injury to the druggist, or another patient deprived of the drug, etc.

Marc Hauser argues, on the basis of Noam Chomsky's linguistic theories, animal studies that demonstrate that other mammals display similar basic "moral" responses, and studies those like those using the trolley car dilemma, that humans have a universal moral grammar, an instinctive, unconscious tool kit for constructing moral systems (Hauser, 2006). Other researchers, although not necessarily as deterministic, expect to find a high degree of consensus on such basic issues as the unacceptability of murder and incest, and an important role for culture in shaping the development of the mind to react to more culturally specific issues (Robinson & Kurzban, 2007). Although the ability of legal analysis to incorporate the insights from the new science is in its infancy, greater understanding of the neurological basis for moral judgments changes the nature of Kohlberg's and Dau-Schmidt's undertakings – and sooner or later takes us back to Gilligan.

## 5. GILLIGAN IN BIOLOGICAL CONTEXT

Research on the biological basis of gender differences has mushroomed in recent years, and the scholarly taboos against acknowledging gender differences may be waning. At least three explanations are immediately apparent: first, the study of biology necessarily involves consideration of gender and the existence of at least some biological differences is obvious and undeniable; second, more sophisticated research techniques make more nuanced findings possible and essential to the study of diseases as diverse as breast cancer and autism; and third, a generation of women researchers have spearheaded the efforts.

The emerging literature on gender is vast and rapidly increasing. In considering the implication for law, economics, and feminism, however, we wish to focus on two areas: game theory and the autism research that considers child development and a "theory of mind." Both rediscover (not always with attribution) the qualities Gilligan associated with the stereotypically feminine. We examine these findings, however, with a note of caution. The existence of differences in brain structure, development, and function do not necessarily explain complex behavior, and even where some differences may be innate, they do not necessarily indicate either incapacity or immutability. Instead, gender may be more important in shaping preferences than abilities.

### *5.1. Game Theory in Feminist Context*

Game theory, as we have discussed earlier, allows the empirical investigation and modeling of strategic decision-making. This empirical investigation allows researches to separate out the interaction of numerous attributes (including, most importantly for our purposes, gender) and preferences in studying behavior. Perhaps the best-known "game" is the prisoners' dilemma in which two prisoners will receive short sentences if neither testifies against the other, but if one defects whereas the other remains silent, the first will go free, whereas the second will receive a very lengthy sentence. Game theory began in the 1940s as a branch of mathematics, but it drew increasing interest in the 1970s as the combination of cooperation and retaliation outperformed more "selfish" strategies in computer simulations (see Ridley, 1996 for a summary of these developments). As the role of cooperation captured increased academic attention, so too did interest in testing gender differences in game theory performances.

Economists Croson and Gneezy (2004) have performed a meta-analysis of scores of studies involving the trust, dictator, ultimatum, and other prisoner dilemma games conducted over decades of study. They find that:

> We believe, as suggested by Gilligan (1982), that men's decisions are less context-specific than women's. Participants of both genders are likely maximizing an underlying utility function, but the function that men use is less sensitive to the conditions of the experiment, information about the other party, and (even) the other party's actions, than the function that women use. This causes what appear to be inconsistent results in our experimental studies; sometimes men appear more altruistic than women and other times, women appear more altruistic than men. But primarily what we see is women's behavior is more *context-dependent* than that of men. (p. 38)

Moreover, in subsequent research, they found that men tended to view trust more strategically than women, who instead focused on the relationships at issue (Croson & Gneezy, 2004). Part of the way in which women are more context-dependent is that their responses are more likely to vary if they can see the other person than if they are dealing with an anonymous subject behind a screen, or if they are given information such as a gender-linked name (see also Croson & Buchan, 1999). In the ultimatum game, for example, the initial offers vary relatively little between men and women or from one type of game to the next. The responders' behavior, however, varies considerably. Where the parties could see each other, both men and women were more likely to accept offers from women, and women were significantly more likely than men to accept low offers (Croson & Buchan, 1999). When the subjects sat behind a screen where they could not see each other, however, offers made by women were more likely to be rejected than offers by men (*ibid.*). Women were also more likely to reject offers in the second study than in the first. The authors emphasize that not only does women's behavior change in the two studies, but also the swings in behavior are substantially larger than the male swings, suggesting greater sensitivity to social context (*ibid.*).[32]

The authors also examine studies designed to judge generosity. Here, they find that, when efficiency is not a factor, women give more than men. Where efficiency considerations are added, men give more to the extent the donations enhance efficiency; women prefer more equal outcomes (Croson & Buchan, 1999). More recent research confirms these differences. A spring 2006 study attempted to distinguish between those motivated by the desire to maximize social surplus (i.e., to increase the size of the pie) and those motivated by a desire to avoid inequity. The report finds "that those other-regarding individuals who can be classified are almost evenly split between inequity aversion and social surplus maximization. However, men and women have systematically different preferences, with women significantly more likely to be inequity averters and men more likely to be social surplus maximizers" (Kamas & Preston, 2006).[33] The authors conclude that some studies that attempt to measure altruism produce inconsistent results about gender effects if they do not distinguish between the different motivations.

Even more intriguingly, game theory experiments suggest that the interaction between men and women may change outcomes. In a carefully structured experiment, several economists found that when charitable giving was anonymous, women gave significantly more than men. When the charitable decisions were made in pairs, however, pairs consisting of one man and one woman give more than same-sex pairs, and all-male pairs give the least (Kamas, Preston, & Baum, 2008). The authors concluded that, "men and women act more altruistically when in the presence of someone of the opposite sex suggesting that increased participation of women in economic affairs may lead people to behave more altruistically" (*ibid.*).

These findings suggest that for the studies that attempt to tease out the elements of cooperation that make societies and markets function effectively, gender matters and women do, in fact, display an ethic of care. Economics by itself, however, can say very little about the source or persistence of the observed behavior. Nonetheless, as we have emphasized throughout this chapter, biology helps us understand the behavior we observe, and it may help structure understandings about the parameters of social as well as natural construction.

### *5.2. Biology and Gender Revisited*

Speculation about the biological basis of gender has a long and checkered history. Much has been made of differences in brain size between men and women, but the latest studies seem to show that the effects, if any, are proportional; smaller people have smaller brains without effect on function (see Darlington, 2002; see more generally Dekaban & Sadowsky, 1978; see also Reiss, Abrams, Singer, Ross, & Denckla, 1996).[34] More recent work on brain structure continues to show some gender differences in both shape and function, but it is not clear that these differences have much effect on complex behavior (Haier, Jung, Yeo, Head, & Alkire, 2005).[35] Finally, studies that show that men and women in fact use different parts of the brain in solving problems do not necessarily conclude that men and women come up with different answers (Spelke, 2005).[36] Nonetheless, a growing body of research has focused on at least two areas that appear to find biological roots for the differences Gilligan observed.

The first involves the effect of hormones in priming fetal development. Male and female fetal development begins to diverge in the 8th week of pregnancy (Brizendine, 2006). At that time, males typically experience a testosterone surge that kills off cells in the communication centers of the brain and contributes to the growth of more cells in the sex and aggression centers. Female fetuses, in contrast, experience much greater growth in the centers of the brain that process communication and emotion (Brizendine, 2006; Knickmeyer, Baron-Cohen, Raggatt, & Taylor, 2005).[37]

These fetal differences correspond to observed differences in toddlers. Higher rates of exposure in utero to testosterone, for example, are associated with diminished eye contact when a baby is one-year-old and smaller vocabularies, but increased abilities at mental rotation during childhood (*The Economist*, 2006; Marano, 2003; Lutchmaya, Baron-Cohen, & Raggatt, 2002). Conversely, girls' ovaries produce a large amount of estrogen during their first two years of life, which may correspond to greater empathy and capacity for communication. Louann Brizendine (2006, pp. 16–17), for example, reports that:

> A University of Texas study of twelve-month-old girls and boys showed the difference in desire and ability to observe. In this case, the child and mother were brought into a

> room, left alone together, and instructed not to touch an object. The mother stood off to the side. Every move, glance, and utterance was videotaped. Very few of the girls touched the forbidden object, even though their mothers never explicitly told them not to. The girls looked back at their mothers' faces ten to twenty times more than did the boys, checking for signs of approval or disapproval. The boys, by contrast, moved around the room and rarely glanced at their mothers' faces. They frequently touched the forbidden object, even though their mothers shouted, "No!" The one-year-old boys, driven by their testosterone-formed male brains, are compelled to investigate their environment, even those elements of it they are forbidden to touch.

Although not all of the developmental differences associated with gender translates into adult differences, researchers hypothesize that if gender is a factor in the socio-cognitive factors that determine facility in the type of relational skills associated with Gilligan's gender analysis, then they would expect to see differences in three areas: facility in reading non-verbal cues, language, and theory of mind (Geary, 2002). With respect to the first, facility with non-verbal cues, studies generally do show significant gender differences. In an effort to tease out whether, as Mackinnon suggested, status effects may explain these differences, Judith Hall reports that for traits such as loud voice, interruptions, and speaking times, status parallels gender effects, with women demonstrating behavior associated with lower status (Hall, 2006). However, with respect to traits thought to be associated with higher status, such as facial expressiveness, the ability to express emotions through non-verbal cues, and to accurately decode non-verbal cues in others, women outperformed men. Women also did so with respect to traits (smiling, gazing, touching, gesturing) thought to be unrelated to status (*ibid.*). These findings suggest that with respect to the traits most closely associated with non-verbal communication, women's greater abilities may be independent of higher or lower status.[38]

The second category, language, is the most complex of the three. Most studies agree that women demonstrate greater verbal ability than men, but the studies show, for example, that whereas girls' language development proceeds more quickly than boys', resulting in greater vocabularies for girls at younger ages, gender differences in vocabularies do not persist into adulthood. However, women do outperform men in verbal memory, spelling, and verbal fluency through adulthood (Knickmeyer et al., 2005).

Finally, Simon Baron-Cohen and his associates at the Autism Research Center at Cambridge University have linked gender development to theory of mind, that is, the ability to make inferences about the intentions, beliefs, and emotions of other people in order to predict and explain their behavior (*ibid.*). These researchers hypothesize that "girls theory of mind may develop earlier in females and that girls and women are, on average, better at making inferences about people's mental states and adjusting their behavior accordingly" (*ibid.*).

Although some studies suggest that these differences in ability may be attributed to, or accentuated by, differences in the social interests of girls and boys, a second category of newly developed research speculates that these capacities may be associated with the performance of mirror neurons. Indeed, the cover of *Scientific American* in November, 2006 featured a story on "Mirror Neurons and Autism," which explored the evidence associating mirror neurons with the abilities involved in theory of mind, reporting that "dysfunctions of this neural system could explain some of the primary symptoms of autism, including isolation and absence of empathy" (Ramachandran & Oberman, 2006). The article noted that studies of people with autism show a lack of mirror neuron activity in several regions of the brain, at the same time, that earlier studies have associated autism spectrum disorders with gender. These studies show, for example, that "[i]ndividuals with autism perform poorly on tests where females are usually superior to males, such as the 'Reading the Mind in the Eyes' test ... , but perform better than people without autism on tests where males usually outperform females, such as the 'Embedded Figures Task'" (Knickmeyer et al., 2005).[39]

A new study, published in July 2006, follows through on the implications of this research and attempts to test the relationship between mirror neurons and gender. Using the same EEG measurements that linked mirror neurons to autism, this research tested 10 girls and 10 boys to determine whether gender was a factor in mirror neuron functioning (Cheng, Tzeng, Decety, Imada, & Hsieh, 2006). The study showed that gender was, in fact, a factor, with the mirror neuron system in the women responding more strongly to pictures of a moving hand, whereas the men's mirror system reacted more strongly to pictures of a moving dot, whereas women's systems did not respond to the dot at all. The researchers concluded that the findings "appear in accordance with psychological and cognitive gender dimorphism, that is, women are stronger empathizers and men are stronger systemizers in the general population" (*ibid.*).[40] Taken together, these results suggest that the hormones that produce gender may also be linked to interpersonal skills;[41] girls on average may in fact bring greater sensitivity to the kind of relational issues Gilligan discussed (*ibid.*; see also Ramachandran, 2001).[42]

At this point we have come full circle. We are back to Gilligan and the traits she associated with the stereotypically feminine. Women *are* on average more relational, more sensitive to the reactions and emotions of those around them, more motivated by the desire to have an effect on others.[43] Although the discovery of mirror neurons is only 10 years old, and their significance is not fully understood, we have laid out the growing case that these differences in behavior do correspond to differences in the organization and function of the brain. Ironically, however, these traits may be most closely associated with the neural evolution – viz., that of mirror neurons – that researchers are hailing as the key to human learning and flexibility (Cheng et al., 2006; Ramachandran, 2001).[44] Men and women, of course, both have mirror neurons, and even if they involve different levels of sensitivity, they permit a theory of mind for both sexes. In addition, as performance across repeated iterations of the various modeling games indicates, both men and women are capable of altering their behavior in response to the reactions they receive from others. Just as we have come back to Gilligan, nature and nurture are increasingly coming together in a more comprehensive explanation of the feedback loops that nature provides to guide the social construction of human behavior (Spelke, 2005).[45]

## 6. CONCLUSION

In this chapter, we have attempted to identify the importance of gender for what we predict will be a new, progressive research agenda. We believe that both law and economics have shifted their focus from the obstacles to freedom and markets to the necessary attributes of a well-functioning society. Behavioral economics, which has multiplied the exceptions to the rational actor model, and institutional economics, which has increasingly sought to understand the creation and function of collective entities, have underscored the limitations of neoclassical economics as an imperial discipline. As the research agenda has changed from identification of the reasons why state interventions have failed to determination of the institutions, private or public, that work, attention has turned to trust, cooperation, cultural norms, social meaning, and altruism. Although articulation of a new paradigm has not yet occurred, we predict that a new model will differ from the rational actor model in that:

(1) It will seek to explain not just individual decisions, but the coordination of behavior. Although conventional economics considers equilibrium points that arise from competition, social stability is a more complex construct. As Kahan (2003) notes, the reciprocity model produces more than one equilibrium point, with the creation of a high trust society resulting from the production of shared norms, internalized through

something more than the profit-oriented incentive effects that attend individual transactions.

(2) It will focus on the preference-shaping process, necessarily relaxing any assumption of exogenously determined choices and values. Examination of "virtuous cycles," after all, necessarily involves consideration of the feedback loops that motivate behavior.

(3) It will be sensitive to the allocation of resources and entitlements. Cognitive psychologists document the existence of an "endowment effect," which suggests that there is an "increased value of a good to an individual when the good becomes part of the individual's endowment" (Kahneman, Knetsch, & Thaler, 1990). Accordingly, the perceived fairness of a transaction may well depend on the extent to which it accords with the expectations that follow from such allocations, and the perceived legitimacy of the entitlements.

(4) It will consider the degree to which legal rules empower or frustrate collective responses. In other words, the ability of more socially conscious druggists to develop norms that facilitate access may be more effective than formal distribution programs.

(5) It will consider the balance between empowering innovation, potentially destabilizing existing hierarchies and creating new ones, and providing support for an ethic of care.

The most important new tools contributing to this research are likely to incorporate evolutionary analysis, behavioral genetics, and neuroscience, and with these techniques will necessarily come renewed attention to gender. Attention to the biological basis of difference, gender or otherwise, carries undeniable risks. Indeed, growing research on stereotype threat (the risk of confirming a negative stereotype about one's group) suggests that there may be a biological component to the perception of and internalization of role expectations (see, e.g., Steele, 1997; Steele & Aronson, 1995; Kang & Banaji, 2006; McGlone & Aronson, 2006). And Judith Harris's new research on peer influence, undeniably an environmental factor in development, has been interpreted in terms of the tendency of the species to take small differences (with gender differences among the most obvious to pubescent teens) and exaggerate them as the basis for specialization and exchange (see Harris, 1999; Ridley, 2003).

Despite these risks, we believe that the reexamination of the biological bases of gender differences is inevitable, and that it offers more opportunities than risks for a progressive agenda. First, as the growing gender literature attests, the research is likely to be done whether or not feminists participate. Second, as developments in biology indicate, the research agenda itself changes when women participate (Hrdy, 1999). Third, as the research focus changes from self-interested behavior to cooperative behavior, so too do the opportunities for more progressive policies.

We have argued in this chapter that as the scholarly paradigm across the social sciences shifts to place greater emphasis on trust and reciprocity, the issue of gender has been notable largely to the degree to which it has been relegated to the margins of the new discourse. There is, however, at least one remarkable exception. In 2001, the World Bank issued a policy research report, "Engendering Development – Through Gender Equality in Rights, Resources, and Voice," which focused on the broad economic and social implications of gender issues in developing and transitional countries (World Bank Report, 2001; see Stotsky, 2006).[46] The report found a correlation between the rights of women and the countries' economic and social well-being, and concluded that granting women more equal decision-making power produced benefits for the society as a whole. In reaching these conclusions, the report focused on two areas that illustrate the potential of the new thinking and contain suggestions for a broader research agenda.

First, the report seconds the conclusion that might be expected from an evolutionary account. In examining the allocation of resources at the household level, the study finds that:

> [H]ousehold resources are allocated in the face of competing preferences and unequal bargaining power among members. This conflicts with the traditional view of economists and policymakers that household members pool their resources and allocate them according to a unified set of preferences. One implication is that the distribution of resources within a household, not just the level of resources, matters. Policies that alter the distribution of resources among household members shift the balance of power among those members, with implications for gender equality and family welfare. (World Bank Report, 2001)

At a practical level, what this means is that women are more likely to spend additional resources on their children, whereas men are more likely to spend them on status enhancing purchases – including cars, alcohol, and mistresses. The report further finds that:

> [a] growing body of evidence indicates that more resources in the hands of women mean greater household allocations to children .... In Brazil additional income in the hands of mothers is associated with substantially larger improvements in child survival and nutrition than additional income in the hands of fathers. For child survival the marginal effect of female income is nearly 20 times larger than that of male income. And for child nutrition, the effect is four to eight times larger." (*ibid.*)

The research further correlates child vaccination rates with the mother's educational levels. These studies emphasize that the allocation of power within families matters for reasons that lay the foundation for the well-being of the next generation. Although feminists have sought to separate issues involving women from those involving children, it is clear that in matters as disparate as the financial status of women post-divorce and the subsistence levels of women in the developing world, a focus on women benefits those for whom women provide care.

Second, the World Bank concludes that greater gender equality correlates with better governance and less corruption. The empirical studies on which the report relied find that higher representation of women in the legislature went together with lower levels of corruption (Dollar, Fisman, & Gatti, 1999). The more intriguing issue is why. The study begins by observing how little research has been done on the role of gender in governance. It cites work done during the 1990s suggesting that women may be less "selfish" than the stereotypical rational man, score higher on measures of ethics and integrity, and react more generously in making economic decisions (*ibid.*). Although these studies remain controversial, the authors refer to the work of a Russian political scientist who argues that women "rarely succumb to authoritarian styles of behavior and prefer not to maintain the sort of expensive entourage which often accompanies high-placed (male) officials," and they speculate that "the presence of women in the higher echelons of the hierarchical structures exercises an extremely positive influence on the behavior of their male colleagues by restraining, disciplining and elevating the latters' behavior" (*ibid.*).

The World Bank used this report to support greater gender equality as a tool in development. Of course, gender equality is an outcome that could be justified directly rather than instrumentally, and the comments, which rest on empirical research on correlations without persuasive evidence of causation, too easily lead to essentialist views about men and women. But the findings nonetheless complement the issues that arise from behavioral biology and suggest that the qualities associated with the stereotypically masculine and feminine, if not always men and women, may play important roles in the well-being of society.

This approach represents a fundamental departure from the rational actor model as it considers the operation of the group rather than individual transactions, the differing contribution based on gender to collective well-being, the effect of initial entitlements on long-term results, the creation of feedback loops that spur virtuous as opposed to vicious cycles, and the role of law in encouraging the process (see Cahn, 2006, see generally

Dallas, 2003).[47] And – as Gilligan might suggest – it acknowledges the importance of the balance between the masculine and the feminine in producing these results, finding value in emphasizing what women contribute.

We believe that to realize the potential a new paradigm will require revisiting the issue of feminism and, as the World Bank example illustrates, it will require reconsidering two issues. The most fundamental is the relationship between stereotypically masculine and feminine preferences. The former, associated with men but certainly not characterizing all men, involve the tendency to establish hierarchies, challenge the existing order when it enhances status to do so, prizes innovation and risk-taking, and resorts more readily to violence. In contrast, the stereotypically feminine devotes greater attention to relational concerns, places a greater premium on inclusion and equality, is more attentive to interpersonal transactions, and contributes more to stability and productivity. We believe that all successful institutions, the military notably among them, carefully balance the tensions among these traits, whatever the identity of individuals who constitute them.

In addition, for society more generally, the relationship between the masculine and feminine requires attention to the connections between home and family. Post-industrial societies are undergoing a major redefinition of family life as fertility rates fall, relationships become more fragile, and women join men in the paid workforce accelerating the changing boundaries between public and private, commercial and domestic. The role of family nonetheless remains important in the transmission of culture, values, and norms between generations, and in providing the primary emotional bonds that connect individuals to a sense of community.

Both these dimensions are critical in understanding the creation of cooperation and trust in complex societies. And both issues are critical to the creation of a comprehensive new paradigm. After all, at this point in the life of the academy, the question of whether or not Heinz will (or should) steal the drug is not particularly interesting.[48] The far more interesting questions are Amy's: why did not the druggist sell to Heinz in the first place? Greed, institutional or personal indifference, or a market based rationing system? And what is the legal system to make of the theft? We suspect that Amy might be a fraction of a second quicker than Jake to guess that if Heinz were black and the druggist white, the result of a conviction might be a riot; whereas if Heinz's theft caused the death of a sicker patient higher up on the rationing list, even Heinz's wife might condemn him. The construction of social trust, or norms, has replaced the abstract articulation of moral justifications as the more important question of the day.

# NOTES

1. See, for example, economist Robert Prentice's observations that "[t]he premise of a rational actor that is fundamental to much law and economics theory is simply wrong, meaning that this scholarship often generates explanations that are unpersuasive, conclusions that are unverifiable, predictions that are unreliable, and policy prescriptions that are unsatisfying"(Prentice, 2003).

2. This construct is also known as "Chicago Man."

3. In this debate between Tony Kronman and Richard Posner, Posner argues that wealth maximization is an acceptable substitute for utility maximization because of the difficulties of determining utility.

4. Hamilton theorizes that "natural selection favors characteristics that cause an organism's genes to be passed on, regardless of whether the organism produces offspring directly." An uncle who contributes to a niece's well-being, for example, helps promote the survival of a child who will pass on a significant portion of his own genes. See also Jones and Goldsmith (2005, pp. 430–431) on kin selection.

5. Trivers predicted that, for all species, the sex that invests more in children will be more discriminating in the selection of mates, whereas the sex that invests less will be more competitive for sexual access to the high investing sex. He also predicted a conflict of interest between parents and children, with parents sometimes, for example, weaning an infant at a less than optimal time for the infant in order to bear additional children. Also see Trivers (1974).

6. Toobey and Cosmides observed that "Darwin took [a] . . . radical step toward uniting the mental and physical worlds, by showing how the mental world – whatever it might be composed of – arguably owed its complex organization to the same process of natural selection that explained the physical organization of living things. Psychology became united with the biological and hence evolutionary sciences."

7. The six stages, found at http://www.nd.edu/~rbarger/Kohlberg.html, are

| Level | Stage | Social orientation |
|---|---|---|
| Pre-conventional | 1 | Obedience and punishment |
| | 2 | Individualism, instrumentalism, and exchange |
| Conventional | 3 | "Good boy/girl" |
| | 4 | Law and order |
| Post-conventional | 5 | Social contract |
| | 6 | Principled conscience |

8. Abrams noted that opposition to gender essentialism became an important component of feminism following Gilligan.

9. Friedman, Robinson, and Friedman (1987) find no differences between men and women. Thomas (1986) finds that when such factors as education and socialization are accounted for, women score higher than men. Walker (1984) finds when education and socialization factors are removed, women score no different than men. Rothbart and Albert (1986) tests college students and finds that, although

both men and women used different types of reasoning, women were somewhat more likely to respond in terms of care and men in terms of rights. Ford and Lowery (1986) find that more feminine males were more likely to use the ethic of care than less feminine males.

10. See also Gilligan, 1986 (commenting on exchange). Gilligan (1985) has responded to the controversy over men's and women's test scores by arguing that critics have mistakenly viewed *In a Different Voice* as a statistical argument for sex differences in moral development, an argument which these critics then rebut by showing no sex differences exist. She asserts that her argument is interpretive and not empirical, and that women constitute themselves in a morally different way even when they score no differently then men. Gilligan (1986) maintains that women are more inclined than men are to use a "care" orientation. Summarizing the findings of six different studies, Gilligan has noted that among the 92 percent of the women who stated that they used a "care" orientation, 62 percent preferred it; among the 62 percent of the men who stated they used a "care" orientation, only 7 percent preferred it. Among the 77 percent of the women who stated they used a "justice" orientation, 38 percent preferred it; 100 percent of the men stated they used a "justice" orientation and 93 percent preferred it. Men's preferences are decidedly more one-sided than women's: not only do all men overwhelmingly prefer the "justice" orientation (93 percent), a large minority of men (38 percent) exclude the "care" orientation completely.

11. Prof Kathryn Abrams (2001) describes the demise of the "first generation care," maintaining that its downfall was its essentialism in suggesting that care was a central activity in most women's lives, and its failure to produce specific policy prescriptions or legal approaches.

12. Indeed, in the cases in which non-material interests are paramount, law and economics often labels and marginalizes such concerns by referring to them as "psychic benefits." For example, one author argued that the only interest a wife might have in pursuing paid employment, rather than the supposedly efficiency maximizing role of specializing in domestic chores, was her "psychic satisfaction" in having her husband perform more housework. Carbone has argued elsewhere that "[m]issing altogether from ... [this] analysis is the fact that many women prefer their jobs to remaining at home, that society accords greater prestige to paid employment, and that economic independence has a dramatic effect on the power relationships within marriage and on women's status within society generally."

13. Summarizing the different theories.

14. Friedman, however, does not claim that all utility maximizing acts should necessarily be legal.

15. Indeed, Friedman (2000) explains that if the legality of theft were to be determined solely in accordance with a utilitarian calculus (that is, a determination that theft was permissible whenever the gain to the thief outweighed the loss to the owner), it would encourage rent-seeking, and therefore wasteful expenditures by both potential thieves and those seeking to secure their possessions. After all, many thefts may be utility enhancing without involving legal necessity (e.g., a thief who values a gold chain more than the wealthy owner, but lacks the resources to be able to purchase it).

16. Carbone explains that any decline in specialization between men and women when women entered the workforce in greater numbers was minor in comparison with the increase in specialization that occurred as women traded the generalist role of wife and mother for more specialized market functions, and used specialized market services to discharge their continuing domestic responsibilities.

17. Indeed, Victor Fuchs, in a more sophisticated analysis of the family and labor market patterns underlying the transformation in women's roles, argued that it was the fact women cared more about children, not the fact that they cared for children, that guaranteed their economic subordination.

18. Ridley comments on B.F. Skinner's work and the conclusion that Skinner's fiction, which envisions a world entirely produced by conscious human design, is a fascist state.

19. Epstein also alleged, "[s]ome radical feminists have taken the view that androgyny – the elimination of all sex-specific roles – is appropriate not only for the workplace but for the greater society at large ... I incline to the view that the biology of sex differences is profound, and influences not only the activities immediately related to courtship, reproduction, and child rearing, but also virtually every other aspect of human conduct" (Epstein, 1992b).

20. The issue of causation is itself, however, incredibly complex. The association of activity in a given area of the brain with a particular behavior, for example, does not prove causation, nor does it determine the origin of the brain activity itself. But some controlled experiments may show, for example, that the injection of a neurotransmitter in fact alters certain behavior, or that blocking receptors for the hormone produces the opposite effect. Even these studies do not "prove" that a particular evolutionary explanation is correct, or the presence or absence of such receptors is necessarily determined by genetic inheritance.

21. Culture seems to be the cart, not the horse – the consequence, not the cause – of some change in the human brain.

22. "Santos's talk gives a history of women in architecture," http://web.mit.edu/newsoffice/2005/santos-0302.html

23. As Nelson (2005, p. 16) suggests, "[s]ome economists ... have begun to explore the empirical implications of a richer psychological model of human behavior. This could lead to a very useful rethinking of core economic assumptions ... Or it may not. I believe that the ultimate usefulness of this research will depend on how willing my discipline is to *let go* of its one-sided worship of the ideals valorized in" the rational choice model.

24. Indeed, the political dominance of the neoclassical model arguably begins with Van Hayek's *The Road to Serfdom*, which argued that state intervention in the market, because of its intrinsic limitations, inevitably produced authoritarian regimes. Steven Ramirez observes, "There is no gentle way to put this: people all over the world are perishing upon the altar of the failed ideology of market fundamentalism. So says the 2001 Nobel laureate in Economics, Joseph E. Stiglitz, in Globalization and Its Discontents. This brand of market fundamentalism, emphasizing free markets, or market liberalization, and minimal government intervention in the economy, is the direct spawn of the efficiency obsession that dominates law and economics."

25. The significance of human capabilities to development is drawn from Amartya Sen's (2000) work.

26. Kahan (2003) observes that, "[f]inally, the conventional theory and the reciprocity theory differ on the variability of preferences across individuals. The conventional theory imagines that the disposition to free ride in collective-action settings is relatively uniform. In contrast, the evidence on which the reciprocity theory rests suggests that the disposition to cooperate varies. In public-goods experiments that generate multiple equilibria, for example, neither universal cooperation nor universal defection is the final resting point."

27. Zak (2008) rejects what the popular understanding of "free enterprise" as resting on self-interest and argues instead that market transactions depend on cooperation, which in turn reflects the internationalization of values such as honesty and trustworthiness.

28. Snarey (1985) finds support for the cross-cultural application of Kohlberg's scheme.

29. Nisbett and Cohen attempted to link different cultural responses to physiological markers, such as rises in testosterone or cortisol levels after certain encounters.

30. These dilemmas are drawn from Judith Jarvis Thomson (1986).

31. Greene, nonetheless, argues for the bankruptcy of deontology as a form of moral philosophy because of the extent to which it rationalizes the results of emotional judgments. Greene believes that pushing the fat man off the bridge may be as justifiable as pulling the switch on the trolley car.

32. For example, when women are responders, they reject the offer 18 percent more often when they cannot see the proposer, whereas men reject offers only eight percent more often.

33. Showing that women were four times more likely than men to be inequity averters.

34. In Dekaban and Sadowsky (1978), "Brain weight is greater in males than in females at all corresponding ages ... The average difference for all ages in 9.8%." Reiss et al. (1996) found in a study of children that the absolute cerebral volume, which is the sum of the gray matter, white matter and cerebrospinal fluid, is approximately 10 percent larger in boys than in girls.

35. In a recent study of 48 people, researchers examined general intelligence tests and MRI brain scans to determine any correlation between intelligence test scores and the amount of gray or white matter in the subjects' brains. The gray matter volume that correlated with the intelligence test constituted 9.6 percent of the full gray matter volume in males' brains, but only 1.7 percent of the gray matter volume in females' brains, whereas the white matter volume correlated to the test was 0.1 percent of the total volume in male brains, and 1.3 percent of the total volume in females' brains. Each of the different types of brain material is associated with different strengths: white matter involves connecting various parts of the brain, whereas gray matter is involved in the processing of more localized information. Gray matter provides "concentrated processing power" and the capacity to connect thoughts, whereas white matter distributes processing capability but also promotes focus. The differences in brain composition and function did not correspond to differences in intelligence, though they may correspond to the way the brain coordinates the two hemispheres (Haier et al., 2005).

36. For example, on tests that involve navigating by geometric or landmark location, women use landmarks and men use maps. But when there is only one of those two sources of information available, then men and women perform equally.

37. These stereotypical differences, of course, refer to the average male and average female. The testosterone levels and corresponding brain development differ among males and females. For a discussion of the possible role of testosterone in what Simon Baron-Cohen has referred to as "extreme form of the male brain" implicated in autism (see Knickmeyer et al., 2005).

38. Of course, this study cannot rule out the hypothesis that women enjoyed greater evolutionary advantages than men in developing these capacities because of their greater vulnerability.

39. The "mind in the eyes" test determines whether an individual can accurately decode the emotion expressed in photos of people's eyes. The embedded figures task involves picking a figure out of a background as in "Where's Waldo," a children's game that requires finding the character "Waldo" in a crowded scene.

40. We should emphasize, however, that the study included a number of caveats, including the suggestion that, whereas they deliberately chose a gender-neutral looking male hand, that the study should be repeated with other more masculine or feminine hands. In addition, the research subjects were deliberately chosen to include only heterosexual men and women who reported no same-sex partners or sexual attraction.

41. The researchers also looked at the role of fetal testosterone levels in social interactions among four-year-olds, and found that higher testosterone levels in boys in fact correlated with weaker social skills and narrower interests.

42. There is much speculation that researchers will some day be able to show that these correlations are causal, that is, that fetal development spurred by the presence or absence of testosterone and other hormones affects the development of mirror neurons and their associated receptors, which in turn determines the level of individual social skills. See, for example, Brizendine's (2006) speculation that women have more receptors for mirror neurons and the *Scientific American* suggestions that autism is related to a deficit in mirror neuron function. At this stage, however, scientists cannot prove with certainty what function mirror neurons serve with respect to complex behavior, much less that these correlations in fact determine gender differences or autism.

43. Steven Pinker's summary of six primary areas of difference emphasizes preferences more than capacities: First, men and women generally differ with respect to their priorities, with men more likely to choose status rather than their families, and women being more balanced. Second, men and women show different vocational interests, with women more likely to choose to work with people, and men with things. Third, men are more likely to take risks. Fourth, men are better at three-dimensional mental rotation and perception. Fifth, whereas women are better at mathematical calculations, men are better at math-based work problems. Finally, men show more difference in variability than do women (Pinker & Spelke, 2005).

44. Ramachandran speculates, for example, that, "The discovery of mirror neurons in the frontal lobes of monkeys, and their potential relevance to human brain evolution ... is the single most important "unreported" (or at least, unpublicized) story of the decade. I predict that mirror neurons will do for psychology what DNA

did for biology: they will provide a unifying framework and help explain a host of mental abilities that have hitherto remained mysterious and inaccessible to experiments."

45. Indeed, Janet Shibley Hyde (2005) suggests that studies should be interpreted through a "gender similarities" rather than a gender difference model. According to her meta-analysis, most studies have found only minimal differences. Where there are differences, the largest ones appear in studies of motor coordination, such as distance in throwing a ball, sexuality measures, such as masturbation and attitudes toward sex outside of committed relationships, and aggression, with men more likely to exhibit physical aggression and women to exhibit verbal facility.

46. The World Bank, available at: http://www-wds.worldbank.org/external/default/main?pagePK=64193027&piPK=64187937&theSitePK=523679&menuPK=64187510&searchMenuPK=64187283&siteName=WDS&entityID=000094946_01020805393496, last visited August 1, 2007.

47. Indeed, we would view the two obvious legal issues arising from this type of analysis as polygamy, where a long literature addresses the role of the family (and monogamy) in the creation of democracy, and corporate governance, where constraint of risk-taking, deception and fraud are important regulatory objectives.

48. Indeed, the far more interesting question may be the circumstances in which our hypothetical Heinz might not steal the drug.

## ACKNOWLEDGMENTS

The authors thank the participants at the Seattle conference "Law and Economics: Toward Social Justice" and at Martha Fineman's Uncomfortable Conversation on Sociobiology, Evolutionary Psychology, and Feminist Legal Theory at the Mid-west Law and Economics Association, Jack Kirkwood, Dana Gold, and Kathy Baker for their comments, and Reetuparna Dutta, Talita Kiper, and Kasia Solon for their research assistance.

## REFERENCES

Abrams, K. (1992). Social construction, roving biologism, and reasonable women: A response to Professor Epstein. *DePaul Law Review*, *41*, 1021–1040.

Abrams, K. (2001). Commentary: The second coming of care. *Chicago-Kent Law Review*, *76*, 1605–1617.

Al-Shebab, A. J. (2002). A cross-sectional examination of levels of moral reasoning in a sample of Kuwait University faculty members. *Social Behavior and Personality*, *30*, 813–820.

Baker, K. K. (2000). Biology for feminists. *Chicago-Kent Law Review*, *75*, 805–835.

Bartlett, K. T. (1990). Feminist legal methods. *Harvard Law Review*, *103*, 829–888.

Becker, G. S. (1981). *A treatise on the family*. Cambridge, MA: Harvard University Press.

Becker, M., Bowman, C. G., & Torrey, M. (2001). *Feminist jurisprudence: Taking women seriously*. Minneapolis, MN: West.

Brizendine, L. (2006). *The female brain*. New York, NY: Morgan Road Books.

Browne, K. R. (1995). Sex and temperament in modern society: A Darwinian view of the glass ceiling and the gender gap. *Arizona Law Review*, *37*, 971–1106.

Cahn, N. (2006). *The contribution of transformational leadership*. Unpublished manuscript.

Carbone, J. (1990). Economics, feminism, and the reinvention of alimony: A reply to Ira Ellman. *Vanderbilt Law Review*, *43*, 1463–1500.

Carbone, J. (2000). *From partners to parents: The second revolution in family law*. New York, NY: Columbia University Press.

Carbone, J., & Cahn, N. (2004). The biological basis of commitment: Does one size fit all? *Women's Rights Law Reporter*, *25*, 223–248.

Caspi, A., Sugden, K., Moffitt, T. E., Taylor, A., Craig, I. W., Harrington, H. L., McClay, J., Mill, J., Martin, J., Braithwaite, A., & Poulton, R. (2003). Influence of life stress on depression: Moderation by a polymorphism in the 5-HTT gene. *Science*, *301*, 386–389.

Chamallas, M. (1988). Consent, equality and the legal control of sexual conduct. *Southern California Law Review*, *61*, 777–862.

Cheng, Y. W., Tzeng, O. J., Decety, J., Imada, T., & Hsieh, J. C. (2006). Gender differences in the human mirror system: A magnetoencephalography study. *Neuroreport*, *31*, 1115–1119.

Chorvat, T., & McCabe, K. (2004). The brain and the law. *Philosophical Transactions of the Royal Society of London*, *359*, 1724–1736.

Cohen, J. D. (2005). The vulcanization of the human brain: A neural perspective on interactions between cognition and emotion. *Journal of Economic Perspectives*, *19*, 3–24.

Crain, W. C. (1985). *Theories of development*. Upper Saddle River, NJ: Prentice-Hall.

Crespi, G. S. (1997a). Does the Chicago school need to expand its curriculum? *Law and Social Inquiry*, *22*, 149–168.

Crespi, G. S. (1997b). Reply: Putting the Chicago school debate in proper perspective. *Law and Social Inquiry*, *22*, 201–206.

Croson, R., & Buchan, N. (1999). Gender and culture: International experimental evidence from trust games. *American Economic Review*, *89*, 386–391. Available at http://opim.wharton.upenn.edu/~crosonr/research/%5B59%5D.pdf. Accessed on November 26, 2006.

Croson, R., & Gneezy, U. (2004). *Gender differences in preferences*. Unpublished manuscript. University of Pennsylvania. Available at http://opim.wharton.upenn.edu/~crosonr/research/%5B59%5D.pdf. Revise and resubmit *Journal of Economic Literature*, p. 38.

Dallas, L. (2003). Law and socioeconomics in legal education. *Rutgers Law Review*, *55*, 855–902.

Darlington, C. (2002). *The female brain*. New York, NY: Taylor & Francis.

Dau-Schmidt, K. G. (1997). Smoking in the washroom of the Chicago school: A reply to Crespi. *Law and Social Inquiry*, *22*, 171–182.

Dawkins, R. (2006). *The selfish gene* (3rd ed.). New York, NY: Oxford.

Dekaban, A. S., & Sadowsky, D. (1978). Changes in brain weights during the span of human life: Relation of brain weights to body heights and body weights. *Annals of Neurology*, *4*, 345–356.

de Quervain, D. J., Fischbacher, U., Treyer, V., Schellhammer, M., Schnyder, U., Buck, A., & Fehr, E. (2004). The neural basis of altruistic punishment. *Science*, *314*, 475–478.

Dollar, D., Fisman, R., & Gatti, R. (1999). *Are women really the "fairer" sex? Corruption and women in government*. Policy Research Report on Gender and Development. Working Paper Series No. 4. Available at http://siteresources.worldbank.org/INTGENDER/Resources/wp4.pdf

Epstein, R. (1992a). The authoritarian impulse in sex discrimination law: A reply to Professors Abrams and Strauss. *DePaul Law Review*, *41*, 1041–1056.

Epstein, R. (1992b). *Forbidden grounds: The case against employment discrimination laws*. Cambridge, MA: Harvard University Press.

Epstein, R. (1992c). Gender is for nouns. *DePaul Law Review*, *41*, 981–1005.

Fishkin, J. S. (1984). *Beyond subjective morality: Ethical reasoning and political philosophy*. New Haven, CT: Yale University Press.

Ford, M. R., & Lowery, C. R. (1986). Gender differences in moral reasoning: A comparison on the use of justice and care orientations. *Journal of Personality and Social Psychology*, *50*, 777–783.

Friedman, D. D. (2000). *Law's order: What economics has to do with law and why it matters*. Princeton, NJ: Princeton University Press.

Friedman, W. J., Robinson, A. B., & Friedman, B. L. (1987). Sex differences in moral judgments? A test of Gilligan's theory. *Psychology of Women Quarterly*, *11*, 37–48.

Fuchs, V. R. (1988). *Women's quest for economic equality*. Cambridge, MA: Harvard University Press.

Geary, D. (2002). Sexual selection and sex differences in social cognition. In: A. McGillicuddy-De Lisi & R. De Lisi (Eds), *Biology, society, and behavior: The development of sex differences in cognition*. Greenwich, CT: Ablex Publishing.

Gilligan, C. (1982). *In a different voice: Psychological theory and women's development*. Cambridge, MA: Harvard University Press.

Gilligan, C. (1985). Feminist discourse, moral values, and the law – A conversation. *Buffalo Law Review*, *34*, 11–87.

Gilligan, C. (1986). Reply by Carol Gilligan. *Signs*, *11*, 324–333.

Goodenough, O. (2008). Values, mechanism design, and fairness. In: P. Zak (Ed.), *Moral markets: The critical role of values in the economy*. Princeton, NJ: Princeton University Press.

Greene, J., Sommerville, R. B., Nystrom, L. E., Darley, J. M., & Cohen, J. D. (2001). An fMRI investigation of emotional engagement in moral judgment. *Science*, *293*, 2105–2108.

Greene, J. D. (2002). The terrible, horrible, no good, very bad truth about morality and what to do about it. Department of Philosophy, Princeton University. Available at http://www.wjh.harvard.edu/~jgreene/GreeneWJH/Greene-Dissertation.pdf

Greene, J. D. (2007). The secret joke of Kant's soul. In: W. Sinnott-Armstrong (Ed.), *Moral psychology, Vol. 3: The neuroscience of morality*. Cambridge, MA: MIT Press.

Habermas, J. (1990). *Moral consciousness and communicative action*. (Translated by Lenhardt, C., & Nicholsen, S.W.). Cambridge, MA: MIT Press.

Haier, R. J., Jung, R. E., Yeo, R. E., Head, K., & Alkire, M. T. (2005). The neuroanatomy of general intelligence: Sex matters. *NeuroImage*, *25*, 320–327.

Hall, J. A. (2006). Nonverbal behavior, status, and gender: How do we understand their relations? *Psychology of Women Quarterly*, *30*, 384–391.

Hamilton, W. D. (1964). The genetical evolution of social behavior, I and II. *Journal of Theoretical Biology*, *7*, 1–52.

Harris, J. (1999). *The nurture assumption: Why children turn out the way they do*. New York, NY: Touchstone.

Hartwell, S. (1995). Promoting moral development through experiential teaching. *Clinical Law Review*, *1*, 505–539.

Hauser, M. D. (2006). *Moral minds: How nature designed our universal sense of right*. New York, NY: Ecco.

Hayek, F. A. (1944). *The road to serfdom*. Chicago, IL: University of Chicago Press.

Henderson, L. (1987). Legality and empathy. *Michigan Law Review*, *85*, 1574–1653.

Henrich, J., Boyd, R., Bowles, S., Camerer, C., Fehr, E., Gintis, H., McElreath, R., Alvard, M., Barr, A., Ensminger, J., Hill, K., Gil-White, F., Gurven, M., Marlowe, F., Patton, J. Q., Smith, N., & Tracer, D. (2005). 'Economic man' in cross-cultural perspective: Ethnography and experiments from 15 small-scale societies. *Behavioral and Brain Sciences*, *28*, 795–855.

Hrdy, S. (1999). *Mother nature: A history of mothers, infants, and natural selection*. New York, NY: Pantheon Books.

Hyde, J. S. (2005). The gender similarities hypothesis. *American Psychologist*, *60*, 581–591. Available at http://www.apa.org/journals/releases/amp606581.pdf

Jolls, C., Sunstein, C., & Thaler, R. (1998). A behavioral approach to law and economics. *Stanford Law Review*, *50*, 1471–1550.

Jones, O. D. (1997). Evolutionary analysis in law: An introduction and application to child abuse. *North Carolina Law Review*, *7*, 1117–1242.

Jones, O. D., & Goldsmith, T. H. (2005). Law and behavioral biology. *Columbia Law Review*, *105*, 405–502.

Kahan, D. M. (2003). The logic of reciprocity: Trust, collective action, and law. *Michigan Law Review*, *102*, 71–103.

Kahneman, D. (2003). Maps and bounded rationality: Psychology for behavioral economics. *American Economic Review*, *93*, 1449–1475.

Kahneman, D., Knetsch, J. L., & Thaler, R. H. (1990). Experimental tests of the endowment effect and the Coase theorem. *The Journal of Political Economy*, *98*, 1325–1348.

Kamas, L., & Preston, A. (2006). *On measuring compassion in social preferences: Do gender, price of giving, or inequality matter?* Available at http://www.scu.edu/business/faculty/research/2005-06-papers/upload/wp-05-06-17-kamas.pdf

Kamas, L., Preston, A., & Baum, S. (2008). Altruism in individual and joint-giving decisions: What's gender got to do with it? *Feminist Economics*, *14*(3), 23–50.

Kang, J., & Banaji, M. R. (2006). Fair measures: A behavioral realist revision of "affirmative action". *California Law Review*, *94*, 1063–1118.

Knickmeyer, R., Baron-Cohen, S., Raggatt, P., & Taylor, K. (2005). Foetal testosterone, social cognition, and restricted interests in children. *Journal of Child Psychology and Psychiatry*, *4*, 198–210.

Kronman, A. T. (1980). Wealth maximization as a normative principle. *Journal of Legal Studies*, *9*, 227–242.

Lutchmaya, S., Baron-Cohen, S., & Raggatt, P. (2002). Foetal testosterone and eye contact in 12-month-old infants. *Infant Behavior and Development*, *25*, 327–335.

Ma, H. K. (1984). Problems in the cross-cultural study of moral judgment development. *The Chinese University of Hong Kong Education Journal*, *12*(2), 50–55.

Ma, H. K., & Cheng, C. (1996). A cross-cultural study of moral stage structure in Hong Chinese, English, and Americans. *Journal of Cross-Cultural Psychology*, *27*, 700–713.

Marano, H. E. (2003). The new sex scorecard. *Psychology Today*. Available at http://www.psychologytoday.com/articles/pto-2832.html

McGlone, M. S., & Aronson, J. (2006). Stereotype threat, identity salience, and spatial reasoning. *Journal of Applied Developmental Psychology, 27*, 486–493. Available at http://www.eric.ed.gov/ERICWebPortal/custom/portlets/recordDetails/detailmini.jsp?_nfpb = true&_&ERICExtSearch_SearchValue_0 = EJ746411&ERICExtSearch_SearchType_0 = eric_accno&accno = EJ746411

Nelson, J. (2005). *Rationality and humanity: A view from feminist economics*. Available at http://ase.tufts.edu/gdae/Pubs/wp/05-04RationalityHumanity.pdf

Nisbett, R. E., & Cohen, D. (1996). *The culture of honor: The psychology of violence in the south*. Boulder, CO: Westview.

Parry, J. T. (1999). The virtue of necessity: Reshaping culpability and the rule of law. *Houston Law Review, 36*, 397–469.

Pinker, S., & Spelke, E. (2005). *The science of gender and science: Pinker vs. Spelke. A debate*. Available at www.edge.org/3rd_culture/debate05/debate05_index.html

Posner, R. (1980). The ethical and political basis of the efficiency norm in common law adjudication. *Hofstra Law Review, 8*, 487–507.

Posner, R. (1998). *Economic analysis of law* (5th ed.). New York, NY: Aspen.

Prentice, R. (2003). Chicago man, K-T man, and the future of behavioral law and economics. *Vanderbilt Law Review, 56*, 1663–1777.

Purdy, J. (2006). The promise (and limits) of neuroeconomics. *Alabama Law Review, 58*, 1–40.

Ramachandran, V. S. (2001). Mirror neurons and imitation learning as the driving force behind 'the great leap forward' in human evolution. *Edge, 69*. Available at http://www.edge.org/documents/archive/edge69.html

Ramachandran, V. S., & Oberman, L. M. (2006). Broken mirrors. A theory of autism. Overview/mirror neurons and autism. *Scientific American*, Vol. 295. Available at http://www.sciam.com/article.cfm?articleID = 00014C1A-8576-152E-BF1F83414B7F0000

Ramirez, S. A. (2003). Book review. Market fundamentalism's new fiasco: Globalization as Exhibit B in the case for a new law and economics. [Review of Joseph E. Stiglitz, globalization and its discontents]. *Michigan Journal of International Law, 24*, 831–853.

Reiss, A. L., Abrams, M. T., Singer, H. S., Ross, J. L., & Denckla, M. B. (1996). Brain development, gender, and IQ in children: A volumetric imaging study. *Brain, 119*, 1763–1774.

Ridley, M. (1996). *The origins of virtue: Human instincts and the evolution of cooperation*. London, England: Penguin.

Ridley, M. (2003). *Nature v. Nurture*. New York, NY: HarperCollins.

Robinson, P. H., & Kurzban, R. (2007). Concordance and conflict in intuitions of justice. *Minnesota Law Review, 91*, 1829–1907.

Rothbart, D., & Albert, M. (1986). Gender differences in moral reasoning. *Sex Roles, 15*, 645–653.

Sanfey, A., Rilling, J., Aronson, J., Nystrom, L., & Cohen, J. (2003). The neural basis of economic decision-making in the ultimatum game. *Science, 300*, 1755–1758.

Sen, A. (2000). *Development as freedom*. New York, NY: Knopf.

Snarey, J. R. (1985). Cross-cultural universality of social-moral development: A critical review of Kohlbergian research. *Psychological Bulletin*, 202–232.

Spelke, E. (2005). Sex differences in intrinsic aptitude for mathematics and science? A critical review. *American Psychologist, 60*, 950–958.

Steele, C. (1997). A threat in the air: How stereotypes shape the intellectual identities and performance of women and African-Americans. *American Psychologist, 52*, 613–629.

Steele, C., & Aronson, J. (1995). Stereotype threat and the intellectual test performance of African Americans. *Journal of Personality and Social Psychology, 69*, 797–811.

Stotsky, J. (2006). *Gender and its relevance to macroeconomic policy: A survey*. IMF Working Paper No. 06/233. Available at SSRN: http://ssrn.com/abstract=941295

Strauss, D. (1992). Biology, difference, and gender discrimination. *De Paul Law Review, 41*, 1007–1020.

Sunstein, C. (2006). A new progressivism. *Stanford Law and Policy Review, 17*, 197–231.

Tavris, C. (1992). *The mismeasure of women: Why women are not the better sex, the inferior sex, or the opposite sex*. New York, NY: Simon & Schuster.

*The Economist*. (2006). The mismeasure of women. *The Economist*. Available at http://www.economist.com/science/displaystory.cfm?story_id=7245949

Thomas, S. (1986). Estimating gender differences in the comprehension and preferences of moral issues. *Developmental Review, 6*, 165–180.

Thomson, J. J. (1986). *Rights, restitution, and risk: Essays in moral theory*. Cambridge, MA: Harvard University Press.

Tooby, J., & Cosmides, L. (1992). The psychological foundations of culture. In: J. H. Barkow, L. Cosmides & J. Tooby (Eds), *The adapted mind* (pp. 19–136). New York, NY: Oxford University Press.

Trivers, R. (1972). Parental investment and sexual selection. In: B. Campbell (Ed.), *Sexual selection and the descent of man* (pp. 136–179). Chicago, IL: Aldine.

Trivers, R. (1974). Parent–offspring conflict. *American Zoologist, 14*, 249–264.

Tsui, J., & Windsor, C. (2001). Some cross-cultural evidence on ethical reasoning. *Journal of Business Ethics, 31*, 143–150.

Walker, L. (1984). Sex differences in the development of moral reasoning: A critical review. *Child Development, 55*, 677–691.

West, R. (1988). Jurisprudence and gender. *University of Chicago Law Review, 55*, 1–72.

World Bank Report. (2001). *Engendering development: Through gender equality in rights, resources, and voice*. New York, NY: Oxford University Press.

Zak, P. J. (2008). *Free enterprise: Values in action conference series, 2005–2006. Moral markets: The critical role of values in the economy*. Princeton, NJ: Princeton University Press.

## Cases

*General Electric Co. v. Gilbert*, 429 U.S. 125 (1976).

# RACE TO THE TOP OF THE CORPORATE LADDER: WHAT MINORITIES DO WHEN THEY GET THERE*

Devon W. Carbado and Mitu Gulati


## ABSTRACT

*Racing to the top of the corporate hierarchy is difficult, no matter how qualified or capable the candidate. Producing more widgets than one's competitors is not enough. Negotiating the political landscape of the institution is also required. More specifically, individual corporate officers have to be appeased, powerful interest groups have to be co-opted and made allies, and competitors have to be undermined or eliminated. The more bureaucratic the organization and the more opaque the promotion process, the more important this institutional game to climbing the corporate ladder. This chapter identifies the kind of racial minorities or racial types who are likely to play this game well and, consequently, race to the top of the corporation. It then explains why these racial types might not have the racial commitment, or feel institutionally empowered, to lift other people of color as they climb the corporate ladder.*


* This chapter is a redacted version of D. Carbado and M. Gulati (2004).

**Law & Economics: Toward Social Justice**
**Research in Law and Economics: A Journal of Policy, Volume 24, 237–270**

**ISSN: 0193-5895/doi:10.1108/S0193-5895(2009)0000024013**

# 1. INTRODUCTION

There is a widespread assumption that people of color at the top of the corporate hierarchy will help those on the bottom. But is that assumption reasonable? We argue that it might not be. More specifically, this chapter suggests there is reason to believe that the racial minorities at the top of the corporate hierarchy will neither racially reform the corporation, nor engage in door-opening activities for minorities on the bottom.

This might seem counterintuitive, particularly given the supposed commitment among people of color – and, in particular, among black people – to "lift as we climb."[1] In this respect, we are not arguing that senior people of color, in the context of the workplace, do not help junior people of color. Surely some do, but to what extent, we do not know. This chapter aims to explain why some people of color at the top of the corporation might not perform this kind of anti-racist institutional work. To do so, we first identify several benefits that theoretically should flow from having people of color in senior management positions. Drawing on insights from both economics and Critical Race Theory, we then discuss why realizing these benefits might prove difficult (see Carbado & Gulati, 2003a, pp. 1757–1828).

# 2. THE THEORETICAL TRICKLE-DOWN BENEFITS OF RACIAL MINORITIES IN CORPORATE LEADERSHIP

There are a number of benefits that one might expect to "trickle down" from the presence of racial minorities at the top of a corporation to those on the bottom. Seemingly, the very success of minorities at the top would help negate racial stereotypes. Further, their presence would cause other corporate leaders to monitor their discussions for bias and also make the corporation more accountable for its decisions that implicate race. In addition, people of color in management positions could facilitate cooperation among racial groups within the corporation and help to reduce token minority hiring (tokenism). Finally, senior racial minorities could serve as role models for and provide mentoring to their junior minority associates. Before explaining why these expectations may not be realized, we elaborate on the nature of each benefit.[2]

### *2.1. Stereotype Negation*

A significant amount of discrimination today is a result of stereotypes, not explicit and conscious animus.[3] Corporations seeking to improve the racial climate of their workplace therefore might try to negate those stereotypes. One strategy for negating minority stereotypes is to promote or hire minorities to senior positions, the theory being that the simple fact of minority success will undermine, if not completely disrupt, negative racial stereotypes about work ethic and competence. If Johnny, who is black and male, makes his way to the top of the corporate hierarchy, the theory goes, his success sends both an individual and a group message – namely, Johnny has the capacity and the commitment to lead a corporation and so do other black men.[4] The combined effect of these messages increases the likelihood that the corporation will promote other junior black men.

Minority success provides another, more subtle type of stereotype negation. Many social psychologists now believe that people of color underperform when they perceive the risk that any negative performance on their part will confirm racial stereotypes (see generally Steele and Aronson (1995) and Aronson, Quinn, and Spencer (1998)). The classic example is blacks scoring poorly on standardized tests because of the concern that their performance will confirm stereotypes about black intellectual inferiority. Claude Steele (1997) attributes this phenomenon to "stereotype threat." The presence of successful people of color could reduce this threat in at least two ways. First, junior people of color could conclude from the presence of successful people of color that the corporation is racially tolerant and that the corporate culture is not corrupted by negative racial stereotypes; there is no "threat in the air" (*ibid.*, p. 613). Second, the success of senior people of color could suggest to the juniors that corporate leaders do not interpret the mistakes of nonwhites as a confirmation of existing racial stereotypes. To the extent that junior people of color respond to the success of seniors in either or both of these ways, they will likely experience less of a stereotype threat and greater workplace autonomy. Moreover, they are likely to perform their jobs more effectively. In theory, the cumulative effect would be to mitigate negative racial stereotypes.

### *2.2. Racial Monitoring*

The presence of minorities at the upper echelons of the corporate hierarchy, even in limited numbers, produces racial monitoring.[5] To appreciate how, imagine a law firm that has been asked to represent a conservative organization trying to strike down affirmative action. The mere presence of some black partners on that firm's executive committee, which decides what cases to take, produces at least two monitoring effects – a discourse effect and an outcome effect. At the most basic level, white members of the executive committee will engage the issue of whether to take the case with the awareness that what they say may offend their black colleagues. In other words, the tone and substance of the conversation – the discourse will be shaped by the perception (which may or may not be real) that the black partners present are racially monitoring the conversation. In addition to the discourse effect, black presence could also determine whether the partners accept the case. The white partners could believe that taking the case would anger or alienate their black colleagues to such a degree that it would be against their long-term institutional interests to do so.

One can imagine these monitoring effects occurring at other institutional moments as well. For example, during firm meetings about hiring and promotions, the presence of some minorities on the hiring and promotion committees might temper those who might otherwise be tempted to make arguments based on racial stereotypes – the discourse effect – and shape the bottom-line decisions the partners make about who to hire and promote – the outcome effect. Both discourse and outcome racial monitoring effects can be intensified by affirmative conduct by the person of color.[6] If, in the above example, a black member of the firm's executive committee speaks to the racial implications of the firm taking an anti-affirmative action case, white partners will be even more careful about how they discuss the issue, and they will, perhaps, be less likely to take the case.[7] Active engagement, then, produces stronger monitoring effects than mere presence.[8]

### *2.3. Racial Accountability*

Related to racial monitoring is racial accountability – the idea that white decision makers will have to account for any institutional decisions that negatively affect minorities. Consider a firm that is contemplating extending offers to 10 white attorneys. The accountability costs of the firm doing so is directly related to the number of people of color, particularly partners, at the firm. Put differently, the more people of color at the firm in leadership positions, the more difficult and costly it will be for the firm to "account" for an entering class with no, or very few, people of color. The presence of people of color increases the pressure that the firm will feel to justify its decisions. That justification could require additional meetings to discuss the matter as well as reports that describe the firm's current and historical hiring practices and the diversity they have yielded. These kinds of institutional activities take time and resources and are, therefore, costly to the firm. Moreover, conversations about race are difficult to have at an institutional level and can generate hurt feelings and affect collegiality. This, too, is a cost that a firm might want to avoid. The greater the number of people of color in leadership positions, and the smaller the number of people of color hired, the more vulnerable the firm is incurring the foregoing cost. To avoid the cost, firms would therefore continue to seek to hire people of color.

### *2.4. Racial Cooperation*

Much corporate labor is performed in teams, and the success of any given team depends on team members trusting each other. The greater the level of trust among team members, the more efficient the team, and the more efficient the team, the more successful individual team members are likely to be. Race can be a barrier to establishing team trust. Nonwhites may question how much their white colleagues have invested in cooperating with them; whites may wonder whether nonwhites can be trusted to subordinate their racial identity commitments for the good of the team.

People of color in leadership positions can reduce racial distrust and facilitate racial cooperation. Senior minorities can provide input into the formation of teams to maximize opportunities for racial cooperation and minimize the likelihood of racial tensions and anxieties. Additionally, the very presence of senior people of color might suggest to whites that nonwhites can work effectively in teams and can be trusted; nonwhites might conclude from senior minority presence that racial cooperation is possible. In short, the greater the presence of senior persons of color, the greater the probability that nonwhites and whites will be more trusting of each other. They might even conclude that the differences among them are superficial,[9] and therefore that race ought not be a basis for judging a person's willingness and capacity to work in teams.

### *2.5. Racial Comfort*

Part of the difficulty people of color experience working in predominantly white workplaces relates to racial comfort: because nonwhite identity is "different," people of color have the burden of making whites feel comfortable with their nonwhite identity. The fewer people of color within the organization and the fewer minority success stories, the heavier the racial comfort burden. Conversely, the more people of color within a firm and the more minority success stories, the less different minorities appear to be than their white colleagues. In this way, first-generation minority successes help to diminish racial difference and the amount of racial comfort work second-generation employees have to perform.[10] Put another way, first-generation successes reduce the demand for, and the supply of, racial comfort work.[11]

### *2.6. Role Modeling*

A standard argument for racial diversity is that it provides positive role models for people of color seeking advancement.[12] The argument maintains that at least one barrier to people of color moving up the corporate hierarchy is the difficulty they have imagining themselves there (Delgado, 1991). The greater the extent of racial underrepresentation at the upper echelons of the corporation, the more difficult this racial imagining. Conversely, the more diverse the corporate boardroom and the more successful the people of color there, the greater the likelihood that junior people of color will imagine themselves occupying similar positions of power and authority. Notably, this claim is less about what people of color actually do at the top of the corporation and more about the fact that they are there.[13] As Richard Delgado puts it,

> The role model argument, in simplest form, holds that affirmative action is justified in order to provide communities of color with exemplars of success, without which they might conclude that certain social roles and professional opportunities are closed to them. Role models are expected to communicate to their communities that opportunities are indeed available and that hard work and perseverance will be rewarded. (*ibid.*)

The Supreme Court has rejected the idea that the benefits of role modeling can justify affirmative action.[14] But the basic role modeling insight – that the presence of people of color at the top sends a positive message to people of color at the bottom that they, too, can ascend the corporate hierarchy – continues to have traction in academic and social contexts.[15]

### *2.7. Reduction in Tokenism*

Tokenism refers to instances in which a firm hires a small number of persons of color and then does little to integrate them into the firm culture.[16]

A firm's reason for practicing tokenism will not always be invidious, but whatever the reason for the practice, one of its effects is to legitimize the existence of a predominantly white workplace and provide the firm with a defense against discrimination. Firms that engage in tokenism can say: "It is true that most of our associates are white. However, it is not true that we discriminate against Asians. We hired Mathew, a Korean American, last year, and we hope that we will hire more people like Mathew in the future."

Tokenism burdens people of color in three significant ways. First, tokenism burdens the token with the weight of representing his entire race. The cost of his failure is imposed not simply on him but on his race as a whole. Consequently, the token's every action is potentially racially representative (Yelnosky, 2003, pp. 1390–1399). He becomes his race and, more particularly, an indication of the potential – or lack thereof – of his race. Second, tokenism limits the token's sense of autonomy. His interactions will likely be overdetermined by his awareness of his status as a representative of his race. For example, Mathew, the Korean-American executive, might avoid interacting with technical support staff out of a fear that he will racially represent his group as technically but not creatively inclined. A third problem with tokenism is that it requires the token to think about whether he belongs. The token could believe that the reason he is a token likely derives from the perception (which may or may not be conscious) that members of his race do not belong or that they cannot fit in. The token has to be careful not to internalize these ideas, and he has to be vigilant about counteracting them (indeed yet another burden on the token).

The success of the first generation (most of whom were tokens) and their presence at the top of corporate hierarchies reduces the racial representation burdens of later-generation employees. The later employee's conduct will be less racially representative, giving them greater autonomy to navigate the workplace and a greater sense of entitlement and belonging.

### *2.8. Mentorship*

To succeed within most large bureaucratic organizations, new employees must gain access to tacit information about both the organization (for example, how to negotiate institutional politics) and the job (for example, how to communicate with clients).[17] Such information has to be conveyed in person. What this means is that senior employees have to take junior employees under their wing. Ideally, senior employees "group mentor" junior employees, providing as a group a network of information for the juniors.[18] This network would then give juniors invaluable official and unofficial knowledge about the institution, its governance structure, and power brokers.

The reasons that people of color typically do not have access to this kind of institutional knowledge are complicated, and the answer is not simply intentional racial animus.[19] Part of the problem may be that scarce mentorship resources are allocated to those with whom the mentors are most comfortable, and these may tend to be juniors of the same race and gender as the mentors.[20] An alternative explanation is that tacit information is often conveyed in informal settings – settings in which people are relatively comfortable engaging in office gossip about the ins and outs of workplace politics. People of color may have limited access to these settings, again because after-work socialization tends to be among same-race colleagues.[21]

First-generation minorities who succeeded did so despite minimal access to information networks. In some cases their successes were a result of exceptional skill, in other cases it was luck, and in still other (presumably rare) cases there was some nonminority who was willing to reach outside an established ingroup to provide mentorship and network opportunities to a minority protégé.[22] The workplace presence and success of the first generation means that succeeding generations of minorities will have access to at least a minimal amount of mentorship and networks, reducing the need to rely on exceptional skill, luck, benevolence, and outside connections.

Taken together, the trickle-down benefits from the first-generation minority successes should provide greater opportunities for junior minorities to advance in the workplace. While the benefits appear plausible on their face, they depend on the assumption that successful minorities will choose to use their senior positions to change corporate culture and to extend opportunities to their junior minority associates. To examine whether this assumption is correct, we ask, "What are the characteristics of the minorities most likely to succeed?" Our exploration of this question shows that those who are likely to rise to the top may not provide the benefits many of us hope would accrue from their success.

## 3. THOSE MOST LIKELY TO SUCCEED

Assuming that racial minorities are subject to negative stereotypes – negative presumptions about work ethic, loyalty, trustworthiness, and collegiality, among other things – minorities who succeed in predominantly white corporate cultures will likely share certain characteristics and strategies. As will become clear, minority success is a function of choices. We do not deny the institutional constraints of being a person of color in a modern corporate culture. Indeed, it is precisely because of these constraints that we focus on choices such as how minorities exercise the limited discretion they have with respect to work assignments, and on what we call racial agency – how senior and presumably successful minorities manage the presence of other junior minorities within the corporation. We argue that being a "successful racial type" is related to the exercise of racial agency. More particularly, the racial types who race their way to the top of the corporate hierarchy are not likely to exercise racial agency to "lift others as they climb." To substantiate this claim, we need to first explicitly articulate the nature or identity characteristics of successful racial types. This is done as shown later.

### *3.1. Risk-Taking, Luck, and Overconfidence*

The simplest models of employee promotion center on production. According to these models, the employee who produces the most widgets at the cheapest cost will be promoted. The theory is that the employer is competing with other employers to produce the cheapest and best widgets; therefore, the employer who does not promote the best widget-producers will lose them to the job market and ultimately be driven out of business.

The reality in most large organizations is quite different. Employee performance is often difficult to measure; moreover, many corporate tasks are structured so that employees are required to exercise discretion. If minority employees are often subject to stereotypes that they are less capable, how will they exercise this discretion? In another article, we argued that there is an incentive for them to work their identities to counteract or to undermine the negative stereotype about competence (Carbado & Gulati, 2000b). One way in which minority employees can do so is to assume primary responsibility for high-risk tasks, tasks that are well beyond their skill level and that have the potential to make them stand out among their peers. High-risk projects, when performed successfully, yield high returns. Taking on and successfully completing a difficult project that people at low levels of experience do not usually attempt might catch the attention of the corporate leaders and cause them to rethink their racial assumptions.

It makes sense, then, for people of color seeking advancement to make this high-risk choice.

This will not necessarily be the case for whites. Because whites are not subject to negative stereotypes, they will experience less pressure to take on high-risk assignments. If we assume that whites and nonwhites are in a competitive race to the top of the corporation, one way for minorities to gain a competitive edge, or at least mitigate a racial disadvantage, is to perform high-risk tasks. And indeed, employment discrimination scholars have at least marginally suggested that the people of color who are most likely to succeed in the corporate context (apart from the true superstars) are those who take big risks and for whom the big risks (sometimes by luck) pay off.[23]

While successful risk-taking helps explain minority corporate success, we believe that another factor plays a role as well: overconfidence. If the firm attributes an employee's successful risk-taking to luck, the firm probably will not promote that employee. Nor is the firm likely to look favorably upon excessive risk-taking behavior, particularly if the firm bears the costs of the failures. Consequently, the employee who is seeking to outperform her colleagues cannot stop at taking higher risk gambles. She must also be able to persuade the firm's decision makers that the successes that result from these gambles were earned and *not* happenstance. Likely, excessively self-confident minorities will be persuasive on this score. The firm will perceive these employees to be "authentic" in their claim that their success was a function of talent, not luck.[24] In sum, risk-taking, luck, and overconfidence together affect whether minorities will ascend the corporate hierarchy.

### *3.2. Teamwork and Racial Fit*

As discussed before a large amount of corporate work is performed in teams. Thus, one's ability to climb the corporate ladder is going to be determined at least to some extent by one's competence and reputation as a team player. Several scholars have suggested that corporate leaders may presume that people of color will not fit comfortably within team-oriented environments.[25] The presumption, more specifically, is that the loyalties of people of color reside outside the institution, and that they have suspicions about, feel uncomfortable around, and are also distrusting of their white counterparts. To the extent that people of color are aware of this negative presumption, they have an incentive to demonstrate not simply that they can, in fact, engage in teamwork,[26] but that they can do so more effectively than their white (typically male) counterparts.[27] Put more controversially, there is an incentive for minorities to prove that they can be better insiders than white men. And those who exhibit the greatest insider-group affinity are most likely to receive promotions.

### *3.3. Managing Other Minorities*

The reality of the modern workplace is that racial minorities are going to be present. The "racial problem" for firms is no longer how to keep people of color out but rather (a) deciding which ones to let in and (b) developing strategies for managing them. In other words, firms are going to want to hire and promote *some* minorities. With respect to hiring, firms will screen for racially palatable nonwhites – for example, a black person who "looks" but does not "act" black.

With respect to promotion, firms likely will have an additional concern, a concern that derives from what we call residual racial difference. Notwithstanding the firm's best screening efforts, the minorities that the firm hires will still be different. They cannot perform their way completely outside their racial identity because most will always be recognizable as nonwhite – less nonwhite than other people of color, to be sure, but nevertheless nonwhite. Firms will want to promote people of color who can help manage this residual racial difference or racial "excess." A crucial element of that task will be to provide and to receive information across the group. In other words, the more intelligence corporate leaders have on people who are residually racial different, and the more information it can get funneled to that group, the better position the corporation is in to manage racial excess. Minorities in key management positions can be effective conduits for this information. There is an incentive, then, for firms to promote those minorities with the capacity to help them better manage and communicate with the larger group of minority workers in the workplace.

This management concern may also extend to minority groups outside the firm. If a firm needs to cultivate customers or clients in minority communities, and there is a perception that minority employees are better able to serve as conduits, the firm will be inclined to promote at least some minority employees who can assist in managing these external relationships.

In short, minorities at the top of the corporation likely will share some or all of these characteristics. But is this type of racial minority likely to ameliorate discrimination and provide trickle-down benefits to junior minority workers? We now turn directly to this question.

# 4. THE LIKELIHOOD OF AMELIORATIVE TASKS BEING PERFORMED

Once a minority employee has raced her way to the top of the corporation, it would seem that the ameliorative tasks she is to perform would be easy. Indeed, many of these tasks get "performed" simply as a function of her presence at the upper echelons of the workplace. Yet there are meaningful "barriers"[28] to performance of these tasks, each of which relates to stereotypes. Below we discuss how these barriers diminish the likelihood that senior corporate minorities will lift as they climb.

## *4.1. Stereotype Negation*

As suggested earlier, there are two stereotype-negating strategies that senior minorities can employ: racial group negation strategies and individual identity negation strategies. The assumption is that either or both of these strategies will racially improve the corporation for junior minorities. However, seniors have a greater incentive to perform individual identity negation strategies than group negation strategies, and the former unfortunately do little to improve the advancement opportunities of junior minorities.

## *4.2. Racial Group Negation Strategies*

### *4.2.1. Direct Intervention*

Imagine that Marco, a Latino, is interested in convincing the decision makers at his firm that Latinos are not lazy and that they are just as competent as whites. He could, in the context of a hiring meeting, simply remind his colleagues of the way stereotypes work and suggest that they be careful not to allow their decision making to be informed by those stereotypes. This need not be done in a confrontational manner. Indeed, Marco might even employ humor to raise the racial consciousness (Cha & Roberts, 2004, pp. 6–9).

However, this kind of direct intervention – speaking out about racial stereotypes in the context of a hiring meeting – is not likely to occur. To understand why, think of the hiring meeting as a high visibility moment, a moment in which one's institutional identity is salient. Recall now the composite of the people of color who are most likely to ascend the corporate hierarchy; these people will probably be overconfident about their abilities, be willing to take high levels of risk, and be able to credibly demonstrate an affinity for the dominant group. Given the nature of the modern corporation (complex hierarchies with decentralization), high visibility moments are few and far between (Carbado & Gulati, 2000a, pp. 103–107). They are occasions, therefore, in which an incentive exists for employees, especially nonwhite employees, to behave in ways that positively construct their *individual* workplace identity. This incentive makes the hiring meeting an inopportune time for Marco to confront authority – even via humor.[29] Likely Marco will want to use the hiring meeting to bolster his reputation as an affable and nonhostile person of color, who is loyal to the firm and committed to its institutional projects.

One might reasonably ask why Marco's risk-taking tendencies would not make him likely to intervene. Being silent during a hiring meeting in which the operation of stereotypes could limit opportunities for people of color hardly seems like something a risk-taker would do. But note that Marco's risk-taking is in respect to his own job assignments, not overall institutional politics. He engages in risk-taking only to the extent that he perceives a stereotype negation payoff, and none seems to flow from admonishing one's colleagues to avoid using stereotypes when making hiring decisions.

The above seems to suggest that Marco has two choices: (1) silence, a passive move that leaves his racially affable institutional identity in tact, or (2) speaking out against the operation of racial stereotypes, an active move with the potential to disrupt his "positive" racial image. However, Marco also has a third option: to very subtly sanction his colleagues' utilization of stereotypes. In the context of the meeting, he might simply say something like,

> Some of you have expressed concerns about the small number of people of color – especially Latinos – in the pool. One of you made the point that we cannot have another year in which we fail to hire at least one Latino. As a Latino myself and a member of this firm for over twelve years, I would certainly like to see others at this firm. But I don't think we should lower our standards, and I don't think we should be paternalistic. Let's not forget that, up until two years ago, there were three other Latinos in this firm. Two left to pursue other opportunities and one was denied partnership for good reason. He simply was not a team-player, and he did not have the best work ethic. That's not a bad racial record. Could it be better? Perhaps. I would need to do some more thinking about it. To be clear: none of this is to say that we should ignore the possibility that our hiring process results in fewer minorities at the firm. What I am suggesting is that there is no indication here that this is the case. From where I sit, then, I think we should stop beating ourselves up about this. I say all of this as a Latino who is deeply concerned about the well-being of Latinos inside and outside of this firm.

Marco's speaking out in this way solidifies his image as a team-player who is loyal to the institution, invested in merit, and willing to subordinate racial group identity politics for the good of the firm. His colleagues could read his comments to say, with respect to hiring, the firm is doing nothing wrong; to the extent there are few Latinos at the firm, that is a function of the limited number of qualified Latinos, not racial discrimination. If so, Marco will have demonstrated to his white colleagues in power (a) a lack of resentment about the possibility of their holding negative racial stereotypes and (b) an affirmative belief in the meritocratic nature of the workplace.[30] In all of this Marco remains authentic as a Latino. At no time does he disidentify with the identity category "Latino" or with the idea of race or racial organization.

Marco's "subtle" intervention could signal an even stronger commitment to the firm and a weaker commitment to racial group identification. Marco could make the point that, given affirmative action, it is particularly important to pay attention to the institution's standards when hiring minorities. This might translate into Marco applying a higher level of scrutiny to minority applicants; he may even insist that marginal minority candidates not be hired, even where marginal candidates from other groups are hired. If Marco adopts this strategy, it will likely allay any concerns about his institutional commitment. But it will also provide those colleagues with an external justification for their negative actions regarding minority issues. For example, it is a lot easier for a law firm to defend some egregiously discriminatory position being advanced by a client if it is able to assert that its minority lawyers insisted, on the grounds of principle, that they not deny that client representation. Along similar lines, it would help the firm defend a discrimination case filed by a former employee of color if the people who led the charge for the denial of promotion were themselves members of a minority group.

Whether, in the above hypothetical, Marco would go so far as to lead the charge against hiring another Latino is not clear. What is clear is that there is little incentive for him to employ a direct interventionist strategy to negate racial stereotypes at the group level. That strategy carries the potential cost of disrupting the impression of him as an affable racial minority and a good institutional citizen.[31]

#### *4.2.2. Indirect Intervention*

Is there an indirect way for Marco to negate racial stereotypes at the group level? The most obvious way for Marco to do so is through his own work performance. More specifically, the quantity and quality of Marco's work may suggest to the firm's decision makers not only that Marco is a smart, hardworking, and conscientious worker but also that these characteristics apply to Latinos as a group. Marco's work performance might very well be outstanding enough to provide that signal. But if Marco is perceived to be exceptionally good – a superstar – or even just very good, the firm might engage in racial exceptionalism. In other words, the firm could tell itself: *Marco may be a Latino, but he is not like other Latinos. He is exceptional. Therefore, the stereotypes we hold about Latinos should not be applied to Marco.* Note that the firm has not revised its negative impressions of Latinos, only its impression of Marco.

Assuming that Marco is not a superstar, he can still attempt to negate group-based stereotypes through the choices he makes about work. That is, Marco can be even more high-risk with respect to work assignments than he otherwise would be. The problem with this strategy is this: the greater Marco's risk-taking, the greater the possibility of large failure, failure which would confirm, rather than disrupt, racial stereotypes. The problem is compounded if other Latinos (or other minorities) in the firm adopt this strategy. The failure rate of the group will rise, creating the overall impression that Latinos or other minorities are irrational and rash. The end result is an exacerbation rather than an elimination of negative racial presumptions.

Another problem with group-based negation strategies that rely on work performance is that most jobs do not involve tasks where each employee's production can be separated and ranked against that of others. Instead, many high-level jobs tend to involve production in teams and fuzzy individual outputs. This limits the extent to which any one individual can, through the quality of his work, challenge racial stereotypes at the group level. At best, such individuals can preempt the application of the negative stereotype to themselves. Returning to our hypothetical, although Marco's work performance may rebut assumptions about *his* competence and work ethic, it will be inadequate to the task of rebutting negative assumptions about Latinos as a whole.

### *4.3. Individual Identity Negation Strategies*

Given both the cost and difficulties of negating stereotypes at the group level, minorities may attempt to disrupt stereotypes at the individual level. We have already discussed one barrier to this: racial exceptionalism. There is another, potentially more problematic barrier. Consider again Marco.

If Marco's individual stereotype negation strategy takes the form of distancing himself from his racial group, it exacerbates rather than ameliorates negative stereotypes about Latinos as a group. Assume, for example, that Marco informs his majority colleagues that he is frustrated with the low standards of work among his fellow minorities and their failure to act as team players.[32] There is little reason to conclude that this individual identity negation strategy will trickle down to benefit junior people of color.

### *4.4. Racial Monitoring*

Recall our assumption above that the presence of successful minorities would have the effect of racially monitoring the institution. White colleagues would be more conscious of racial issues when making decisions in the presence of their successful minority colleagues than they would in their absence. This accountability effect could impact both the firm's labor market decisions, including those relating to promotion and hiring, and its other interactions with the outside world, including choices about what products to manufacture, how to market them, and others. But are these assumptions about racial monitoring correct?

Imagine that Marco has just been promoted to partner. Assume that hiring decisions are made by partners, that Marco is about to participate in his first hiring meeting, and that he is only one of two minorities present. Will Marco's presence have a monitoring effect? There are several reasons to answer that question in the negative. First, Marco has likely participated in numerous socialization rituals in which his racial palatability was both demanded and supplied. Indeed, Marco's very success within the firm was probably a function of his capacity to practice racial comfort and individual identity stereotype negation (Carbado & Gulati, 2003a, pp. 1803–1806). Members of the partnership, then, would not feel excessively racially policed by Marco's presence.

Second, if this is Marco's first partnership meeting about hiring, he has an incentive to use the moment to assure his partners that his status as a partner will not change his institutional or racial identity. In other words, Marco might view this meeting as a high-visibility moment in which he, as a partner, needs to demonstrate institutional fit, loyalty, and team orientation.[33] Further, he would want to find a way to convey the idea that he is not interested in disrupting the selection and socialization processes that (racially) produced him. This would send a message to the partners that Marco is willing to help the firm "manage" other racial minorities and residual racial differences. The foregoing suggests that there are good reasons to question that Marco's presence would operate as a racial monitor. This conclusion is not undermined by the risk-taking aspects of Marco's identity, which, again, are directed at work assignments as part of a broader strategy to negate racial stereotypes.

### *4.5. Racial Accountability*

Another assumption we made about senior minorities is that they would produce racial accountability. The idea, again, is that the presence of these minorities would require the firm to account for – explain or justify – apparent racial inequities in the firm. The reasons senior people of color may not produce racial monitoring also explain why racial accountability may not occur. In short, the firm would expect that the people of color it promotes (a) are committed to the norms of the firm, even norms that adversely affects minorities in hiring and promotion and (b) would continually demonstrate that commitment.[34] As a result, the presence of minority seniors would not necessarily exert any pressure on the firm's decision makers to account for racial disparities or inequalities within the firm.

### *4.6. Racial Cooperation*

Earlier we posited that the presence of senior minorities would facilitate racial cooperation. The notion was twofold. First, seniors would help form teams that would maximize opportunities for racial trust; and second, their very success would eliminate or mitigate racial anxieties and suggest to nonwhites and whites alike that racial cooperation is possible. Here again the question is whether these theoretical benefits can be realized. The short answer is only marginally so.

Senior minorities are not likely to structure teams in a race-conscious manner. Their firm socialization would suggest to them that this is a bad thing to do. It would render their own racial identities less palatable, or, in other words, weaken their institutional fit. Further, if these seniors have worked hard to demonstrate their capacity for racial cooperation on their own, they may expect other minorities to do the same.

Nevertheless, the presence of successful senior minorities will probably provide some racial cooperation payoff. Their presence will suggest that people of color – of a particular type – can work cooperatively with whites. Thus, the firm's decision makers will not likely adopt an absolute position that minorities cannot work cooperatively with whites. Instead, decision makers will likely assume that minorities can work cooperatively, but only so long as they are of the same racial type as the ones who survived the promotion process. In this sense, the racial cooperation payoff from the mere presence of senior nonwhites is likely to be marginal.

### *4.7. Racial Comfort*

A related assumption we made is that senior people of color will reduce the supply of and demand for racial comfort work in predominantly white corporations. The thinking was that the presence of senior people of color would diminish anxieties about racial difference, thus reducing the need for juniors to supply racial palatability. Just the opposite may be true, however. Recall that minorities who succeed in climbing the corporate hierarchy will probably have adopted strategies that negate racial stereotypes only as they apply to them. Consequently, even with the presence of seniors who survived several promotion tournaments, the firm's decision makers will still base their hiring and promotion decisions on the idea that, as a general matter, racial differences cause grit not grease. They will thus continue to scrutinize junior minorities for their capacity to supply grease – that is to say, comfort. The greater the presence of racial comfort at the senior level, the greater the expectation that racial comfort should be supplied at the junior level. As we have argued elsewhere [cite law and economics of critical race theory], to be efficient, firms already have an incentive to achieve sameness (Carbado & Gulati, 2003a, pp. 1788–1802). To the extent possible, firms will want to realize the efficiency gains of sameness while maintaining some degree of racial diversity (*ibid.*). The success of senior people of color creates racial precedent for how to satisfy both demands: skin-deep diversity; diversity that is based on phenotype and sameness in performance of workplace identity. Rather than reducing the demand for racial comfort then, the presence of successful minorities might actually increase it.

### *4.8. Role Modeling*

We also assumed that the presence of people of color at the top of the corporation would send a message to people of color at the bottom that they can reach the top. But once we move past the generic category "people of color" and the simple fact of their presence to discuss instead racial types and racial performance, it becomes less clear that the people of color at the top of the corporation will function as role models for the people of color at the bottom. The minorities on the bottom of the corporation may view those at the top as "sell outs" – people who sold their racial identities for career opportunities. And even where this is not the case, the racial palatability of senior people of color may make it difficult for the junior people of color to identify with them – that is, to view them as role models.

The foregoing arguments assume that the minorities at the bottom of the corporation will want to forge a racial connection with those at the top. However, this may not be the case, particularly if the corporation is successful in screening for racial palatability. The more successful the corporation is at performing this screening, the less likely people of color at the top will have racial tension or disconnection with those on the bottom. More concretely, if Marco, a junior Latino executive, was the product of the corporation's successful screening for racial palatability, he will probably not be concerned that senior executive Pablo (who goes by Paul) does not seem to be motivated by an affinity for his racial group. Indeed, Marco might see Paul as a role model precisely because Paul lacks this kind of racial investment. This may be the unexpected message that successful racial types send. But this message is not about the success of racial difference but rather the success of racial palatability.

### *4.9. Tokenism*

With respect to tokenism, our assumption was that minority successes are likely to reduce the costs of tokenism, such as the weight of representing one's race and a diminishment in one's sense of workplace autonomy and belonging. Once again, there is reason to question this assumption. Consider first the burden of racial representation. Assume once more that Marco has just been promoted to the partnership. If one of the reasons the partners promoted Marco is that they perceived him to be different from other Latinos, his presence will do little to reduce the racial representation burden of junior Latinos. They too will have to prove that they are not like other Latinos, and they assume the risk that their job performance and overall institutional identity will suggest that they are. In other words, precisely because Marco's promotion was based, at least in part, on racial exceptionalism, other Latinos will have to prove either that they, like Marco, are exceptional or that racial stereotypes about Latinos are inaccurate. Marco's success, therefore, will not necessarily ameliorate the racial representation burdens of junior Latinos.

Nor is Marco's success likely to increase the workplace autonomy or sense of belonging of junior Latinos. Paradoxically, the more entrenched the firm's perception of Marco as a racial exception, the heavier the burden on junior Latinos to repudiate negative stereotypes. The logic of this dynamic derives from the simple notion that, by definition, exceptions are not the norm. The firm's decision makers could conclude that if Marco is the exception, the others are not. For example, assume that in addition to Marco, there are two other Latinos at the firm. This demographic backdrop could invite the firm's decision makers to ask, *How likely is it that we have three racially exceptional Latinos working for us?* In this way, Marco's perceived exceptionalism might actually decrease rather than increase the workplace autonomy of junior Latinos. Because of his exceptionalism, juniors will have to structure their workplace interactions to rebut the presumption that, while Marco is a racial exception, they are not. They have the freedom to simply interact.

### *4.10. Mentorship*

As discussed above, the first few generations of successful minorities likely had trouble finding mentors; people who would transfer to them not only the tacit knowledge required to excel at their jobs, but also an understanding of the informal norms and politics of the workplace essential for institutional survival and advancement. But how likely is it that those who made it despite the lack of mentorship will mentor successive generations?

At least two of the characteristics we attribute to minorities at the top of the corporation, overconfidence and the need to demonstrate affinity for the dominant group, suggest that the answer is "not very likely." First, consider overconfidence. Recall our suggestion that senior people of color firmly believe, or convey the idea that they firmly believe, that they deserve their success and that it was not a product of chance or circumstance.[35] This overconfidence enables the minority who uses high-risk strategies to succeed and to persuade others that her success was not the product of chance but of merit, but a person of color who succeeds without mentoring may believe that other minorities do not or should not need any mentorship because, after all, she made it on her own merit. She may even construe affirmative mentoring as "special help," or help that could function to confirm the very stereotypes she spent much of her time attempting to disrupt.

The second characteristic that cuts against mentorship is that the successful minority needs to continually demonstrate that she is a team player. Sharing her human capital with other minorities might suggest that she is a special interest player. If the senior minority perceives that her colleagues are scrutinizing her mentorship choices for signs of racially specific mentorship, she may consciously avoid mentoring too many or, indeed, any minorities.

A final reason why senior minorities might not mentor juniors derives from the investment on the part of seniors in continued corporate success. If a senior perceives that minority juniors have a poor success rate, and if having a stable of successful mentees is important to one's long term success, there is a disincentive for the senior person of color to mentor junior nonwhites.[36]

## 5. CONCLUSION

Central to this chapter is the idea that an employee's ability to race to the top of the corporation is not solely a function of traditional qualifications and capability. Producing more widgets than one's competitors is not enough. To succeed, employees have to effectively negotiate the political landscape of the institution. They have to appease individual corporate officers, co-opt and make allies with powerful interest groups, and undermine competitors. The more bureaucratic the organization and the more opaque the promotion process, the more important this institutional game is to climbing the corporate ladder.

Broadly stated, our aim has been to identify the racial types who are likely to play this game well and, consequently, race to the top of the corporation. Because the racial minorities at the top of the corporation are in a position to ameliorate discrimination for those on the bottom, identifying these racial types is crucial to making corporations more welcoming to racial minorities. It is this intuition that helps to explain why many corporate governance and employment discrimination scholars rest some of their hope for the establishment of colorblind corporate cultures on the assumption that successful racial types will actively seek out and perform anti-discriminatory institutional work.

As shown earlier, there is reason to believe that the racial minorities at the top of the corporate hierarchy will not racially reform the corporation or open the door for the minorities on the bottom. Indeed, strong incentives exist for minorities to race to the top of the corporation and pull the ladder up behind them when they get there.

This is a sad place to end. In this respect, we should emphasize that we are not making an empirical claim. People act against incentives all the time.

Perhaps people of color at the top of the corporate hierarchy are doing precisely that. But perhaps they are not, in which case we should be even more concerned at the current status of anti-discrimination law.

# NOTES

1. The expression originated as a slogan of the National Association of Colored Women's clubs (see Tangenberg, 2003, p. 381).

> The [NACW] clubs were established in 1896 to provide support to African American women and to combat negative racial stereotypes. The slogan adopted by NACW, "Lifting as we climb," was used to refer to the commitments of club members to lift each other socially, economically, and spiritually as their communities suffered the profound effects of racial discrimination.

It continues to have currency inside and outside the black community. For an indication of its continued usage in the black community, see al-Hakim (2001), stating, "[i]t astounds me that this man, this black man, has forgotten where he has come from. He has completely neglected the idea that we have in our community to 'lift as we climb.' Instead, he is kicking as he climbs, kicking those hot on his heels. He is a disgrace to beneficiaries of affirmative action, and as a member of the black community."

2. Though they are interrelated, for purposes of simplicity, we discuss them separately.

3. This has been one of the most consistent criticisms of the Supreme Court's conceptualization of racism as a problem of conscious intentionality. See *Washington v. Davis* (1976) (holding that to establish an equal protection claim, the plaintiff must prove intentional racial decision making on the part of the state).

4. Because racial stereotypes often have gender specificity, Johnny's success would not necessarily send a strong signal about the capacity of black women to succeed in that corporate environment. See generally Crenshaw (1989) (articulating the concept of intersectionality to suggest, among other things, that race and gender intersect to affect black women's and black men's vulnerability to discrimination differently).

5. See Carbado and Gulati (2003b) (explaining that the mere presence of racial minorities can affect speech).

6. The obligation to act affirmatively is discussed in a series of articles by David Wilkins about the "obligation thesis" (see Wilkins, 1998). For examples of Wilkins's research focusing on the related questions of (a) the obligations of those in the minority community who succeed in the corporate world to help their community and (b) whether the economic pressures that apply within institutions like corporate law firms allow for "doing well by doing good" (see generally Wilkins, 1998; Wilkins, 1993).

7. Research suggests that the effect of making salient the danger that decision makers might be acting in a prejudiced manner can reduce the amount of prejudice (assuming that acting with prejudice is a disfavored behavior) (Spencer, Fein, Strahan, & Zanna, 2004, pp. 113–132).

8. Active engagement will produce the strongest monitoring effect when it takes the form of institutional criticism. If, for example, a minority employee consistently engages the institution in conversations about the relationship between minority under-representation and the firm's selection and promotion processes, the partners may perceive that every hiring and promotion decision is being monitored. This perception could shape the outcome of the firm's hiring and promotion practices.

9. The statement in the text is an oversimplification. As research into the "contact" question has demonstrated, a number of conditions, such as equality of status, need to be satisfied before contact between the groups effectively can reduce prejudice. The research to this question derives from and builds on the classic work *The Nature of Prejudice* by Gordon W. Allport, who set forth a set of conditions under which intergroup contact would reduce prejudice and enhance tolerance that have since been examined, modified, and re-examined. For a discussion of this hypothesis and the literature following Allport, see generally Brewer and Brown (1998), Hewstone (1996), and Wittig and Grant-Thompson (1998). For a discussion of this literature in the legal arena, see generally Estlund (2000).

10. Racial comfort work is part of broader identity management strategy people of color employ to navigate predominantly white workplaces. For recent research on the topic of minority self-presentation and identity construction in majoritarian work settings, see generally Roberts (2005) and Cha and Roberts (2004). For a fascinating treatment of the extra costs that minorities bear in terms of the consumer purchases (e.g., purchasing high status goods like Remi Martin cognac, Brooks Brothers or Armani suits, and BMW cars) they make in order to counteract negative stereotypes, see generally Lamont and Molnár (2001).

11. For descriptions of the dynamics of this presentational dilemma and the risks that minorities face in negotiating their everyday identities in the workplace, see generally Carbado and Gulati (2000b), Carbado and Gulati (2000a), and Carbado and Gulati (2001).

12. Edward Chen (2003, p. 1116) articulates the standard role modeling argument for racial diversity as follows:

> Diversity can establish the credibility of an institution, build bridges to other communities, and increase sensitivity to and awareness of diverse clientele and constituents. This is true whether the context is a union seeking to organize in a minority or immigrant community, a business looking to expand its markets to new communities, or a social service agency seeking to serve minority or culturally isolated populations. ... [D]iversity provides role models for those historically excluded. It can provide a source of hope and inspiration for those who would otherwise limit their horizons and aspirations.

See also Higginbotham (1999, p. 207) ("The existence of minorities in positions of prestige and power provides role models to young impressionable children. Having minorities employed in fields which have largely been dominated by white's [*sic*], opens children's eyes to many career possibilities") and Alger (1999, p. 194) ("[O]ne argument [seeking to justify faculty diversity], often called the role model theory, holds that faculty of color in a variety of disciplines are seen as role models for underrepresented students of color").

13. See, for example, Ifill (2000, p. 481) (claiming that Justice Clarence Thomas was confirmed as a Supreme Court Justice because of his status as a role model). Ifill states

> [Clarence] Thomas was the first Supreme Court nominee who came to the nomination proceedings almost exclusively as a role model. Distinguishing himself in neither ... big law firm practice nor academia ..., Thomas's supporters advanced his race and his perseverance in overcoming childhood poverty and racism to the public as his principal qualifications for service on the Court .... Thomas and his backers used Thomas's race and his experience with poverty to create an image of Thomas as the ultimate role model (*ibid.*).

Ifill goes on to say,

> While Thomas's backers viewed him as a black role model, to many blacks, Thomas was not a role model. In fact, given his record ..., his political views, ... and his disparaging remarks about well-regarded black leaders, most blacks would have considered Thomas the very opposite of a role model ... .
>
> Despite [many black leaders' and civil rights organizations'] disagreement with nearly all of Thomas's positions on civil rights issues, a majority of blacks supported Thomas ... . Some advocated supporting Thomas because they feared that if Thomas were not confirmed, President Bush would appoint a white candidate to fill the position. (*ibid.*, pp. 482–483)

See also Addis (1996, p. 1384, n. 20) (referring to Cornel West's analysis of Justice Thomas's confirmation). Addis states

> Discussing what he saw as the racial reasoning of the black leadership that prevailed during the Clarence Thomas/Anita Hill Senate hearing, [Cornel West] comments: "Unfortunately, most black leaders remained caught in a framework of racial reasoning – even when they opposed Thomas and/or supported Hill. Rarely did we have a black leader highlight the moral content of a mature black identity, accent the crucial role of coalition strategy in the struggle for justice, or promote the ideal of black cultural democracy. *Instead, the debate evolved around glib formulations of a black 'role model' based on mere pigmentation ... .*"

(*ibid.*, quoting West, 1993, p. 31) and Angelou (1992, p. 35) ("Because Clarence Thomas has been poor, has been nearly suffocated by the acrid odor of racial discrimination, is intelligent, well trained, black and young enough to be won over again, I support him"). For a more general discussion of the race and gender politics implicated in Clarence Thomas's judicial appointment, see Carbado (1997, pp. 77–81).

14. See *Wygant v. Jackson Board of Education* (1986) (refusing to utilize the role model theory) and *Regents of the University of California v. Bakke* (1978) (refusing to consider remedying the amorphous effects of past "societal discrimination" a compelling state interest).

15. See, for example, White (2004, p. 2168, n. 241) (commenting that the contours of the academic debate over affirmative action are well known). White states

> Supporters [of affirmative action] retort that the relationship between African Americans and whites is hardly symmetrical, and that racial preferences are necessary to remedy discrimination, to provide role models for the disadvantaged, and to increase diversity ... Although little new can be said about these arguments, the dispute continues with no sign of resolution. (*ibid.*)

Tilles (2004, p. 460) (explaining some scholars' arguments that the *Grutter v. Bollinger* (2003) opinion seems to approve of the role model theory that Wygant rejected and countering that "the closest *Grutter* comes to arguing in favor of the role model theory is ... [that it advances] the legitimacy of societal leadership, not models for minority students to follow").

16. The classic work on tokenism and the burdens that come associated with it is Kanter (1993), *Men and Women of the Corporation*. Kanter's focus was on women, and the dynamics with respect to other groups such as racial minorities are likely to be different. For more recent discussions, see Roth (2004, pp. 208–210) (finding that tokenism effects are diminished in the presence of objective evaluations, mentors, and specialized skills); Yelnosky (2003, pp. 1389–1399) (reviewing and discussing the recent literature on tokenism).

17. In the law firm context, this information is described in Wilkins and Gulati (1996). See generally Smith (2000, pp. 389–390), Murray and Owen (1991), and Seibert, Kraimer, and Liden (2001).

18. Individuals rely on not just a single mentor for developmental support, but on a "relationship constellation" (Higgins & Kram, 2001).

19. David Wilkins describes the importance of having access to networks that can provide such information in the context of the story of Lawrence Mungin, a black lawyer who makes a number of strategic errors in his attempt to move up the corporate hierarchy (Wilkins, 1999a, 1999b) (describing how Mungin cut himself off from possible sources of information about the law firm's informal processes in the black community). The importance of having access to social networks forms the basis for much of Glenn Loury's writing about the economics of discrimination (Loury, 1998, pp. 119–121) (arguing that social networks, which largely determine one's access to resources, allow past discrimination to persist over time and can have deleterious impacts on skills among minorities and significantly contribute to racial inequalities).

20. See Thomas and Gabarro (1999, p. 26) (observing, in the context of a study of the difficulties that black executives face in advancing up the corporate hierarchy, that white men often find it more comfortable working with other white men). See generally Friedman and Holtom (2002) (describing the background literature on the barriers to mentorship for minority employers and finding that the presence of "network groups" can help alleviate that problem) and Thomas (1993) (describing the barriers that racial differences can erect to the creation of effective mentorship relationships). On the importance of mentorship relationships for lawyers in general and minority lawyers in particular, see generally Higgins and Thomas (2001) (finding that a lawyer's portfolio of mentoring relationships is crucial in determining the occupational path he or she takes) and Thomas and Higgins (1996) (describing how minority employees, who can be at a disadvantage in terms of accessing intrafirm networks of information, are sometimes able to reach outside their own firms' race-based networks of information).

21. See Wilkins and Gulati (1996, pp. 569–570) (arguing that black associates at large firms often have a difficult time of establishing mentoring relationships necessary to be privy to tacit information partly because white mentors prefer associates who remind them of themselves); see also Benokraitis and Feagin (1993, pp. 334–335) (describing the informational inadequacy problem that arises as a result of being excluded from informal social groups at the workplace).

22. See, for example, Kaufman (1998, p. A1) (describing a mentoring relationship between two Jewish partners at a major New York law firm and a young black associate who later became a partner). As Thomas (1993) describes, there are significant barriers to such cross-group mentorship. What Wilkins (1999a; 1999b, pp. 30–31) interestingly finds in the law firm context is that the first generation of minority successes often came in laterally, after what was usually a distinguished career in public service. Wilkins (2004, pp. 29–30) argues more recently that minority associates and partners, because of their reduced access to intrafirm networks, often have to tap into networks outside their firm – networks that often involve public service to the larger minority community. In other words, they did not succeed in the usual manner. The fact that they came in laterally at a later stage, however, usually meant that they did not have a large store of institution-specific tacit knowledge to help their successors. Indeed, despite their partner status, they were usually struggling for survival themselves (*ibid.*, pp. 35–47).

23. See, for example, Carbado and Gulati (2000b, pp. 1289–1290) (describing how the dynamic can occur in everyday workplace image management choices); Charny and Gulati (1998) (explaining the structural dynamic that produces an incentive for minority workers to take on high-risk gambles); Wilkins and Gulati (1996, pp. 522–523) (explaining this dynamic in the context of law firm promotions). Although not often explicitly described as a high-risk gamble, scholars in the gender discrimination area have also identified the same dynamic as occurring when women employees have to attempt to negate the stereotypes of being meek but then risk overcompensating and activating the other negative stereotype of being unfeminine or pushy. See, for example, Valian (1998, pp. 133–137) (re-examining the tradeoffs of appearing masculine or feminine); cf. Miller and Meyers (1998, p. 212) (describing how the attempt to compensate for negative stereotypes can sometimes result in overcompensation where someone talks too fast, laughs too loud, or comes on too strong, and ends up putting off other people instead of pleasing them). Finally, for those outsider employees who try to demonstrate affinity for the dominant group, there is also the danger of being perceived as a traitor by their own group. See Branscombe and Ellemers (1998, p. 258) (discussing the long-term risks and benefits that individuals who remove themselves from their group face).

The dynamic described in the text is particularly likely to occur in up-or-out settings where both the rewards for success and the penalties for failure are large. If, however, the penalty for failure in that partner game is not large, then the high-risk dynamic described in the text can be reversed in a way that those with an a priori lower likelihood of success are pushed towards excessive risk aversion. In law firms, even though there is supposedly an "up-or-out" system, the "out" part is not generally a high penalty, because those who fail in obtaining partnership can generally get "high" or "efficiency" wage jobs elsewhere.

24. On the importance of authenticity for effective impression management, see Cha and Roberts (2004, pp. 33–36) (citing to studies to support the point that those who demonstrate authenticity are likely to be more effective in their impression management strategies).

25. The development of open, trusting, and genuine relationships is crucial for the setting up of effective teams. See Edmonson (1999, pp. 354–355) (stating the importance of trust at the team level rather than just among team members). There are two bodies of research that bear on this point that racial minorities are likely to have difficulty in matching up to their white male counterparts on these criteria. First, research shows that perceived similarity and ingroupness positively influences the likelihood of trust and liking, crucial precursors for setting up effective teams. See generally Kramer, Brewer, and Hanna (1996, p. 357), Nemeth (1986), and Polzer, Milton, and Swann (2002). And then there is a large body of research on the types of negative stereotypes racial minorities face that, depending on the minority identity in question, can include laziness, untrustworthiness, lack of intelligence, lack of creativity, and foreignness. See generally Devine (1989), Jeanquart-Barone (1996), Sinclair and Kunda (1999), and Cha and Roberts (2004).

26. See Flynn, Chatman, and Spataro (2001) (finding that demographically different persons who are better able to self-monitor are more likely to be able to succeed in workplace settings).

27. Along these lines, a number of commentators recommend that outsiders – those with different social identities – de-emphasize those social identity differences and instead emphasize work-related commonalities so as to achieve cohesion and unity at the workplace. See generally Allison and Herlocker (1994), Chatman, Polzer, and Barsade (1998), and Dovidio, Kawakami, and Gaertner (2000).

There is a body of research that finds that the above prescriptions do not always need to hold for diverse teams to function effectively. If the organizations themselves set up structures that value social identity differences, then employees will feel less of a need to adopt the kinds of strategies mentioned above. Instead, their differences can, in some cases, be harnessed to achieve productivity gains. See Ely and Thomas (2001, pp. 240–243) (examining the potential value of diverse individual cultural experiences to the group process); Ely and Thomas (2004, pp. 26–31) (analyzing the impact of racial learning environments on performance measures); see also Barreto and Ellemers (2002) (finding that a person's identity presentational choices, including which aspects of their identity to emphasize and which aspects to de-emphasize, are a function of how the organizational culture treats those different identities).

28. We put barriers in quotes because, as will become clear, we are talking about behavioral incentives.

29. Cf. Bell (1994, pp. 9–25) (providing "models for confrontation").

30. See Anderson (1999, p. 9) (describing how many successful blacks internalize conceptions of the organization as a meritocracy and are willing to blame whatever bad experiences they have had on aberrant individuals); cf. Thomas (2004, p. 102) (noting, in a description of IBM's recent strategic initiative to improve diversity at the firm, how members of the black task force advocated for a conservative approach to diversity because of the fear that they would be perceived as asking for "unearned preferences, and, even worse, might encourage the stereotype that blacks are less capable").

31. On a related note, experimental research shows that when outsider group members are allowed even minimal entrance into the dominant group (that has a higher status), these outsider group members tend to strengthen identification with the group into which they seek entrance. See generally Ellemers (1993) and Wright, Taylor, and Moghaddam (1990). All outsider group members, however, do not react to the opportunities for individual advancement versus group advancement equally. Those outsiders with lower levels of identification with the outsider group and who contest their being placed in the lower status group, as one might expect, are more willing to leave their fellow outsiders behind if presented with an opportunity for individual advancement. See Branscombe and Ellemers (1998, pp. 245, 257) (discussing studies about the identification levels of group members). The result then can be that these peripheral outsider group members (who are the ones most likely to advance) take on strategies that serve the interests of the dominant group and do not best advance the interests of their marginalized outsider group. See Carbado and Gulati (2003a, p. 1813, n. 202) (citing to research by Stephen Wright and others in making this point) and Major, Quinton, McCoy, and Schmader (2000, p. 211) (discussing how people may not respond to social identity threats or negative stereotyping if the emotional energy required to respond to correcting those problematic perceptions is too high). See generally Lamont (2001) (finding that successful and elite African-Americans, while often espousing racial solidarity, often adopt strategies of self-presentation that are not truly inclusive, but instead only allow the advancement of a few minority group members to the privileged position of insiders).

32. There is a large literature on "outsiders" using distancing strategies to advance in the workplace. These distancing strategies can come in at least two forms. First, there can be distancing in that the employee might try to emphasize aspects of her identity that are the nonminority aspects. In other words, she may try to make her race less salient. So, if her colleagues are Catholic or from the same college that she went to or if they all play chess, she may try to emphasize those commonalities and deemphasize the racial and gender differentials. Alternatively, the minority employee might try to make herself exceptional and comfort her colleagues about the negative views that they have about minorities. So, she may tell them that she also thinks that it is a problem that so many minorities are lazy and obsessed with race issues. Of the two strategies discussed above, the second one is obviously more harmful to the group's interest (because it involves the active confirmation of stereotypes). But the first strategy is also problematic in that it involves deemphasizing (making invisible) the race of the successful minority and, therefore, reducing the chances that success will be used by others to revise their views about the racial group.

Roberts articulates the distinction that we make above in terms of "assimilation" versus "decategorization" (Roberts, 2005, pp. 25–26). Assimilation refers to emphasizing distinctiveness from one's social group and similarities to the more dominant group. "Passing" is an extreme form of assimilating behavior. Decategorization also involves reducing the salience of one's racial identity, this time by emphasizing the nonstigmatized portions of one's identity, such as one's identity as an engineer or a sports fan or a UCLA graduate. Similarly, avoiding issues of race in one's conversations is another method of achieving decategorization. See Thomas (1993, pp. 178–180) (discussing how minorities may sometimes suppress race in order to develop relationships with mentors who are uncomfortable with racial issues). On both sets of strategies in a variety of contexts, including race, gender, and sexual orientation, see generally Chrobot-Mason, Button, and Diclementi (2001), Dovidio et al. (2000), Ellemers, Spears, and Doosje (2002), LaFromboise, Coleman, and Gerton (1995, p. 489), Ely (1994), Ely (1995), Rudman (1998), and Rudman and Glick (1999).

33. In her classic work, Kanter (1993, pp. 227–229) describes this (in the gender context) as women being subject to "loyalty tests" where, as a requirement of fitting in, women are expected to put down other women on occasion. Kanter describes three ways in which women can pass loyalty tests: they can let slide biased statements about other women, they can allow for jokes about women to be made without resistances, and they can accept their situation (*ibid.*). See also Mizrahi (2004) (suggesting the continued applicability of Kanter's work to the gender discrimination context today).

34. Patricia Hewlin and Ashley Rosette (2004) argue that even white male employees will often feel pressured to avoid pointing out instances of discrimination (even while thinking that it is wrong) so as to avoid being stigmatized as nonteam players. Hewlin and Rosette draw on a larger literature on organizational silence. For examples of articles in this area, see generally Milliken, Morrison, and Hewin (2003), Pinder and Harlos (2001), and Near and Miceli (1987). In the context of studying the disclosure securities practices of organizations, Langevoort taps the management literature to understand how and why it is that lower level employees are often reluctant to report bad news to their superiors (and, indeed, will often spin the news in a positive fashion so as to please their superiors). See generally Langevoort (1997).

There are at least two other dynamics that can also produce this silencing. One of them is where those who have been promoted feel a sense of obligation to the organization for having promoted them and, therefore, remain silent in the face of injustice (Kanter, 1993, p. 229) (explaining how women demonstrate loyalty). The other relates to the perception of the institution as a just, fair, or meritocratic place. Research shows that those who hold these "just world" beliefs are less likely to perceive discrimination. See Kaiser (2005) (discussing the "study examining individual differences in chronic endorsement of the [Belief in a Just World]") and Major and Kaiser (2005, pp. 13–15) (examining the "[b]elief systems that justify hierarchical and unequal relationships among groups in society"). Conversely, research also suggests that outsiders who attribute negative events to discrimination, even when those events are blatant, are likely to be perceived as troublemakers, that is, hypersensitive and irritating). See Kaiser and Miller (2003, pp. 234–236) (discussing results of experiment).

Given the foregoing, it seems reasonable to predict that an institution will have an interest in promoting those who both feel grateful to the institution for promoting them and those who perceive the institution as meritocratic and fair. These individuals, after all, are going to be less likely than others to perceive discrimination.

35. See Anderson (1999, p. 12) ("For ... blacks [at the higher status levels of an organization] there is a strongly felt need to believe they are present in the organization not solely because of the color of their skin but because of their own excellence in the general business world").

36. The phenomenon of inadequate mentorship by outgroup members has been observed at length in the literature on gender (Mizrahi, 2004, pp. 1590–1592) (examining the phenomenon of "female-on-female workplace hostility"). More broadly, see generally Heim and Murphy (2001). Research by scholars such as Ely

and Thomas (2001), however, suggests that there is nothing necessary about this dynamic. Organizations can be structured in ways that women (and other outsiders) are comfortable enough in their difference that they are able to help others of their group (Ely, 1994, p. 206) ("In settings in which women can perceive their group favorably relative to men, as when there is evidence of women's advancement, women's identifying with women will be a positive experience and can serve to strengthen relationships among them").

# REFERENCES

Addis, A. (1996). Role models and the politics of recognition. *University of Pennsylvania Law Review*, *144*(20), p. 1384.

Alger, J. (1999). When color-blind is color-bland: Ensuring faculty diversity in higher education. *Stanford Law & Policy Review*, *10*, p. 194.

al-Hakim, B. (2001). Letters to the editor: UC regent: A disgrace to his race. *The Daily Californian Online*. Available at www.dailycal.org/article.php?id = 4243

Allison, S., & Herlocker, C. E. (1994). Constructing impressions in demographically diverse organizational settings. *American Behavioral Scientist*, *37*, p. 637.

Anderson, E. (1999). The social situation of the black executive: Black and white identities in the corporate world. In: M. Lamont (Ed.), *The cultural territories of race: Black and white boundaries* (p. 9). Chicago, IL: University of Chicago Press.

Angelou, M. (1992). I dare to hope. In: R. Chrisman & R. L. Allen (Eds), *Court of appeal: The black community speaks out on the racial and sexual politics of Clarence Thomas vs. Anita Hill* (p. 35). New York, NY: Ballantine Books.

Aronson, J., Quinn, D. M., & Spencer, S. (1998). Stereotype threat and the academic underperformance of minorities and women. In: J. K. Swim & C. Stangor (Eds), *Prejudice: The target's perspective* (pp. 83–103). San Diego, CA: Academic Press.

Barreto, M., & Ellemers, N. (2002). The impact of respect versus neglect of self-identities on identification and group loyalty. *Personality and Social Psychology Bulletin*, *58*, p. 629.

Bell, D. A. (1994). *Confronting authority: Reflections of an ardent protestor* (pp. 9–25). Boston, MA: Beacon Press.

Benokraitis, N. V., & Feagin, J. R. (1993). Sex discrimination: Subtle and covert. In: J. M. Henslin (Ed.), *Down to earth sociology* (7th ed., pp. 334–335). New York, NY: Free Press.

Branscombe, N. R., & Ellemers, N. (1998). Coping with group-based discrimination: Individualistic versus group-level strategies. In: J. K. Swim & C. Stangor (Eds), *Prejudice: The target's perspective* (p. 258). San Diego, CA: Academic Press.

Brewer, M. B., & Brown, R. J. (1998). Intergroup relations. In: D. T. Gilbert, S. Fiske & G. Lindzey (Eds), *The handbook of social psychology* (pp. 554–594). New York, NY: Oxford University Press.

Carbado, D. W. (1997). The construction of O.J. Simpson as a racial victim. *Harvard Civil Rights-Civil Liberties Law Review*, *32*, 77–81.

Carbado, D. W., & Gulati, M. (2000a). Conversations at work. *Oregon Law Review*, *79*, p. 103.

Carbado, D. W., & Gulati, M. (2000b). Working identity. *Cornell Law Review*, *85*, p. 1259.

Carbado, D. W., & Gulati, M. (2001). The fifth black woman. *Journal of Contemporary Legal Issues*, *11*, p. 701.

Carbado, D. W., & Gulati, M. (2003a). The law and economics of critical race theory. *Yale Law Journal, 112*, 1757–1828.
Carbado, D. W., & Gulati, M. (2003b). What exactly is racial diversity? *California Law Review, 49*, p. 1149 (book review).
Carbado, D., & Gulati, M. (2004). Race to the top of the corporate ladder: What minorities do when they get there. *Washington and Lee Law Review, 61*, p. 1643.
Cha, S. E., & Roberts, L. R. (2004). Asian American journalists' performance of ethnic and professional identities. On file with the *Washington and Lee Law Review*. Unpublished manuscript.
Charny, D., & Gulati, M. (1998). Efficiency-wages, tournaments, and discrimination: A theory of employment discrimination law for "high-level" jobs. *Harvard Civil Rights-Civil Liberties Law Review, 33*, p. 79.
Chatman, J. A., Polzer, J., & Barsade, S. (1998). Being different yet feeling similar: The influence of demographic composition and organizational culture on work processes and outcomes. *Administrative Science Quarterly, 43*, p. 749.
Chen, E. M. (2003). The judiciary, diversity, and justice for all. *California Law Review, 91*, p. 1109.
Chrobot-Mason, D., Button, S., & Diclementi, J. (2001). Sexual identity management strategies: An exploration of antecedents and consequences. *Sex Roles, 45*, p. 321.
Crenshaw, K. (1989). Demarginalizing the intersection of race and sex: A black feminist critique of antidiscrimination doctrine, feminist theory and antiracist policies. *University of Chicago Legal Forum*, p. 139.
Delgado, R. (1991). Essay: Affirmative action as a majoritarian device: Or, do you really want to be a role model? *Michigan Law Review, 89*(5), p. 1223.
Devine, P. G. (1989). Stereotypes and prejudice: Their automatic and controlled components. *Journal of Personality and Social Psychology, 56*, p. 5.
Dovidio, J. F., Kawakami, K., & Gaertner, S. L. (2000). Reducing contemporary prejudice: Combating explicit and implicit bias at the individual and intergroup level. In: S. Oskamp (Ed.), *Reducing prejudice and discrimination*. Mahwah, NJ: Lawrence Erlbaum Associates.
Edmonson, A. (1999). Psychological safety and learning behavior in work teams. *Administrative Science Quarterly, 44*, 354–355.
Ellemers, N. (1993). The influence of socio-structural variables on identity management strategies. *European Review of Social Psychology, 4*, p. 27.
Ellemers, N., Spears, R., & Doosje, B. (2002). Self and social identity. *Annual Review of Psychology, 53*, p. 161.
Ely, R. J. (1994). The effects of organizational demographics and social identity on relationships among professional women. *Administrative Science Quarterly, 39*, p. 203.
Ely, R. J. (1995). The power in demography: Women's social constructions of gender identity at work. *Academy of Management Journal, 38*, p. 589.
Ely, R. J., & Thomas, D. A. (2001). Cultural diversity at work: The effects of diversity perspectives on work group processes and outcomes. *Administrative Science Quarterly, 46*, 240–243.
Ely, R. J., & Thomas, D. A. ( 2004). Team learning and the racial diversity-performance link. August, pp. 26–31. On file with *Washington and Lee Law Review*. Unpublished manuscript.
Estlund, C. L. (2000). The changing workplace as a locus of integration in a diverse society. *Columbia Business Law Review, 2000*, p. 331.

Flynn, F. J., Chatman, J. A., & Spataro, S. A. (2001). Getting to know you: The influence of personality on the impression formation and performance of demographically different people in organizations. *Administrative Science Quarterly*, *46*, p. 419.

Friedman, R. A., & Holtom, B. (2002). The effects of network groups on minority employee turnover intentions. *Human Resources Management*, *41*, p. 405.

Heim, P., & Murphy, S. (2001). *In the company of women: Turning workplace conflict into powerful alliances*. New York, NY: J.P. Tarcher/Putnum.

Hewlin, P. F., & Rosette, A. S. (2004). Stigma avoidance: A precursor to workplace discrimination. On file with the *Washington and Lee Law Review*, August. Unpublished manuscript.

Hewstone, M. (1996). Contact and categorization: Social psychological interventions to change intergroup relations. In: C. N. Macrae, C. Stangor & M. Hewstone (Eds), *Stereotypes and stereotyping* (p. 323). New York, NY: Guilford Press.

Higginbotham, F. M. (1999). Affirmative action in the United States and South Africa: Lessons from the other side. *Temple International & Comparative Law Journal*, *13*, p. 207.

Higgins, M. C., & Kram, K. E. (2001). Reconceptualizing mentoring at work: A developmental network perspective. *Academy of Management Review*, *26*, p. 264.

Higgins, M. C., & Thomas, D. A. (2001). Constellations and careers: Toward understanding the effects of multiple developmental relationships. *Journal of Organizational Behavior*, *22*, p. 223.

Ifill, S. A. (2000). Racial diversity on the bench: Beyond role models and public confidence. *Washington and Lee Law Review*, *57*, p. 481.

Jeanquart-Barone, S. (1996). Implications of racial diversity in the superior–subordinate relationship. *Journal of Applied Social Psychology*, *26*, p. 935.

Kaiser, C. R. (2005). Dominant ideology threat and the interpersonal consequences of attributions to discrimination. In: C. van Laar & S. Levin (Eds), *Stigma and group inequality: Social psychological approaches*. Mahwah, NJ: Routledge/Lawrence Erlbaum Associates.

Kaiser, C. R., & Miller, C. T. (2003). Derogating the victim: The interpersonal consequences of blaming events on discrimination. *Group Processes & Intergroup Relations*, *6*, 234–236.

Kanter, R. M. (1993). *Men and women of the corporation* (2nd ed.). New York, NY: Basic Books.

Kaufman, J. (1998). Inside outsiders: As blacks rise high in the executive suite, CEO is often Jewish. *Wall Street Journal* (April 22), p. A1.

Kramer, R. M., Brewer, M. B., & Hanna, B. A. (1996). Collective trust and collective action: The decision to trust as a social decision. In: R. M. Kramer & T. R. Tyler (Eds), *Trust in organizations: Frontiers of theory and research* (p. 357). London, UK: Sage Publications.

LaFromboise, T., Coleman, H. L. K., & Gerton, J. (1995). Psychological impact of biculturalism: Evidence and theory. In: N. R. Goldberger & J. B. Veroff (Eds), *The culture and psychology reader* (p. 489). New York, NY: New York University Press.

Lamont, M. (2001). Everyday anti-racism: Competence and religion in the cultural repertoire of the African-American elite. On file with the *Washington and Lee Law Review*, May 3. Unpublished manuscript.

Lamont, M., & Molnár, V. (2001). How blacks use consumption to shape their collective identity: Evidence from marketing specialists. *Journal of Consumer Culture*, *1*, p. 31.

Langevoort, D. (1997). Organized illusions: A behavioral theory of why corporations mislead stock market investors (and cause other social harms). *University of Pennsylvania Law Review*, *146*, 101–172.

Loury, G. C. (1998). Discrimination in the post-civil rights era: Beyond market interactions. *Journal of Economic Perspectives*, *12*(2), 119–121.

Major, B., & Kaiser, C. R. (2005). Perceiving and claiming discrimination. In: L. B. Nielson & R. Nelson (Eds), *The handbook of employment discrimination*. Dordrecht, The Netherlands: Springer.

Major, B., Quinton, W., McCoy, S., & Schmader, T. (2000). Reducing prejudice: The target's perspective. In: S. Oskamp (Ed.), *Reducing prejudice and discrimination* (p. 211). Mahwah, NJ: Lawrence Erlbaum Associates.

Miller, C. T., & Meyers, A. M. (1998). Compensating for prejudice: How heavyweight people (and others) control outcomes despite prejudice. In: J. K. Swim & C. Stangor (Eds), *Prejudice: The target's perspective* (p. 212). San Diego, CA: Academic Press.

Milliken, F. J., Morrison, E., & Hewlin, P. (2003). An exploratory study of employee silence: Issues that employers don't communicate upward and why. *Journal of Management Studies, 40*, p. 1453.

Mizrahi, R. (2004). 'Hostility to the presence of women': Why women undermine each other in the workplace and the consequences for title VII. *Yale Law Journal, 113*, p. 1602.

Murray, M., & Owen, M. A. (1991). *Beyond the myths and magic of mentoring*. San Francisco, CA: Jossey-Bass.

Near, J. P., & Miceli, M. P. (1987). Whistle-blowers in organizations: Dissidents or reformers? In: L. L. Cummings & B. M. Straw (Eds), *Research in organizational behavior* (Vol. 9, p. 321). Greenwich, CT: JAI Press.

Nemeth, C. J. (1986). Differential contributions of majority and minority influence. *Psychology Review, 93*, p. 23.

Pinder, C. C., & Harlos, K. P. (2001). Employee silence: Quiescence and acquiescence as responses to perceived injustice. In: G. Ferris & K. Rowland (Eds), *Research in personnel and human resources management* (Vol. 20, p. 331). Kidlington, Oxford: JAI Elsevier Science.

Polzer, J. T., Milton, L. P., & Swann, W. B. (2002). Capitalizing on diversity: Interpersonal congruence in small work groups. *Administrative Science Quarterly, 47*, p. 296.

Roberts, L. M. (2005). Changing faces: Professional image construction in diverse organizational settings. *Academy of Management Review, 30*(4), 685–711.

Roth, L. M. (2004). The social psychology of tokenism: Status and homophily processes on Wall Street. *Sociological Perspectives, 47*, 208–210.

Rudman, L. A. (1998). Self-promotion as a risk factor for women: The costs and benefits of counterstereotypical impression management. *Journal of Personality & Social Psychology, 74*, p. 629.

Rudman, L. A., & Glick, P. (1999). Feminized management and backlash toward agentic women: The hidden costs to women of a kinder, gentler image of middle managers. *Journal of Personality and Social Psychology, 77*, p. 1004.

Seibert, S. E., Kraimer, M. L., & Liden, R. C. (2001). A social capital theory of career success. *Academy of Management Journal, 44*, p. 219.

Sinclair, L., & Kunda, Z. (1999). Reactions to a black professional: Motivated inhibition and activation of conflicting stereotypes. *Journal of Personality and Social Psychology, 77*, p. 885.

Smith, P. J. (2000). Failing to mentor sapphire: The actionability of blocking black women from initiating mentoring relationships. *UCLA Women's Law Journal, 10*, 389–390.

Spencer, S. J., Fein, S., Strahan, E., & Zanna, M. (2004). The role of motivation in the unconscious: How our motives control the activation of our thoughts and shape our actions. In: J. P. Forgas, K. Williams & S. Laham (Eds), *Social motivation: Conscious and unconscious processes* (pp. 113–132). New York, NY: Cambridge University Press.

Steele, C. M. (1997). A threat in the air: How stereotypes shape intellectual identity and performance. *American Psychologist, 52*, p. 613.

Steele, C. M., & Aronson, J. (1995). Stereotype threat and the intellectual test performance of African Americans. *Journal of Personality and Social Psychology*, *69*, p. 797.

Tangenberg, K. M. (2003). Linking feminist social work and feminist theology in light of faith-based service initiatives. *AFFILIA: Journal of Women and Social Work*, *18*, p. 381.

Thomas, D. A. (1993). Racial dynamics in cross-race developmental relationships. *Administrative Science Quarterly*, *38*, p. 169.

Thomas, D. A. (2004). Diversity as strategy. *Harvard Business Review* (September), 98–102.

Thomas, D. A., & Gabarro, J. J. (1999). *Breaking through: The making of minority executives in corporate America* (p. 26). Cambridge, MA: Harvard Business School Press.

Thomas, D. A., & Higgins, M. C. (1996). Mentoring and the boundaryless career: Lessons from the minority experience. In: M. B. Arthur & D. M. Rousseau (Eds), *The boundaryless career: A new employment principle for a new organizational era* (p. 268). New York, NY: Oxford University Press.

Tilles, E. A. (2004). Lessons from Bakke: The effect of Grutter on affirmative action in employment. *University of Pennsylvania Journal of Labor and Employment Law*, *6*, p. 460.

Valian, V. (1998). *Why so slow? The advancement of women* (pp. 133–137). Cambridge, MA: The MIT Press.

West, C. (1993). *Race matters* (p. 31). Boston, MA: Beacon Press.

White, J. V. (2004). What is affirmative action? *Tulane Law Review*, *78*(241), p. 2168.

Wilkins, D. B. (1993). Two paths to the mountaintop? The role of legal education in shaping the values of black corporate lawyers. *Stanford Law Review*, *45*, p. 1981.

Wilkins, D. B. (1998). Essay: Identities and roles: Race, recognition, and professional responsibility. *Maryland Law Review*, *57*, p. 1556.

Wilkins, D. B. (1999a). On being good and black. *Harvard Law Review*, *112*, p. 1966 (book review).

Wilkins, D. B. (1999b). Partners without power? A preliminary look at black partners in corporate law firms. *Journal of the Institute for the Study of Legal Ethics*, *2*, 30–31.

Wilkins, D. B. (2004). Doing well by doing good? The role of public service in the careers of black corporate lawyers. *Houston law Review*, *41*, 29–30.

Wilkins, D. B., & Gulati, M. (1996). Why are there so few black lawyers in corporate law firms? An institutional analysis. *California Law Review*, *84*, p. 496.

Wittig, M. A., & Grant-Thompson, S. (1998). The utility of Allport's conditions of intergroup contact for predicting perceptions of improved racial attitudes and beliefs. *Journal of Social Issues*, *54*, p. 795.

Wright, S., Taylor, D., & Moghaddam, F. (1990). Responding to membership in a disadvantaged group: From acceptance to collective protest. *Journal of Personality and Social Psychology*, *58*, p. 994.

Yelnosky, M. J. (2003). The prevention justification for affirmative action. *Ohio State Law Journal*, *64*, 1389–1399.

## Cases

*Regents of the Univ. of Cal. v. Bakke*, 438 U.S. 265, 305–10 (1978).

*Washington v. Davis*, 426 U.S. 229, 239–40 (1976).

*Wygant v. Jackson Bd. of Educ.*, 476 U.S. 267, 275–76 (1986).

# WORKPLACE RACIAL DISCRIMINATION AND THE PROFESSIONALS AT THE CENTER OF CORPORATE HIERARCHIES

Cheryl L. Wade

## ABSTRACT

*Why do so many African Americans get stuck near the bottom or at the middle of the corporate ladder? Why do so many continue to complain about discriminatory pay and promotion decisions many decades after the enactment of anti-discrimination laws? Law and economics commentators who have written about the issue of employment discrimination have failed to address the complexity of the problem of implicit bias and the effects of the frequently inaccurate heuristics used by some white workers when making judgments about their black colleagues. Economic theory without context is useless. But with context, law and economic analysis can help us understand and address specific problems like workplace discrimination that persist within corporate cultures because of an overestimation of the cost of anti-discrimination efforts and an underestimation of the gravity and likelihood of workplace discrimination.*

*In this chapter, I explore the economic and socioeconomic reality of African American low and mid-level corporate managers in order to capture a more complete picture of the costs of discrimination in the*

**Law & Economics: Toward Social Justice**
**Research in Law and Economics: A Journal of Policy, Volume 24, 271–306**

**ISSN: 0193-5895/doi:10.1108/S0193-5895(2009)0000024014**

*corporate workplace. I also explore the heuristic assumptions that are made about African American professionals and the effects those assumptions have on the black community. Finally, to understand the gravity of the harm to individuals, their families and the communities to which they belong, narratives about the economic and psychological harm caused by discrimination are essential. I offer the narratives of six middle managers and low-level professionals who faced discrimination in the corporate workplace to provide an important context about discrimination's real costs.*

## 1. INTRODUCTION

One afternoon in the spring of 2006, I spent some time in the Central Park Conservatory Garden. The garden was closing and I waited with about 20 others for the park attendant to let us out of the locked gate. A well-dressed, seemingly affluent white woman asked me if I worked in the garden. Volunteers who work in the park wear knee-pads or gardening gloves and carry gardening tools. I carried a Nike tote bag in which I had books and a compact disc player. All park attendants wear uniforms. Their shirts are a pale green, and their khaki pants a deeper shade of green. The only aspect of my appearance that was similar to the Central Park attendants and workers was my brown skin. Other than the fact that I am African American, I looked like the others who toured and enjoyed the park that spring day dressed in jogging or hiking shoes, exercise clothes, and carrying tote bags.

As I walked home from the park, I thought about going out to buy newer, more expensive-looking exercise clothes. Maybe then I would not be mistaken for "the help."[1] Then I remembered my experience at Bliss Day Spa in Manhattan the year before. While in the locker room, one of the white patrons had assumed that I was the locker room attendant who was also a black woman. When she made this assumption, I was dressed in the thick white terry-cloth robe and slippers that all clients wear on their way to their massages and facials.

Another incident occurred when, after seeing a movie, I stood and waited for my friend to come out of the women's bathroom. Without excusing himself, a white man brusquely asked me where the men's room was. I was annoyed and responded with a question, "why would I know where the men's room is?" He responded, "well, I asked because you're standing there looking as though you work here."

Similar interactions occurred with regularity in the professional workplace. When I worked as a lawyer in a large New York City law firm, colleagues and clients who did not know me, or who did not know me well, frequently assumed that I was a messenger, or a secretary. One particular example makes the point graphically: while I waited in the reception area, dressed in a navy blue business suit, the white receptionist received a call from the person for whom I was waiting, asking her to let me know that he was running late. I later found out that he asked whether there was an associate waiting in the reception area. I recall that while on the phone, the receptionist looked over at me and said to the person with whom she was speaking, "no, she's not here." (I did not know at that time that she was talking with the person for whom I waited.)

I call these incidents professional misidentifications, and the accumulation of these types of interactions has made me intolerant of them. These personal stories about my experiences in New York City are not unique.[2] African Americans suffer daily indignities, mild annoyances, and micro-inequities that accumulate day after day and rob us of our individuality and inner peace.[3] I describe these experiences because they offer insight into the assumptions some whites make about the type of work that African Americans do.[4] Clearly, working as park or locker room attendants are honorable ways to make a living. It is true that many if not most of these jobs are filled by black Americans, at least in some urban areas. But not *all* black Americans work at such jobs. These stories reveal the inability of some whites to see much of anything beyond brown or black skin. In anonymous interactions such as the ones I describe in the preceding paragraphs, socioeconomic differences and educational attainment are irrelevant.

So many black Americans can tell personal stories similar to the ones I tell in the immediately preceding paragraphs.[5] I have heard many black lawyers mistaken for mail room workers, or defendants; black doctors mistaken for nurses or orderlies; black business executives mistaken for secretaries. The common thread throughout all of these interracial misunderstandings is that although the lawyers, executives and doctors were dressed like, and behaving like, members of their profession when the misidentifications occurred, they did not look like lawyers, executives or doctors to the whites who misidentified them because they looked like African Americans. My point here is not that these professional misidentifications are actionable discrimination, or even that they are morally blameworthy. If they say anything at all about race, the messages are indirect, unconsciously transmitted, almost imperceptible, and perhaps innocuous. The incidents are mere annoyances in the daily lives of African Americans.

But sometimes anonymous interracial interactions are blatantly racist and clearly communicate a belief in black inferiority and white supremacy. These are hurtful exchanges rather than mere annoyances. For example, two years ago I encountered another well-dressed, seemingly affluent white woman, walking directly in my path. I was walking to my right, she to her left.[6] As she passed me, she mumbled something about moving out of her way. As we continued walking, in opposite directions, I turned to say something about my rules for pedestrian traffic. As we passed each other, continuing to walk in opposite directions, she yelled over her shoulder, "Go back to the ghetto! If you're not going to act civilized, you should just go back to the ghetto!"

The implicit – and explicit – messages communicated in the anonymous interracial exchanges I describe here reveal perceptions about black Americans – where they deserve to live, the work they should do – regardless of that black person's socioeconomic status and level of education. In other words, differences in socioeconomic status and educational achievement among black Americans become irrelevant, at least in the eyes of some whites.

My white neighbors who presumed that I worked at the park, spa, and movie theatre may have come to these conclusions through the use of heuristics. Heuristics are cognitive shortcuts that individuals use in their decision making when they have limited amounts of time and information. Using these shortcuts is not inherently racist, but as the interactions I describe above demonstrate some of the very real assumptions about African Americans, their use can negatively impact the professional advancement of African Americans when heuristics are employed in the workplace.

In the workplace, interracial exchanges are not anonymous, but the expectations that some white Americans have about the kind of work black people are best suited to do follow them into the workplace. This is primarily because relationships between black and white employees are typically not close enough to overcome the messages that African American features convey in the minds of some whites.[7] Slavery's legacy, particularly the myth of white supremacy and black inferiority, coupled with educational deficiencies among many black Americans, and the seemingly intractable poverty in which a disproportionate number of black citizens live today, combine to create low expectations regarding black achievement. Expectations about the kind of work for which black employees are best suited are likely rooted in the fact that a disproportionately large number of black Americans work in menial jobs that require little education, and a disproportionately small number of black Americans are at the top of workplace hierarchies.

Low expectations for black achievement inevitably lead to discriminatory employment practices. African Americans are hired because "[w]hite-only work forces can create public relations problems" (Carbado & Gulati, 2003, p. 1757). But what happens after African Americans enter corporate workplaces? Will unexamined, subtle and implicit bias about the kind of work African Americans can and should do lead to discriminatory pay and promotion decisions? Do differences in pay and promotion rates between black and white employees and managers exist because of an unacknowledged bias concerning the professional ability and intellectual acuity of African Americans? Why are so few African Americans at the top of corporate hierarchies? Why do so many African Americans get stuck near the bottom or at the middle of the corporate ladder? Why do so many African Americans continue to complain about discriminatory pay and promotion decisions many decades after the enactment of antidiscrimination laws?

Answering these questions is critical to the goal of ending racial discrimination in the corporate workplace. Most analyses of the problem of race discrimination against African American professionals in the corporate setting omit the wide-ranging nature of the costs of that discrimination. In this chapter, I attempt to capture a fuller picture of those costs by describing the *context* of workplace discrimination against African American professionals – its history, its effects on the African American community as a whole, and its effects on individual victims of discrimination. By offering narratives – my own, as described above; those of individual African American female plaintiffs in an anti-discrimination lawsuit against Home Depot; and those culled from other sources – I seek to encourage a more complex and honest conversation about racism and discrimination that will fuel structural changes in the corporate setting to promote racial and economic justice.

## 2. LAW, ECONOMICS, AND DISCRIMINATION: RACIAL ASSUMPTIONS AND COSTS IN CONTEXT

Law and economics commentators who have written about the issue of employment discrimination have failed to address the complexity of the problem of implicit bias and the effects of the frequently inaccurate heuristics used by some white workers when making judgments about their black colleagues. Supreme Court Justice Byron White commented on the limitations of applying economic theory in legal analysis, observing that they "may have the appeal of mathematical exactitude and scientific certainty" but they are "nothing more than theories which may or may not prove accurate ..." (*Basic, Inc. v. Levinson*, 1988, p. 254).

Problematic assumptions about "efficiency" touted by traditional law and economics scholars are found in Professor Richard Epstein's comments on the disadvantages that antidiscrimination laws pose in the workplace.

> ... [t]he greater the disparity in taste among ... workers, the more difficult it will be for employers to provide a single homogenous environment equally pleasing to all. One way employers may avoid this problem is to eliminate some of the divergence by *grouping workers according to common tastes, which implies some degree of discrimination among them. As long as workers' tastes are correlated by race, religion, sex and age ... some forms of discrimination routinely condemned under the Civil Rights Act actually work to the advantage of [white and minority] employees.* (Epstein, 1996, p. 580, emphasis added)[8]

Epstein sees discrimination that produces a racially homogenous workforce as potentially advantageous for white employees *and* employees of color. He assumes that employees who do not have to work with employees of another race will be more productive because they are happier to be with people who are like themselves. Epstein concludes that because workers in homogenous groups will be more productive, employers will be able to pay these homogenous groups of workers more.[9]

Professor Richard Delgado (1993, p. 1196) criticizes law and economics commentators who argue that anti-discrimination legislation is inefficient because these scholars "focus on individual choices ... when the essence of racism and other forms of prejudice is much broader than that." Delgado writes of the structural nature of racism and the fact that this "irrationality [is] built into [the] very structure" of society (*ibid.*). Delgado explains that ubiquitous racist stereotypes preclude most non-discriminatory employment practices (*ibid.*). The professional misidentifications I describe in the Introduction illustrate Delgado's point. Racist and sexist assumptions and stereotypes about the intellectual acuity and professional ability of women and some racial minorities will prevent the professional advancement of these disadvantaged groups. Women and workers of color will work in the homogenous groups that Epstein finds beneficial, but it is likely that these groups will work at or near the bottom of corporate hierarchies. If they climb the corporate ladder at all, they are likely to get stuck at the middle.

Devon Carbado and Mitu Gulati shed light on Epstein's argument about the efficiency of homogenous workplaces. They explain that "many employers ... use teams to manage their workplace culture to achieve trust, fairness, and loyalty" among workers as a strategy to minimize transaction costs by reducing the need for direct oversight over employee performance and to facilitate information sharing (Carbado & Gulati, 2003, p. 1789). According to Epstein, the trust, fairness, and loyalty that creates efficiency is more likely to exist in homogenous groups, so employers have an incentive to seek workplace homogeneity as an efficient way to conduct business. Epstein believes that race is one of the ways to determine whether workers have common tastes and would therefore work well and efficiently together (*ibid.*, p. 1790).

This sort of approach ignores the diversity of the black American community. It ignores all that middle-class African Americans have in common with white professionals, managers and colleagues in the workplace. Racial heterogeneity in the workplace will work if we recognize commonalities beyond race. The white Americans who assumed that I was a park worker, locker room attendant, or that I belonged in the ghetto failed to see, or look for, commonality; they saw only my phenotypical characteristics. They failed to see how much we may have had in common – that though I am African American, I enjoy the garden in Central Park and a spa massage. Working in teams in the workplace provides an opportunity to see beyond phenotypical differences and acknowledge what individuals from different races have in common. Their work and the best interests of the corporation are two obvious examples of what black corporate professionals have in common with their white colleagues.

Trust, fairness, and loyalty become even more important as workers ascend corporate hierarchies. Teams of managers and senior executives are monitored far less and more indirectly than their subordinates. This means that the homogeneity that engenders trust, fairness, and loyalty becomes more essential among managers and executives. This, in part, explains workplace racial stratification. Employers seek out employees of color to enhance diversity. But, at the top of corporate hierarchies, where teamwork, trust, fairness, and loyalty become even more important, racial homogeneity is more likely.

Carbado and Gulati (2003, pp. 1798–1799) offer some hope for addressing the type of race discrimination that occurs when employers pursue homogeneity among workers.

> ... It is helpful to conceptualize heterogeneity/diversity as operating in a two-stage process. At stage one, superficial differences in terms of variables like race cause distrust, difficulties in communication, and a reluctance to cooperate. However, under the right conditions of intergroup contact–equal status, opportunities for self-revelation, egalitarian norms, and tasks that require cooperative interdependence – diverse team

> members can, at stage two, gain each other's trust, *begin to see commonalities*, work cooperatively, and realize the benefits of working as a diverse team. Central to this theory is the notion that there are meaningful things an employer can do at stage one – the initial contact stage–to facilitate cooperative behavior at stage two (emphasis added).

As Delgado argues, institutional and structural racism is grounded in ubiquitous racial stereotyping. The interracial interactions I describe in the Introduction demonstrate how embedded and pervasive the negative stereotypes are about African Americans and the work they are able to do. These negative stereotypes make trust, fairness, and loyalty difficult to achieve within racially diverse groups of employees. Carbado and Gulati conclude, however, that racially heterogeneous groups *can* be successful if employers control certain aspects of corporate culture and context in a way that encourages group members to explore what they have in common, in spite of racial differences.

Professor Lynn Stout's work also addresses the possibility of creating a corporate context and culture that promote certain goals. Law and economics scholars predict that humans inevitably act in self-interested ways. Therefore, in order to ensure that self-interested executives and directors make decisions that are in the corporation's best interests, they are given stock and stock options that will align the corporate agents' interests with the success of the company and the interests of other shareholders. Stout challenges this assumption by observing that most corporate directors are "other-regarding" corporate agents who do not behave in self-interested ways (Stout, 2003).

Stout explores empirical research that establishes that people are not completely self-interested. People behave altruistically, especially when they are encouraged to do so (*ibid.*, pp. 11–12). Stout observes that other-regarding behavior is enhanced and encouraged by establishing a social context that values consideration of others' interests; such a context is more likely achieved if actors perceive that others will benefit from the consideration of their interests (*ibid.*, p. 13). Given that African American professionals in the corporate workplace have middle-class values, corporate actors are more likely to perceive that their decisions will benefit that segment of the minority population. In other words, corporate managers and executives who will most likely conclude that they have little in common with the urban poor because of differing value systems may feel differently about the black managers and professionals to whom middle-class values are likely to be attributed.

The second factor that helps to create a social context that encourages other-regarding behavior involves the sharing of a "sense of common social identity" (*ibid.*). When it comes to race, this is a problem. Corporate managers and executives, most of whom are white and male, are not likely to share a sense of common social identity with female and minority employees. And, not only is a common social identity unlikely because of racial and gender differences, it is unlikely also because most senior executives and managers are relatively affluent when compared to other employees. However, it is possible that officers and managers will focus on the characteristics they do happen to share with black professionals. Those characteristics will relate to class identity issues, such as the value of education, hard work, and saving for one's future, rather than racial identity. The question becomes whether class will trump race to find common ground among different racial groups.

According to Stout, cost is also relevant when considering how to inspire other-regarding behavior (*ibid.*, pp. 17–19). If the costs of other-regarding decision making are low, other-regarding behavior is more likely. Here is the problem: real anti-discrimination efforts are costly. Diversity rhetoric costs relatively little. So, what incentives do managers and boards have to spend more in order to move beyond the cosmetic efforts they already make? What incentives do they have to seriously monitor and address the problem of discrimination?

The microeconomic theory relating to risk-utility or cost-benefit analysis helps us in this regard. It is true that real monitoring and anti-discrimination costs are high. The relevant question for economists, then, is to compare the costs of preventing the harm with the gravity of the harm to be prevented and the likelihood that the harm will occur.

This formula is used to determine whether actors are negligent under tort law. If it costs too much to prevent harm that is not that serious, and that is not likely to occur, an actor is not negligent when she fails to take precautions to prevent that harm. Apply this analysis to Stout's assertion that corporate actors are more likely to behave in other-regarding ways if it does not cost too much. Cost-benefit analysis would help corporate actors understand the true nature of the cost of preventing discrimination. The costs of serious anti-discrimination efforts seem high – too high – only if directors and officers ignore both the likelihood that discrimination will occur and the gravity of workplace discrimination.

Economic theory without context is useless. But *with* context, law and economics analysis can help us understand and address specific problems like workplace discrimination that persist within corporate cultures because of an overestimation of the cost of anti-discrimination efforts and an underestimation of the gravity and likelihood of workplace discrimination.

Therefore, in this chapter, I explore the economic and socioeconomic reality of African American professionals in order to capture a more complete picture of the costs of discrimination in the corporate workplace. I also explore the heuristic assumptions that are made about African American professionals, and the effects those assumptions have on the economic core of the black community, in order to offer insight into how and why discrimination manifests in the corporate workplace. Finally, to understand the gravity of the harm to individuals, their families and the communities to which they belong, narratives about the economic and psychological harm caused by discrimination are essential.[10] Narratives also provide the context that demonstrates that harm from discrimination is very likely to occur.[11] I offer the narratives of six middle managers and low-level professionals who faced discrimination in the corporate workplace. Their narratives provide important context about discrimination's real costs.

## 3. THE ECONOMIC COSTS OF WORKPLACE DISCRIMINATION

The complex variations in the social and economic circumstances of black American life are frequently overlooked in academic and popular literature and culture.[12] Much has been written about African Americans who are at the top of the socioeconomic hierarchy. These Americans include the black elite, some of whom have been economically privileged for decades, even centuries. At the other end of the spectrum are the urban poor. Their lives, like the black elite, are well examined in academic and popular literature. However, at what I refer to as the "economic core" of black American life are mid-level and low-level professionals, skilled workers and certain service employees who work for public companies. Members of this economic core worked hard for the credentials that enabled them to enter the corporate workplace. They earned an education. More often than not, they conformed to dominant cultural expectations. They have done all the things that the black urban poor have been criticized for not doing (Dyson, 2005). A focus on the relationship between public companies and black Americans is important because public companies employ large numbers of Americans of African descent who form this "economic core" of the black American community.

Discrimination in the workplace creates economic inequality that leaves this economic core particularly vulnerable. These Americans sit on the fence that separates poverty from middle class life. They, along with the working poor, are uniquely vulnerable when discriminatory employment practices are tolerated in racially toxic corporate cultures. Very often, members of this economic core are only a paycheck or two away from poverty. Mid-level and low-level African American professionals who work for public companies may ascend further into solid middle class life if corporate decisions are equitable. Or, they may slip from the ranks of the middle class and fall dangerously closer to poverty as a result of workplace hiring, pay and promotion decisions that are tainted by structural, institutional and individual racism that is frequently subtle, unacknowledged or even unconscious.

Here are some of the dismal facts regarding disparities in wealth, unemployment and income between black and white Americans. "[T]he median net worth of African American families is ... about 15 percent of that for whites ..." (Klein, 2004, p. A1). "The unemployment rate for blacks remains nearly double the national rate ..." (*ibid.*).[13] Census reports for 2005 and 2006 reveal that the average household income for African Americans is significantly lower than the average household income of the total U.S. population (DeNavas-Walt, Proctor, & Smith, 2007, p. 5).

Economic disparities between black and white Americans cut across class boundaries. In 2000, middle-class black Americans worked almost three months longer than their white counterparts in order to earn the same income (Mishel, Bernstein, & Boushey, 2003). Middle class "black families are three times more likely" to file for bankruptcy as their white counterparts (Warren, 2004, p. 1779). "[T]he net worth of African American and Latino *college* graduates is similar to the net worth of white *high school* graduates, and the net worth of African American and Latino high school graduates is similar to the net worth of white high-school dropouts" (Scholz & Levine, 2004, p. 898).

Randall Robinson (2002, p. 271) observed that "[a]ll of the socioeconomic data confirm that [African Americans] trail the American mainstream in every area of critical measure." After acknowledging the troubled socioeconomic status of black Americans, Robinson commented that "[t]his should surprise no one. No people could endure what [African Americans] alone have endured in America for more than three and a half centuries and not suffer badly for it" (*ibid.*). Commentators have offered more specific explanations for wealth and income disparities between black and white Americans. For example, the higher rates at which middle-class black homeowners declare bankruptcy may be the result of predatory lending "and other subprime credit that drain billions of dollars out of the pockets" of racial minorities (Warren, 2004, p. 1779). Professors Emma Coleman Jordan and Angela P. Harris discuss and provide sources that describe discriminatory practices in banking and real estate that begin to explain disparities in wealth between black and white families "with identical job, income, and credit information" (Jordan & Harris, 2006, p. 618).

Professor Elizabeth Warren (2004, p. 1779) suggests that "job difficulties" may, in part, explain why more black and Latino families file for bankruptcy than do whites. The question I explore in this chapter also relates to "job difficulties" – specifically, corporate workplace discrimination. Racial discrimination in the workplaces governed by public companies may be one source of the socioeconomic plight of the black American community. Discriminatory pay and promotion practices adversely affect not only the economic well-being of individual workers and communities of color, they affect the entire nation. Consider predictions about demographic changes in the United States. "One half of the U.S. population will be nonwhite by 2050 … ."[14] If workplace and other types of economic discrimination continue to contribute to the financial insecurity of people of color, the effects on the entire nation will be dire. The entire country will suffer as the number of people of color grows if disproportionately high numbers of them continue to face financial insecurity. "Projections suggest that within 15 years the gaps in opportunity experienced by African Americans and Latinos today will result in declining education and income levels that will affect the overall productivity and economy of the country" (Wheary, 2006, p. 3).

Moreover, workers and professionals who form the economic core of the black community are uniquely vulnerable to workplace discrimination (see later). First, they are educated, but not as highly credentialed as high-level professionals. They are not graduates of elite schools. They do not possess the indicia that help more credentialed African Americans climb the corporate ladder. Second, *white* middle class Americans face challenges in today's economy that are similar to those faced by their counterparts in the black community. Middle and low-level black managers are particularly vulnerable because they must supervise white subordinates whose own economic vulnerability may make them resent the relative success of their black managers.[15] Considering the impact of workplace discrimination on mid-level and low-level professionals of African descent is imperative because discriminatory employment practices keep so many black professionals and managers both stuck at the middle of corporate hierarchies and at risk of falling even lower.

## 4. WORKPLACE DISCRIMINATION: THE EFFECTS OF RACIST HEURISTICS IN THE CORPORATION

Today, the workplaces governed by public companies are more racially diverse than they have ever been. With more diversity, however, workplace discrimination and racism become increasingly significant issues with which many corporate managers have yet to deal.[16] Racial stratification remains the hallmark of corporate workplaces where people of color are stuck at the lower and middle levels of corporate hierarchies.[17] At some companies "high-potential professionals of color ... become mired in middle management."[18] Even at companies that have good diversity records, professionals and managers of color who hover near or at the middle of corporate hierarchies face potentially career-chilling racism (Thomas, 2001). Although discriminatory practices keep some professionals and managers of color at the bottom or middle of corporate hierarchies, others are underpaid when compared to their white counterparts.[19] Discriminatory employment practices persist in spite of legislative enactments and judicial pronouncements that prohibit them.[20]

Heuristics about the abilities of black workers and managers frequently arise regardless of their socioeconomic status, even when they are well educated, and contribute to discrimination in the workplace. Very successful black managers and executives are suspect in the eyes of some whites.[21] Some whites become even more suspicious of the workplace successes of black workers and managers if they pay attention to corporate discourse about race. Corporate spokespersons, web sites, and disclosure documents do not mention discrimination, but speak only of diversity and equal opportunity (Wade, 2004, p. 1541). These communications make it appear that discrimination is no longer a problem that continues to taint workplace relationships (*ibid.*). Because of communications such as these, many whites, who are not targets of racial discrimination in a predominantly white firm, may conclude that workplace discrimination is no longer a problem. White workers may resent black managers if they believe that black professionals ascend to positions of authority not because they are qualified, but because of a company's diversity efforts. White workers may fear that equal opportunity and diversity efforts exist to their detriment.

Discussions about diversity and equal opportunity have become meaningless and obfuscating rhetoric that obscure, and even foster, the discrimination with which African Americans continue to grapple in the corporate workplace (*ibid.*). Structural impediments to racial equality in the corporate workplace are fortified by equal opportunity and diversity rhetoric that has no real substance.

The sentiment that black workers ascend corporate ladders because of some unfair advantage provided them because of their minority status conflicts with what many black workers, managers and executives say about their ability to thrive in the corporate workplace. Many of the African American executives interviewed for a book describing the issues black executives face echoed a recurring theme about how black employees and managers have to work harder in order to succeed (Cobbs & Turnock, 2003, pp. 18, 27, 75–100, 228–232). Alfred Little, Jr., a retired Vice President of Newport News Shipbuilding said the following: "I've learned to accept that as an African American, you're somewhat vulnerable. Knowing that, I use it to push myself to higher levels of excellence" (*ibid.*, p. 75).

Ira D. Hall, who served as Texaco's Treasurer before retiring, similarly explained, "I did not want to leave any question. My record would be the best record of anybody who'd ever worked there" (*ibid.*). Cobbs and Turnock explained that "[f]or many black Americans the compulsion to work twice as hard and to be twice as good, no matter how physically and emotionally exhausting, is how they make their mark" (*ibid.*, p. 76). Generations of black parents have taught their children that black Americans have to "[b]e twice as good" in order to succeed in the workplace (*ibid.*, p.228). Cobbs and Turnock (p. 1) observe that "[o]rganizations are complicated" for everyone, but African Americans must deal with "added layers" of complexity that include doubt in their abilities. To overcome this doubt, many African Americans "work twice as hard," and the authors acknowledge the emotional toll and the psychological strain this imposes (*ibid.*, pp. 5, 27).

Whether or not black employees and managers decide to work harder in order to counteract negative workplace stereotypes, tacit or even unconscious doubts about the intellectual acuity and professional ability of black workers cuts across class boundaries. The social stigma that questions black professionalism attaches to black workers and managers at every level of the corporate hierarchy.[22]

Understanding this heuristic baggage, which is rooted in the bitter historical relationship between the exploitation of African American labor and the economic success of the United States and its wealthiest white citizens, is a critical part of transcending racism in the workplace. This exploitation began with chattel slavery[23] and continues today with the privatization of prisons, a service traditionally provided by government.[24] One aspect of slavery's legacy includes stereotypes of African Americans that render them unfit for corporate success in the eyes of corporate decision makers who subscribe to them, perhaps on an unconscious level.

In her book, *Post Traumatic Slave Syndrome*, Dr. Joy DeGruy Leary examines the persisting psychological impact of slavery on the descendants of the enslaved. Leary (2005, p. 13) provides historical perspective in order "to understand how African Americans adapted their behavior over centuries in order to survive the stifling effects of chattel slavery, effects which are evident today."[25]

Leary's work is about slavery's present-day impact on African Americans. Just as relevant is slavery's present-day impact on white Americans. In order to justify the institution of slavery, white enslavers dehumanized enslaved Africans. Enslavers attempted to justify slavery by claiming that enslaved Africans were not human, or capable of feeling pain. Enslaved Africans were constructed as morally and intellectually inferior beings. The myth of white supremacy and black inferiority was formed as part of the effort to justify slavery. The myth grew, took on a life of its own, persists today, and is particularly deleterious in workplace interracial relationships (Cobbs & Turnock, 2003, p. 4).

> Blacks ... struggle daily just to turn down the background noise of "You are inferior," however muted, in order to function effectively. Even though experience and time have moved the bias to a different level of consciousness, the barely veiled negative assumptions – you're not as well trained, you're not as smart, you're replacing a better-qualified white man – continue to attach themselves despite what your resume shows and your work proves. You are asked, or worse, not asked, questions about your ability that others don't face. You are excluded from meetings, activities, and memos that are important to your particular project. However these events may be rationalized, you recognize the message. *Your white male colleagues enjoy an atmosphere of positive assumptions about their abilities, unless or until they perform poorly. You, on the other hand, must prove your ability in an endless cycle of "guilty until proven innocent."* (*ibid.*, p. 27, emphasis added)

The enduring myth of white supremacy and black inferiority infects workplace decisions about who should be hired, promoted, and paid well. The harm the myth inflicts on perceptions about black Americans and their qualifications at work affects *all* black Americans, regardless of gender, class and other differences in personal circumstances and sensibility.[26]

The growth of the Latino and Asian population far exceeds that of African Americans. I do not focus, however, on workplace discrimination against Asians because "[d]ata on the Asian population shows that in relation to economic opportunity this group has a much stronger position than African Americans and Latinos. Not only are Asian median incomes dramatically higher than African American and Latino incomes, they are in fact higher than white incomes" (Wheary, 2006, p. 4). Work that focuses attention on workplace discrimination against Latinos is crucial. I do not do so in this chapter, however, because of differences in the historical and present-day relationships that Latinos and African Americans have with the United States and its white citizens.[27] Professor Roy Brooks explains that "blacks were the *main target* of slavery and Jim Crow. No other American group inhabited the peculiar institution. No other American group sustained more casualties or lengthier suffering from slavery and Jim Crow .... White-on-black oppression is ... different from other white-oppression syndromes, whether racial or gender" (Brooks, 2004, p. 161).

I do not intend to suggest that the workplace discrimination that Black employees face is worse than the discrimination that taints the lives of white women or other people of color. The discrimination with which Black employees deal is not worse than the discrimination that others face, but it is different, and therefore warrants exclusive attention in this chapter.

In his remarkable and impelling book, *The Reckoning*, Randall Robinson (2002, p. 273) questions the wisdom of focusing on certain discrete issues that affect the black community.

> We lament racial profiling, as indeed, we should. But, we appear to do this without understanding that racial profiling is the tree, not the forest. Perhaps we have misfocused so badly because of considerations driven by class. Racial profiling affects *all* blacks. The warehousing of poor blacks in prisons affects only *them*, as if [the fates of poor black people] were not indissolubly bound up with all the rest of ours.

Is workplace discrimination, like racial profiling, just another single tree in the forest of problems the black community faces? The fates of poor blacks *are* inextricably tied to the fate of the black community and the entire nation. The fates of black Americans at the middle of the economic hierarchy are similarly intertwined with the fates of the black poor, the black elite and the entire country. If the economic core shrinks because its members lose ground and join the poor, this harms the once-middle-class-but-now-impoverished family. It also makes our tasks in attending to the needs of the poor (which is what Robinson advocates) more difficult as their numbers swell. There will be fewer successful Americans who will be able to contribute to the well-being of impoverished Americans.

Even though they face seemingly intractable workplace discrimination, black Americans at the middle and near the top of corporate hierarchies subscribe to an impressive work ethic that yields success, but not parity, with their white colleagues with substantially similar, identical, or in some instances, fewer credentials. The workplace successes that many black Americans achieve enable them to fight their way up the American socioeconomic ladder and confer wealth and opportunity to their children. All of this demonstrates the importance of work and its connection to the inter-generational upward mobility of black Americans.

Workplace discrimination, to use Robinson's metaphor, is in fact one tree in a forest of problems that African Americans face, but it is the tree that provides the rotten fruit and inadequate shade that make even basic survival difficult. Attending to this particular tree of workplace discrimination is crucial. Parents who receive fair compensation and promotion opportunities can better clothe, feed and educate their children. The link between workplace equity and the survival of black families is obvious. Racial equity in the workplace is the tree that bears the fruit of inter-generational upward mobility within the black community. And racially discriminatory employment practices will inflame and proliferate in corporate cultures unless the problems of racism and discrimination are acknowledged and confronted, and structural changes are made.

## 5. AFRICAN AMERICAN VICTIMS OF WORKPLACE DISCRIMINATION

The largest race discrimination class action settlements in U.S. history,[28] and many of the more recent race discrimination suits demonstrate that workplace discrimination is a significantly intractable issue for African Americans. Some recent instances of workplace discrimination against African Americans involve specific acts of racial harassment,[29] but a great deal of today's workplace race discrimination is subtle, sophisticated, ambiguous, pervasive, and experienced on a daily basis (Deitch et al., 2003, p. 1299). African Americans face workplace discrimination in hiring, promotion and pay. Workplace discrimination affects African Americans who are near or at the bottom of corporate hierarchies, and also professionals and managers at the middle or near the top.

Researching three large public U.S. corporations, David Thomas (2001, p. 98) of the Harvard Graduate School of Business Administration compiled what he described as strikingly consistent data revealing that whites and minorities competed on two distinct tracks for ascending corporate hierarchies. White employees enjoyed a fast track up the corporate ladder. The ascension of minority workers was significantly slower. For example, even after earning his bachelor's degree at a leading college, it took one African American participant in Thomas' study nine years to reach middle management when his white colleagues ascended into middle management in approximately five years (*ibid.*).

Thomas also found that some companies "have revolving doors for talented minorities, recruiting the best and brightest only to see them leave, frustrated, and even angered by the barriers they encounter" (*ibid.*). Other companies "have failed to achieve racial balance within their executive teams .... [O]thers have minorities in their executive ranks, but only in racialized positions, such as those dealing with community relations, equal employment opportunity, or ethnic markets" (*ibid.*).

A vivid example of the type of workplace discrimination that affects African Americans involves bias in hiring practices. Researchers from the University of Chicago and MIT conducted an experiment in Boston and Chicago where they chose 1,300 newspaper advertisements for entry-level jobs and submitted thousands of resumes from make-believe job seekers (Krueger, 2002, p. C2). The researchers submitted two types of resumes, some with first names that are typically associated with African Americans, others with first names that are typically associated with whites. Other than the first names, the job applications for the black job seekers were identical to those of the white job seekers. "Applicants with white-sounding names were 50 percent more likely to be called for interviews than were those with black-sounding names" (*ibid.*).[30] Earlier research also showed that black candidates who applied for jobs in person were not as likely to be given an interview or a job as whites who applied in person (*ibid.*).

I focus on the black community's economic core because the economic survival of its members is essential to the well-being of the black community in general. And, because a significant number of black households are headed by women, some of them caring for minor children, the financial well-being of black *women* is essential to the well-being of the black community, and the entire nation.[31] This is, in part, the reason why I devote the rest of this chapter to the narratives about discrimination against six black female entry-level middle managers – the Home Depot Plaintiffs.

## 6. THE HUMAN COST OF WORKPLACE RACIAL DISCRIMINATION: NARRATIVES OF THE "HOME DEPOT SIX"

Even though women of color are "the fastest growing segment of the work force," corporate diversity efforts "have failed to recruit and retain" women of color (Tucker, Wolfe, Viruell-Fuentes, & Smooth, 1999, p. 12).[32] Only two percent of senior management or executive positions are held by women of color (*ibid.*). Also, many women of color "report that they have limited opportunities for advancement within their respective companies and that they doubt top management's commitment to diversity" (*ibid.*). They describe the corporate cultures in which they work as "uncomfortable, hostile, and unsupportive" (*ibid.*).

Various facets of the problems of workplace discrimination faced by women can be seen in the stories of the "Home Depot Six." In June 2004, six black women, middle, and low-level managers at The Home Depot, Inc. (the "Home Depot Six" or "Home Depot Plaintiffs")[33] filed a racial and sexual discrimination and harassment suit against the company.[34] I use the stories of the Home Depot Plaintiffs to shed light on the often ignored uniqueness of the workplace discrimination black women confront.[35] The discrimination that plagues black women is similar to, but different from the type of discrimination that white, Asian women, and Latinas face. The type of bias that black women face is similar to, but different from the type of bias that infects the professional lives of black men.

As is true for other women of color, black women are vulnerable because they are women. They are sometimes exposed to workplace sexual harassment that threatens their physical, emotional, and mental well-being. Race and gender stereotyping and bias combine to tarnish the professional lives of all women of color. But the unparalleled history of black Americans presents challenges for black women with which white Asian women, and, Latinas (who are not of African descent) do not have to deal. It is a history that includes the type of racism that causes some whites to continue to question the intellectual acuity of black Americans. At the same time, the workplace experiences of black women differ from those of black men because black men generally do not have to deal with sexual harassment that threatens their physical well-being.

Examining the experiences of the Home Depot Plaintiffs provides important insight into the economic core of the black community. The Home Depot Plaintiffs' narratives also reveal much about the complexity, subtlety and sophistication of workplace racial discrimination (U.S. Senate Judiciary Committee Hearing, 2006), and their stories present an opportunity to consider significant race, class and gender issues.[36] Telling the stories of these six black women, and acknowledging the professional barriers they face, help to ameliorate the impact of workplace discrimination by giving voice to the most ignored victims of workplace bias.[37] As Mary Helen Washington (1989) wrote, "[t]hese gendered and racial voices speak not just for the individual but for a community . . . . This is the language of resistance because it reasserts a community which the dominant culture seeks to control and silence."

The complaint filed on behalf of The Home Depot Six described toxic workplace cultures where women and minorities were treated unfairly and differently from their white counterparts or male colleagues, and faced retaliation when they complained.[38] The complaint portrayed a corporate culture in which managers "commonly used" racial slurs and made racist comments.[39] The plaintiffs described the Company's culture as one in which managers tolerated frequent sexual harassment and intimidation of women workers.

James Vagnini, now a partner at the New York law firm Valli, Kane & Vagnini, was a member of Leeds Morelli & Brown when he represented the Home Depot Six. He arranged for me to meet with two of the plaintiffs – Glenor Cyrus and Kari-Ann Kerr. I first met them one evening in the fall of 2005 when they generously agreed to visit with me and several of my students in my Race and Business seminar. Both women were possessed with a dignified, quiet presence that belied their youthful appearance. They described pervasive and systemic discrimination in promotion and pay decisions at Home Depot. Much of what I have learned about their case I found in several documents I received from James, including a mediation statement and the complaint that was filed on the plaintiffs' behalf. Some of the documents were prepared by the plaintiff's lawyers, others were documents submitted to Leeds Morelli & Brown on behalf of Home Depot.

The Home Depot Plaintiffs also alleged more pervasive and systemic discrimination in promotion and pay decisions. One unusual aspect of this part of the plaintiffs' case was their claim that in its communications with the Equal Employment Opportunity Commission (the "Commission" or the "EEOC") the company claimed that these black women employees were white.[40] The company changed the plaintiffs' race from black to white on paper because their salaries were significantly lower than the salaries paid to white employees with the same or lesser qualifications who performed substantially the same work. Instead of paying them a fair salary, the company misled the Commission by making it appear that white employees, not black employees, received the unfairly low pay.

When each of The Home Depot Six applied for promotion, the company changed its records to reflect that the women were black, not white. The company, however, denied the promotion requests of some of the black female applicants, claiming that they lacked the requisite education and experience. White employees, however, were promoted even when they had less education and experience than their black counterparts. Some of the women were promoted, but with no increase in salary, and others were promoted with only a "negligible" increase in salary. This meant that these black women workers were paid significantly less than their white counterparts, both male and female, and less than their black male counterparts (*Glenor Cyrus et al. v. Home Depot, Inc.*, Complaint, 2004).

Glenor Cyrus, one of the plaintiffs, described troubling events at Home Depot. Attempting to perform her duties as an Associate Development Supervisor in Human Resources, Cyrus reviewed a report stating that a white manager had made a racist remark to another employee. Cyrus alleged that the same white manager who was the subject of the report pushed her out of his way and destroyed the report while asking, "What the fuck do you think you are doing?" Cyrus complained about this incident to her immediate supervisor and to a Human Resources Manager, both white men. The manager who pushed Cyrus and destroyed the report about his allegedly racist remark was never disciplined. As far as she can determine, Cyrus' complaint was ignored until the Human Resources Manager to whom she complained joked about the incident at a Christmas party. A few months after this incident another Home Depot employee complained about the same white manager who had pushed Cyrus. Again, the allegations were about racism, and when Cyrus attempted to investigate she was told not to do so.

As is true with many black women, the workplace harassment that Cyrus confronted related not only to race, but also to gender. A white assistant manager hired to work in Cyrus' store about a year after she was hired tormented her with jokes that were sexual in nature. Cyrus asked the assistant manager to stop and complained to two white male managers, but the jokes continued for the entire tenure of Cyrus' employment. The jokes and her managers' refusal to investigate her claims made Cyrus sick – literally. She began to suffer severe headaches (*ibid.*).

In spite of the harassment, Glenor Cyrus remained committed to her work at Home Depot. She interviewed for a promotion from Associate Development Supervisor in Human Resources to Human Resources Manager. When she was not promoted, Cyrus complained that she was denied promotion because she was pregnant, black, and female. Cyrus made the complaint to a Human Resources Manager-a black, woman. The manager refused to investigate Cyrus' complaints about the interview process (*ibid.*).

At this point, the emotional toll on Cyrus worsened and she was diagnosed with hypertension, depression, and anxiety. On August 10, 2002, approximately two years after coming to Home Depot, Cyrus left the company, alleging that she was constructively discharged. Her replacement was white (*ibid.*).

LaTanya Martin-Avery joined Home Depot as an Associate Development Supervisor, and in approximately a year and a half interviewed for a promotion to Store Human Resource Manager. She claims that she was granted the interview only because some managers thought she was white because she had been classified as such in EEOC documents. She was chosen for the position but was told that she would get a raise of only $1500, and that she would be fired if she did not accept the position. Martin-Avery discovered that some of her white women colleagues were given a raise of at least $10,000 when they were promoted to the same position even though they had less experience and education (*ibid.*).

The rest of the complaint filed by The Home Depot Six contains similar descriptions of systemic and pervasive discriminatory promotion and pay practices. For example, when June DeBourgh interviewed for a promotion to Human Resource Manager, she was not given the information about the interview process which included a test, while external candidates received the information. Gayna Samuel described preferential treatment given to her white female partner, who was assigned to special projects that enabled her to improve her skills (*ibid.*).

The Home Depot Six also alleged that they suffered harassment. At a staff meeting, Samuel was told that several managers hated her. Carolyn Saunders was demoted after she complained of demeaning treatment that included white store managers who repeatedly asked her what she had done to get her job, suggesting that she exchanged sex for employment.

James Vagnini, the Home Depot Six's lawyer, described processes where promotion decisions were based on files that contained photographs of the candidates. Vagnini claimed that this enabled managers to quickly pass over black candidates for promotion (Vagnini, J., personal interview, October 6, 2006). One white female candidate was promoted even though she scored significantly lower on a test than the Home Depot Plaintiffs. And, in corporate documents obtained during discovery describing the results of the test that determined who would be promoted, the letter "B" appeared next to the names of The Home Depot Six. "Alongside all the black names there were 'B's written in-black, black, black" (*ibid.*).

The discrimination and harassment imposed a significant emotional toll on the Home Depot Plaintiffs. June DeBourgh suffered insomnia, back pain, depression, and skin problems caused by stress. She received medical treatment for all of these conditions (Complaint, 2004). La Tanya

Martin-Avery also became ill from the stress and had to seek medical attention (*ibid.*). When I met Glenor Cyrus and Keri-Ann Kerr, I learned more about their personal and emotional suffering. Keri-Ann described her frustration and anger, and admitted that the ordeal depleted her self-confidence and zest for work, stating "It affected my entire being. I was confused, depressed" (Kerr, K., personal interview, 2006). Glenor suffered from nightmares and headaches because of the discrimination and harassment (Cyrus, G., personal interview, October 6, 2006).

The detailed clarity of the Home Depot plaintiffs' evidence is rare in most discrimination cases. Because of enormous amounts of money paid out to settle two race discrimination class actions in the 1990s, companies have become particularly vigilant about ensuring that there is no record or memorialization of discussions or processes that could be construed as discriminatory (Wade, 2002a, 2002b). The Home Depot plaintiffs, however, were able to provide their lawyers with evidence to which most discrimination plaintiffs have no access because they happened to be Human Resource specialists, which provided them with access to important information and documents. I have access to the details about the plaintiffs' ordeal at Home Depot because at the time the complaint was filed, the Home Depot Six no longer worked for the Company,[41] so they felt free to come forward with details. Many employees who endure workplace discrimination remain silent because they are still employed by the company and fear retaliation.

## 7. MITIGATING THE IMPACT OF DISCRIMINATION IN THE CORPORATE WORKPLACE

Workplace discussions about race are infrequent and deficient,[42] so in the introduction to this chapter, I look beyond the workplace to personal narratives about anonymous interracial interactions for insight into interracial relationships at work. The autobiographical subplot I offer is coupled with historical and social commentary that reveals what some whites expect from black Americans as far as work is concerned.

Americans disagree about race discrimination, whether it exists, and if it does exist, why it persists.[43] It is only with anecdotal evidence that subtle implications and concealed attitudes can be examined. The anecdotes in this chapter are true and accurate. Most disturbing is the fact that they describe details that are similar to events in the lives of scores of black Americans with whom I have spoken about this topic. The narratives I share in this chapter that describe interaction outside the workplace reveal some of the subtlety and complexity of the negative assumptions, perceptions, and stereotypes about black Americans and the work they can and should do. These assumptions, perceptions, and stereotypes follow black Americans into the workplace. The professional misidentifications that I describe in the Introduction that occurred within the workplace provide evidence of this.

I confine consideration of workplace discrimination to the factories, offices and businesses governed by large public companies, rather than the workplaces of federal, state and local governments, or the workplaces of small private corporations. A focus on public corporations is critical because of the huge impact they have on the lives of the millions of Americans they employ. I focus on public companies also because of the promise of structural amelioration of racial inequities. Corporate governance decisions about how public companies are to be governed offer some possibilities for dealing with workplace discrimination other than litigation. Mitigating the impact of workplace discrimination will require the types of structural approaches that can be undertaken through corporate governance processes. Litigation alone is not an effective tool. As Senator Biden (2006) observed during confirmation hearings for Justice Samuel Alito, "[I]t's harder to make a case of discrimination even though there's no doubt that it still exists."

Narrowing the discussion to corporate workplaces is crucial also because the discourse about race in the private sector is strikingly different from the discourse in which government employers now engage. Because of anti-affirmative action activism and debate (Masci, 1998; Krueger, 2003), public sector employers have circumscribed some of their rhetoric about creating more racially diverse workforces. Private sector employers, however, remain emphatic in their proclamations about the virtues of diversity and equal opportunity (Wade, 2004). The rhetoric of corporate spokespersons, however, typically does not include discussion of racism and discrimination. This means that the discourse about race within corporate cultures is anemic and superficial, and may explain why corporate workplaces remain racially stratified. There is a troubling dichotomy between what corporate spokespersons say about diversity and equal opportunity, and the corporate cultures that impede the attempts of workers of color to attain parity with their white counterparts (*ibid.*).

Even though race discrimination in hiring, promotion, and pay persists (Lee, 2006), corporate workplaces provide a unique opportunity for improving race relations because of the nature of corporate culture in general. Corporate cultures demand compliance and uniformity.[44] Employees who do not conform to corporate practices and expectations must leave the company. Meaningful discussions about race, racism, and discrimination, along with committed anti-discrimination discourse and efforts, can create a corporate cultural expectation of racial equity. Those who do not conform to anti-discrimination ideals will not survive in a corporate workplace culture that takes anti-discrimination efforts seriously.

The corporate workplace provides a limited possibility for interracial healing because it is the one place where Americans of different races come together. The workplace also offers hope for decreasing the vulnerability and fragility of the economic core of the black community. The poorest black Americans who are unemployed are almost completely isolated from the rest of the nation. Because of their isolation, the poorest black Americans are forgotten or ignored by more privileged citizens. Working class, and low-level and mid-level professionals, however, come together in the workplace with the rest of America, and are not as isolated as the poorest, unemployed black Americans. It is arguably more difficult for affluent Americans to ignore those who form the economic core of black economic life because Americans of different classes interact in the workplace.

The workplace provides the opportunity for more privileged classes of black Americans to help black workers on the lower rungs ascend corporate hierarchies. Educated and affluent black Americans uplifting the race by assisting disadvantaged blacks – this is a vintage theme in the black community.[45] Black professionals at the top should assist those in the middle, and professionals in the middle should assist workers at the bottom in ascending the corporate hierarchy.

Black Americans, however, cannot and should not be expected to do the kind of work that will uplift other black workers without the help of their white colleagues.[46] White senior executives and officers must take anti-discrimination efforts seriously. For example, after women employees at Wal-Mart filed a class action claiming that the company engaged in discriminatory employment practices,[47] the company's CEO announced "that he would cut executive bonuses if the company fail[ed] to meet diversity goals," and that "[t]he company will reduce executive bonuses by up to 7.5 percent this year and 15 percent next year if [Wal-Mart] fails to promote women and minorities in proportion to the number that apply for management positions" (Greenhouse & Hays, 2004, p. A1). This is the kind of serious anti-discrimination and diversity effort that may help to transform corporate cultures that tolerate discrimination.

As with executive bonuses linked to diversity goals, any additional suggestions for dealing with workplace discrimination should be extralegal at this point. Of course, when aggrieved, employees should continue to resort to discrimination litigation. But, changes in basic corporate practices, training, and governance have the potential to transform corporate cultures, and this may avoid some discrimination litigation. For example, formal training of mentors should encourage interracial workplace relationships where racial differences and problems are openly and honestly acknowledged and discussed (Thomas, 2001, p. 98). David Thomas of the Harvard University Graduate School of Business Administration recommends "educating managers ... by teaching them how to mentor effectively" (*ibid.*). Thomas acknowledges that all workers, regardless of race, benefit from good mentor relationships, but he acknowledges that for minorities, good mentors are essential in garnering company-wide support for employees of color. Minority employees, more than their white colleagues, need mentors to protect them from disadvantages and criticism that are tinged with racism, such as creating opportunities that others would deny them (*ibid.*).

When I met with Glenor Cyrus, one of the Home Depot plaintiffs, she explained that the Human Resources department and professionals – of which she was one – were not taken seriously (Cyrus, G., personal interview, October 6, 2006). Her lawyer confirmed this, adding that "employment discrimination is usually not a matter that really gets that far up the chain in the corporate structure. It is not a matter that anyone is really concerned about. They issue the policies, they issue all the programs on diversity but truthfully it has always been a matter that's dealt with at a very low level in any corporation" (Vagnini, J., personal interview, October 6, 2006). The most significant cultural change that U.S. corporations can make would be to ensure that Human Resource departments and professionals, and anti-discrimination efforts become serious priorities that receive attention from workers, managers, and leaders at all levels of corporate hierarchies.

Addressing discrimination in the workplaces governed by large public companies is crucial. Instead of attempting to convince one individual at a time that racial prejudice continues to disgrace the nation and defile the lives of people of color, tackling the issue of discrimination in corporate workplaces has greater transformative power. Discrimination in corporate workplaces is best addressed by creating corporate cultures in which racism is acknowledged and not tolerated. As corporate cultures change, the behavior of hundreds of individuals changes. Individuals change because they must conform to corporate culture, norms, practices and expectations in order to keep their jobs. Russell Simmons, music and entertainment entrepreneur, observed that corporations "have longer lives than people" (Gates, 2004, p. 59). The positive effects of attending to corporate workplace discrimination will be more durable, and will last as long as the company is in business, and this typically will be longer than the lifetime of a single human. These positive effects may be socially transformative also. Behavior not tolerated *in* the workplace may eventually cease *beyond* the workplace.

## NOTES

1. "According to a 1997 study by the Boston-based Initiative for a Competitive Inner City in association with the PricewaterhouseCoopers accounting firm, African Americans buy almost thirty percent more clothes than the average American consumer ... . Even inner-city blacks spend almost 11 percent more on clothing ... than the average U.S. household ... " (Robinson, 2002, p. 142). My experiences may explain this apparent frivolity on the part of African Americans who overspend on clothing. Living in New York City, I have had taxis refuse to stop for me; store clerks who refused to accept my American Express Gold card without picture identification; retail sales people have ignored me thinking I do not have enough money to spend in that particular store. Black Americans are judged based on their appearance in ways that other Americans are not. Like me, other African Americans, especially those living in poverty, may attempt to counteract the negative assumptions that are made when some whites see brown skin. One way to do this is to dress well.

2. In his book, *The Reckoning*, Randall Robinson (2002, pp. 12–13) described a similar story told to him by Jesse Jackson. "[W]hen [Jackson] was running for president and was featured on the cover of virtually every national magazine, he had emerged from his New York hotel having had lunch with Zimbabwe's President Robert Mugabe before rushing off to other high-level meetings at the United Nations ... In the lobby of the hotel, the Reverend Jackson's eyes found the beaming face of an elderly white woman .... Pressed for time, he managed a gracious patience as the old woman struggled to say her piece: 'I really couldn't leave without thanking you for all that you have done.' ... Moving away, the old woman pressed a dollar into the Reverend Jackson's hand: 'I never would have been able to lift those heavy bags. Thanks again and here's a little something for you.' "

3. Speaking directly to African Americans and offering them advice about how to navigate the corporate workplace, Cobbs and Turnock (2003, p. 3) observe that African Americans "have years of experience in a world that sees [them] not as an individual, but as a bundle of stereotypes, most of them negative."

4. Cf. Cobbs and Turnock (2003, p. 149): African Americans "work against a backdrop of conflicting assumptions, more muted than in the past but still a part of many peoples' thinking. Rather than the old stereotypes of dumb and lazy, you may be viewed as too cautious, too sensitive, or too aggressive."

5. In conversations I have had on this topic with scores of African American professionals, each one has shared with me a comparable story of professional misidentification. If you, the reader, are white and have not heard similar stories from black friends, acquaintances or colleagues, ask them whether they are willing to talk to you about their experiences with professional misidentification. The kind of frank discussion that may ensue would begin to advance meaningful interracial discourse on race that rarely takes place in American life.

6. I have created my own rules for pedestrian traffic in New York City. We should use the right side of the sidewalk, not the left. These are my own personal rules and no one has to follow them, but traveling in our city would be so much more pleasant if we walk the way we drive, and in fact, cultural sidewalk etiquette in the United States seems to generally follow this rule.

7. David L. Hinds retired as Managing Director at Deutsche Bank. In an interview in which he is asked to give advice to African Americans in the corporate workplace, he comments on what some whites think of their African American colleagues: "There will always be someone asking, 'Why are you here?' You cannot influence the speculation about you, the conversations behind your back ..." (Cobbs & Turnock, 2003, p. 7).

8. Epstein's assumptions about tastes that vary according to race and sex are dangerously essentialist. Epstein ignores the diversity among women and minorities by assuming that women and racial minorities have tastes that differ from those of white men as a general matter.

9. The law and economics scholars' theory that the market will correct discrimination if it is inefficient is typical in the debate between conservatives and progressives. Conservatives escape responsibility for theories and practices that cause harm to others by relying on markets that they assert are objective. Conservatives decry the desire of liberals for more government intervention. But, as one author observes, conservatives rely on governmental intervention themselves. For example, conservatives benefit from government policies like limited liability for corporate shareholders. In other words, it is, according to conservatives, acceptable when the government intervenes for the benefit of corporate shareholders – typically the most powerful in our society (Baker, 2006).

10. Because a significant number of black households are headed by women, workplace discrimination against black women harms individuals, families, and the black American community in general. There is psychological harm in single-parent and two-parent families. And, in two-parent families, the fact that black women are likely to earn more than their black male partners means that the economic harm to the family remains significant. And, because in a matter of decades, half of the U.S. population will be non-white, discrimination that threatens the financial stability of racial minorities will threaten the economic stability of the entire nation.

11. Moreover, with respect to the likelihood that harm will occur, in large public companies, with many employees, and in a society in which racism and sexism continue to thrive, discrimination and the harm it causes may be inevitable.

12. See Graham (1999, pp. xi, ix) (describing the "families, organizations, schools, fraternities, and summer resorts" of the black elite, and observing that "[t]he stereotype of the working-class black or impoverished black is one that whites, as well as

blacks, have come to embrace and accept as an accurate and complete account of the black American experience").

13. Also see Havemann (2005) ("[T]he proportion of African Americans of all ages who were working fell to 56.5%, its lowest level in nearly 10 years").

14. Wheary (2006, p. 3) ("Between 2000 and 2050, the white population will grow 7 percent. In contrast, the African American population will grow 71 percent, the Latino population will increase 188 percent and the Asian population will grow 213 percent").

15. Notably, one of the Home Depot Plaintiffs, Keri-Ann Kerr, whose experience with workplace discrimination I narrate later, describes the resentment against her expressed by a white woman she supervised. In an altercation with the woman, Keri-Ann's subordinate told her that Keri-Ann held her job only because she was a black woman (Kerr, K., personal interview, October 6, 2006).

16. Professor Rachel Moran (2005) describes varying types of racism and discrimination as defined by critical race theorists and law and economics scholars and considers their application in the business setting.

17. See Leonhardt (2005) ("Today, the corner offices of the nation's largest companies are dominated by white men in a way that few other parts of society still are .... The top of the corporate [world] remains largely closed to women and minorities").

18. See, for example, Thomas (2001) ("Diversity has become a top priority in corporate America. Despite corporations' best intentions, however, many have failed to achieve a racial mix at the top levels of management").

19. For example, one African American woman moved from middle management to more senior status at Kaiser Permanente (Cobbs & Turnock, 2003, pp. 127–129). But, even as a corporate officer, and after more than one stellar success, she discovered that she "wasn't even on the first step of [her] salary range" and was significantly underpaid. This discovery was fortuitous and was precipitated by unrelated personnel changes (*ibid.*, pp. 169–170).

20. Title VII is the most important legislation in this context. Notably, the landscape of workplace racial discrimination has changed since passage of the Civil Rights Act. As (then) Senator Joseph Biden has described, "discrimination has become very sophisticated ... [and] very much more subtle than it was ... 50 years ago .... [E]mployees don't say any more ... 'We don't like blacks in this company ....' They say things like, 'Well, they wouldn't fit in ... .' [I]t's harder to make a case of discrimination even though there's no doubt that it still exists" (U.S. Senate Judiciary Committee Hearing, 2006).

21. Reginald Lewis's experience vividly illustrates the point that obviously talented black corporate elites must grapple with the less than favorable perceptions that some whites have about African Americans. Although Lewis did not work in a public company, he was "[a] successful corporate lawyer who remade himself into a financier and buyer of corporations [who] bought the McCall Pattern Co. for $22.5 million, guided it to record earnings and ... sold it for $65 million" (Lewis & Walker, 2005, p. xiii). Lewis bought "Beatrice International Foods, a global giant with 64 companies in 31 countries, for just under $1 billion" (*ibid.*, p. xiv). "His net worth was estimated by Forbes at $400 million when he died [in 1993], putting him on the magazine's 400 list of wealthiest Americans" (*ibid.*, p. xv). In spite of his

entrepreneurial brilliance, Lewis "share[d] stories" with another successful black male acquaintance, "about how we were perceived, or different standards that we were held to ... and some of the things you have to do that most people don't think about" (*ibid.*, p. 276).

Another experience provides insight into the perceptions that some whites have about the abilities of well educated and bright African Americans. Lewis' talent went unrecognized when he started his legal career at a large, prestigious corporate law firm in New York City. Two years after Lewis graduated from Harvard Law School, "a partner at the firm implied that Lewis might not make partner; however, he told Lewis that the firm could get him a teaching position..." (*ibid.*, p. 75). (On a personal note, when I started my own legal career at the same firm in 1988, this story had become a legend that was whispered among the few black associates with whom I worked. By that time, Lewis had become one of the firm's most prestigious clients.)

22. Significantly, intra-racial class boundaries melt away when black executives or managers near the top of corporate hierarchies get help from black workers at the bottom. One black woman executive acknowledged the help and information she received from another black woman, an administrative assistant, who was invaluable in helping the executive navigate a difficult corporate environment (Cobbs & Turnock, 2003, p. 46).

23. "Today we view slavery as a kind of blur in the history of this country. Yet America is too young for the memory of slavery to be so old. The existence of slavery is too close to be thought of as so far away. When one considers the economic origin of America, it was Africa and her people who subsidized America's development. After all, two hundred years without wages is an African subsidy to America ..." (Jackson, 2004, p. 345).

24. Privatization occurs when local, state, or federal governments transfer the operation or ownership of correctional or detention facilities from local, state or federal governments to private corporations (Stephan, 1997, p. 2). Add to this privatization trend the fact that a disproportionately high number of the prison population is African American (Marable, 2002, pp. 153–154). Prison privatization plus disproportionately high incarceration rates for black Americans create a situation where white shareholders profit from the cheap labor of blacks. As Randall Robinson (2002, p. 3) notes, "[p]ublic funds are being used to subsidize a national private prison industry whose growth depends on higher incarceration rates .... The investors are disproportionately white. The prisoners are disproportionately black. Inside the new private hells, prisoners toil for private companies, earning but a pittance ... ."

To understand the import of this phenomenon, consider the fact of discriminatory practices within the criminal justice system that contribute to the disproportionately high incarceration rate for black Americans. For example, "the U.S. Commission on Civil Rights ... found that while African Americans ... constitute only 14 percent of all drug users nationally, they account for 35 percent of all drug arrests, 55 percent of all drug convictions, and 75 percent of all prison admissions for drug offenses" (*ibid.*, p. 154). In other words, the disproportionately high numbers of black prisoners is the result of racism rather than a propensity for criminal activity that exceeds that of whites. Black prisoners are not only a source of wealth for shareholders of prison-privatization companies, their incarceration provides employment for government workers also. "There are more employees at work in the American prison industry than in any Fortune 500 corporation, with the one exception of General Motors" (*ibid.*, p. 155).

25. Leary describes present-day behavior of African Americans that derives from slavery's legacy. For example, she describes an African American mother at a recent school meeting who downplays her child's accomplishments when speaking with another parent who is white. Leary explains that understanding the mother's reticence about her child's success is best understood by providing historical context. Enslaved mothers denigrated their children when speaking with the whites who enslaved them. Enslaved mothers who boasted about their children risked that the trumpeting of their children's virtues would make them seem more attractive in the eyes of plantation owners. Daughters and sons would be sold and separated from the parents who loved them if enslaved mothers acknowledge beauty or strength in their children. An enslaved mother's acknowledgment of her daughter's beauty risked that enslavers would rape her child. Leary writes, "[s]lave mothers and fathers had been belittling their children in an effort to protect them for hundreds of years. Yet what originally began as an appropriate adaptation to an oppressive and danger-filled environment has been subsequently transmitted down through generations. It is evidenced today by behaviors like those exhibited by the black woman at the school meeting. While on the surface seemingly harmless, such behavior serves to both humiliate and injure the young black children of today, who cannot understand why their mothers and fathers, who are obviously proud of them, speak so poorly of them. All too often these children ... internalize the demeaning criticisms" (Leary, 2005, p. 15).

26. By sensibility, I refer to black Americans, particularly black conservatives who insist that they are largely unaffected by racism. Whether they perceive it or not, some whites prejudge them on the basis of race.

27. "In building the middle class ... the United States must contend with a legacy of past discrimination that will structure patters of wealth and opportunity well into the 21st century .... Many programs conceived in theory to support all Americans were limited in practice to helping whites find and keep well-paying jobs, achieve economic security and build assets. For example, many African Americans were prevented from taking advantage of the hallowed GI Bill because numerous all-white universities denied them admission ... " (Wheary, 2006, p. 4). This kind of historical discrimination does not impact Latinos (unless they are Latinos who are of African descent) in the same way it affects the present-day financial security of black Americans.

There are many historical incidents that distinguish African Americans from other racial minorities with respect to their status in this nation. One example is the complete destruction of a section of Tulsa, Oklahoma where black Americans thrived and prospered. "In a 36-square block section of North Tulsa, over 600 thriving black businesses prospered .... There were several black millionaires [who] owned private airplanes, a bus line, restaurants, general stores ... real estate companies, hotels, a bank, schools ... two theaters" during the early 1900s" (Wilson & Wallace, 2004, p. 17). "... [B]lack communities all over America were beginning to emulate [the thriving black Tulsa enclave]. There were over fifty-two all black towns in America, during that time. All were systematically destroyed either by violence or the government's so-called urban renewal plan" (*ibid.*, pp. 19–20).

Other examples include the "Black Codes" enacted during Reconstruction in the aftermath of the passing of constitutional amendments intended for the protection of African Americans (Tye, 2004, pp. 18–19) ("[S]outhern whites … lashed out at Negroes, tearing down as many of the new freedoms as they could, including even the liberty to learn to read and write").

28. The two largest racial discrimination class action settlements were brought by hundreds of African American employees against two major corporations, Coca-Cola and Texaco, Inc. (White, 1996, p. 33; Winter, 2000, p. A1).

29. For example, the one black employee out of 100 workers suffered physical attacks and racist taunts while working for Commercial Coating Service Inc., but the company took no steps to stop the racial harassment even after the Equal Employment Opportunity Commission sued the company (Lozano, 2006).

30. The results were consistent for men and women.

31. In 2004, 30.4% of black Americans headed their households with no husband present, while only 12.6% of the total U.S. population lived in female-headed households (U.S. Census, 2007).

32. See also Sarra (2005) (explaining how the racial, gender, and class composition of corporate boards precludes the advancement of women and people of color in the workplace).

33. The six plaintiffs are Glenor Cyrus, June DeBourgh, Kari-Ann Kerr, LaTanya Martin-Avery, Gayna Samuel, and Carolyn Saunders.

34. Home Depot is the world's largest home improvement retailer and the second largest retailer in the United States. According to the legal complaint filed by the Home Depot Plaintiffs, Home Depot is a public corporation, employing thousands in the United States and operating more than 1,500 stores in the United States, Canada and Mexico. In 2003, Home Depot's revenue was $63 billion dollars. Home Depot is a Fortune 500 company. Complaint (2004).

35. See, for example, Fairfax (2005) (discussing barriers faced by women of color in joining corporate boards).

36. Even though black women's experiences with racism and sexism are often eclipsed by those of black men, or white women, black women have been at the forefront in two significant workplace discrimination cases. At least one of the named plaintiffs in the Wal-Mart sex discrimination suit is an African American woman (Abelson, 2004, p. C1). The named plaintiff in the race discrimination class action against Texaco was also an African American woman (Roberts & White, 1998, p. 2).

Women of color who face discrimination also face unique problems under the law. See, for example, Crenshaw (1989) (describing interpretations of Title VII that ignore the unique experiences of women of color) and Scales-Trent (1989) (recommending the use of "sub-categories" in constitutional law in order to fully confront the issues women of color face).

37. Richard Delgado (1989, pp. 2415, 2439) explains that it is imperative that people of color tell their stories as part of the "struggle for racial reform" and that whites should listen to the stories "in order to enrich their own reality."

38. The complaint was filed in the United States District Court in the Eastern District of New York on June 1, 2004. The case was brought pursuant to Title VII of

the Civil Rights Act of 1964, as amended, 42 U.S.C., Section 2000e, et seq.; 42 U.S.C., Section 1981, the Equal Pay Act, 29 U.S.C., Section 206; New York State Executive Law, Article 15, Section 290 et seq.; New York Labor Law, Section 740 et seq.; New York City Administrative Code, Section 8-102, et seq.

39. The plaintiffs alleged that managers frequently used the word "nigger." Some of the racist comments had sexist overtones. For example, one store manager told another employee to "tell that nigger to blow on your pencil" (Complaint, 2004). The plaintiffs claimed that Home Depot managers destroyed documents containing racist remarks.

40. This was done in reports sent to the Commission at the time the Home Depot plaintiffs were employed (Complaint, 2004).

41. Glenor Cyrus alleged that she was constructively discharged after working for Home Depot for two years. Kari-Ann Kerr also claimed that she was constructively discharged after a nine-year tenure with the Company. Home Depot terminated the employment of June DeBourgh and LaTanya Martin-Avery after approximately three years at the Company. Gayna A. Samuel and Carolyn Saunders were terminated after approximately two years with Home Depot.

42. See Wade (2004) (describing and providing examples of corporate rhetoric about diversity and equal opportunity that obfuscate racism and discrimination in corporate workplaces).

43. This is not a new or recent debate. In 1998, Congressional Quarterly Inc. reported that while there were many black Americans who acknowledged that racial discrimination continued to be a problem, there were some blacks and whites who thought that racism was no longer an issue at the end of the 20th century (Masci, 1998, pp. 56–58).

44. Cf. Green (2005) (arguing that a focus on work culture is crucial to corporate anti-discrimination efforts).

45. Professor Manning Marable (2002, p. 166) records one of the first articulations of W.E.B. Du Bois' idea that the fates of the "Talented Tenth" of the African American population who had attained an education and some amount of professional success were linked to less educated and less affluent black Americans. "African Americans who one hundred years ago were fortunate enough to gain access to a higher education were obligated to serve those who were economically and socially disadvantaged." The notion that successful black professionals should uplift less privileged black citizens is an idea expressed by several prosperous African Americans interviewed by Henry Louis Gates Jr. (2004, pp. 37, 45, 96, 99). Assisting less privileged black Americans is also an obligation that Reginald Lewis took seriously (Lewis & Walker, 2005, pp. 283–288, 302).

46. See Wade (2006). It is important for whites to talk about white supremacy, rather than "asking people of color to do all the work" (Grillo & Wildman, 1991, p. 407); see also Carbado and Gulati (2004, p. 1658), arguing that "[t]he shape that diversity takes" in the corporate workplace "will be a function of what ... white men want."

47. Approximately 1.6 million current and former female Wal-Mart employees provided statistical and anecdotal evidence of discriminatory compensation and promotion practices, and gender stereotyping (*Dukes v. Wal-Mart Stores, Inc.*, 2004)

This sex discrimination class action is the largest workplace-bias suit in the history of the United States (Greenhouse & Hays, 2004, p. A1).

## ACKNOWLEDGMENT

My sincere thanks to Aru Satkalmi, a talented, extraordinary, and tireless librarian.

## REFERENCES

Abelson, R. (2004). Suing Wal-Mart but still hoping to move up. *New York Times*, June 23, p. C1.

Baker, D. (2006). *The conservative nanny state: How the wealthy use the government to stay rich and get richer*. Washington, DC: LULU. Available at http://www.conservativenannystate.org

Brooks, R. (2004). *Atonement and forgiveness*. Berkeley, CA: University of California Press.

Carbado, D., & Gulati, M. (2003). The law and economics of critical race theory. *Yale Law Journal, 112*, p. 1757.

Carbado, D., & Gulati, M. (2004). Race to the top of the corporate ladder: What minorities do when they get there. *Washington and Lee Law Review, 61*, 1645, 1658.

Cobbs, P. M., & Turnock, J. L. (2003). *Cracking the corporate code: The revealing success stories of 32 African-American executives*. New York: AMACOM.

Crenshaw, K. (1989). Demarginalizing the intersection of race and sex: A black feminist critique of antidiscrimination doctrine, feminist theory and antiracist politics. *University of Chicago Legal Forum, 139*, 139–167.

Deitch, E., Barsky, A., Butz, R., Chan, S., Brief, A., & Bradley, J. (2003). Subtle yet significant: The existence and impact of everyday racial discrimination in the workplace. *Human Relations, 56*, p. 1299.

Delgado, R. (1989). Storytelling for oppositionists and others: A plea for narrative. *Michigan Law Review, 87*, 2411, 2415.

Delgado, R. (1993). Rodrigo's second chronicle: The economics and politics of race. *Michigan Law Review, 91*, p. 1196.

DeNavas-Walt, C., Proctor, B., & Smith, J. (2007). Income, poverty, and health insurance coverage in the United States: 2006, p. 5. *U.S. Census Bureau*. Available at http://www.census.gov/prod/2007pubs/p60-233.pdf

Dyson, M. (2005). *Is Bill Cosby right? Or has the black middle class lost its mind?* New York, NY: Basic Civitas Books.

Epstein, R. (1996). The subtle vices of the employment discrimination laws. *John Marshall Law Review, 29*, p. 575.

Fairfax, L. (2005). Some reflections on the diversity of corporate boards: Women, people of color, and the unique issues associated with women of color. *St. John's Law Review, 79*, p. 1105.

Gates, H. L. (2004). Jesse Jackson: Restitution, reinvestment. In: *America behind the color line: Dialogues with African Americans*. New York, NY: Warner Books.

Graham, L. (1999). *Our kind of people: Inside America's black upper class*. New York, NY: Harper Perennial.

Green, K. (2005). Work culture and discrimination. *California Law Review*, *93*, p. 623.

Greenhouse, S., & Hays, C. (2004). Wal-Mart sex-bias suit given class-action status. *New York Times*, June 23, p. A1.

Grillo, T., & Wildman, S. (1991). Obscuring the importance of race: The implication of making comparisons between racism and sexism (or Other-isms). *Duke Law Journal*, 397–412.

Havemann, J. (2005). U.S. reports accelerating job growth: Payrolls grow by 262,000 positions in February. But the unemployment rate increases to 5.4%. *Los Angeles Times*, March 5, p. 1.

Jordan, E., & Harris, A. (2006). *When markets fail: Race and economics*. Eagan, MN: Foundation Press.

Klein, A. (2004). A tenuous hold on the middle class. *Washington Post*, December 18, p. A1.

Krueger, A. (2002). Sticks and stones can break bones, but the wrong name can make a job hard to find. *New York Times*, December 12, p. C2.

Krueger, A. (2003). Economic scene: The Supreme Court finds the 'mushball middle' on affirmative action. *New York Times*, July 24, p. C2.

Leary, J. (2005). *Post traumatic slave syndrome: America's legacy of enduring injury and healing*. Portland, OR: Uptone Press.

Lee, C. (2006). Job police or not, the EEOC is busy with discrimination. *Washington Post*, March 7, p. A13.

Leonhardt, D. (2005). Who's in the corner office? *New York Times*, November 27. Available at http://www.nytimes.com/2005/11/27/business/yourmoney/27ceo.html?_r = 1&scp = 1&sq = leonhardt%20who%27s%20in%20the%20corner%20office&st = cse.

Lewis, R., & Walker, B. (2005). *Why should white guys have all the fun? How Reginald Lewis created a billion-dollar business empire*. Baltimore, MD: Black Classic Press.

Lozano, J. (2006). Company to pay former worker $1 million. *AP Online*, March 23.

Marable, M. (2002). *The great wells of democracy*. New York, NY: Basic Civitas Books.

Masci, D. (1998). The black middle class. *CQ Researcher*, January 23, pp. 56–58.

Mishel, L., Bernstein, J., & Boushey, H. (2003). *The state of working America 2002–03*. Washington, DC: The Economic Policy Institute.

Moran, R. (2005). Whatever happened to racism? *St. John's Law Review*, *79*, p. 899.

Roberts, B., & White, J. (1998). *Roberts v. Texaco: A true story of race and corporate America*. New York, NY: Harper Perennial.

Robinson, R. (2002). *The reckoning: What blacks owe to each other*. New York, NY: Dutton Adult.

Sarra, J. (2005). Class act: Considering race and gender in the corporate boardroom. *St. John's Law Review*, *79*, p. 1121.

Scales-Trent, J. (1989). Black women and the constitution: Finding our place, asserting our rights. *Harvard Civil Rights-Civil Liberties Law Review*, *24*, p. 9.

Scholz, J., & Levine, K. (2004). U.S. black–white wealth inequality. In: K. M. Neckerman (Ed.), *Social inequality*. New York, NY: Russell Sage Foundation Publications.

Stephan, J. (1997) *Census of state and federal correctional facilities*, p. 2. U.S. Department of Justice.

Stout, L. (2003). On the proper motives of corporate directors (or, why you don't want to invite homo economicus to join your board). *Delaware Journal of Corporate Law, 28*, p. 1.

The Home Depot. (n.d.). *Did You Know?* Available at http://corporate.homedepot.com/wps/portal/!ut/p/c1/04_SB8K8xLLM9MSSzPy8xBz9CP0os3gDdwNHH0tDU1M3g1APR0N31xBjAwgAykfC5H1MzN0MzDycDANMYdIGBHT7eeTnpuoX5EaUAwDOvP5h/dl2/d1/L2dJQSEvUUt3QS9ZQnB3LzZfMEcwQUw5MTU1RjBVSEExR0xUMzAwMDAwMDA!/. Accessed on December 23, 2008.

Thomas, D. (2001). The truth about mentoring minorities: Race matters. *Harvard Business Review, 79*(4), p. 98.

Tucker, J., Wolfe, L., Viruell-Fuentes, E., & Smooth, W. (1999). No more "business as usual": Women of color in corporate America. *Center for Women Policy Studies*, p. 12.

Tye, L. (2004). *Rising from the rails: Pullman porters and the making of the black middle class*. New York, NY: Henry Holt & Co.

U.S. Census Bureau. (2007). The American community – Blacks: 2004. Available at http://www.census.gov/prod/2007pubs/acs-04.pdf

U.S. Senate Judiciary Committee hearing on Judge Samuel Alito's nomination to the Supreme Court. Washington Post (courtesy of Federal Document Clearinghouse e-media). Available at http://www.washingtonpost.com/wp-dyn/content/article/2006/01/10/AR2006011000781_pf.html

Wade, C. (2002a). Racial discrimination and the relationship between the directorial duty of care and corporate disclosure. *University of Pittsburgh Law Review, 63*, p. 389.

Wade, C. (2002b). Corporate governance as corporate social responsibility: Empathy and race discrimination. *Tulane Law Review, 76*, p. 1461.

Wade, C. (2004). 'We are an equal opportunity employer': Diversity doublespeak. *Washington and Lee Law Review, 61*, p. 1541.

Wade, C. (2006). Transforming discriminatory corporate cultures: This is not just women's work. *Maryland Law Review, 65*, p. 101.

Warren, E. (2004). The economics of race: When making it to the middle is not enough. *Washington and Lee Law Review, 61*, p. 1777.

Washington, M. H. (Ed.) (1989). *Black-eyed Susans/midnight birds: Stories by and about black women*. New York, NY: Knopf Publishing Group.

Wheary, J. (2006). African Americans, Latinos and economic security in the 21st century. *Demos Future Middle Class Series*, p. 3.

White, J. (1996). Texaco's high-octane racism problems. *Time*, November 25, p. 33.

Wilson, J. J., & Wallace, R. (2004). *Black wallstreet*. Long Island City, NY: Seaburn Publishing.

Winter, G. (2000). Coca-cola settles racial bias case. *New York Times*, November 17, p. A1.

## Cases

*Basic Inc. v. Levinson*, 485 U.S. 224, 254 (1988).

*Dukes v. Wal-Mart Stores, Inc.*, 222 F.R.D. 137 (N.D. Cal. 2004).

*Glenor Cyrus, et al. v. Home Depot, Inc.* (No. CV 04 2250) (Complaint, 2004).